ISLAM IS A FOREIGN COUNT

NATION OF NEWCOMERS: IMMIGRANT
HISTORY AS AMERICAN HISTORY
General Editors: Matthew Jacobson and Werner Sollors

Islam Is a Foreign Country

American Muslims and the Global Crisis of Authority

Zareena Grewal

NEW YORK UNIVERSITY PRESS

New York and London

NEW YORK UNIVERSITY PRESS
New York and London
www.nyupress.org

References to Internet websites (URLs) were accurate at the time of writing.
Neither the author nor New York University Press is responsible for URLs
that may have expired or changed since the manuscript was prepared.

LIBRARY OF CONGRESS CATALOGING-IN-PUBLICATION DATA

Grewal, Zareena.
 Islam is a foreign country : American Muslims and the global crisis of authority / Zareena
Grewal.
   pages cm
 Includes bibliographical references and index.
 ISBN 978-1-4798-0088-9 (hardback) — ISBN 978-1-4798-0056-8 (pb)
 1. Muslim youth—United States—Attitudes. 2. Muslim youth—Religious life—United
States. 3. Islam—United States. 4. Ummah (Islam) 5. United States—Ethnic relations.
6. Social integration—United States. I. Title.
 E184.M88G74 2013
 297.5'70835—dc23
                              20
New York University Press books

Manufactured in the United States of America

10 9 8 7 6 5 4 3 2 1

Also available as an ebook

For Hamada
"Here I go out the window!"
And you came with me.
Home is wherever you are.

In that Empire, the Art of Cartography attained such Perfection that the map of a single Province occupied the entirety of a City, and the map of the Empire, the entirety of a Province. In time, those Unconscionable Maps no longer satisfied, and the Cartographers Guilds struck a Map of the Empire whose size was that of the Empire, and which coincided point for point with it.
—Jorge Luis Borges, "On Exactitude in Science,"
translated by Andrew Hurley

CONTENTS

ACKNOWLEDGMENTS

It is my pleasure to thank the people and institutions that have made this book possible. First and foremost, I am deeply indebted to the long list of Muslim students, teachers, and public intellectuals in the US and the Middle East patient and generous enough to allow me to interview them. The small parts of those lives shared with me have enriched my own in unexpected ways that were never small. Although I only refer to religious leaders widely known to American Muslims by name in this book, I learned a great deal about sincerity and passion from each and every one of the learned men and women I encountered over the years, at times through our strong disagreements.

Thanks to the families that hosted us abroad, the Mahayni and Al-Azem families in Syria, the Zagha family in Jordan, and the Stino family in Egypt. Research and writing were made possible by grants from the Interdepartmental Program in Anthropology and History, the Ramsdell Foundation, the Rackham Merit Fellowship and Rackham Humanities Fellowship at the University of Michigan, and the Center for the Study of American Muslims at the Institute for Social Policy and Understanding and by the Fulbright's Islamic Civilization Grant, which also afforded me an official affiliation with AlAzhar University that was critical to my research. Librarians and archivists Kathryn DeGraff, Munir Muhammad, and Catherine Morse provided essential help with research. Omer Bajwa and Mahan Mirza assisted in obtaining difficult sources. Kirin Tahir was a patient and resourceful research assistant. I am grateful to NYU Press's editorial director, Eric Zinner, editors Ciara McLaughlin and Alicia Nadkarni, and the series editors, Werner Sollors and Matthew Jacobson, for their oversight and great care in making the long process to the publication of this book smooth, efficient, and rewarding. I thank NYU Press's two anonymous reviewers whose feedback improved the arguments. Publication costs were offset by a generous grant from the Frederick W. Hilles Publication Fund at Yale. Laura Helper-Ferris and Maysan Haydar offered additional editorial support at key junctures. I am very indebted to David Lobenstine, who elevates editing to an art form and whose brilliant ideas and gentle insistence radically transformed the structure of this book. Special thanks to Matthew Jacobson for his warm, steady encouragement and friendship and for believing in the book and in me from day one.

As a graduate student at the University of Michigan, I benefited from being part of a thriving and warm intellectual community in the interdepartmental program in anthropology and history that included David Cohen, Fernando Coronil, Julie Skurski, Ann Stoler, Chandra Bhimull, Edward Murphy, Monica Patterson, Sonja Luherman, Ilana Feldman, and Mamadou Diouf. In the history department, Juan Cole, Michele Mitchell, and John Carson offered critical advice. While "writing up" in New York, I had the good fortune to take a seminar, "The Idea of Tradition," with Talal Asad, who has been a sensitive and insightful critic and profound influence on my intellectual development. Sincere thanks to the scholars on my committee who helped me conceptualize the research project this book is based on and guided me through its different phases. Barbara Metcalf proved a gentle but serious interlocutor, and her encouragement to forgo chronology and write an allegorical history of American Muslims made a world of a difference. Andrew Shryock's enthusiasm and hard questions kept me reading widely and agonizing in productive ways. Ruth Behar's elegance, poetic instinct, and sharp mind first inspired me as an undergraduate, and she continues to be a model as a teacher, scholar, and artist. Without her encouragement and example, I would not have had the courage to make myself vulnerable in the text by including my own story. Sherman Jackson first urged me into graduate school and out of Islamic studies, and he has been a nurturing mentor and a generous friend ever since. The precision, urgency, and moral strength that he brings to research and his impatience with anything that smacks of intellectual cowardice combine to make him a challenging critic and a model public intellectual. I offer my sincere gratitude to all my teachers, for their time, kindness, guidance, and friendship over the years.

In the course of research and writing, I have presented pieces of this book in its various stages at dozens of conferences and workshops. At the earliest stages of writing, important feedback from Hussein Agrama, Umar Faruq Abd-Allah, Gelya Frank, Saba Mahmood, Aminah McCloud, Ebrahim Moosa, Bruce Lawrence, Enseng Ho, John Bowen, Brian Edwards, and Brinkley Messick helped sharpen my ideas. I am especially grateful to the community of young scholars in our "Islam in/and America" collective, convened with Rosemary Corbett and Juliane Hammer. These scholars and friends include Nayan Shah, Hishaam Aidi, Zaheer Ali, Edward Curtis, Zain Abdullah, Sally Howell, Su'ad Abdul Khabeer, Sylvia Chan Malik, Tim Marr, Amina ElAnnan, Sohail Daulatzai, Moustafa Bayoumi, Debra Majeed, Maryam Kashani, and Junaid Rana.

At Yale, the Program in Ethnicity, Race, and Migration, Religious Studies, and American Studies have been exhilarating and warm places to think, read, write, and teach. I am grateful for the intellectual camaraderie of Steve Pitti, Alicia Schmidt Camacho, Jon Butler, Joanne Meyerowitz, Katie Lofton, Mary Lui, Sally Promey, Patricia Pessar, Muneer Ahmad, Laura Wexler, Jean Cherniavsky, Vicki Shephard, Birgit Rasmussen, Kate Dudley, Inderpal Grewal, and Matt Jacobson. In Middle East Studies, I thank Marcia Inhorn, Frank Griffel, Narges Erami, Andrew March, and Jonathan Wyrtzen. I am especially grateful for the manuscript colloquium organized by Steve Pitti and Matt Jacobson that afforded me the opportunity to workshop my book-in-progress with three generous and insightful scholars, Kevin Dwyer, Sherene Razack, and Bob Orsi. Their enthusiasm and thoughtful engagement with an early iteration of the book transformed the final product in so many ways, particularly in helping me think through a way to make my own place in the narrative a window into the perspectives of the Arab teachers on their American students. I owe heartfelt thanks to the students in my "Muslim Diasporas" and "Crisis of Islam" courses for their feedback on early drafts and for inspiring me with their curiosity.

My family and closest friends endured this long, arduous project and made it bearable when I feared it might not be. In the Middle East, Jeremy and Catherine Morse, Suleman and Fawzia Siddiqui, and Nausheen Masood transformed what were supposed to be short study breaks into world adventures. Farid Senzai made me see public scholarship and *Three's Company* with new eyes, and at ISPU he made a real team out of our ragtag group of friends. Sherine Hamdy shared beaded necklaces and ideas-all-night on both sides of the Atlantic. Dave Coolidge and Sumaiya Balbale made me think hard and laugh harder and showed faith in my blind stabs in the dark. Rabia Bajwa provided sincere advice, tribal solidarity, and comic relief in difficult moments. For more than twenty years, Catherine Morse has held a light and a mirror for me; her friendship is the greatest source of joy and inspiration I have ever known. During those frantic semesters as a graduate student when I half lived with my in-laws, Ismat and Batul Hamid showed enormous patience with the clutter caused by my paperwork and suitcases. They also showed enormous resilience as they watched another war destroy the Iraq they once knew. I learned much from them and my friend Kirk W. Johnson about working hard for peace, but they each know when and how to stop and have a little fun. My husband's relatives fleeing the war, Rana, Muad, and Huthayma AlAni and Najm and Suhair Yasin, made our rented apartments in Amman and Damascus into real homes, filled with laughter, good food, and unshakable hope. Special thanks to my own extended family and the friends we consider family in the mosque communities of greater Detroit, especially the Mandahar clan now spread around the world. My cousins, aunties, and uncles in Detroit, Gujranwala, Lahore, Mandi Bahauddin, Philadelphia, and San Francisco cheered me on from afar. The humanist vision of my father, Nisar Grewal, is surely one of the seeds of this book. I am deeply indebted to my siblings, Nasir and Lubna Grewal, for all their little favors along the way. Nasir's relentless skepticism shaped and improved my arguments. The love, support, and prayers of my mother, Amina Grewal, are my greatest and most treasured constant. My daughter and playmate, Bayan Noor, is the light that makes it all clear. As an infant, toddler, and little girl, Bayan napped or played silently as she waited for yet another academic conference to end before she could take me into her world of ideas, where puddles are really oceans and hotel lobbies, fantastical palaces. Her smiling baby brother, Zayd Hakim, arrived just in time to make last-minute revisions even more last minute; I thank him first and later Zaky Yasin for sleeping so soundly and sweetly in my lap as I typed all night. Finally, loving thanks to Hamada Hamid Altalib, who understands that I think most clearly in motion; without him, it might have been just circles and circles, no direction chosen.

Introduction

Unmapping the Muslim World

On a sweltering July afternoon, I absently drove through a neighborhood known as the heart of Arab Detroit. The quiet suburb of Dearborn, Michigan, is famously home to the headquarters of the Ford Motor Company and also home to at least thirty thousand Arab Americans. "The Middle East in the Midwest," as Dearborn is often dubbed, is a regular stop for journalists and TV crews searching out Muslim man-on-the-street sound bites or exotic b-roll footage—the street signs along Michigan Avenue written in Arabic, halal McNuggets at McDonalds, or burqa-clad women rollerblading. That is why, driving along in the summer of 2007, I barely took notice of the cameramen setting up on the street corner. But then I came upon a swarm of police cars blocking off the street for at least a mile. Anxiously, I craned my neck to see what the gathering onlookers were fixed on. I could hear muffled cries in Arabic and a growing crowd of teenagers waving Iraqi flags further down Warren Avenue. Hoopties with boys piled on the roofs and Arabic radio stations blaring were slowly circling the police lines, Iraqi flags and outstretched arms hanging out the windows. In the distance, drums pounded. A little boy darted between the squad cars waving his Iraqi flag and ignoring the reprimands of the police.

I scanned through the car's radio stations for news coverage of the war in Iraq. A white police officer directing traffic off Warren Avenue waved me toward a side street. Leaning out of my car window, I asked him, "Did something happen?"

He studied the amorphous mob of Arab teenagers in the distance. "A lot of things are happening right now," he muttered.

The fear in his eyes made my thoughts race. A few months earlier, I consulted on a major survey on Muslims in the US for the Pew

Foundation; the report had just been publicly released and caused a bit of a media stir. Despite the overall rosy findings of the report (reassuringly titled *Muslim Americans: Middle Class and Mostly Mainstream*), Fox News and other conservative media focused on the findings highlighting the political disaffection of Muslim American youth.[1] Anti-Muslim right-wing bloggers and pundits made alarmist arguments in the media about how the report proved that neighborhoods like "Dearbornistan" constituted a "home grown threat."[2] This is what was on my mind as I turned onto a residential street. Seconds after I rounded the corner, loud gunshots fired. My heart sank as I imagined the headlines, the photographs: Muslim youth, born and bred in America, holding violent demonstrations. I spotted a middle-aged woman with a hot-pink scarf tied over her hair bouncing a toddler in her lap in the shade of her front porch.

"*Shoo sar?*" I asked from my car window.

"Iraq won the Asia Cup!" she yelled back, smiling broadly.

Then she lifted her hand in the air and shot an imaginary, celebratory bullet into the sky.

Dearborn may be a quaint "Little Lebanon," but it is also a domestic front in the War on Terror. Locals pride themselves on producing the best Arabic food outside the Middle East and the first Muslim Miss USA. But Dearborn also has the distinction of being the first American city to get its own office of Homeland Security after September 11th, even before New York. Across the US, Muslim American communities such as Dearborn inspire fear and fascination; they are constantly scrutinized and talked about by researchers, by law enforcement officials, by pundits on the nightly news. For all this attention, Muslim Americans are still rarely heard. Millions of dollars are spent on survey research on the Muslim American population to answer burning questions about their demographics, their political views, the degree of their devotion to Islam, even their happiness.[3] The goal is always the same: to discern "good" Muslims from "bad" ones, "Little Lebanon" from "Dearbornistan"; when surveys find Muslim Americans have strong commitments to Islam and strong attachments to Muslims in other parts of the world, the statistics are routinely treated as ominous, threatening, as if religiosity and a global sense of religious community are an obstacle to the cultivation of attachments to Americans and America. These surveys

Fig. I.1. Iraqi American teens in Dearborn celebrate Iraq's Asia Cup win as the US-led forces remain at war in Iraq against opposition forces that see "Operation Iraqi Freedom" and "Operation New Dawn" as military occupations. (Photo courtesy of Reuters)

promise a window onto the Muslim American "street," but the love of soccer and the emotional and psychological significance of the Iraqi win in Dearborn are, needless to say, impossible to capture in a survey. These surveys are like a picture taken from far away, and the details are often so blurry that a jubilant celebration can look like a riot degenerating into chaos.

A more intimate picture might capture the finer textures of some of the most important issues facing Muslims in communities such as

Dearborn: what does it mean to be Muslim and American in our global age? What ties Muslim Americans to Muslims around the world? Who speaks for the stunningly diverse population of American Muslims? These questions are inextricably linked to questions about the nature of American citizenship as well. What are the cultural criteria of national belonging that allow one to be recognized as American? In Dearborn, everyone understands that citizenship is more than a legal status, that national belonging is fragile and that it can be withheld from those who are deemed foreign and different even if they are technically legal citizens. These days at ethnic events and citywide Islamic holiday parties in Dearborn, recruiters from the US armed forces, the FBI, and the CIA are regular sponsors but not always warmly received ones. Amid the carnival rides and food carts at the Arab International Festival, Arab children receive free balloons and spy swag at the CIA's air-conditioned "Top Secret Lounge" and scale the US Army's rock-climbing wall as stories of wrongful arrests and the scents of grilled kabobs swirl through the crowds below.

The gap between legal citizenship and social citizenship belies the idea that the nation is a natural entity, merely a territorially bound political unit; rather, the United States is a place both physical and also imagined, one that is produced and perpetually reproduced by a community of citizens who collectively imagine that they share a deep, horizontal kinship.[4] On the nightly news, the weather report presents our national borders as natural features of geography, crossed by cold fronts and warm fronts. These simplified maps are one of innumerable representations that naturalize the moral geography of the nation, treating cultural difference like a feature of the terrain. The imagined community of the nation is often apprehended in geographic terms. When we talk about the US as the "City on the Hill," the "Leader of the Free World," or the "Nation of Immigrants," we construct the nation as an exceptional community in the world, but these national mythologies also conjure an imagined geography of an exceptional, value-laden place. Moral geographies are constituted by a set of ethical and political assertions about a piece of land that produce a shared, conceptual map among that land's inhabitants.[5] The ethical and political assertions that accompany a moral geography are so taken for granted, so integral to the identity of the place, that they are "facts" of life, silent, unspoken. As Donald Pease notes, "a nation is not only a piece of land but a narration about the people's relation to the land."[6] The collectively imagined affiliations among American citizens—and the corresponding imagined separation from people outside the nation's borders (as well as outsiders within), the perpetually appealing notion of "us" versus "them," of "We the people" in contrast to the "Others"— sustain the imagined community of the nation, the idea that the nation is a container of a singular, all-encompassing culture, a national way of life bound by the water's edge.

Like the nation, the Orient is also a moral geography of an exotic but inferior culture that is treated as though it were merely a place. The late cultural critic Edward Said argues in his classic book *Orientalism* that centuries of Western production of artistic and scholarly representations of the Oriental (Muslim) Other as weak, decadent, depraved, irrational, and fanatical operate as a form of backhanded self-flattery, confirming through contrast that the West is civilized, dynamic, and superior. The central point of Said's *Orientalism* is to challenge the authority and political neutrality of this body of self-referential knowledge about the (Muslim) Other, this powerful discourse that operates independently of and in political service against the actual lands and peoples it claims to represent.[7]

Americans have inherited this centuries-old discourse. When Americans refer to the "Muslim World," they reproduce, amend, and complicate Colonial Europe's moral geography of the Orient. Often Americans mistakenly use the terms "the Muslim World" and "the Middle East" interchangeably; both terms refer to far more sweeping groupings of peoples and lands than those defined by the specific and narrow American political and cultural interests in these geographies over time. Historically, American popular attitudes and US foreign policies toward the Middle East have been neither uniformly hostile nor consistent: as "the Holy Land," it has been a site of religious significance since the country's founding; as a source of oil, it has been an economic linchpin since the Second World War; as a proxy, bloody, Cold War battleground against the USSR, the region became a site of national, geopolitical interest; as a source of terrorist threats in the late twentieth century and even more dramatically in the twenty-first, the region became a site of national security interest.[8] In addition, American minorities, particularly African Americans, have contested the dominant American discourse about the Muslim World, developing their own alternative investments in Islamic peoples and places as inspirations of racial justice; their transnational attachments to Muslims abroad who are not Americans destabilizes the idea of a "people" at the heart of citizenship.[9] In contrast to European colonialists' sustained preoccupation with the Orient, historically, American interests in the "Muslim World," those of whites or racial minorities, are characterized by spurts of cultural and political attention and material investment "followed by virtual silence," cycles of discovery and forgetting, reimagining and remapping.[10] Today the "Muslim World" figures as a place and an idea that is strategically important to the US despite being, in the eyes of most Americans, regressive, dangerous, and distant, both geographically and culturally.

Of course, cultures, peoples, ideas, and beliefs do not actually map themselves onto the terrain of the earth in this simple way. There is, in other words, no place we can call the "Muslim World." If the "Muslim World" is the modern equivalent of Islamdom (lands ruled by Muslims), it would refer only to Muslim-majority countries; countries with significant minorities of Muslims, such as China, will be left out. If the "Muslim World" is a euphemism for the Middle East (sometimes including Afghanistan and Pakistan), it fails to account for the indigenous populations of Christians and Jews and other religious minorities throughout the region as well as the fact that 1.9 billion Muslims live outside the Middle East.[11] Ultimately, the term "Muslim World" implies both that Muslims live in a world of their own and that Islam is an eastern religion and there is a foreign place—a distant, contiguous part of the world—where Islam properly belongs. Where does that leave the American Muslims who are the focus of this book? Do places like Dearborn make the United States part of the "Muslim World"?

Islam Is a Foreign Country unmaps the moral geography of the "Muslim World" as a place and a people outside American geographic and cultural borders by mapping an alternative, transnational *Muslim world* imagined by American Muslims that includes them and the US. To mark the dominance of the moral geography of the "Muslim World" as a foreign place and a source of foreigners in the West, I capitalize both words; when referring to Muslims' aspirational moral geography, the "Muslim world," I do not. Rather than a foreign region, the Muslim world is a global community of Muslim locals, both majorities and minorities who *belong* to the places where they live and who, in their totality, exemplify the universality of Islam.

Central to this book are Muslim American youth at the dawn of the twenty-first century who are preoccupied by this conundrum, one that American Muslims have been grappling with for decades: What makes Islam belong to a place? Can Islam be an American religion without being compromised, diluted, disfigured, assimilated? Living with both the possibility and the impossibility of Islam being an American religion, American Muslims have internalized what the great black scholar W. E. B. Du Bois referred to as double consciousness, "a peculiar wrenching of the soul, a peculiar sense of doubt and bewilderment. Such a double life, with double thoughts, double duties, and double classes, must give rise to double worlds and double ideals, and tempt the mind to pretense or to revolt, to hypocrisy or to radicalism."[12] Through the journeys of American Muslim seekers abroad, through their studies, struggles, and soul-wrenching debates about their place in the US and in the world, *Islam Is a Foreign Country* offers an account of deeply religious and politically disaffected American Muslim youth. They are not "homegrown" terrorists, but they fit what has become the de facto profile of "radicalized" Muslim youth, in their opposition to the political status quo, their global vision of justice, their attachments to Muslims abroad, and their sense of alienation from the American mainstream. Perhaps it is their idealism that is most radical, the persistence with which they desire a home.

The War on Terror shows us how high the political stakes and the costs of imagining Islam in terms of geographic borders and imagining American citizenship in terms of cultural, religious, and even racial criteria can be. Immediately after September 11th, President George W. Bush cautioned Americans against lashing out at fellow citizens just because they were Muslim; despite his insistence that the terrorists did not represent "real" Islam, the underlying message of his "with us or against us" mantra rang loud and clear: unless proven "good," every Muslim was presumed to be "bad."[13] War on Terror policies at home and abroad collectively punish Muslims for the 9/11 attacks. Iraq and Afghanistan became formal battlefields in retributive military conflicts an ocean away. Lebanon, Iran, Pakistan, Sudan, Somalia, Syria, and

Yemen became informal battlefields, their populations subject to economic sanctions, missile and drone attacks, covert operations, and targeted killings undertaken by the US government. Domestically, Muslim
Americans became the mass targets of surveillance and a wide range of
punitive US government policies that systematically criminalize Muslims and "Muslim-looking" people through a body of legislation that
is race-neutral in its language but targets and racializes these special
populations in its effects.[14] Most prominently, immigration legislation is
now a proxy for legal measures that are selectively applied to brown and
black Muslim populations through incarceration, mass deportation,
and denial of entry without the due process of law. Such policies and
attitudes are not simply a reaction to the 9/11 terror attacks; like other
cases of scapegoating American minorities, these policies and attitudes
depend on preexisting social conditions that treat Muslims both within
and outside US borders as people who would readily participate in or
approve of terrorism and, therefore, populations who ought to be held
collectively responsible for the attacks.

Before September 11th, there was a growing political consensus on
the right and the left that racial profiling was an inefficient, ineffective,
and unfair policy. Ironically, at a campaign event in Dearborn in 1999,
then presidential candidate Bush promised to roll back the profiling of
Muslims.[15] After September 11th, the national consensus flipped, with
people on the right and even many on the left embracing the profiling
of Muslims in the name of national security. In the wake of 9/11, Gallup
polls found significant approval for the internment of Arab Americans
(one-third of New Yorkers polled), and in 2006, a Gallup poll showed
that 39 percent of Americans believe all Muslims, even US citizens,
should be forced to carry special identification cards.[16] Just as punitive
immigration legislation is selectively applied to Muslim cases by the
government, the profiling of Muslim-looking people is often recast as
patriotic vigilance. The same perverse logic that undergirds racial profiling is simply taken to its logical extreme by those who commit acts
of "backlash" violence: the hunt for terrorists is a hunt for "Muslim-
looking" people. Hate crimes against Muslims are treated like crimes of
passion; while the violent effects of the perpetrators' displaced anger are
roundly condemned, their anger over 9/11 and their love of the nation
are widely shared emotions.[17] In contrast to terrorist violence, which is

consistently represented in the media as incomprehensible, hate violence meted out against "Muslim-looking" people is typically represented as unfortunate but predictable, regrettable but understandable.

Muslim Americans are long familiar with being treated with suspicion; however, the political pressures and the hyperscrutiny of their communities, whether from the government, the media, their neighbors, or even researchers, intensified dramatically after September 11th. Immediately after, many Muslims draped their bodies, cars, homes, and workplaces with American flags, sometimes as much out of fear of racial violence as out of patriotic mourning.[18] The appearance of the flags also signaled the disappearance of other "marking" signs; many Muslim women quietly removed their veils (just as "Muslim-looking" Sikh men removed their turbans) in anticipation of the backlash, or after suffering its real and sometimes violent consequences. A few days after September 11th, I was saddened to find a few Dearborn housewives bent over the back fenders of their minivans, carefully peeling off their "I ♥ Islam" bumper stickers. What, after all, could be more American than an "I ♥ ——" bumper sticker?

This picture of the tenuous quality of American citizenship, the contradictory assertions of inclusion and exclusion that pervade Muslim communities such as Dearborn, are rarely highlighted by journalists and television producers covering the Arab/Muslim American street. They usually use Dearborn's photogenic mixture of exotica and American small-town charm to tell a far more optimistic story about the nation, about the American Dream, a story that echoes the same foundational myth as America's many Chinatowns and Little Italys and sustains the national narrative of Americans as a quintessentially diverse and tolerant people, the moral geography of the US as a Nation of Immigrants and a Land of Opportunity.

In contrast to most Muslim-concentrated neighborhoods in the US today, the Arab community of Dearborn dates back to the early twentieth century, made up mostly of Ellis Island immigrants (Ottoman peddlers and laborers from what is now Lebanon, Syria, and Israel/Palestine) who settled down as factory workers in auto plants and whose grandchildren and great-grandchildren still make up a major population of the city. Like many ethnic enclaves in the US, there are families who have been there for generations and who continue to bring their relatives to the US, as well as new immigrants who have just arrived. Dearborn is a diverse community in terms of religion, including Arab Christians and Muslim Sunnis and Shias, and diverse in terms of nationality and ethnicity, with immigrants from Syria and Lebanon, Palestine and Iraq, Egypt and Yemen. Historically, immigrants in Dearborn enjoyed upward class mobility, and in many ways they have fared better in an increasingly anti-Muslim political climate than have newer, less established Muslim communities in other parts of the US.[19]

This is a fair portrait of Dearborn, but on closer inspection, Dearborn also tells us a less optimistic and far more fractured story about America. Dearborn's changing demographic picture reflects a history of domestic policies that are profoundly racist, such as the introduction and reversal of immigration laws over the course of the twentieth century which denied or limited entry of nonwhite immigrants through quotas, as well as a long history of US involvement in bloody, military conflicts in the Middle East—refugee populations came to Dearborn as a result of the creation of Israel and the subsequent wars between Arab states and Israel, the civil wars in Lebanon and Yemen, the Iran-Iraq war, and the US-led wars in Iraq.[20] The shifts in Dearborn's population also reflect the booms and busts of greater Detroit's economic history. When Henry Ford doubled the average factory worker's pay to five dollars a day in 1914, he revolutionized the auto industry and started a "gold rush" to Detroit by drawing thousands of people from around the country, including many Arab Americans. As the auto industry has dramatically shrunk and weakened after decades of capital flight and urban decay, the population of Detroit has also shrunk, with Arab Americans searching for economic opportunity in other parts of the country and even abroad, some returning permanently to the Middle East. Today the working-class Arab neighborhoods act as a (brown) racial buffer zone between (black) Detroit and the (white) more affluent, western half of the suburb, a legacy of the history of "white flight" (and capital flight) from the city to the suburbs in the sixties and a reminder of the persistence of racial tensions that segregate greater Detroit.

Both local racial tensions and global conflicts in the Middle East heighten suspicions of the Arab community of Dearborn, of their political loyalties. Although not quite white, Arab Americans enjoy certain racial privileges not accorded to blacks in neighboring Detroit, such as the privilege to be able to live and work in a predominantly white suburb such as Dearborn. Yet Arab Muslims lack the social citizenship that blacks enjoy in a post-civil-rights America, in which blacks are frequently represented as quintessentially American even as they continue to suffer the brutalities of American racism.[21] As the African American case demonstrates, attaining social citizenship is not always equivalent with attaining social justice; however, many American Muslims cling to this hope, this particular American myth, that the former leads to the latter. Moustafa Bayoumi argues in his book *How Does It Feel to Be a Problem?*, which lifts its title from Du Bois's 1904 *The Souls of Black Folk*, that the obstacle that prevents Arabs and Muslims from attaining social citizenship is not a lack of representation. He argues that the problem is that Arabs and Muslims have too many representations that dissolve too easily into abstractions, leaving these communities unknowable, perpetually foreign. Our pop culture is awash in the images of Arabs and Muslims, yet, he notes, "sometimes when you are everywhere, you are really nowhere."[22] "Nowhere" is the point on the map of the nation where you are demanded to perform your citizenship and belonging as the very possibility of real inclusion is denied in the same breath. "Nowhere" is a place American Muslims, like me, have navigated all our lives.

Native Orientalist

Not all of the Muslim neighborhoods in Detroit are as telegenic as the Arab community of Dearborn. My earliest childhood memories are of living in a working-class Punjabi neighborhood in Detroit. Like many other first-generation immigrants, my parents came to the US from Pakistan as economic refugees, trying to escape the poverty and political corruption endemic in postcolonial countries like Pakistan that although independent from formal colonial control remain locked in a state of dependency on the US.

When I was four, we moved because my father landed a job as a technician at Ford Motor Company, radically changing our class status and planting us firmly in suburbia. I was lonely in our new, white neighborhood of evenly spaced single-family homes and English-speaking children. In order to help me make friends and learn to speak more

English, my parents enrolled me in a private nursery school in the afternoons. Quickly I began speaking almost exclusively in English, but my parents were most surprised by the fact that I spoke "black English." At first they assumed that this was just the English I had heard first, in Detroit, and that, eventually, living in a white community, I would learn "proper English." But as the months went by, I seemed to be picking up more and more black colloquialisms. (My mother, in her thick accent, would drill into me, "Don't say 'ain't I,' say 'amn't I.'" Years later, I would have to drill "amn't" out of my vocabulary.) The teacher's aide finally solved the mystery of how I was learning "black English" in a white school when she confessed to my father that the head teacher was a racist. My teacher prevented me and the only other nonwhite student in my class, a black girl named Kecia, from participating in class activities and sitting at the main table, relegating us to a separate table in the back of the room.

My father was livid. He was a university student and a political activist (and a hippie) in the US during the sixties, active in the civil rights movement, which he saw as part and parcel of a global anticolonial, human rights struggle that connected Detroit to Karachi. Since he worked the evening shift at Ford, he began a kind of "sit-in" during my afternoon classes, stonily reading a newspaper in the back of the room, at the table that had been for Kecia and me. In the end, my parents pulled me out of the school in disgust. I learned then that my place at that table had to be fought for, that sitting at the table was not the same as being welcome at the table.

That kind of overt, biting racism was the exception for us, however, not the norm. I made new friends easily in our sleepy suburb, and my parents developed warm friendships with our white neighbors and a few other families that were also new to the neighborhood, immigrants from Albania, Iraq, India, and Vietnam. We kept in touch with the families from our old neighborhood, and one by one each of those Punjabi families followed our lead and moved to the suburbs once the men secured auto assembly-line jobs.[23] For my father, however, our suburban life was a holding pattern; America was a turnstile, not our destination. He always insisted that we would eventually move back to Pakistan, which was why we should not accumulate too many toys or clothes or replace unreliable appliances or cars too quickly. And, every few years, our family went through the same process of almost moving back: my father would start a small import-export business on the weekends, our house would go up for sale, and my father would make a dramatic scouting trip to Pakistan, to see if we could really do it. The end was always the same: his dejected return to America and to Ford, followed by weeks of cross-Atlantic phone feuds over inheritance with his family and, finally, by his failing business shuttered and all our savings gone. Then my mother would dig the "For Sale" sign out of the front yard and persuade my father not to give up on the American dream: "This is the best country in the world, the land of opportunity."

Slowly, we began to socialize with a wealthier, suburban Muslim community that shared my mother's dream of a permanent and prosperous future in America. The suburban Muslim community was very different from the Punjabi neighborhood of my earliest memories. Primarily made up of a professional class from Pakistan and India, the collective obsession was on "arriving," fulfilling the American dream of wealth and privilege while assuaging the guilt of realized dreams with immigration sponsorship papers for relatives left behind and vacation suitcases heavy with store-bought gifts from *Amreeka*. Within this subculture of South Asian immigrants, often termed "a model minority" for their comparative economic success and the ease by which they move in (and into) white neighborhoods, those of us in the second generation were largely geared toward two career fields: medicine and engineering (even law school was considered risky). Anthropology and other social sciences ("the sciences that don't raise you," as my father-in-law dubbed them) are particularly suspect because they are dangerously close to philosophy (a discipline he blamed for "our civilization's downfall"). As a graduate student attending my parents' dinner parties on holidays and weekends, I explained to our friends and relatives with embarrassment that anthropology is the study of culture and that I planned to research the global Islamic revival and debates about Islamic authority—hastening to add that I would be improving my Urdu alongside my Arabic. I was usually met with open and predictable disapproval.

I was challenged on two fronts simultaneously: Why I would want to learn about Islam from Orientalists? And why I would waste money on a career without job security? Our Punjabi friends and relatives would remind me of stories I knew too well, of my distant uncle who read borrowed books by street light in the little town of Faisalabad and came to the US on a scholarship; he was the one who took pity on his orphaned cousin, my father, and helped him get a partial scholarship to the University of Michigan. My father was an excellent student but struggled to pay his tuition and rent; he worked at the library and secured babysitting jobs by impressing American children in the park with his expert kite-flying skills, but it was never enough and he was forced to drop out after only three semesters. Here I was, they marveled, thirty years later, the overeducated daughter of a simple kite-runner-turned-technician, studying with Orientalists!

Yes, I would admit, I was guilty of the luxuries of a college girl—reading important books so that I might become Something and spending our hard-earned Ford dollars on university classes to learn languages I had half forgotten and the history of our subjugation. I knew my parents' friends had not read Said's book; they did not realize what an insult it was to call me an Orientalist. These friends would ask me, politely, expectantly, how many more years were left before I would actually *be* an Orientalist? My parents found this hilarious, and it continues to be something of a running joke for us: my PhD in Orientalism. And I always laugh. But, in a way, it is really not that funny.

It is a half-innocent mistake but also a reminder that the discipline of anthropology has been intimately linked to the history of colonization that haunts my family, that haunts Pakistan, and that continues to aid the imperial interests of the US government. Immediately after the attacks of 9/11, I watched an earlier generation of discredited anthropological scholarship become reenergized as weapons for use by the US military's wars in Iraq and Afghanistan, books such as anthropologist Raphael Patai's *The Arab Mind*; it was painfully clear that the sudden surge of academic interest in Islam and the sudden bounty of funding for research in the Middle East was not politically neutral.[24] For my parents, this half-serious joke is also a way to remind me to remember where I come from, to remind me that while I studied in one of the finest universities in the country and am now afforded the luxury to write books, I could have just as easily been married off out of high school, living in an urban ghetto like my friends from our old neighborhood. Or I could have been like my cousins in Pakistan, dreaming of a Green

Card, mailing flattering pictures to the pre-med sons of Pakistani immigrants scattered throughout American suburbs, praying to somehow get to *Amreeka* while cursing its bombs. My picture travels across borders in the haughty navy-blue vinyl of a US passport, announcing to the border patrol in pastel stamps that I can go (almost) anywhere, that I am nobody's mail-order bride, that romance and research and travel are luxuries I can afford. Still, such luxuries are a responsibility and do not count as "real" work in my family; even now, so many years later, when voices are raised and doors slammed, my suspicious "college books" are cursed. Things might have been different, so I had better think twice.

And I have thought about it, countless times over the years, what it means for me to inherit anthropology.[25] Just as the Orientalist's scholarly authority and cultural superiority rests on a detachment and *distance* from the eastern object/region of his expertise, so too is the anthropologist's discovery of cultural difference through travel predicated on a physical and, more importantly, ontological distance, preserving the essential framework by which "we" study "them." Muslims in the communities that I grew up in are keenly aware of the political and ontological distance that separates them from scholarly experts on Islam; but at the same time, most know little about the ways in which disciplines such as anthropology have reinvented themselves in the wake of Said's *Orientalism* and other path-breaking critiques. Anthropologists, along with scholars in literature, history, area studies, and a wide range of disciplines similarly invested in cultural analysis, now look more closely and critically at the scholarship produced by their disciplines about cultural Others, a movement known loosely as postcolonial studies.[26] On the first day of my first seminar as a graduate student, the class grappled with Said's challenge to redefine the discipline of anthropology, "to forget itself and to become something else [or] remain as a partner in [imperial] domination and hegemony."[27] Whatever nervous jitters or romantic fantasies about the world of ideas that I brought with me into that seminar room on that first day were suppressed by the urgent pitch of the debate around the conference table. Could anthropology salvage itself from its imperial history, or would that be another futile phantom chase, like anthropologists salvaging disappearing cultures, dying languages, and endangered noble savages?[28] After all, the discipline was born out of the Western desire to know others in order to better rule them, to disparage them, or, as Said famously illustrates, to fuel fantasies about the West itself. Was anthropology anything more than a discipline premised on race and difference, doomed to a perpetual cycle of reproducing and deconstructing its own representations? Our class agreed that anthropology could redeem itself by reinventing itself, although we could not agree on what it was that made anthropology worth salvaging as a discipline.[29] Sitting around that long conference table on the first day of class, faced with a history intertwined with imperial interests and a methodology appropriated so easily that its intellectual distinctiveness seemed to evaporate before our eyes, the insistence on the importance of rigorous training in a discipline with an identity crisis, a discipline urged to forget itself, seemed hollow, insular, like a narcotic buzz, like false bravado—or, maybe, a bad omen.[30]

Strangely, being trained during a time when anthropology was mired in its own crisis of authority better equipped me to approach Muslim debates about the crisis of Islamic authority that are the subject of this book. Muslims in the US and around the world grapple with a basic, burning question: who defines Islam today? In the process of mapping Muslims' own global debates about Islamic authority and Islam's place in the US and in the world, I found myself seeing problems and debates that I was trying to document and analyze with new eyes, and often anthropology's crisis acted as a kind of illuminating mirror. Anthropologist Arjun Appadurai describes the challenge to reformulate anthropology for the global age as the unraveling of a conundrum: "what is the nature of locality, as a lived experience, in a globalized, deterritorialized world?"[31] It occurs to me that Muslim Americans ask the same question in religious terms: what might an authentic, American Islam look like in the context of a mobile, heterogeneous, transnational community of believers? What makes a religion, a people recognizably American? Of course, I did not search out the burning questions that drive the religious debates I map in this book; I learned them first as my parents' different and competing visions of America, as my father's great dilemma: is the US only a turnstile, or can it be a home for us? Inheriting anthropology has put me in the position to turn those questions into objects of analysis, to narrate the lives of Muslim American youth and the lives of those debates, to claim a kind of expertise.

The Trouble with the Native Point of View

Classic anthropology's intellectual mission is split at its root; the oxymoron of its method, "participation observation," involves a double move of intimation and distancing: immerse yourself among them and then, once the grant money runs out, come back home, translate all you saw and heard. But I never expected to be able to simply dust myself off and leave the subjects of this study behind me because the conversations that constitute this ethnography, and all ethnography, are ongoing and unfinished, what anthropologist Ruth Behar likens to rabbinical scholars' commentaries upon commentaries on Jewish ritual law that stretch over generations.[32] Fears of anthropologists "going native" in the field and suspicions about whether "native anthropologists" can be truly objective are long outdated, absent in the critical anthropology taught in college classrooms today. Anthropologists no longer imagine the "field" as a distant location where the anthropologist lives among the ____ people; rather, fieldwork is defined in terms of a politics of location, of shifting insides and outsides, of affiliations and distances.[33] The fierce debates among anthropologists about the politics of representation that were my introduction to the discipline taught me to see the fragility and shifting quality of what determines whether I am inside or outside the communities I study at any given moment. What I also learned as a graduate student, and not from my professors, is that in the wake of September 11th the demand in the American book market for tell-all accounts written by "native informants" (especially brown or black Muslim women) has only grown stronger—as the authority of the "native anthropologist" has fallen out of currency in the discipline. Browse an "Islam" shelf in any American bookstore, and alongside (and often indistinguishable) from scholarly books, you will be sure to encounter several best-selling treatises penned by Muslim women "experts" who will explain the real cause behind terrorism (Islam), the global oppression of Muslim women (Islam), every episode of violence in Muslim history (Islam).

Foremost among them is Irshad Manji, a Bengali-Canadian gay rights activist and media personality who is a regular expert on Islam on American radio and television programs. Usually, my Muslim family and friends are not up-to-date on who's who in the world of Ivy

League fellowships, but they follow Manji's career with grave interest. I found myself explaining to them, again and again, why, after all those years and dollars and books, she and I ended up with the same professional title, at the same elite university. ("Why did your Yale make her out to be some kind of expert on Islam?") Manji is one of a growing number of what cultural critic Hamid Dabashi names "native informers," experts whose authority is derived by the twin sources of their status as "natives" (although they often describe themselves as "former" or "recovering" Muslims) and the facility by which they reproduce the tropes, images, and obsessions of Westerners through the classical Orientalist methodology of circular citations, only referencing evidence that confirms the thesis of Muslims' racial and cultural inferiority.[34]

Manji's claim to fame is a *New York Times* best-seller titled *The Trouble with Islam: A Muslim's Call for Reform in Her Faith*, intended as an open letter and "wake-up call" to the global Muslim community, which she describes in her book as "an army of automatons [marching] in the name of Allah."[35] Manji's neo-Orientalist argument is a simple, pure form of what anthropologist Mahmood Mamdani calls "culture-talk": in the West, we have culture, but in the East, their culture has them. Our culture is creative, heterogeneous, and constantly evolving, while Muslim culture is constructed as empty habit, monolithic, mindless conformity to lifeless customs and mummified rules in ancient texts. Culture-talk reduces Muslims to a destructive and "museumized peoples [who cannot] make culture, except at the beginning of creation, . . . people . . . incapable of transforming their culture, the way they seem incapable of growing their own food."[36] Like classic Orientalism, the sheer scale of culture-talk allows it to wield considerable cultural authority as a kind of "common sense" about Muslims and Islam, even when it makes little sense, reproducing and exacerbating the imbalances of power between Westerners (including Muslim Westerners such as Manji) who claim to know Muslim lands and peoples and the actual societies and peoples in question. Manji diagnoses the "Muslim mind" as pathological (brutally violent, barbaric, oppressive, misogynistic, inherently intolerant and racist), and she traces these pathologies back to the original Arab "desert-mindset" of the seventh century, the founding period of Islam, such that devout Muslims, wherever they are and whoever they are, can only march in deadened lockstep behind progress, blind both to the oppressive qualities of their "brain-dead" religion, as she calls it, and to the freedoms offered by the West.[37] Manji promises her Western audiences "insider" information, and ultimately, the dirty, little, Muslim secret that only she has been brave enough to reveal confirms what they already suspected: that everything Muslims do is motivated by Islam!

From the perspective of scholarly critics of native informers, the trouble with Manji and her ilk is that their explanations of what drives Muslims and Islamic history are nonexplanations, crude replications of long-discredited Orientalist arguments.[38] From the point of view of Manji's lay Muslim critics, the trouble with her work is not that her critique of Muslim violence or sexism or Muslim history is a betrayal of "her people" but that the premise of her "reform," like classic Orientalists, aligns her with a number of insidious and imperialistic political agendas. Manji intends her nonmilitary, religious reform campaign, "Operation *Ijtihad* [Reason]," to enter Iraq and Saudi Arabia behind US tanks, offering it as a way to ensure the US's national security.[39] Manji is hardly alone in her prescriptions of religious and cultural solutions for Muslims in theaters of military conflict rather than political ones or in her assumption that these religious and cultural reforms ought to serve the US government's interests. In official and unofficial discourses in the US, from the right and the left, diagnoses of Islam's various "crises" are ubiquitous: the crisis of violence, of backwardness, of stasis, of women's oppression. In fact, within the post–September 11th US political sphere, the reform of Islam became an explicit national interest, and parallel to preserving our national security, military interventions in the Middle East and South Asia are justified by their promise to reform Islam and "resolve" Islam's crisis.[40] In the mainstream US media, political commentators and pundits incessantly proclaim that acts of religious "terror" committed by Muslim actors are indicative of a "clash of civilizations" and "the crisis of Islam"—both terms made famous by Orientalist Bernard Lewis, who argues that the crisis of Islam is a symptom of its pathological essence.[41] As a native informer, Manji echoes Lewis's culture-talk but modifies it by offering good Muslim reformers such as herself as a source of redemption for this doomed civilization. "The cancer begins with us [Muslims]," Manji writes, and she locates that cancer in "nasty" verses of the Quran.[42] Manji rejects the veracity of the Quran itself, not just particular interpretations of the text. This makes her a bold reformist in the eyes of many Americans who are convinced that Islam is in dire need of a reformation and who wrongly equate the Quran's normative status in Islam to the Bible's normative status in Christianity or Judaism. In fact, the Quran's status is more akin to Jesus's status among believing Christians, as the divine incarnate, the Word; but that does not mean that the way Muslims understand the text is set in stone, nor does it render the message of the Quran beyond debate. The Quran itself invites readers to reflect and interpret its verses, both those that are self-evident in their meaning and those that are metaphorical and difficult to decipher. Rather than Manji engaging the ongoing debates about the meanings of Quranic verses that trouble her, she essentially calls Muslims worldwide to rip out the offending pages of their Qurans. Since from a normative Muslim perspective the Quran is inviolate, Manji's directive is widely perceived as absurd and outside the conversation of reform, just as Christians would not recognize the denial of Jesus Christ as a legitimate reform of their faith. Manji also dismisses the Prophetic hadith (traditions of Muhammad) wholesale, which are the second source of revelation for Muslims, because of the possibility of forgeries (a favorite obsession of Orientalist scholars). In addition to rejecting both sources of revelation, Manji parrots a long string of stereotypes and historically baseless myths about Islam, from the idea that Islam was "spread by the sword" to the classic and widely discredited Orientalist narrative of twelfth-century Muslim scholars closing the doors to reason (*ijtihad*), a crude distortion of the history of Islamic law.[43] As a final example of her provocative and profoundly insulting tactics, Manji compares the Prophet Muhammad to terrorists at length, making a parallel between his military victories against the pagan armies that outmatched him in seventh-century Arabia to the ways "Bin Laden's cavalry used box-cutters to attack a superpower."[44]

Native informer "tell-all" accounts do not explain how Islam figures in local contexts or in a broader history; they simply demonstrate that Islam explains every episode of Muslim violence in history, at every scale, from a dysfunctional nuclear family to a war between medieval empires. Manji's troubled childhood is the basis for her authority: she grew up witnessing the brutal violence of her abusive father in her home, and she links this experience to the stultifying

Sunday-school lessons in her mosque in Canada, which she characterizes as a "madrasa" where her white chador flattened her hair and her
spirit.[45] (This is why my Muslim friends joke that Manji's book ought
to have been titled "The Trouble with My Childhood" rather than *The
Trouble with Islam*.) Manji's memoir serves as a point of departure for a
long list of episodes of oppression and violence at the hands of Muslims
throughout history (when non-Muslim parties are implicated partners
in the same violence, she simply omits them), and she insists again and
again that Islam is the cause of this oppression. Manji identifies herself
as the ideal "good" (albeit barely) Muslim, a courageous voice of dissent
against Islam and (only) Muslim governments.[46] Manji's book combines polemic and memoir, disparate and distorted historical accounts
filled with an exhausting number of inaccuracies, a passionate defense
of the governments of the US and Israel and conservative policy recommendations. She applauds George W. Bush, the Patriot Act, and racial
profiling and pushes for more loans from nongovernmental organizations in poor Muslim-majority countries and assaults multiculturalism,
yet her best-selling book received nearly universal praise in the liberal
as well as conservative US press.[47] Indeed, despite her clear disgust with
Islam's founder (and Arabs, in general), many people (even Oprah)
consider her the ideal candidate to lead what are presumed to be the
necessary global political and religious reforms to resolve Islam's "crisis." Aside from her Security Studies fellowship at Yale, followed by an
endowed faculty position at New York University, Manji was the first
recipient of Oprah's O magazine Chutzpah Award, an award that recognizes courageous women activists, because she stands up to "Islamic
bullies and terrorists."[48]

For me, the trouble with native neo-Orientalists such as Manji is
the pervasiveness of their ideas. I have to explain again and again that
their ("native") explanations are different from my ("native") explanations because mine are based not on the color of my skin or my individual experience in Sunday school but on years of research, on the
disciplined study of history and culture. As a researcher, the question
of whether Islam is "in crisis" is a point of investigation for me, not an
assumed fact as it is in the polemics of native informers. My questions
guided me through hundreds of hours of piecing materials together in
archives and through hundreds of interviews with American Muslim

youth in the Middle East and the US. This book does not offer a definitive reform program in order to resolve Islam's presumed crisis; rather,
it offers a far more complex and revealing picture of global debates both
about and among Muslims that get at the heart of anxieties (both most
Americans' and Muslims' own) about Islam's place in the world.

Although in earlier periods of American history Islam was associated with Eastern wisdom and scholasticism, albeit in romantic and
Orientalist terms, today many Americans imagine Islam to be a profoundly anti-intellectual tradition devoid of reason, an assumption bol-
stered by headlines about the extreme measures of a few Islamist militant movements, such as the Taliban in Afghanistan and Pakistan and
the Boko Haram in Nigeria. For most Americans, these troubling cases
have made the word *madrasa*, which in Arabic simply means "school,"
synonymous with mind-numbing lessons in guerrilla warfare. In this
hyperpoliticized context—when capturing the hearts and minds of
Muslim youth is the goal of a war both global and endless and when
madrasas are seen as medieval outposts and bastions of anti-intellectual
dogma—I sought out beauty and complexity in precisely these unlikely
places, in unofficial communities of Islamic learning in the Middle East
that attract Muslim American youth. In these pedagogical networks
overseas, American Muslims debate the place and future of Islam in the
US as they grapple with their obligations both to their country and to
their *umma*, the global community of believers, and as they study their
tradition. They also debate what constitutes religious authority, how to
resolve what they deem Islam's crisis of authority. Calls from outside for
resolving the "other" crisis of Islam, the crisis of violence, of backwardness, of stasis, come from multiple directions and political locations
and, in this study, act as a distant but relentless buzz of background
noise. Through the journeys and studies of Muslim American youth in
the Middle East, this book foregrounds Muslims' own debates about the
reform of Islam, debates that are rarely understood on their own terms.

Questions about Islamic learning, specifically questions about its
nature, purpose, and scope, are at the core of Muslims' own global debates
about religious reform. However, these debates bear little resemblance to
the diagnoses of Islam promulgated by Manji or the State Department,
which casts the "problem" with Islamic learning as a thinking problem
and a curriculum problem: the curriculum taught in madrasas fails to

instill the reflexive questioning of modern thought. The notion that the Islamic intellectual tradition has somehow escaped the process of squaring itself with secular critical inquiry that Christianity and Judaism have successfully undergone is a false problem. Contrary to the stereotype of an unchanging, medieval madrasa system that has somehow survived into our day, and a religious tradition that is only recently grappling with the challenges of modernity, Islamic education around the world has undergone dramatic, modern reforms for over a century, reforms that have profoundly redefined Islamic religious authority for Muslims around the world. Anthropologist Robert Hefner writes, "Islamic education is characterized, not by lock-step uniformity, but by a teaming plurality of actors, institutions, and ideas. . . . Indeed, if there is a struggle for the hearts and minds of Muslims taking place around the world, which there certainly is, madrasas and religious education are on its front line."[49] Rather than passive objects, hearts and minds to be won in a war without end, I engage with American Muslim youth as subjects in these global debates about Islamic authority and reform.

A Map in Fragments

Critical anthropologists have abandoned the modern conception of the discipline as an objective, exact science and with it the conceit of closure and finality for our analyses.[50] Today anthropologists pay close attention to the ways knowledge is produced, reading all positions as contingent, all histories as local, all subjects as constructed, and all claims as competing, including our own. I offer this book as a critical and, I hope, artful translation of global Muslim debates in the form of a fragmentary map that destabilizes the boundaries of the US and the Muslim World and deterritorializes the anthropology of Islam. As anthropologist Fernando Coronil writes, "Points on maps make a point. Like lines in a play, they become meaningful by being joined to each other by the authors and publics who join them. . . . They represent an external reality from within it. Their truth is measured by their exactitude as models of the world they image, but it is realized by the world they help create."[51]

This book is a map of our world in fragments; each point in it corresponds to a place and a point in history. This map corresponds not to the exactitude of my scholarly methods of research but to the exactitude of what appeared significant to me as I tracked these global debates about Islam's crisis of authority in the Middle East and in US mosques and the mainstream American media. My critical mapping of these debates is not a filling of gaps in knowledge so much as an attempt to "create useful knowledge—producing [a map] that can guide us toward, and define, desirable ends."[52] By concentrating the work and words of devout Muslims onto these pages, I stretch and fragment a set of debates about American citizenship and the reform of Islam not only to make a text about the world but to capture the textures of our world. By focusing on the "site" of the Muslim world as it is variously imagined by Muslims in global debates about Islamic authority and Islamic knowledge, this historical ethnography is anchored in many different and discontinuous spaces on both sides of the Atlantic.

This book is divided into two parts. Part 1 situates the debates about authority and the place of Islam in the US that preoccupy young Muslim American seekers today in a twentieth-century history of the transformations of Islamic authority and of American Muslims' transnational moral geographies. Part 2 maps the movement of ideas and intellectuals between the Middle East and the US through an ethnography of students and teachers in global pedagogical networks and, more recently, in the American media spotlight. In chapter 1, I offer a conceptual key to this fragmentary map and an introduction to these unofficial networks of learning in the Middle East. The global networks that connect US mosques to Muslim intellectuals in the Middle East have a genealogy to the reclamation projects of earlier generations of Muslim American seekers and intellectuals; chapters 2 and 3 offer a kind of conceptual history which excavates earlier Muslim American intellectuals' claims to Islamic knowledge and expertise through study and travel, both real and imagined, intertwined with their claims to American citizenship. The ethnographic chapters in part 2 each take up different sets of debates that animate the global pedagogical networks, destabilizing conventional assumptions about the stasis of Islamic learning, the authority of women, and a monolithic view of the US in the Middle East. Chapter 4 maps debates about Islamic pedagogy and reform, contextualizing them in terms of the history of colonial and postcolonial secular reforms to Islamic education and the emergence of the global Islamic revival. Chapter 5 explores the ways religious authority is conceptualized, with a particular focus on the challenges of Muslim American female intellectuals in these networks. Chapter 6 tracks the ways the diagnosis of an authority crisis constrains debates about Islam's future in the US. Finally, in chapter 7, I return to the lives of debates about reforming Islam in the US, represented in the mainstream US media as a battle for hearts and minds, with prominent American Muslim intellectuals on the front lines. These American Muslim leaders represent an earlier generation of seekers who studied Islam abroad; navigating a fraught, post–September 11th America, these intellectuals negotiate their Islamic authority and their American identities in US mosques, the official spaces of the state, and the mainstream American media.

Islam Is a Foreign Country intervenes not only in the debates in my scholarly fields but in the debates that are the object of this study, debates about Islamic orthodoxy and authenticity, debates about the meaning of American citizenship in a global age. I could not divorce my emotional and ethical investments in these debates any more than I could erase those of the subjects; it is precisely these emotional and political investments and our shared experiences of displacement that give this book's debates—both the arguments I develop and those I document—their urgency. I must admit I worry about the different eyes roaming these pages for recognition, from different traditions, with different sets of expectations and, maybe, different kinds of disappointment. After all, my own claim to authority, to integrity and competence, both intellectual and cultural, is precariously balanced on these unsteady pages.[53] Over the course of my research, I had to reconcile the intrinsic tensions between the different intellectual traditions I navigate, the ways in which anthropology necessarily disciplines and secularizes my analyses, ways in which I may not always be conscious. As Said notes, geographical "dislocation, secular discovery, and the painstaking recovery of implicit or internalized histories . . . stamp the ethnographic quest with the mark of a secular energy that is unmistakably frank."[54] While for Said these qualities are a mark of anthropology's worldliness, my Muslim friends and family, in their own words, identify them as intellectual limits, limits they have been warning me to anticipate since I first started out on the path of becoming a scholar.

As a way of sensitizing myself to these tensions and limits, I became the student of a Ghanaian scholar and Islamic jurist, a shaykh, throughout my first few years of graduate school. Although he also holds a PhD in Islamic studies from the University of Michigan in addition to his religious credentials, he often urged me to balance my secular education as he bemoaned the fact that so many Muslim academics know more about Western philosophy than they do about their own intellectual tradition. Eager to maintain my intellectual footing in both canons, I struggled to supplement my university course packs with the reading required by my "other" education, but it remained hopelessly imbalanced, always more "high" theory than Islamic legal theory. After a long week of seminars and heavy reading loads, on Saturday afternoons I would drive out to an old, quiet Detroit neighborhood, where my shaykh had converted an old blue house neighboring his own into a modest, free counseling service center for Muslim families. Here, the other students and I would pile into a tiny, dusty room and crowd around a wobbly table for our *halaqa*, an Islamic study circle. For hours we would go over an Arabic text on Islamic legal theory at a painfully slow pace due to our difficulties with the classical Arabic. Occasionally, the class would be interrupted by one of the shaykh's small children hunting his deep pockets for a lollipop or by a new convert with a quick question or by a troubled, worn-out couple needing an argument mediated. Although we took our studies seriously, the study circle also became a springboard for innumerable tangential discussions. The shaykh welcomed these, made that dusty room a safe place to make any criticism or ask any question. This is where I would voice my frustrations with the racism, classism, sexism, and political impotence that permeate the Muslim communities that I work in, both in the US and in the Middle East.

The study circle also became a place to bring questions from my other intellectual world, the world of graduate classes, course packs, and postmodern dilemmas that sometimes would snowball into faith crises. Often the shaykh would be unable to satisfy my questions and doubts or even to allay my frustrations with a Muslim history replete with not-so-"Islamic" episodes. I complained to him about feeling stifled by the plaintive expectations of my community, desperate for me to write about our Golden Age, when "we" were the most "civilized" and Europe slept through the Dark Ages until the Enlightenment ("which we gave them, anyway," they remind me). I would also express my own doubts about the value of my work in the current political climate, the futility of trying to represent Muslim hearts and minds as anything other than objects to be won or lost in a global battle of civilizations. Still, I was inspired and comforted by how the shaykh would listen to my often overly tortured ranting or my painful questions and remain utterly unmoved by what I found so disappointing. Many of the issues that kept me up at night hardly fazed him. He would simply say that Islam could not be reduced to Muslims, often hastening to add that America too fell far short of its ideals; he would remind me that although we can only approximate justice in this world, human failures cannot diminish the ideal of justice that binds us all. And although I admit I never felt a faith so pure and strong, it always made me feel better knowing that it existed out there, in the wise, kind eyes of my shaykh, in his open, brilliant smile. I would pray for his solid faith, his easy courage, and that my work might touch people the way his kindness had touched me.

It was over a year before I discovered that I was passing by my old childhood neighborhood every week on my way to the *halaqa*. I am not sure why it never dawned on me, but memory works in strange ways. It did not look like the home I knew from faded photographs and monochromatic memories. It looked like a ghetto: sad, dirty, small streets, crumbling houses that seemed like slumped shoulders, garbage in piles, just another poor black neighborhood surrounded by too many empty warehouses and liquor stores, indistinguishable and unrecognizable to me. That discovery forced me to think more carefully about why it was that as I was mastering a canon, training to be a scholar, maybe even an expert; I found myself seeking knowledge and authority elsewhere, too, traveling across the borders of class and race, across the borders of secular and religious, across the borders of English and Arabic, now and then, across the borders between who I had been, who I might have been, and who I was becoming. The questions I explore here emerged out of those personal links between place, authority, and identity.

PART I

The Roots and Routes of Islam in America

1

Islam Is a Foreign Country

Mapping the Global Crisis of Authority

THE BABYSITTER

With the first blue light of morning, Usman waits at Damascus International Airport for a young Muslim American stranger.[1] As always, Usman will help him with the heavy suitcases; he will find him a suitable, furnished, and reasonably priced apartment and make the introductions to appropriate tutors; he will escort him to the embassy and patiently go through the red tape; he will take him on guided tours of the city and share its secrets; he will act as translator and, when a faux pas is committed, a diplomat; he will listen to daydreams deep into the night and impart advice with humility; he will even cook feasts of American Chinese food for his homesick friends with queasy stomachs.

Each year, dozens and dozens of Western student-travelers in Damascus cross Usman's path and receive his help at no cost. They are beneficiaries of the extraordinary hospitality he and his wife lavish on strangers. In their circles, Usman is known as the Babysitter. His babysitting career has made him a kind of expert on his "clients" and, therefore, a "key informant" for an anthropologist with her own heavy suitcases. Usman explains this strange world to me with the patient eyes of experience: "The two-monthers have goatees and wear clothes from the Gap, and the six-monthers try to buy traditional clothing and they don't really know why they're doing it. Romantic stuff. Us long-term ones, we don't really care, anymore. That is, unfortunately, how a lot of people experience Damascus: superficially. If they're here for two months, they're into their romantic thing, or they can't handle the cockroaches, and that's all they remember. The guy who thought he was in heaven on earth, the guy who thought he went back in time, and the guy who will say Damascus is nothing but huge cockroaches in a giant ashtray of a city, they are all wrong."

Since Usman spends so much time arranging for student-travelers' pedagogical needs, he often plays the role of sounding board for wistful ambitions. "The first thing I tell [Americans] is that learning is a commitment; it's not a package, not ready-made. Islam is not going to pick you up at the airport—I am. You can call it a lot of things: finding their identity, Islamic escapism, romantics looking for an island of tradition, spiritual tourism, whatever. They all get disappointed because Damascus is not a utopia. All of the Americans are good people, but [their educational] goals are different, and so the experience is gonna be different."

Usman expects the Americans' romantic notions of Damascus-as-utopia to dissipate on their own after a few months, but he feels obligated to disabuse them of romantic notions about their self-important social activism back in the US. "Damascus is not MSA training-ground," he says, referring to the Muslim Students Association, a popular group on American college campuses. "The goal is not to return to America as more effective public speakers or Muslim celebrities but to become mu'minin [true believers].

"In the US, in MSA, instead of bars and clubbing, [Muslim youth] work to plan these events on campus: Islam Awareness Week, Eid dinners, and it's very self-congratulatory. But if you say, 'OK, we're gonna have a qiyam [all-night prayer vigil],' those same activists will walk out. Something is wrong. At some level, the activism thing is a dunyawi [worldly] thing, halal [good, clean] fun. But do Muslim Americans actually know what they are working for? What? An Islamic state? What's the goal? Why do we need an Islamic state—as a safe haven from our corrupt dictatorships? What does establishing Islam in America mean? Raw numbers of converts? That we want a Muslim president? I mean, is that what Allah wants us to do? I don't think so.

"I'm not into discussing what Islam needs, and Syrians don't use that kind of vocabulary. So, when Americans say 'Islam needs a renaissance,' it's like, 'Allah doesn't need a renaissance.' Islam is just the system, the means. Allah is the end. Sometimes Muslims go about it backwards. At the end of the day, it's more than leaving a mark. It's what's happening to your soul."

Then Usman's face and voice soften. "I'm like this, too, by the way," he confesses. "I'm much more intellectual than spiritual. I'm much more inclined to reading than praying, and I know I need to change that, and I learned that here." As an Egyptian American who arrived in Damascus not only with broken Arabic but with broken Arabic in an Egyptian colloquial accent, Usman endured years of chiding from his Syrian peers who could not forgive his parents for speaking so much English in their American home. Seven years later, Usman's Arabic is good enough for him to pass as a Damascene local, a pipe dream for most American student-travelers. But despite his affection for Damascus, Usman admits he still does not feel at home.

"I don't know a single Westerner that really feels at home here. Damascus taught me that I am [an American] no matter how good my Arabic gets. In that way, I really am like a babysitter. I can help you, I'll take care of you while you're here, but it's not my house and I will leave."

A Crisis of Authority, a Crisis of Epistemology

The religious imagination of American Muslims is a profoundly geographic one. This book takes up Muslims' own debates about the crisis of Islam, specifically a crisis of religious authority, and how this sense of crisis is intertwined with the notion that its resolution is located somewhere else, and often some time before. In the essay "Imaginary Homelands," Salman Rushdie inverts novelist L. P. Hartley's famous opening line, "The past is a foreign country, they do things differently there." Rushdie argues that it is the present that is foreign "and that the past is home, albeit a lost home in a lost city in the mists of lost time."[2] Lost homelands and lost glories have dominated the religious imaginations of Muslim Americans for at least a century, reflecting an enduring sense of being out-of-place in the US. African American Muslims speculate about their roots in Islamic Africa, about the learned princes and princesses ripped from their land, forcibly turned slaves on US plantations, forcibly turned Christians in their slave-masters' churches. Nostalgic immigrants remember the lives they traded for their American dreams in a familiar but distant East, where time moved slowly enough for daily congregational prayers in the neighborhood mosque and for daily visits over tea with relatives. Their American children have few if any memories of the old country and often identify strongly with their religious heritage without necessarily feeling attached to their parents' countries of origin. Devout Muslim American youth are often nostalgic for a deeper history, in an Islamic East that is not an airplane ride away but an epoch away, when Islam was a global superpower, a thriving, rich civilization, all lost to the rise of the West and its subsequent imperial domination of the East. Many, like Usman, travel to the intellectual centers of the Muslim world in the hope of recovering their tradition's lost knowledge, lost dignity.

The subjects of this study, self-identifying devout American Muslims as well as their coreligionists in the Middle East, believe that Islam is under attack from all sides. There is a strong sense of crisis, a sense that the predictability of life is breaking down, a sense of unstoppable, damaging change. They speak of the crisis of Islam as a generalized condition, and the sources of danger they name are diffuse, including the cultural and political legacies of colonialism and the pressing realities of American empire in the Age of Terror but also internal conflicts, hot debates over the definition of Islamic authority that they fear could implode their tradition. I locate global debates over Islamic authority in specific historical and cultural contexts in the US as well as in the Middle East in order to isolate and analyze one strand of the amorphous body of issues that are so often glossed as a singular crisis of Islam.

One animating question of the crisis—how to define Islamic authority—is, ironically, a result of the contemporary, worldwide Islamic revival. Today, across Muslim societies all over the world, men and women without seminary educations are reinvigorating Islamic public discourse; these revivalists are aided by advancing levels of education and new media. Although they lack the philosophical sophistication of seminary-trained theologians and jurists, the revivalists dominate the Islamic public sphere and blogosphere; their voices echo from speakers in mosques, cars, computers, and television sets, their pamphlets, books, essays, and columns pervade bookstores, newsstands, and the Internet. The sheer popularity of these lay Muslim activists challenges the exclusive claim of seminary-trained scholars to interpret revelation and to develop an Islamic vision of social justice. Of course, this story of the modern fragmentation of Islamic authority has a darker side; voices of individuals such as Osama bin Laden are also amplified as a result of the widening access to Islamic public discourse, and although his lethal religious and political vision does not compel the masses, he successfully captured the imagination of a small but dangerous Muslim following around the world.

The question of who speaks for Islam—the question that preoccupies the devout Muslims in this study—is about more than the struggle to respond to Muslim terrorists and native informants in the mainstream US media, and it is also more than determining who should be the imam in their local mosque. American Muslim youth share a historical narrative of the fragmentation of Islamic authority with their coreligionists around the world, but their invocations of crisis also index a very particular, very American set of racial conflicts and religious anxieties. My aim is not to offer a resolution to what devout Muslims deem a crisis of authority but to show what their sense of crisis produces and forecloses, what it makes possible and impossible, what it makes thinkable and unthinkable. To this end, this chapter serves as an introduction to these global intellectual networks and the debates that animate them; it offers a kind of conceptual key to this fragmentary map, defining analytical terms such as *tradition, counterpublic, crisis,* and *orthodoxy.* As we follow the journeys of Muslim American youth in the US and in the Middle East, these conceptual tools will aid us in accounting for the ways that the global and the local converge in their debates about religious authority and Islamic knowledge, debates rooted to particular places but also shared across borders.

Today the phenomenon of young Muslims traveling abroad for religious study is a common feature across the diverse spectrum of US mosques. The overwhelming majority of American student-travelers abroad plan to return to the US, meaning that their Islamic education abroad is not an end in itself but a means to retrieve tools to help resolve Islam's crisis. American Muslim youth are a cross-section of the heterogeneous American Muslim population spread across much of the US as a whole and vary a great deal in their degrees of religiosity. Like most faith communities in the US, only a fraction of Muslim Americans are "mosqued" Muslims, and even among those who are, many are not particularly aware of these debates about religious authority and Islamic knowledge, in contrast to individuals such as Usman who are deeply invested in these debates; in fact these debates drew him to Damascus.[3]

Urban intellectual centers, such as Damascus, have attracted Muslim seekers and students from around the world for centuries. Those students once came and continue to come from far distances, from Timbuktu, from Jakarta, from Grenada. Today Muslim student-travelers also come from Boston and San Diego, but their religious studies are energized by a strong sense of urgency, of crisis.

Muslim American student-travelers seek a way to imagine a future for Islam in the US, a way to resolve the contemporary religious crisis in their US mosques, and thus their hopes for religious study are merged with a particular moral geography of the Islamic East (not always the Middle East) as an Archive of Tradition. Although they hope to revive their tradition, Muslim American student-travelers often talk about their tradition in simple, static terms, as an object that can be found, excavated, and brought home, a view that corresponds to the term's older usage in anthropology. Anthropologist A. L. Kroeber's classic definition of tradition as the "internal handing on through time" of culture traits renders tradition a static object.[4] Although Muslims often sound like an older generation of anthropologists when they talk about their tradition as an object waiting for discovery abroad, to be extracted and brought back to the US, as we will see, the processes of studying, teaching, and arguing over what constitutes tradition are far more complex and challenging than the retrieval of a souvenir.

The crude construction of tradition as a fixed body of practices and ideas that move through time unchanged and unchallenged, except when abandoned, will not take us very far in understanding the religious lives and debates of Muslim students and teachers in the global networks explored here. This commonsense usage of the term *tradition* operates on the assumption that "normal" tradition requires an unthinking conformity to the past that opposes reason. Therefore, this view of tradition as fixed cannot account for the arguments within a tradition and as a result, arguments within tradition are always represented as exceptional, as a problem, a rupture in the flow of tradition. In contrast to this impoverished understanding of tradition, I draw on an alternative understanding of tradition developed by critical anthropologists of Islam who place argument and reason at tradition's center. In this more rigorous understanding of tradition, debate itself becomes a testament to the health of the tradition.[5]

Talal Asad, in his now classic literature review "The Idea of an Anthropology of Islam," first redirected scholars studying Muslim societies away from debates about the right scale of their analyses to a more productive set of questions about which concepts could best capture Muslims' lives. Following Alasdair MacIntyre, Asad recuperates tradition as an analytical tool, as a set of discourses connected to an exemplary past and to interpretations of foundational texts that Muslims draw on in their ordinary lives.[6] Just as the Orientalist claims to have the tools to be able to get at the heart of Islam, anthropologists of Islam claim that their method allows them to access the point of view of their Muslim subjects, their interior worlds, Muslim hearts and minds, so to speak.[7] Although anthropologists interested in social structure and historical causation, such as Ernest Gellner, are typically seen as very different from symbolic anthropologists such as Clifford Geertz, Asad argues that they all treat Islam as a total system. Whether they construct Islam as a distinctive historical totality or deterministic system or as a body of Islamic symbols, these anthropologists represent Islam dramaturgically. Asad writes, "Gellner's Islamic actors do not speak, they do not think, they *behave* [within a fixed social structure] . . . for Geertz, as for Gellner, the schematization of Islam as a drama of religiosity expressing power is obtained by omitting indigenous discourses, and by turning all Islamic behavior into *readable gesture*."[8] Asad rejects the idea that anthropologists might be able to isolate "Islamic" social systems, as Gellner claims, or "Islamic" experiences, as Geertz attempts to do. Instead, Asad argues that by thinking of Islam as a discursive tradition, an unfolding of arguments over shared foundational texts across space and over time, anthropologists could discern Islamic practices and styles of reasoning. In other words, in lieu of Muslim subjects who "behave" or "act" out their roles, Asad urges anthropologists to examine the arguments, logics, and styles of reasoning and interpretation of Muslim subjects who *think*.[9] Asad's complex and open-ended definition of Islam as a discursive tradition best captures the religious debates about authority and Islamic pedagogical practices in the US and in the Middle East that I map here.

It is important to note that whether in the US or in the Middle East, the crisis of authority and epistemology that preoccupies devout Muslims is a qualified crisis, not a total crisis of authority. In these Muslim networks, the normative belief in the Quran and the Prophet Muhammad's example as authoritative sources of divine revelation are taken for granted. Rather than the core sources of revelation, the debates about Islamic religious authority in these networks are over the scholarly disciplines built around revelation. The Quran is believed to be the divine word as revealed to Muhammad in the seventh century through the medium of the angel Gabriel. As a human prophet receiving direct divine guidance over twenty-three years, Muhammad's own life example, as recorded in the *hadith* traditions and ancillary literatures, is a second source of revelation for Muslims. The death of the Prophet in 632 meant the loss of religious authority based on cultural and temporal proximity to the event of divine revelation. To the extent that the Prophet was inerrant, to the extent that even his human errors—and there were a few, as the Quran itself points out—were rectified through divine intervention, Prophet Muhammad's moral vision for his followers was overall the yield of a divine process and, therefore, a process not beholden to human rationality. Even when the Prophet made rational decisions, devout Muslims believe that Muhammad's decisions and actions had God's implicit sanction if they were left to stand. When his rational decisions or human errors displeased God, the Prophet was corrected through new revelations brought by the archangel Gabriel. In sum, although Muslims believe Muhammad was human and not divine, his exemplary life shares divine authority with the Quran. After the Prophet's death, the interpretive process of engaging revelation and the political leadership of the umma passed to his followers, who could not make claims to inerrancy that would be recognized by the majority of the community. The question of inerrancy and political leadership is what led to the Shia/Sunni schism, with Sunnis ultimately taking the position that the period of direct, explicit, binding divine communication ended with Muhammad's prophecy and Shias extending the Prophet's divine authority to his descendants. Thus, the interpretations of those who succeeded Muhammad, regardless of whether they are the Prophet's blood relatives, are not considered by Sunnis to have legitimacy through divine endorsement the way Muhammad's life had.

In the eighth and ninth centuries, Muslims (Sunni and Shia) developed a strong scholarly tradition and established an interpretive community of scholars to formalize a range of disciplines around the core sources of revelation. In the absence of the final Prophet, the early Muslim community had to replace its source of divine communication with a rational infrastructure linking their educated guesses about what God wanted in the here and now to the fixed revelation, both the Quran and the moral example of Muhammad's life. The formation of scholarly communities and disciplines was a direct result of the rapid expansion of the Muslim community from seventh-century Arabian city-states into a world empire that stretched as far west as Spain and as far east as India in less than two hundred years. The emergence of Islamic scholarly disciplines—linguistics, exegesis, philosophy, poetry, theology, and law—in the urban centers of the Islamic empire and the popularization of mystical sufi orders that developed formal and informal religious vernaculars were directly tied to the spread of Islam to lands and peoples that were separated from the Prophet's life and message by space, time, and often language and culture. Core elements from encounters with non-Muslim intellectual interlocutors were borrowed and integrated into the new Islamic disciplines, and Islamic pedagogy was institutionalized in a range of ways. Although the growth of converts was far slower than the growth of the Islamic empire, contrary to the myth that Islam was spread by the sword, within a few generations a critical mass of the subjects of Muslim rulers were themselves Muslims. In an effort to preserve the interpretive integrity of the tradition in the face of this increasingly diverse, heterogeneous umma, new scholarly disciplines reconstituted religious authority as decentralized and provisional by abstracting it; religious intellectuals divorced religious authority from Arab cultural (but not linguistic) primacy. For example, Islamic law settled on an objective discourse of law rather than an ontological one, such that students of the law from different walks of life and cultural and linguistic backgrounds had equal access to revelation through the medium of an intricately constructed public reason and scholarly methodology. The Islamic disciplines and their associated methodologies form a canon, and for devout Muslims, that canon is a kind of cumulative answer to the question of how believers ought to reflect on and engage the world. The contemporary sense of crisis among devout Muslims in the US and around the world emerges from the fear that the answer—that is, those bodies of traditional knowledge—is either an inaccessible or an inadequate answer to the challenges devout Muslims face today.

By the ninth century, the terms of Sunni religious authority based on scholarly study produced a plural, robust, decentralized, ethnically diverse, and global intellectual community. Parallel to the emerging class of Islamic scholarly authorities, local men and women captured the imagination of lay Muslims and accrued authority based on their reputations for piety and spiritual insight, and they developed followings among Muslims who considered these pious men and women saints. The sheer variety of religious perspectives and interpretations increased exponentially with the dramatic growth of the Islamic empire and the umma, and, for some Muslims, this created a sense of religious crisis. In the ninth century, a state inquisition was set up to impose a unitary, theological doctrine because there was a growing sense that the diversity of Muslims' theological opinions threatened the future of the tradition. Despite the inquisition's brutality, it failed, and no single school of law or theology has ever been able to become hegemonic. Historians emphasize the enormous importance of this failed inquisition to the development of the highly decentralized structure of Sunni Islam in particular, noting that had the inquisition succeeded, it may have formed a hierarchy similar to those in other religious traditions.

This deep history of contested and competing forms of Islamic authority looms large in the religious imaginations of American Muslims, who often make parallels between debates about authority in their own growing, diverse communities and the disagreements over the definition of authority in this foundational history, disagreements that were also exacerbated by the umma's rapid growth in size and diversity. Arguments over religious authority in US mosques are shaped by the global flows of Islamic intellectuals and ideas from all over the world. American Muslims construct Islamic knowledge as something forgotten or lost over the generations through the trauma of colonialism and postcolonial modernization programs of educational reform that have marginalized classically trained scholars, resulting in a crisis of authority. American Muslims' debates also carry the imprint of a particular American history by which race and class shaped Islamic authority in the US over time, and the search for traditional knowledge abroad is offered as an explicit attempt to transcend that fraught, local history. The conditions of contemporary mosque life in the US reflect broad and widely disputed definitions of interpretive authority and religious leadership, and as a result, American mosque communities are often deeply divided on the question of who should lead their mosque. Muslims in the US make up the most demographically diverse national Muslim population in the world, and mosques are among the most diverse American houses of worship.[10] While Muslim Americans often offer the diversity of their congregations as a point of pride, this diversity is also a source of divisive conflicts over religious authority. As Muslim Americans debate who ought to lead their mosque congregations, questions of authority and authenticity that reflect the ethnic, racial, sectarian, and class divisions in US mosque communities are at the forefront of their debates. (Although there is a parallel sense of an authority crisis among Shia Muslims, their constructions of Islamic authority are more rigidly defined in terms of the Prophet's bloodline and a clerical class than the decentralized construction of authority of Sunni Muslims; due to these differences, parallel American Shia debates and global pedagogical networks abroad rarely overlap with the Sunni networks and debates I focus on here.)[11]

Disagreements over the criteria that make one a religious authority do not in and of themselves constitute a crisis, because crisis is more than mere confusion, even communal confusion, as a result of an unresolved religious debate. The sense of crisis derives from the sense that religious debates are becoming incoherent. In other words, healthy argument and debate within a tradition depends on coherence (but not uniformity or consensus); crisis emerges out of the sense of incoherence, the loss of a common vocabulary. Consider Thomas Kuhn's discussions of knowledge in *The Structure of Scientific Revolutions*.[12] Kuhn explores how counterfactuals create gaps in scientific theories and how coherence is maintained despite these gaps. Kuhn argues that once the theory's explanatory power falls below the level of effort it takes to sustain the theory itself despite the gaps—once the counterfactuals hit a critical mass that the theory of knowledge cannot account for—there is a crisis, a scientific revolution. The old theory is exchanged for a new one that reorders the world. The new reordering, inevitably, will also be constituted by gaps, an incomplete circle that functions as though it were closed, until enough counterfactuals accumulate and yield yet another crisis, and so on. The same cycle characterizes the life of tradition, from its creation and establishment of authoritative knowledge and practices, to the emergence of crisis to the resolution of crisis through knowledge and practices that are not necessarily new but that reorder the world in a new way.

In the nineties, training in the classical Islamic disciplines began to be seen by many devout American Muslims as a potential source of resolving the debates about defining Sunni religious authority. If there was an increased Islamic literacy and a critical mass of classically trained American Sunni scholars, then intellectual mastery of the tradition could be the new, universal measure of religious authority, trumping ethnic, racial, class, and, for some, even male privilege. The journeys of seekers such as Usman to the Middle East are predicated on this very notion, that the authority of classical Islamic training, the mastery of "traditional" bodies of knowledge, will resolve the authority crisis as it manifests itself in US mosques and will, in Usman's words, "establish" Islam in the US. Throughout these networks, student-travelers also encounter an earlier generation of American expats (often converts) as teachers in the Middle East; they have devoted years to the study of the classical Islamic disciplines, and they act as nodes in these pedagogical networks. These middle-aged American men and women left the US to pursue Islamic higher learning, but in contrast to most of their American students, many of them do not have the ambition to return to the US.

TIME MEASURED IN ANTS

Jawad is happy living in the community of American sufis in Amman. Before devotees could begin the formal stages of spiritual exercises in the sufi order, his white American teacher, Shaykh Nuh Keller, required them to complete forty days of consecutive prayers on time, a seemingly simple task but one that often proved they were less conscientious about their five daily prayers than they realized. For some, such as Jawad, it took months before they could complete the forty days. Shaykh Nuh also had him comb over the careless years of his adolescence in order to calculate all the prayers in which Jawad had made minor ritual mistakes or that he had skipped altogether. Under Shaykh Nuh's guidance, Jawad was making up for these lost prayers, one at a time. Jawad felt a mixture of irritation, guilt, and frustration with himself.

"I haven't missed a prayer since July," Jawad smiles, sheepishly. "That's eight months, and I'd never prayed five times a day for that long before, and its embarrassing." The prayers are not the only condition of the forty days. Expressing anger breaks the cycle, as well. Jawad stands still till the mood passes through him; if it remains, he sits, and if he still feels angry, he lays down. If it persists, he washes his body for prayer as a final anger-management tool and pretends to be coolheaded with the hope that meeting anger with fortitude will become a reflex. Raising his voice for more than a sentence is forbidden, along with cutting remarks, lies, slammed doors, and complaining about others simply "to get it out." Living with strangers in a small slice of a new country, a few blocks built around a small, white mosque on a sloping hillside, leaves Jawad with a strong sense of homesickness and a lot he wants off his chest.

"You just get tired of failing. At first you do it for show. I mean, I'm living with these [American] guys I don't really know, and they are all really smart, sober guys. I don't want them to see me miss a prayer, and pretty soon, I mean, now, I can't imagine not getting up for *fajr* [dawn prayer] even if no one was here. It's like, does Allah want to see your face in the mosque in the morning or not? And if not, forget it, you'll be on the snooze button. Shaykh Nuh says, 'If you want to know your worth in Allah's eyes, then look at what Allah keeps you busy doing.'"

Occasionally, the young Palestinian men in the neighborhood photo lab successfully coax Jawad into indulging in a secret, guilty pleasure: a basketball game in a nearby private gym. Shaykh Nuh espouses the relinquishment of attachments to worldly things as a precondition to spiritual studies. His rulebook for his American devotees is clear enough: "Those who cannot do without the gym, the sauna, fast-food restaurants, amusement parks, hairdressing salons, and so forth are worldlings, not *murids* [devotees], and should not come. People can go elsewhere for these."[13] Jawad did not want to be a worldling, but basketball was an attachment he never could break. His Palestinian friends practice their shots and their English with him and joke about sneaking into the US in one of his suitcases. They call him "*Jawaz Safar*," Passport, a teasing play on his name and the privilege of his mobility.

What his Palestinian friends do not know is that Jawad is not that privileged. In his cold, bare apartment in Amman, Jawad sleeps with thousands of dollars worth of pastel bills stuffed in a pillowcase. (His father owns two cars and a modest house in New Jersey, and he takes great pride in the fact that he has never seen the inside of an American bank.) They also do not know that Jawad's trip to Jordan is not the first time he has bought a one-way international plane ticket to study Islam. This time Jawad is determined not to go back home feeling like a failure. This time Jawad will change.

The Pakistani madrasas on CNN—Jawad sat with those kids wearing white skull caps and rocking back and forth to the rhythm of the Quran. He remembers the rocking and memorizing and swatting flies. Americans do not understand that those kids are not thinking about suicide missions. The students he knew were like him, thinking about hunger pangs and heat and their smarter siblings who might pass them by and make something of themselves yet.

The GED class and the community college courses had been for his mother. Jawad has the kind of mother who cries too easily, from too much of anything, too much excitement, too much to do, even if someone speaks to her in a voice too loud. Nothing brings on her tears like disappointment. When he was a boy, she had convinced herself that he would be a doctor or at least a physical therapist like his cousin. The cigarettes and the detentions and the report card that spelled D-E-A-D-D might have been hints (the A was in physical education).

Jawad was seventeen and did not know what to do, so he convinced his father to sell his car and let Jawad study in a Pakistani madrasa. He could memorize the entire Quran and become a *hafiz*. Although not the same as a physical therapist, it could be something his mother could be proud of. After an eighteen-hour flight, some cups of tea, and a few phone calls, his uncle enrolled Jawad at the Ashrafiyyah in Lahore, the largest madrasa in Punjab. Now that Jawad is in Amman, he regrets not studying in Karachi instead, under the famous Usmani family of scholars. Shaykh Taqi Usmani is the shaykh the other Americans ask him about—although someone told him he would not have had a chance at getting in anyway. Had he studied in Karachi instead, maybe he would have lasted for more than a few months. Too soon he was back home, defeated and depressed. His mother was relieved, thrilled to dote on him and have him tearfully thank her for all she did that went unappreciated, the clean house, the steamy rotis fresh off the iron *tava*, the closet of clean clothes. The Ashrafiyyah transformed his cramped, old house with squeaky stairs and chipping paint in Jersey City into a palace. And his mother was some kind of saint he had done wrong.

Still, a few months was something—not long enough to memorize anything impressive but long enough to understand that time moved more than one way inside you. That was what memorization taught him, taught his body. He could measure time with the ways verses got imprinted on his mind instead of in minutes. He would rock back and forth the way the second hand circles a watch in tiny lunges. He learned to memorize to black ants marching from crack to crevice in a ceaseless line across the ceiling, like black Arabic letters marching in front of his eyes.

Muslim Counterpublics: Not a Movement, People in Motion

Who are the student-travelers that make up these transnational, mobile networks of learning? American Muslim student-travelers are not part of a singular, global movement, nor do they fit any particular demographic picture. They are men and women, married and single, reflecting a diverse range of ethnic, racial, and socioeconomic backgrounds. American student-travelers may study abroad for a summer or for ten years. Some, such as Usman, are fluent in Arabic and pore over ancient monographs; others stumble over Arabic letters and learn basic rites of worship from illustrated pop-up books written for Arab children. Most are in their twenties, but the American students range from young adolescents to middle-aged adults. For long-term students, such as Usman, their pedagogical journeys can be quite expensive, and they must work to support themselves. Usman's studies and his young family have been supported primarily by the odd jobs he has taken over the years but also, if reluctantly, by occasional loans from his parents in the US. For working-class student-travelers such as Jawad, their journeys and studies abroad are far more financially burdensome. Student-travelers may have personal savings or a scholarship, or they may be funded by their mosque communities back in the US who expect them to come back to the US and serve either their mosque or a national Muslim organization on completion of their studies. Americans' destinations are all over the map: Mauritania, Senegal, Morocco, Spain, Sudan, Egypt, Jordan, Syria, Lebanon, Turkey,

Iran, Yemen, Saudi Arabia, India, Pakistan, and Malaysia. These networks are not only linked to the US; Muslims come from Canada, Europe, Latin and South America, Asia, and Africa to study as well.

Through word of mouth in university student groups, email discussion lists, and references from Muslim American religious leaders, American student-travelers establish contacts with scholars and current students overseas. The choice of whom to study with and what subjects to study often (but not always) corresponds to the religious orientation of the student-travelers in the US, since it is often through their American networks that they decide on a particular destination. In some cases, these networks are formal, named, easily identified. For example, the Jerrahi, a mystical sufi order which originated in Turkey, has established US mosque communities in New York, in White Plains, Brooklyn, and the Lower East Side of Manhattan, and their American devotees often travel to Istanbul to study with the head sufi shaykh. In other cases, an American Muslim movement and a pedagogical institution in the Middle East may have an informal association, such as the longstanding but unofficial relationship between the African American Muslim community of Imam Warith Deen Mohammed and the state-sanctioned Abu Nour secondary school and college in Damascus. In most cases, the pedagogical networks and affiliations are general, informal, and overlapping but still identifiable. For example, an American student who identifies as a Salafi will usually gravitate to teachers and peers who are sympathetic to this theological reform movement, choosing a location in order to study with a particular, sought-after teacher or at a specific pedagogical institution. Once abroad, American student-travelers may also "experiment" with other Islamic networks or have an eclectic mix of teachers, reflecting pragmatic concerns for convenience, such as the price of tuition or the commute. A student may choose a teacher who has a center in the neighborhood that he or she happens to rent an apartment in, and, in such cases, previous religious affiliations have little to do with how teachers and students find one another. Importantly, ancestral origins do not necessarily determine their destinations, demonstrating that these educational journeys are more than heritage tourism, more than an effort to merely celebrate one's ethnic or religious roots. Syrian Americans travel to Mauritania, Pakistani Americans to Turkey, African Americans to Pakistan, Bosnian Americans to Malaysia.

This multisite study moves across the US and three bustling Arab metropolises that are popular destinations for American Muslim youth: Amman, Jordan; Damascus, Syria; and Cairo, Egypt. Although cities such as Cairo and Damascus have most recently entered the consciousness of most Americans in the context of the so-called Arab Spring, these cities have long held a special significance for the American Muslim communities examined here. For decades, Cairo has been the most popular pedagogical destination for American student-travelers, not least because it is so easy for American citizens to get and renew visas and because it boasts the most diverse set of networks. With a dense population of over 10 million, Cairo is not only the capital of Egypt; this megacity is the largest in Africa and in any Arab country. Like Cairo, Syria's densely populated capital city of 2.5 million, Damascus, is one of the oldest continuously inhabited cities in the world and a center of global trade and Islamic intellectual activity for centuries. Political changes in the twentieth century led to a decline in Damascus's global prominence, though it maintains its intellectual and economic importance in the region. Amman is the capital city of Jordan, Syria's neighbor to the south. With a population over a million, this capital city is one of the fastest growing cities in the Middle East. Although it is also an ancient city, it does not have the prestige of being an Islamic intellectual center for centuries the way Damascus and Cairo do. Amman attracts Western tourists, and it is seeing a great deal of economic growth, including becoming a favorite hub for multinational corporations in part because it has long been seen as relatively politically stable by observers outside the region and especially since the dignity revolutions (also known as the Arab Spring) that consumed Damascus and Cairo in 2011. While distinct from one another in important ways, Damascus, Amman, and Cairo are connected by a diverse set of unofficial, Islamic pedagogical networks of teachers and students. For example, the sufi community of Shaykh Nuh Keller has established a small enclave in Amman that attracts Muslim devotees from North America and Europe who come to study with him for months or even years; he also has students in Damascus and Cairo.

American Muslim student-travelers are often surprised to find themselves navigating debates about Islamic authority that are just as heated and dizzying in the Middle East as the debates that inspired them to leave the US. In fact, some of these student-travelers enter very politically charged contexts in the Middle East with only a cursory knowledge or a vague sense that the unofficial Islamic communities they seek out are quasi-illegal. The persecution of religious minorities in the Middle East looms large in the American imagination, but many Americans might be surprised to learn that the religious *majority*, Sunni Muslims, also faces government persecution. Throughout the Middle East, governments feel threatened by popular Islamist movements associated with the global Islamic Revival, and many have legislated against essentially any religious activity that does not have explicit government sanction. In a path-breaking ethnography of religious women's networks in Cairene mosques, Saba Mahmood helpfully divides the global Islamic Revival into three strands: (1) Islamist political parties legally working toward political power within the existing state structures (in Egypt, this includes movements such as the Muslim Brotherhood which have organized themselves into political parties and have even won elections, such as President Mohamed Morsi's short-lived victory in 2012 in the wake of the 2011 dignity revolution); (2) militant Islamists committed to subverting the state itself (again, in Egypt, this includes the militant groups that grew out of the Muslim Brotherhood as well as other radical jihadist groups such as AlQaeda); and (3) what she terms the *da'wa movement* or the *piety movement*. Mahmood defines the da'wa movement as a loose network of socioreligious organizations promoting a general and *informal* Islamization of the sociocultural landscape through welfare and charitable services, the dissemination of religious knowledge, and the production of religious media and literature.[14] The da'wa movements make up the bulk of the global Islamic Revival, not only in Egypt but around the world, including in the US, although most scholarly and media attention focuses on Islamist political movements, whether parties operating within the system or militant Islamists trying to subvert governments.

The subjects of my research, both the American student-travelers and their peers and teachers in the Middle East, all unambiguously fall under this third strand of the Islamic Revival, loose and *informal* religious networks promoting a general Islamic influence on their societies through good works but primarily through the dissemination of religious knowledge.[15] I am, however, reticent to adopt Mahmood's term da'wa movement in reference to the pious works and networks examined here. First, the term *movement* implies more of a unified set of goals, mental occupations, and organizational structures than I believe is appropriate for transnational and culturally fragmentary contexts such as US mosques or the unofficial pedagogical networks that American student-travelers move in throughout the Middle East. Second, although the term *da'wa* is often literally translated as "missionizing," American Muslims use the term loosely, primarily to refer to the propagation of faith practices among Muslims themselves and to the labor of disabusing non-Muslims of stereotypes by giving them a more accurate, humanizing, and even beautiful picture of Islam. The ideal of converting Americans operates as a distant, implicit, and abstract goal in this general use of the term *da'wa*.[16] Since the religious conversion of non-Muslims is more of an ideal than a high priority for Muslims in these global networks, I use the general term *revivalist* interchangeably with pious *da'iy* (one who performs da'wa or "invites" other Muslims to a more pious lifestyle and generally recuperates the image of Islam).

In reaction to the policing of unofficial Islamic studies in the Middle East, American Muslim youth generally see their religious studies abroad in tension with state projects, including state-run Islamic universities. In contrast to the "gap year" that many Jewish American young adults spend studying classical Jewish disciplines in a university in Israel before or after college, the religious education that Muslim American student-travelers are primarily looking for rarely involves formal educational institutions. This is due in part to the student travelers' shared perception that there is a general corruption of postcolonial Muslim institutions of religious learning due to their suspect relationship to the state. Most American students arrive on tourist or student visas and study in unofficial study circles or with informally organized religious institutions that present themselves to state officials in the Middle East as language-training programs or tourism companies. American students may enroll in a formal, historical religious institution, in a local secular university language program or language center run by religious graduates of the secular track, or in a government-sanctioned religious institute such as Abu Nour in Damascus and other historic madrasa-universities such as AlAzhar in Cairo, sometimes simply to maintain their student visas. More often than not, they consider this coursework supplemental. The real education in their view is their unofficial, and therefore untainted, religious education in study circles outside the classroom, often held in private homes rather than in public spaces.[17] After they have traveled so far from home, this search for knowledge in the social margins of Arab metropolises becomes yet another displacement.

By analyzing transnational networks that link American Muslims to the global umma, I shed light on one dimension of the crisis of religious authority and Islamic knowledge as it is manifest in US mosque communities, and I destabilize the cultural and scholarly boundary that separates the study of populations in the US from those in the Muslim World. Just as researchers often reproduce an artificial separation between Muslims in the Muslim World and in the US, research on American Muslims also reveals a troubling territorial bias, making hard boundaries of the ethnic, racial, and class lines among American Muslims. Scholars often overterritorialize Muslim American communities, relying far too heavily on demographic variables when dividing Muslim Americans into separate communities, perhaps as a practical concession to their incredible diversity. The isolation of Muslim Americans by nationality, ethnicity, and race creates the illusion of discrete "villages" (Arabs in Dearborn, Iranians in Los Angeles, South Asians in Chicago, Senegalese in Harlem). This "village effect" obscures the fluid and overlapping qualities of Muslim American communities, including their shared investments in distant Islamic places.[18] By mapping transnational circuits of Islamic intellectuals and ideas, I capture the shared debates and shared religious imaginaries of a diverse set of Muslims in the Middle East and in the US without collapsing their important differences.[19]

Despite the incredible diversity of the religious perspectives and goals of American Muslim student-travelers, they do have a shared vocabulary, when they talk about the "crisis" of Islam as self-evident, when they refer to their project of studying abroad and bringing Islamic knowledge back to the US alternatively as "establishing Islam" or "preserving Islam" or "carrying Islam." However, this shared vocabulary does not make them a movement so much as a *counterpublic*, a community of debating Muslims. Muslim American counterpublics are not restricted to physical structures such as a particular mosque or even to a particular denomination of Islam but are constituted by discursive relationships. In other words, these global communities of Muslims hold together through the shared, public deliberation of religious questions about Islamic authority and knowledge, as well as the collective cultivation of Islamic practices, virtues, and dispositions.[20] By taking debates as my point of entry rather than communities anchored to a place or a physical institution, the fluidity and global quality of Muslims' own debates about religious reform emerges alongside their local inflections, whether in Atlanta or Amman. Put simply, American Muslim student-travelers and their teachers and peers in the Middle East make up a collectivity not because their preoccupations, commitments, practices, and backgrounds are identical or even similar but because they are all participating in overlapping, global debates about Islamic learning, religious authority, and the future of their tradition in the US and in the world.

THE CALL

We had a string of American friends who planned vacations to Cairo during my fieldwork. I wanted them to love Cairo as much as I did. I arranged the best tours far in advance, and I went on scouting trips with their shopping lists in hand before they arrived. When Egyptians would tell my American friends that they "lit up all of Cairo," I translated the common colloquialism as a spontaneous compliment.

Playing hostess so often makes the trip to the pyramids with Sakeena my fifth in six months, but her excitement and wonder make it new again for me. One of the reasons Sakeena chose Cairo was because it was where her parents had honeymooned; they had been impressed by how safe Cairo was, and it made it easier for them to let their youngest travel so far from home all by herself. As we ride up through the dunes, Sakeena describes the aged photos she had studied as a child, her mother's bell-bottoms and her father's Afro as they stood arm in arm in front of the pyramids. And now she will see the pyramids for herself.

"I don't know how to describe Egypt," Sakeena tells me, slowly listing the adjectives that come to mind. "Old. Beautiful. Dirty, definitely dirty. Corrupt. Very noisy!" She pauses. "But Egyptians are sweet." Sakeena finds their corruptions sweet, their dreams sweet. The city is exciting and intimidating but also comforting and familiar. "Everything is normal here: *hijab* [scarves], *adhan* [the public call for prayer], being Muslim. I really feel like I am part of this normal Islamic city. But," she adds, lowering her voice, "the bad part of that is the [sexual] harassment. *Hijab* won't protect you in the street 'cause everybody covers [their hair] here. It's normal. [Cairo is] not some perfect bubble, but you feel safe, in a way. You feel Muslim."

The beauty and the force of the stoic structures humble Sakeena, but her heart also breaks for the slaves who died in the name of genius and for Cairo's smudge of black smog in what she calls "Cleopatra's blue sky." Sakeena poses with a horse named Coca-Cola at the foot of the imposing structures, tiny figures in the ancient landscape frozen onto film. The pictures are proof that she has been here, that she galloped through sandy dunes to crawl into a pharaoh's tomb, proof that she is following her parents' path and that of the countless generations of seekers before her. The mood is spoiled only for a moment when our guide explains why the pyramid entrance was built so low. If Sakeena had known beforehand, she would never have entered, stooping in reverence for the pharaoh.

Sakeena wants to absorb it all slowly. We are the last to leave. Khalid, our savvy and amicable eleven-year-old guide, warns that the sun will set soon and that we have to return the animals in time for the laser light show. I convince him to let Sakeena linger long enough to see a Giza sunset and promise we will make it back in time. The desert sun sets in endless colors, the world a box of spilled paints. The sky works over us until the sun sinks beyond sight, until the stillness and natural silence is broken by distant voices.

"*Allahu akbar, Allahu akbar* [God is the Greatest]."

The call to prayer comes from every direction, melodic echoes of men's voices flying on light winds, beginning and ending, notes in chaos rather than unison, one reaching over the next, in a clumsy, beautiful orchestra.

"This is the best thing of the whole day. Thank you," Sakeena smiles at me. "Can we pray *maghrib* here? Please? Ask Khalid if we can just pray here."

Khalid looks around helplessly and reminds me how late it is; there is not a tour group in sight, and, he insists, the laser show is very good, not to be missed. He assures Sakeena that there is an alcove for prayer within walking distance of their shop. Once we return the animals, he will take us, he promises. Gesturing around, he insists that there is no place here to pray, no rugs to pray on, no water for ablutions.

Sakeena is insistent and, as a kind of trump, recites the hadith: "The Prophet, peace be upon him, said: 'The world is my *masjid* [prayer space].'"

Her stilted, formal Arabic makes Khalid giggle despite his explicit training to never laugh at the Arabic of foreigners, especially Westerners. I hand them bottled water for ablutions, and we pray on a patch of thin grass overlooking the pyramids. We press our faces into paper napkins that form into the shape of our features in the softness of the sand.

As we get up from prayer and dust ourselves off, Sakeena wads the napkins into tight balls and places them in a plastic bag of stray garbage she has collected to take back with us. She rakes her fingers through the remaining imprints of our knees, hands, and faces and stands up.

"This place makes life seem fleeting and short, like nothing is permanent," I tell her.

Sakeena shakes her head no. "This spot will be a witness for us on *yawm al-qiyama* [Judgment Day]. We were here. We prayed here."

The Authority of Islamic Landscapes

Like most travelers to cities in the Middle East, Muslim American student-travelers are dazzled by the religious elements of these urban landscapes: the onion-shaped domes of mosques, the minarets like needles in the sky, and the crowds of veiled women and bearded men. And these young Americans are also struck by the colorful, racy billboards, the thickness of polluted air, the familiar sound of a cell phone ringtone derived from an American radio hit, the occasional sighting of a sleek, expensive, imported car. American Muslims' journeys and studies abroad are intended to retrieve bodies of traditional knowledge and make them accessible to American Muslims in US mosques on their return, with the hope that that knowledge will make the debates in US mosques more coherent by introducing a universally authoritative Islamic vocabulary. As they seek out traditional knowledge, American student-travelers debate what makes cities such as Cairo authentic locations for studying their tradition: the presence of learned scholars, diverse and expansive libraries, pious saints, concentrations of blessings in the very geography, or simply what Sakeena relishes, an Islamic social ethos that is the product of being in a Muslim-majority society.[21]

As student-travelers marvel at the presence of Islam in daily, public life in the Middle East, they also bemoan the political corruption, economic destitution, and omnipresent traces of globalization. American student-travelers pursue their Islamic studies in the liminal spaces of somber, imposing mosques that interrupt the colorful, noisy city landscapes of glittering storefronts, honking taxis, loud billboards, and American fast-food franchises. Understanding the religious significance of these particular urban landscapes, the ways that Muslim Americans imbue them with religious meaning, illustrates the slippery quality and shifting configurations of religious authenticity. The process of imbuing particular geographies with religious authority, of making a place an object of pious reflection and sentiment, is simultaneously a material and external process and an internal, imaginative one. Although the imagination is often thought of in highly individualized terms, we must also remember that relationships to places are not lived in solitary moments but most often in the company of others; the religious imagination is personally meaningful, but it is also a social formation that is shared and sustained by a collective, in this case by global Muslim counterpublics.[22]

Sakeena experiences Cairo as being in a Muslim (but not necessarily divine) place. In fact, being part of an Islamic *public* is a novel, striking, and transformative experience for all the American student-travelers I encountered but especially for women such as Sakeena, who is accustomed to the scarf over her hair eliciting stares in the US. In the Middle East, even solitary ritual prayer has a powerfully public feeling to it, in part because it can be performed nearly anywhere, in sharp contrast to public spaces in the US. Among the most striking and moving features of the urban Middle Eastern landscapes for American student-travelers is the aural presence of Islam, especially the sounds of the call to prayer that ring out five times a day and the Quran tapes blaring from taxis, shops, and homes. Anthropologist Charles Hirschkind describes Cairo as a bustling city periodically enveloped in "a sort of heavenly interference pattern created by the dense vocal overlayings. These soaring yet mournful, almost languid harmonic webs soften the visual and sonic tyrannies of the city, offering a temporary reprieve from its manic and machinic functioning."[23]

If we restrict our focus only to the religious studies pursued in these cities, we miss the other equally complex bodies of knowledge that the student-travelers encounter, challenge, and assimilate as they develop pious habits, participate in rituals, and develop relationships with peers, teachers, landlords, and neighbors. After all, Cairo is not made meaningful to Sakeena only through her religious studies but also through the nurturing of affective attachments and imaginative investments in a particular moral geography that envelops both Egypt and the US. By focusing on American Muslim student-travelers' experience of urban places in the Middle East, we deepen our understanding of real people in real settings but at the same time glimpse the lure of imagined places. Religious significance, whether historical or metaphysical, fuses physical landscapes to the religious imagination. Sakeena experiences the Giza desert and the monuments of the pyramids as signs of a lost past which is personally meaningful to her, but she is in Cairo because she is invested in an Islamic future in the US. If we consider the way Sakeena engages the landscape itself and reverses the process of memorialization, how Sakeena's prayer absorbs the desert landscape as a future agent and witness to her piety on Judgment Day, we see that tradition is constituted between past and future, between forward-looking as well as backward-looking imaginaries.

THIRD WORLD RELIGION

Stapled to trees and taped to walls across the University of Jordan campus are small, pink fliers announcing the university's newest technological investment: "One Thousand Computers Project." Thanks to the vision of the young King Abdullah, the modern, Georgetown-educated son with perfect English and accented Arabic, the university was gifted a large number of computers. The posted fliers boast the achievement with glee. Now a thousand students could play video games or chat with each other all at once. Richard complains that it is the only thing the Jordanian students use the lab for, anyway.

Richard is working on a calligraphy project, preparing his portfolio for his applications to graduate schools back in the US. All he needs is to scan a chapter from a precious, centuries-old Quran with beautiful Kufic script that he has on loan from a famous shaykh.

It took nearly two hours and more than a few cigarettes blown in his face just to locate the two scanners on campus in the Computer Science Department. And, of course, there is no cable to hook up the scanners to any of the one thousand computers. One thousand computers, two scanners, no cable, one confrontation.

Richard did not mean to lose his temper. He just wanted to get to the point, and the office was hot and crowded. Fine, there was no cable, could he at least go and buy the cable himself and hook it up? No, no, of course not. And who was he, again? Oh, yes, the American student. The convert. The director of the department was having his coffee now. Come back or talk to the manager. Did he like Amman? Did he find Arabs backward? Maybe he could fill out a form. What kind of papers did he have? Would he like a cold drink while he waited? These questions were a routine for Richard now, each and every time he interacted with a secretary, clerk, or office manager in the university. Initially, he found the lengthy customs of Arab hospitality charming, but now he sees them as painful obligations, what he calls "bureaucratic inertia." The heavyset blond secretary with black roots and heavy, waxy makeup advises Richard about living in Jordan in soothing tones. "In Jordan, you can't just make a demand, in and out like in America. 'Andna protocol. People want to get to know you: Where are you from? Who is your family? They want to respect you, and they want you to respect them."

After Richard's first week, he was ready to change his ticket and go back to the US. His Quran tutor convinced him not to give up, and his landlord found him a nicer apartment. The landlord also persuaded him to forgo his guilty reluctance and hire a housekeeper. Richard began taking Arabic classes at the university alongside his private religious studies in study circles. After a semester in Amman, Richard now knows better than to stack appointments or to expect to complete more than one errand a day, but he is still frustrated by the questions, the permissions, the forms, the never-ending flow of tea and cigarettes, and, most of all, the chain of command.

Finally, a knob turns, and before he knows it, Richard is in an exasperated shouting match with the director of the computer lab, tiny gold cups clanging in tiny gold saucers, sweaty foreheads, bruised egos, and puffed-up chests.

"Do you know who I am?" the director asks Richard.

Richard thinks, "Who do you think you are?" But instead he mutters, "*Ma khasara!* [What a waste!]" That remark seals his fate. No cable today. No scanning today. He tries to convince himself to just forget it.

"And this is supposed to be progress," Richard sighs. "Obviously, I knew about the [Iraq] war, I knew to expect some poverty, but I didn't expect the baggage, the whole colonialism, backwardness complex—the clash of civilizations. Until I actually got here, I honestly didn't really fully get that I had converted to a third-world religion."

Tradition, Modernity, Crisis

In our global age, the world cannot be meaningfully divided into the inherently unequal halves that we are used to: modern/traditional, progressive/backward, West/East, first world/third world. However unwieldy these fraught terms are, it is revealing to examine how they are deployed on the ground. How do devout Muslims, American student-travelers and their Arab peers and teachers in the Middle East, speak to and speak past one another about modernity and about tradition? Of course, the Muslim students and teachers in these pedagogical networks do not see themselves as failed moderns; rather, as moderns, they ask what elements of their tradition's past ought to be preserved for their tradition's future; what will it take for their tradition to survive and thrive in our modern world, specifically in the US? The journeys of these young Muslim Americans are driven by a desire for Islamic authenticity, for a connection to a rich, albeit too often romanticized, past which is important not necessarily (or, at least, not only) because of its pastness but because of what it contains for the future of the tradition. Through their religious studies with their local peers and teachers, American student-travelers in the Middle East debate what is authentic tradition, what elements of the past they deem relevant for the present and the future of Islam in the US and in the world, debates that are implicitly about the nature and meaning of modernity.

In Jordan, Egypt, and Syria, American Muslim student-travelers also encounter, reproduce, and challenge local, Arab discourses about modernity in which the trope of crisis looms large. Kevin Dwyer, in his work on the human rights debate in the Middle East, was among the first American anthropologists to isolate the motif of crisis (*'azma*) as a key, local metaphor in the Middle East, one he inherits from Moroccan sociologist and public intellectual Muhammad Guessous. Guessous, who confesses that he avoids the word himself precisely because it is so overused by Arabs, names this generalized sense of crisis in Arab societies "azmatology." Dwyer describes the incredibly wide range of social and political issues framed by his subjects in Egypt, Morocco, and Tunisia who are subsumed by this general sense of crisis. The social and political issues that are captured by Guessous's term "azmatology" includes the political illegitimacy of rulers, the difficulty of choosing between radically different political ideologies—from democracy, capitalism, socialism, and one-party rule to authoritarianism—the chasm between the rich and poor and the diminishing possibilities of social mobility, censorship, and the intellectual bankruptcy of the educational systems.[24] There is also a profound sense of loss and ambivalence toward globalized American economic and cultural dominance, an anxiety over the erosion of moral values and extended and nuclear family structures. This generalized sense of crisis partly inspired the dignity revolutions that first ignited the region at the end of 2010. Azmatology is not only a sense of crisis over the political and social order; this generalized sense of crisis pervades issues even at the scale of the individual, a discomfort with the strong pressure for conformity and anxiety over the absence of originality in Arab societies, the broadly felt sentiment of failure, the fear of a pervasive "colonized" psychology, which is often contrasted with the ingenuity and dynamism of the West. One way Richard encounters this azmatology with its notions of Western progress and Arab (under)development is in the form of observational questions posed to him, as ordinary Jordanians sometimes use him to gauge whether something is "backward." Although he complains about the "inertia" of Jordanian bureaucracies, Richard is ambivalent about the modernization and development of contemporary Jordan. In fact, Richard sees this modernization and the marginalization of Islam as one source of the more specific crisis of Islamic authority in the Islamic public sphere in the Middle East and in US mosques that preoccupies him; over time, he also becomes invested in crises that are not internal to Islam but are manifest throughout the postcolonial Middle East, political crises which he sees as the product of authoritarian rule and US imperialism.

Scholars grapple with developing an apt analytical language for talking about the modern condition in the "third world," what is now often termed the Global South. Scholars have developed "multiple modernities" and "alternative modernities" frameworks in which modernity is either multiple in its origins and expressions or singular but not hegemonic because it is selectively appropriated in the Global South. In the alternative modernities model, scholars argue that the genealogies of modernity extend far beyond the Western core, and they track the non-Western roots of capitalism, the nation-state, and other modern formations.[25] In the multiple modernities model, scholars emphasize the agency of those who form and develop their own expressions of the modern that reflect the local needs and desires of subjects in the Global South. However, as conceptual tools, *modern* and *modernity*, even in their modified plural forms, have largely lost their analytical value. For example, the alternative modernities framework has come under scrutiny for making modernity so relative a concept as to obscure the global structural inequalities that constitute the gaps between the Global North and the Global South. Similarly, some scholars critique the hybridity of the multiple modernities model because such a characterization often reinscribes the modernity of the West as original and sui generis and the modernity of "others" as derivatives of the original (Western) modernity they intend to destabilize.[26]

Both the alternative modernities model and the multiple modernities model are ultimately inadequate. Rather than trying to settle on a better scholarly definition of *modernity* by pluralizing it, we ought to explore not only the multiple local definitions of *modernity* but also the ways these local iterations of the term are used in different social contexts, whether in tandem or in tension with dominant, global discourses of modernity. The dominant discourse of modernity around the world, including throughout the Middle East, uncritically assumes that the West is the universal example of all that is modern and idealizes its technological advances, consumer products, and secular humanist values. (In many forms of colloquial Arabic, this is marked by the use of the French word *moderne*.)[27] This modern West is often contrasted with

the backwardness and the "underdevelopment" of the Middle East or
the Muslim World generally. This conception of the West—as the core
from which a universal modernity radiates or seeps outward to the rest
of the world—reduces Muslim societies in the Middle East to hybrids of
(Eastern, premodern) tradition and (Western, globalized) modernity.

When we consider the different deployments of modernity in the
context of the pedagogical encounters of these global networks and
contextualize them in social fields of power, we are able to capture the
plurality of experience, interpretation, and understanding of the concept of modernity with which ordinary Muslims grapple in their everyday lives. Many of Jordan's Muslims, Richard complains, believe that
material progress and spiritual progress go hand in hand. Richard is put
off by what he sees as "westoxified" or "Americanized" Jordanians who
reproduce this dominant discourse of modernity. Like many American student-travelers, Richard believes Muslims had enlightenment
(with a lower-case *e*) and civilization in the past but have since lost it.
In Richard's alternative narrative, backward elements are ubiquitous
in contemporary Arab societies, but backwardness here figures as an
absence of the features of the Islamic civilization that he longs for, not
the absence of the Western cultural forms that Richard believes many
Jordanians wrongly fetishize. In other words, his vision of civilizational
progress is of a traditional future. Richard's vision is backward-looking, even romantic, but it is also forward-looking and plural, because it
includes the possibility of multiple, civilized cultures, including that of
American Muslims. For Richard, the time that a medieval calligrapher
spent hunched over parchments thousands of years ago is important
for the future of Islam in the US, an importance that the Muslims he
encounters in the university computer lab in Amman fail to see.

American student-travelers and their peers and teachers in the
Middle East tend to imagine themselves as seekers partaking in a free-
floating pedagogical ritual (the *rihla*); however, their quests for Islamic
knowledge cannot be removed from a whole host of social, political,
and economic factors that make their journeys and studies possible. The
journeys of American Muslim student-travelers such as Usman, Jawad,
Sakeena, and Richard are structured as much by class, race, nationality,
ethnicity, gender, and political conditions as they are by their explicit
religious motives as seekers. None of these social factors necessarily

undermine the sincerity of their religious motives, but they are a crucial—and often unspoken—force in shaping their pedagogical encounters. Yet Muslim American seekers sometimes insist that it is only natural that, as Muslim minorities in the West living beyond the peripheries
of the Muslim World, they are compelled to travel to the Islamic core in
order to gain knowledge. They often cite Quranic verses and hadith, the
recorded traditions of Muhammad's words and moral example, which
exalt such travel for knowledge (and not necessarily sacred knowledge)
as among the best forms of worship, such as this oft-cited Prophetic tradition: "God makes the path to paradise easy for [the one] who travels
a road in search of knowledge, and the angels spread their wings for
the pleasure of the seeker of knowledge, even the serpents in the water
[revere the seeker]. The learned person is superior to the [mere] wor-
shipper just as the moon has precedence over the rest of the stars."
Although American student-travelers often describe their travels as a
discrete, unchanging, and simple Islamic practice of the *rihla*, I draw on
American Muslims' pedagogical encounters in Damascus, Amman, and
Cairo in order to argue for a more robust conceptualization of American Muslims' journeys for knowledge, one that takes their identity as
Americans in these global networks in the Middle East as seriously as
their identity as devout Muslims.

For many Muslim American student-travelers, their search for an
authentic Islam in the Middle East is a search for a way to be whole,
to be an authentic Muslim now, by traveling "back" in space and time.
Their rhetoric conflates traveling "east" with traveling "back," and it has
a genetic link to an old and troubling Eurocentric discourse in which
the practice of travel is constitutive of the Western, modern man.[28] In
eighteenth-century England, travel was a mode of racial, gender, and
class formation; the "grand tour" distinguished the young men of English aristocracy, who enjoyed the privilege of travel, from women, from
lower social classes, and from other races and nations, even as their
travels pivoted on the desire to be immersed elsewhere and to not
be seen as visitors or outsiders.[29] By the nineteenth century, Western
romantic discourses of the traveler-as-hero became fused with emergent forms of scientific authority, discovery, and exploration, including
Western anthropology.[30] This emergent Western discourse of travel as
"eyewitness observation" depended on the construction of the Western

gaze and its "conquering and orgiastic curiosity, so taken with unveiling hidden things."[31] The documentation of European travel practices of leisure, exploration, and scientific discovery were fundamentally in service of colonial empires, visually indexing the European metropolis's insatiable "need to present and re-present its peripheries and its others continually to itself," often combining the desire for that which is exotic and unique and unseen with a contradictory disdain for the "natives" as inferior and/or as increasingly inauthentic as they "modernize."[32] As Inderpal Grewal argues, such Eurocentric constructions of travel have been and continue to be severely limiting because they consolidate national, racial, class, gender, and sexual identities as stable and unitary, not only at the point of departure (our here) but also at the destination point (our there). "[Travel] is a metaphor that [became and remains] an ontological discourse central to the relations between Self and Other. . . . Whether travel is a metaphor of exile, mobility, difference, modernity, or hybridity, it suggests the particular ways in which knowledge of a Self, society, and nation was, and is, within European and North American culture, to be understood and obtained."[33] The construction of those who travel as imaginative, curious, and learned also depends and produces an image of those people who do not or cannot travel.[34] The immobile are both those who are left behind at home and those who wait to be discovered at the traveler's destination. Insofar as their immobility is implicitly or explicitly linked to stasis in time, inertia, parochialism, and complacency, those who do not travel are implicitly characterized as inferior even when they are idealized as the "authentic" and the "real."

The question here is not whether, or to what extent, American student-travelers' quests are polluted by virtue of their being American, that is, whether the journeys of American student-travelers are authentic, true forms of the Islamic quest (*rihla*) or simply a kind of "spiritual tourism," as Usman put it. This line of questioning presumes the *rihla* is a discrete and generic traditional practice that moves through time like an unchanging object. While Muslims living in the US are doing what Muslims all over the world do and have done for centuries, that is, traveling for Islamic knowledge, their journeys also must be contextualized in terms of American legacies of travel and the sociopolitical contexts of the Middle East. We ought to see class, race, nationality, and gender not as mutable, fixed things in the world but as social forms that emerge, transform, and recede in such cultural encounters.

Although travel is often assumed to broaden one's horizons, the act of travel can also narrow one's horizons. Usman expects that the time his American coreligionists spend in Damascus will disabuse them of their fantasies of arriving in an Islamic utopia, but we know that a long sojourn in a distant place is not enough to purge such troubling and persistent Orientalist fantasies. Furthermore, prolonged exposure to the unfamiliar is just as likely to engender alienation and antagonism as identification and attachment between Muslims. Richard's embarrassment and defensiveness about his initial desire to leave Jordan reflect his discomfort with Jordanians' persistent reminders to him of who he is in their eyes (a white, American man) as well as his discomfort with himself and the way he reacts to encountering cultural difference. Rather than minimizing the racial, national, economic, and political differences between Richard and the Jordanians he interacts with, his conversion to Islam only heightens the significance of his race and nationality in Amman. Richard is frustrated by how his identity as an American and a convert to Islam operates in Jordan. Furthermore, Richard does not like who he becomes in Jordan, as he reluctantly adopts the tactics of the socially privileged in a profoundly stratified society. In other words, the explicit conflict (his frustration and antagonistic relationship with some of the university employees in Amman) and his internal conflict are not driven by a disdain for Jordanians so much as a self-loathing produced by having to confront their cultural norms, to live with fewer amenities, to deal with physical and social discomforts, to face their differences in economic and political privilege and cultural norms. All he wanted, all he expected, was religious communion. In traveling, Richard experiences the ironic and unsettling feeling of difference between him and his Jordanian coreligionists, when he expected only familiarity, even solace. This highlighting of difference between Muslims is the ironic counterpoint to travel intended to heighten one's consciousness of the spiritual unity of the umma.[35]

ALGHAZZALI'S DAMASCUS

The afternoon heat is so powerful that even the flies in Damascus seem dizzy. Fawzia wears a long, navy-blue overcoat of georgette. Her white scarf, pressed) and starched, conceals every hair, with the ends characteristically looped and tucked in at the neck. The overcoat and the neatly tied and tucked scarf are a kind of uniform for the Qubaysiyat, a popular underground women's faith movement. Others, similarly clad, pass Fawzia by in the winding alleys of the old city and exchange secretive smiles. Fawzia murmurs greetings of peace.

Despite her clothes, Fawzia never manages to blend in all the way. In the tiny shops, her posture and her shoes betray, long before her broken Arabic, the dollars and the US passport in her purse. Fawzia is a self-described "Cali girl" from Los Angeles, and yet she feels at home in Syria. She has no real interest in visiting her parents' homeland, Bangladesh. "Islam is too cultural there," she explains. "It's too mixed in with Hinduism. You can't even learn real Islam there."

Instead, Fawzia came to Damascus to study Islam. Every morning, except on Fridays, Fawzia has a lesson in the art of melodious Quranic recitation, mastering the strict rules of cadence and rhythm. After her Syrian teacher leaves, Fawzia spends the afternoon memorizing verses and practicing her recitation. She records her own voice and checks it against cassette tapes of internationally renowned reciters, in the hope that she will earn an ijaza, a certificate linking her through a long chain of teachers and students back to the Prophet himself and giving her the authority to teach recitation to students back in the US.

One evening a week, Fawzia attends a religious lecture given by her Qubaysiya shaykha, or ansa. Ansa Tamara Gray is a charismatic, middle-aged, white American expat who has taken Western student-travelers such as Fawzia as her charge, overseeing their recitation lessons. Ansa Tamara opens her class with group singing of English songs with "Islamicized" lyrics; her lectures cover a range of issues related to spiritual purification, complete with assignments such as supererogatory prayers and exercises to develop patience or manage anger, regimens Fawzia performs meticulously.

At night, Fawzia reads books in English that came to Damascus in her suitcases: Rumi's poetry, Muhammad Asad's Quran commentary, and AlGhazzali's The Alchemy of Happiness. Fawzia loves AlGhazzali best; in his time, he was a master theologian, a jurist, a philosopher, and above all, a seeker. Although Fawzia reads AlGhazzali in English, she dreams of knowing him in Arabic.

"He was an intellectual and a poet, and he dealt with the West in his own way, in his own time, by wrestling with Western philosophy. He didn't just reject philosophy wholesale, but he also didn't just accept stuff because Aristotle said so. He didn't just critique them like any Joe Schmoe; he became an expert himself. He engaged the West but still preserved Islam. Half the time, Muslims now don't even know whether or why we [are] for or against certain things."

AlGhazzali came to Damascus in 1095. He left his family, his prestigious academic position, his entire life behind to search for a truth beyond his books and fame and wealth. He became a wandering mystic crisscrossing the desert, a simple ascetic cleaning the bathroom in the Umayyad Mosque on his knees, a humble teacher lecturing in the *zawiya*, a lonely seeker locked away in the minaret of the mosque with his solitude and his hopes of being transformed.

Fawzia is in Damascus almost a millennium later. As she makes her way to the mosque, through tiny, irregular streets of cobblestone, past haggling merchants and children sipping cola through straws from plastic sandwich bags, Fawzia longs for a different time, for AlGhazzali's Damascus. Every Friday, on her way to the Umayyad Mosque, she closes her eyes and runs her fingers against crumbling walls, imagining that she is on her way to sit at the feet of her teacher and to hear his seminal Damascene work, *The Revitalization of the Religious Disciplines*, from his own lips, in the sun-lit corner of the mosque that has since been named after him.

Beyond the Invention of Tradition

Fawzia diagnoses Islam with a particular crisis, a dearth of expert knowledge; however, she is referencing not only the mosques in Damascus but also those in Los Angeles. In tandem with her Syrian and American teachers and peers in Damascus, she invests the US with the hope for the future of her tradition-in-crisis. Fawzia links the contemporary, global crisis of Islam to the private crises of faith and public, philosophical debates of the twelfth-century jurist, theologian, and philosopher AlGhazzali. As she derides the incoherence of her contemporary coreligionists (for not knowing what they believe or why), she offers AlGhazzali's mastery of Aristotelian logic, his refutation of rival philosophers, and his pious training as a kind of hope and instructive example, as a way to resolve Islam's crisis in the here and now. Reproducing the trope of the ancient Greek roots of Western civilization, Fawzia equates Aristotle with "the West"—a category he preceded by thousands of years—but not in order to exalt the nation or the West. She makes this claim in order to project her own sense of crisis, that Islam is and has been under onslaught from "the West," back through the ages, even as she works and prays for a bright future for her tradition in the US. She makes a parallel between the political challenges and cultural pollutants posed by the West to Islam today and the pollutants of Aristotelian philosophy that AlGhazzali was purging from Islamic philosophy in the twelfth century; her hopes for Islam's future are intertwined with a strong ambivalence about her own homeland, the US, and her parents' homeland, Bangladesh.

The category of *tradition* allows us to account for the ways the global and the local converge in Fawzia's account, her travel fantasy and her anachronistic history but also her very serious studies as a devotee of the Qubaysiyat and her positive and negative feelings about the US. As an analytical tool, *tradition* is at once fluid and deterritorialized, precise and magnifying; however, it requires recuperation. The scholarly aversion and suspicion of any and all claims made in the name of tradition is a reaction, in part, to an ugly political reality.[36] Scholars have long trained their gaze on the enormous harm and violence inflicted in the name of tradition in colonial and postcolonial contexts. This type of constructivist argument was first made famous by Eric Hobsbawm and Terence Ranger in their collection *The Invention of Tradition*. Hobsbawm argues that traditions "which appear or claim to be old are often quite recent in origin and sometimes invented."[37] This volume sparked a large body of scholarship that takes as its primary task the debunking of historically baseless claims in service of political projects, particularly in regard to nationalism.

In Muslim-majority societies, we find many troubling examples of contemporary Islamists invoking the authority of tradition as they make claims to political power, what we might call "abridgements of tradition."[38] Historians have demonstrated, in contrast to the boisterous cries of aspiring Islamist politicians, that a theocratic nation-state with a singular *sharia* law is a new political form, not the resurgence of an older one. Modern theocratic nation-states such as Iran and Saudi Arabia are a radical departure from the classical structure of the Islamic caliphate and the plurality of historical Islamic law. Deconstructions of political projects and ideological rhetoric justified in the name of tradition are often instructive; however, such constructivist analyses lose their analytical force when they reduce Islam to a ruse or a mask for the social, political, and economic agendas of Muslims today. Such analyses render Islamists merely political parties in the guise of religion, Fawzia merely an American tourist in the guise of a sincere seeker. Following Hobsbawm, a constructivist analysis will interrogate Fawzia's claims about tradition: Why AlGhazzali, and why now? What genealogy, what context, and against what or whom are Fawzia's claims made? These questions can be quite revealing. Despite all the allusions to Islam's universalism and the continuity of an unbroken intellectual tradition, Fawzia's pedagogical goals are animated in part by a mythic narrative of American exceptionalism, reproduced in tandem with her Arab peers and teachers; the American umma is exceptional, distinguished by its wealth, resources, diversity, talent (due to the brain drain), political privilege, and vision, and, therefore, the agenda for the global umma ought to be set by American Muslims, at least once they are properly trained. These kinds of territorializing claims about the (American) future of Islam are often strikingly unreflective and explicit. For example, Fawzia and her peers open their class by singing the song "I Can Show You Islam" with Ansa Tamara Gray, adapted from a song in the Disney film *Aladdin*, "I Can Show You the World," a score criticized for being replete with racist, anti-Arab lyrics.

A constructivist analysis of Fawzia's rhetoric might debunk such anachronisms and historically baseless claims by dutifully juxtaposing her words against those of a serious scholar, such as the eminent historian Marshall Hodgson, who argues, quite convincingly, that as a tradition, Islam inherits Aristotelian philosophy as much as, if not more than, "the West" does.[39] Such an analysis can be compelling and important. Yet one limitation of the constructivist approach is that it foregrounds historical authenticity as the primary frame for engaging tradition, such that what Muslims claim in the name of tradition is usually only of scholarly interest insofar as it is a *mis*representation of the past.

In reaction to constructivist arguments, some scholars reject any and all questioning premised on degrees of historical authenticity, collapsing the analytical distinction between tradition and ideology altogether. Scholars working in an antihistoricist mode pare down the category of tradition further, taking what we might call a nominalist stance toward tradition, such that anything named tradition is tradition. Anthropologists Richard Handler and Joyce Linnekin argue in favor of such an approach by demonstrating that the transmission of tradition is never a simple process of preservation because the very act of preservation inevitably alters or reconstructs that which it intends to fix.[40] They argue that since authentic tradition is defined in the present, all "genuine" traditions (in Fawzia's case, AlGhazzali) are "spurious," and all "spurious" traditions (Disney's *Aladdin*) are "genuine." Despite often being cast as preservation, they argue, tradition is always new and always invented because authenticity is always defined in the present. Since authenticity, historical and otherwise, implies a standard (or multiple standards) by which to judge information or behavior, the nominalists, as a gesture of their scholarly suspension of (religious) judgment and rejection of authenticity, define Islam as whatever is labeled Islam by their Muslim subjects. The result is an analytical strategy that pluralizes the concept of a singular Islam to "*islams*," but, just as in the case of pluralizing modernity, this approach fails to take us very far analytically. Nominalists treat Islam in the present as unique and independent of the past or the future; they use the terms "traditional" and "new" as interpretive rather than descriptive categories. Nominalists will concern themselves not with the historical AlGhazzali or the historical Aristotle but with interpreting what AlGhazzali, Aristotle, the landscape of Damascus, and the score of *Aladdin* each *means* to Fawzia (and others in her pedagogical network) in the present. Fawzia's "symbolic needs" at this very moment, in other words, are what constitute tradition, constitute her islam.

Like the constructivist approach, the nominalist analysts' pluralizing of Islam flattens tradition to the point that it obscures more than it reveals. The representation of Islam as a totality of fragments on a horizontal axis ("islams") fails to correspond to actual religious discourses (which are never even and are always enmeshed in networks of power) and masks the very heterogeneity of Muslims it intends to capture.

Proofs are required in the context of an argument, in the context of trying to persuade someone to come around to our view of things. Ordinary Muslims such as Fawzia are at least as conscious of the diversity of interpretation and practice of Islam as academics are, evinced here by her dismissal of her Bangladeshi coreligionists, yet Fawzia is still theologically invested in the *idea* of a single Islam and, therefore, in engaging and persuading other Muslims to come around to her view of "real Islam." After all, Fawzia's dream of getting a recitation license, an *ijaza*, pivots on her investments in being recognized as an authority by *other* Muslims, in Syria and back in the US.

The diversity and heterogeneity of Muslims and their widely ranging claims about Islam are not proof of the absence of a coherent tradition; rather they are simply proof of the absence of homogeneity. The nominalists' move to distinguish the "islams" of particular groups, a movement, a village, or even one individual's definition of Islam as sui generis "islams" obscures the relational, contested, communal quality of tradition and erases the social fields of power in which religious debates are always enmeshed. Fawzia's beliefs about the beliefs of other Muslims are her *own* beliefs and cannot be fully appreciated if we treat them as a discrete, sui generis object, Fawzia's "islam" among "islams," as the nominalists frame it.[41] What is left out of nominalist accounts is not merely the "background information" contextualizing the Qubaysiyat as a movement or Damascus as an Islamic intellectual center but, more importantly, the multiple and competing mainstreaming and marginalizing processes by which Muslims assign stigma and prestige and define and debate what counts as authentic tradition. The debates Fawzia has with her coreligionists about where and how darkly the lines of inclusion in and exclusion from authentic tradition are drawn happen in particular constellations of power and resistance, in which Fawzia's American passport, her dark skin, her broken Arabic, her Qubaysi uniform, and her gender are all signs. By focusing on the complexity of these pedagogical encounters, the ways they inherit multiple discourses of travel, my analysis not only discloses what Islam means to Muslims in specific moments but also where, at what moments, and under what circumstances the primacy of tradition, however it is articulated, dissolves in importance, supplanted by other, equally powerful pulls on these individuals.[42] Over the course of my own parallel studies with

Arab intellectuals abroad, I also found that the studies and forms of knowledge production American Muslim youth seek out in order to resolve what they see as a crisis of authority are remarkably akin to the expertise created by anthropologists.

THE MASTERS OF MASTERS

In Damascus, Usman introduced my husband, Hamada, and me to a private tutor. Shaykh Firas was a reserved man of few words, assiduously polite but not warm. With his perfectly pressed linen suits, wire-rimmed glasses, and neatly trimmed beard, he looked more like a young businessman than a shaykh, and, in a sense, he was a professional businessman. Aside from being a part-time imam in a small mosque outside the Jewish quarter of Old Damascus, he ran an Arabic and Islamic studies institute with a satellite campus in Beirut. Institutes such as Shaykh Firas's offer a "crash course" introduction to the classical Islamic disciplines, what Usman teasingly referred to as a "*barnamij* cocktail," a mix-and-match program that focused on disciplines of one's choice, with a little of this classical text and a little of that modern textbook.

On Tuesday and Thursday afternoons, after Shaykh Firas left our apartment, Hamada and I would take a cab to the outskirts of Damascus to study the art of recitation and ritual law with another teacher, Shaykh Jibril. It was a transitional neighborhood, part slum, part historic, dotted with a few older homes. There was a dim promise of new construction in the form of parked and vacant construction equipment and small piles of new cement bricks, a few empty lots filled with broken cement, gravel, and glass where old buildings must have been razed to the ground.

Shaykh Jibril was an imposing figure, always dressed in long, cotton robes and cheap sandals. He was well over six feet tall and three hundred pounds, with a deep, booming voice and thickly knitted eyebrows. He was the opposite of Shaykh Firas in many ways: warm, unkempt, loud, funny. I related to him better, even though it was Shaykh Firas who looked like us, who was middle class and college educated and well dressed and well traveled like us. Shaykh Jibril did not have college degrees, but he had several *ijazas* and a good reputation as a Quran scholar in Damascus. He never ceased to amaze me with his ability to carry the weight of any of our tangential conversations on the politics in the Middle East or American culture and history. Shaykh Jibril was impressed with our intense focus and perseverance in reading through the difficult legal manual. He was brought to exasperated laughter when he heard me recite even short chapters from the Quran. I felt terrible when the sounds of the letters emerged from the wrong spots in my mouth or in my throat or when I forgot a rule. I had spent two months the previous summer learning the phonetic rules of recitation from a Syrian woman who ran a Quran institute in Jordan. After all our hours and exercises and drills, I had retained most but not all of them.

"You Americans amaze me," Shaykh Jibril teased. "You are so advanced in some areas, and in others, my kids could be your teachers. Compared to you, my kids are the masters of masters!"

Shaykh Jibril and his sweet wife had two lovely daughters, and their mischievous son was the baby of their family. Their eldest daughter was nine, and she was the only family member who ever entered the office during our lessons. She would come exactly in the middle of each session, carefully balancing in her pudgy hands a silver tea tray that she primly laid out before offering a shy curtsy and ducking out the door. Shaykh Jibril's middle child was his clear favorite. She was most like him, but he really favored her because as an infant she had almost died and because she suffered from what he suspected was dyslexia. He worried people would always underestimate how smart she actually was. His son was only six, but no one could deny that he was some kind of mechanical genius. His best friend was a screwdriver, and he took apart any toy (though they had very few toys) or any appliance or piece of furniture he could get his hands on before his mother caught him, just to learn how to put it back together again. I once watched him completely disassemble a rotary phone into piles of small pieces and then put it back together while I ate a chicken pita sandwich and read his sisters a book. To be sure that I knew just how clever he was, he had me call his aunt on the reassembled phone, proof that he had done it correctly. They were the masters of masters as far as I was concerned.

Although we would become friends, it took a few weeks before Shaykh Jibril's family felt comfortable enough to talk to us casually and not just as student-clients. I vividly remember the first time one of his daughters, the younger one, spoke to me before I spoke to her. As I was leaving, she stepped into the courtyard and called out to me, "My sister says you bring a different pencil every time!" Her older sister was right behind her but too late to stop her. She gasped and turned beet red, covering her face with her hands. She looked so embarrassed that her younger sister had revealed that she reported every detail about us back to them that I was afraid she might cry. I smiled and looked down at the smooth, pink pencil in my hand with embarrassment. I laid the pencil on the window ledge behind me before I slipped out the door into the alley. I suspected that Shaykh Jibril's children received one pencil at the beginning of the school year and they finished the school year with that very same pencil, just shorter. I never lost another pen or pencil in Damascus.

Toward a Deterritorialized Anthropology of Islam

Like the student-travelers, I developed complicated relationships with the Arab intellectuals in these networks who became my teachers; I include the stories of my encounters with them in order to piece their experiences and perspectives into this fragmentary map. Before Shaykh Firas would allow me to sit in on his classes, he made sure I was disabused of the notion that the intellect is the instrument of dispassionate rationality exalted in modern thought, in which the classic unfeeling scientist is represented as the height of intellectual prowess. In an Islamic ontology, he explained to me, the intellect, the 'aql, is an instrument of perception, defined as "a light that God puts in the heart by which people are able to see things as they truly are." This broader understanding of intellect does not pit emotions against the critical apparatus, since emotions may sharpen one's perception in some cases. Perceptiveness is linked to reflection rather than identification, and, as an illustration, Shaykh Firas cited the famous quote of the sufi Ibn 'Ata Allah Al-Iskandari: "It is reflection that illumines hearts." Thinking about my ethnographic encounters as a process of reflective participation rather than participation-observation undid anthropology's oxymoron of fieldwork, in which participation involves communication and emotional investment and observation requires detachment and objectivity.[43]

Today critical anthropologists labor toward developing critiques that leave open the possibility that they too might be remade, their own thinking and assumptions challenged through the process of engaging a different worldview.[44] The passionate intellectual life of global Muslim networks I track here has a genealogy to an older, broader conception of the intellect, of alternative regimes of reason, one that remade me as a scholar. As we forged links, even difficult links, between different bodies of knowledge, Muslim intellectuals such as Shaykh Firas and Shaykh Jibril taught me to think more carefully about our locations in multiple intellectual communities and the shifting boundaries of each.

Although we traveled together and grappled with the challenge to define authority and expertise together, the purpose and guiding questions of my journey and my studies were very different from those of the Muslim American seekers chronicled here as well. While American student-travelers see their journeys to the Muslim World as an act of religious communion and connection, these pedagogical encounters are also structured by conflicts and their competing visions of Islam. Echoing an earlier generation of anthropologists, Muslim American student-travelers often talk about their travels and mobility in an unreflexive way, with little attention to the complex cultural work travel does, such as when Fawzia's narrative of her journey and studies transforms an airplane into a time machine. As we will see again and again, travel for Islamic knowledge may introduce, define, underscore, and exacerbate differences among Muslims, and it may produce powerful religious and political solidarities, just as the search for ethnographic knowledge creates connections and distances. Following and studying alongside devout Muslim intellectuals and students in these global networks, I found the beauty of concentration, of intense focus, of open curiosity, of rich discipline as I tracked their debates. I also witnessed the ugly and insidious ways Muslim intellectuals suppress dissent and debate under the banner of crisis.

THE SATANIC VERSES

Shaykh Firas was impressed with our strong grasp of Arabic grammar but exasperated by our previous, uneven study of Islamic law and theology. We knew enough of the technical vocabulary of Islamic law to annoy him with irreverent questions as we combed through the readings. American Muslims, Shaykh Firas complained, came at everything the wrong way, as if they could parachute into the tradition.

"I have students from all over the world who come to Damascus to study, but the Americans are so different. Their questions are so strange. They see Islam from the edges, not its center, not its orthodoxy. [For example,] a few American students have asked me about the satanic verses in the Quran. Now, no one accepts this; no one in Syria, even the most serious students, would spend much time on this obviously inauthentic account from the life of the blessed Prophet. Are they learning their religion from Salman Rushdie?" And then he asked me pointedly, "Have you read this book?"

The scandal over Rushdie's novel *The Satanic Verses* was my introduction to the "clash of civilizations," the lesson that impressed me most in junior high. In 1989, Iran's Ayatollah Khomeini made *fatwa* a household word in the US, when he decreed the novelist Salman Rushdie a heretic and put a bounty on his head. In our home, a fatwa was not a death threat but a religious opinion, open to challenge. I grew up in a family in which Islam, what an intellectual such as Shaykh Firas would consider my parents' unlearned "village Islam," with its rich aesthetics and discipline, was deeply revered, its rituals loosely practiced, its small and big questions hotly debated. But the Rushdie affair was a black-and-white issue, us against them. All I knew then was that this strange-looking man ("who was supposed to be Muslim," my mother would shake her head in disbelief) had written a book and in it referred to the Prophet as "Mahound." I did not know then that this name is a medieval European slur of Muhammad that permeates Orientalist literature. I did know that Muslims all over the world were outraged, that he might be killed, and that the *Amreekan* were, predictably, taking his side and buying his book in droves. My social studies teacher echoed Rushdie, explaining the conflict as a category mistake on the part of Muslims who failed to recognize the novel as fiction, as art. I knew my mother could differentiate between fiction and history, and she did not need to read any more than the title to be thoroughly disgusted. I knew, too, that our local Muslim community was, ironically, like Rushdie, in danger because of the book and the fatwa. They were quietly suffering a violent backlash: a friend from our old neighborhood in Detroit was threatened at knifepoint at her junior high school bus stop, and another family friend had his house smoke-bombed. I cringed as the Pakistani man interviewed on the evening news became embarrassingly hysterical and lost his composure and his English and began cursing the other, calm, white professor sharing the panel in Urdu. (I remember he called "the Orientalist" an "*ullu ka phata*," a son of an owl.) Somehow all of these things were Salman Rushdie's fault. My parents laughed and kissed my little brother when he, on his own, cut Rushdie's face out of a *Time* magazine and threw it in the garbage. There stood my little brother, the iconoclast armed with bright, orange scissors, and I wished it had been my idea. I prayed then that I would never do something so bad that would make me stop being Muslim, something that would make my family cut my face out of the pictures in the photo albums lining the shelves in the upstairs closet.

So when Shaykh Firas asked me about the novel, I recognized his question as a test, and I was not surprised at his visible pleasure when I admitted I never had the heart to get past the first chapter. "Our entire religion is based on a total faith that the verses of the Quran were transmitted from God, to [the angel] Gabriel, to the blessed Prophet Muhammad. But [American Muslims] will come and say, yes, but [the twelfth-century theologian] Ibn Taymiyyah believed that the Prophet did receive verses from Satan that allowed concessions to the pagans. The Prophet believed the verses were from God until he received a revelation that those verses were from Satan. In all my studies, I had never heard of this opinion of Ibn Taymiyyah's. And I discovered this opinion did exist, but there is essentially a scholarly consensus that Ibn Taymiyyah was wrong and that there were no satanic verses. It is strange that Muslim Americans who do not know even basic things know this obscure and heterodox opinion which none of us have ever heard of."

I suspected I had the answer to his mystery. I explained to Shaykh Firas that there was a Harvard professor who had written an article about Ibn Taymiyyah's controversial acceptance of the satanic verses account and that this was the kind of article that would be assigned in American college courses, Islam 101. I explained that for many American Muslims, after Sunday school, college would be the first place where they would be seriously, formally studying their religion and where they would encounter obscure opinions and interpretations.

After Shaykh Firas noted whatever I could remember of the citation of the article in his notebook, he gave a lengthy and impassioned refutation of Ibn Taymiyyah's argument and a general criticism of Orientalism for my benefit. I tried to reassure him that I did not find Ibn Taymiyyah's position convincing but that even if Ibn Taymiyyah was right, it did not invalidate the Quran or the divine sanction of prophecy because the verses were stricken by divine command anyway. From my point of view, it was just a minor theological debate among Sunnis, a difference over the nature of Muhammad's prophetic infallibility, whether it was total or cumulative. Did it really matter? It clearly mattered to Shaykh Firas. Over the next few weeks, Shaykh Firas would take the opportunity of our coffee and tea breaks to refute various Orientalist theses, Schacht and Goldziher and several others I had never even heard of, let alone read. I would listen patiently and sympathetically to his criticisms, but my assurances that these theses had long been abandoned and revised in Western scholarship on Islam did not diffuse his anger.

I was amazed at how well he knew the Orientalist literature even though he did not read in English or German. When I asked why he was so concerned with scholars from several generations ago, I was surprised to discover he had a cold reverence for them. "Today's Orientalists are not worth our attention. They do not know Arabic like the generations before them. In the past, the Orientalists were masters of Arabic, masters of masters. The Orientalists today do not know Arabic as Goldziher did. That's why you must learn the tradition from our own sources."

Orthodoxy and the Problem of the "Real"

Like tradition, *orthodoxy* as an analytic category must be distinguished from its commonsense usage. Anticipating the scholarly skittishness associated with the category of orthodoxy, Asad defines orthodoxy not as a body of opinion at the "heart" of Islam but as a distinctive "relationship of power. Wherever Muslims have the power to regulate, uphold, require, or adjust *correct* practices, and to condemn, exclude, undermine, or replace *incorrect* ones, there is the domain of orthodoxy."[45] Fawzia's mapping of "real" Islam onto the Arab world and marking of Bengali (but not Syrian) culture as a pollutant of Islam is one such example. Shaykh Firas's textualist view of orthodoxy as a fixed canon, a bounded body of texts and vetted opinions, one that excludes Ibn Taymiyyah's different definition of prophetic infallibility, is another. Nominalists reproduce the normative Muslim view of orthodoxy as a fixed body of opinion at Islam's core, and in their analyses, they often treat it as a static and coercive instrument.

Following Asad, I understand orthodoxy as a discursive (and dynamic) relationship of power, and I take his prescription regarding the line-drawing work of orthodoxy as an ethnographic directive, not a theological exercise (one that Orientalists engage in as well) or a strictly descriptive one in the nominalists' sense. Orthodoxy in Asad's sense is not simply derived from foundational texts; rather, the relationships of power that constitute orthodoxy are sustained, animated, or undermined by the deployments of foundational texts as well as a whole host of political and social factors that empower some Muslims and not others, everything from petrodollars to the Internet to racial and class hierarchies, and so on.

Rather than reproduce the false binary of traditional/modern, or real/false Islam in my analysis, I represent the Islamic tradition as heterogeneous and dynamic shifting ground by focusing on its many histories, its multiplicities, its material and imaginative forms and fragments. The challenge for those who study religious communities is to remain alert to the tension between tradition claims and abridgements of tradition, without privileging one category over the other. Ideological claims may be constituted by constructions of the past as simple, but the claims themselves ("The personal is political" or "Aristotle is the father of Western civilization" or "*Sharia* is eternal") are just as complex and wide ranging as are claims made in the name of tradition that do not abridge history in this way. Although I complicate and resist the simpler narratives that Muslim American student-travelers offer about their pedagogical journeys, my aim is not only to debunk their own accounts but to demonstrate how Islamic authenticity (and its antecedent orthodoxy) emerges not as a found object in the past or in the "archive" of the Middle East but as a continual process of debate and redefinition that is transmitted over time and space.

In my analysis, I use the term *tradition* in an open-ended way, as the unfolding of arguments among Muslims over time, and I understand *crisis* to be the condition of incoherence that must be resolved by developing new ways of understanding the relationship between the tradition's past and its future. Through the stories of Muslim American student-travelers like Fawzia and intellectuals like Shaykh Firas, we will see that they often talk about their tradition in simple, static (even classical anthropological and Orientalist) terms, as a brittle object moving through time. By tracking the convergences and divergences in the religious imaginations and pedagogical projects of the American students in these networks and their peers and teachers in the Middle East, we see the ways that territorial locality, constructions of home and away, self and other, familiar and foreign shape the very understanding of tradition itself. To a great extent, Muslims in the US and the Middle East are suspicious of Western discourses about (and diagnoses of) Islam. These suspicions shape their religious imaginations in powerful ways and index a "double consciousness," a condition of constantly seeing yourself through the eyes of a more powerful Other, in this case an Orientalist.[46] As we will see, Orientalism haunts and shapes contemporary, global debates among devout Muslims about the nature of Islamic authority, in ways Muslims actively resist and in ways they unconsciously reproduce, just as it continues to haunt debates among anthropologists about the nature of their scholarly authority.

In my view, critical anthropology requires a humility that is more than a simple identification and alignment with the desires, politics, and worldview of those whom we write about, just as it must be more than a process of revealing the misconceptions of Western audiences. The cultural appropriations and mistranslations, even those with Orientalist valences, can be productive and generative for American student-travelers working to "establish" Islam in America and to resolve the crisis of authority, just as they were powerful in shaping the religious imaginaries and political projects of earlier communities of Muslim Americans who were also grappling with their place in the US and in the world. I focus on the imaginative work that makes journeys for knowledge to the Middle East meaningful for American Muslim student-travelers. I track the claims Muslim Americans make in the name of tradition as they engage each other in debates and assign stigma (inauthenticity) and prestige (authenticity) to certain practices and not others; through these claims, we can index the micro- and macroconstellations of power which sustain their competing moral geographies and the contested category of orthodoxy. The allegorical, discontinuous, and deterritorialized history that I construct in the next two chapters jumps back and forth between a diverse set of Muslim American intellectuals and religious leaders and the accounts of the Sunni student-travelers in order to foreground how the process of defining "pure," "authentic," and "orthodox" Islam is always contested and shifting, the labor of specific actors with specific interests.

2

Islamic Utopias, American Dystopia

Muslim Moral Geographies after the Great Migration

MALCOLM'S DICTIONARY

Over and over, Omar stumbles through the same difficult letters, his mumbling accompanied only by the buzz of fluorescent lights and the clicking of *misbah* beads in Ahmad's hand. Hours dragged by: Omar at the uncomfortable classroom desk, head in his hands, and his teacher Ahmad, leaning back in a chair with his eyes closed, listening and nodding. Drill after drill. The Arabic letters: *kha, sad, 'ayn, hamza, dad,* and *qaf.* Mistake after mistake.

"Ka, ka, ka, ka." Omar nearly coughs out the sounds, knowing without looking up that Ahmad is shaking his head no, no, no, no.

Omar always loses his patience first. Ahmad leans toward his student and thumbs back in Omar's notebook to the profile of a man's head he had scrawled onto the lined paper on their first day of class. Each Arabic letter is mapped onto the tongue, lips, and throat, indicating the place the sound was supposed to emerge from, as if seeing the letter *qaf* penciled onto a paper throat would make the sound start in Omar's. Ahmad smiles and pronounces the letter deliberately and effortlessly, "qa," tapping the right spot in the drawn throat with his pencil.

Omar finds it humiliating. Omar is all too aware that he sounds stupid in Arabic. It bothers him that Egyptians sometimes talk around him like he is a piece of furniture. Ahmad is only a few years older than Omar is, but he makes Omar feel like a child. Weeks have gone by, but their sessions still sting.

Omar's loneliness makes the days, hours, minutes spent studying drag. Omar never imagined that Cairo could be lonelier than Cambridge. His high SAT scores had surprised his teachers at his Harlem high school but not his mother. The father he could barely remember had always been a numbers man, a talent that had gotten him only as far as Atlantic City. Even now, she suspected, he was probably dumping quarters into a slot somewhere, cigarette in one hand and the handle in the other. His mother always said Omar had his father's mind and his father's looks but not his bad luck. That was how he ended up at Harvard. Even though he sat in the back of class and rarely spoke, in Cambridge, Omar learned he was smart. In Cairo, Omar is learning he only comes off smart in English. Ahmad had never heard of Harvard before.

Omar forgets his wounded ego in the night, when he sits alone in his Cairene apartment memorizing an Arabic dictionary one page at a time, just as Malcolm X had sat in a Boston prison cell in 1948 with an English dictionary, arming himself one page at a time. The Quran, Malcolm's *Autobiography*, and the dictionary are stacked in that order on the table next to his bed. That way he goes to bed with purpose and wakes with purpose. Arabic words slosh around in his sleep, whispers, one rushing into the next, the way dreams do, like a river, like the Nile, calling his name around every bend.

Transnational Moral Geographies

The nation-state is arguably the most powerful and pervasive moral geography of our modern world. But as we have seen, the imagined community of the nation is always in competition with other imagined communities, including transnational ones. Transnational communities and their corresponding moral geographies produce obligational pulls to places and peoples that eclipse attachments to the state and destabilize the national myth of a horizontal citizenry. American minorities in particular often develop deep attachments to imagined communities that are global and inclusive in ways their experience as US citizens fails to be. In 1964, Malcolm X delivered perhaps his most famous speech, "The Ballot or the Bullet," in Cleveland, Ohio, ten days before embarking on his transformative journey to Mecca for the hajj pilgrimage. In the speech, Malcolm X described the gulf between American legal citizenship and social citizenship for blacks and the strong sense of ambivalence and even hostility toward the nation that it engenders.

I'm not going to sit at your table and watch you eat, with nothing on my plate, and call myself a diner. Sitting at the table doesn't make you a diner, unless you eat some of what's on that plate. Being here in America doesn't make you an American. Being born here in America doesn't make you an American. Why, if birth made you American, you wouldn't need any legislation, you wouldn't need any amendments to the Constitution, you wouldn't be faced with civil-rights filibustering in Washington, D.C., right now . . . No, I'm not an American. I'm one of the 22 million black people who are the victims of Americanism. One of the 22 million black people who are the victims of democracy, nothing but disguised hypocrisy. So, I'm not standing here speaking to you as an American, or a patriot, or a flag-saluter, or a flag-waver—no, not I. I'm speaking as a victim of this American system. . . . I don't see any American dream; I see an American nightmare.[1]

In a tragically shortened life spent agitating for black rights, Malcolm X challenged blacks to see themselves not as an American minority but as part of a global majority, in part by invoking Africa. The appeal of transnational moral geographies is not as predictable or formulaic as we might assume; often they cannot be explained simply in terms of superficial identity markers such as race and heritage.

For example, Malcolm X, like many African Americans, represented Africa as the homeland, the motherland. Yet biological roots are not the sole or even primary reason Africa is meaningful to blacks in the diaspora.[2] Paul Gilroy draws our attention from the language of African *roots* to the shared experiences symbolized by Atlantic *routes*, arguing that the transnational cultural exchanges of blacks and their shared histories of slavery and racism constitute an alternative and more compelling transnational moral geography than Africa as homeland, what he terms the Black Atlantic. Malcolm X's claim to being an African in America rather than an American is a cutting critique of the brutalities of American racism and the ways it systematically excludes and victimizes black citizens, not simply a genealogical claim to a diasporic homeland. Gilroy persuasively argues that routes, emblematic of the shared experience of racism and slavery, have more powerfully captured the imaginations of blacks in the West than their heritage through roots.[3] After all, the privilege of social recognition, the sense of belonging to the nation, eluded blacks in the US long after the Civil Rights Act of 1866 first recognized them as legal citizens. In "The Ballot or the Bullet," Malcolm X's references to Africa invoke the routes of the Black

Atlantic, not blood ties to Africa. For Malcolm X, as for Omar and his fellow Muslim American travelers, alternative, transnational moral geographies, whether Africa or the Islamic East, and alternative, transnational imagined communities, whether the African diaspora or the global Muslim umma, eclipse their attachments to and investments in the nation.[4]

As a young black man and a Muslim, Omar feels a strong attachment to the global umma; he is drawn to the intellectual centers of the Middle East and Africa. The transnational moral geography of the Islamic East as Archive inspires Omar's journey to Cairo for religious study; more specifically, he models himself on Malcolm X as an American social reformer, black leader, and Muslim seeker. Omar struggles to integrate into Egyptian society, and he struggles in particular with the rote pedagogical culture he encounters in Cairo, built on endless repetition and phonetic drills. He hopes his studies will prepare him to be a leader in his mosque community on his return, to establish Islam there. Omar's journey and study of Arabic, theology, and Islamic law connect him to a Muslim past (and fainter African roots), a lost heritage that haunts him and his community in the US; like Malcolm X, his studies abroad are also an investment in an American future. Throughout American history, racial and religious minorities—black Muslims and Mormons, Christian Scientists and Pentecostals, Catholics and Jews—have constructed narratives of their persecution and marginality, narratives of *countercitizenship* linked to alternative moral geographies that compete with those of the nation. Their countercitizenship reflects their ambivalence toward the US and its cultural mainstream, manifest as a seeming embrace of their exclusion and a strong identification as religious outsiders. Historian R. Laurence Moore argues that over time countercitizenship narratives paradoxically "Americanize" religious minorities; in fact, he contends that outsiderhood has been a more powerful force in the process of inventing Americanness than other, more obvious American tropes such as the frontier.[5]

What might a history of Muslim Americans look like if we examine the cultivation of Islamic sensibilities and attachments to the global umma alongside the contradictory processes of becoming American? In this chapter and the next, I historicize the process by which the Islamic East as Archive became a dominant, transnational moral geography in US mosques. My use of the term *US mosque community* is not territorial but shorthand for Muslim American counterpublics that are engaged in common religious debates. Shared debates do not require consensus, only a shared vocabulary. While my use of the term *counterpublic* indexes these shared moral questions in relation to a broader American mainstream, I distinguish it from the politically oppositional charge that characterizes what some scholars refer to as *subaltern counterpublics*. In order to capture that oppositional ethos, I refer to American Muslims' narratives of countercitizenship, which in their transnational formulations of belonging challenge the very underpinnings of the nation. As we will see, while all the American Muslim communities examined here constitute Islamic counterpublics, only a subset produce radical countercitizenship narratives such as the ones that are the subject of this chapter. By embracing outsiderhood, American Muslims have for nearly a century developed transnational moral geographies as Islamic critiques of the contradiction between the universal promise of legal citizenship in the US and the ways they have been excluded from American social citizenship. In this chapter and the next, I track the rise and fall of different transnational moral geographies and the corresponding countercitizenship that posit the umma as an alternative imagined community to the nation.

Muslim Americans' transnational moral geographies challenge the primacy of national affiliations through devotional practices, calls for racial equality, and global religious communion. As we will see, their transnational moral geographies of the Muslim world not only compete with the moral geography of the nation; they are also in competition with one another. Over the course of the twentieth century, through their invocations of roots and routes to the Muslim world, Muslim American religious leaders, many of whom were black, developed a wide range of transnational moral geographies of a utopic Muslim world against the US, which they describe as a racial dystopia.

Just as Omar struggles to master Arabic and Islamic ritual law in order to return to his American mosque community as an authority, many prominent American Muslim religious leaders throughout the twentieth century, such as Noble Drew Ali, Mufti Muhammad Sadiq, Elijah Muhammad, and Malcolm X, also derived their Islamic authority from travels and studies in Islamic lands, whether real or imagined.

These brown and black Muslim leaders attracted followers (most of whom were black) by developing transnational formulations of Muslim belonging that were also powerful Islamic political critiques of the US in the tradition of *Black Religion*, what Malcolm X called "old-time religion."[6]

Black Religion is a modality of what Moore calls religious outsiderhood, a countercitizenship narrative critical of the American mainstream and the dominant religious discourse. Black Religion, not to be mistaken for an umbrella category for all African American religions, is defined by three key features: the subversion of white supremacy, the revalorization of black origins (roots), and the embodied protest and agitation in the service of black liberation and against oppression in cosmic terms.[7] In an account of the transformations of Islamic authority in black communities, Sherman Jackson emphasizes that Black Religion is fundamentally a *religious* tradition that fuses otherworldly salvation and the worldly struggle for liberation and dignity in the face of racial oppression:

> The God of Black Religion is neither specifically Jesus, Yahweh, nor Allah but an abstract category into which any and all of these can be fit, the "God of our weary years," the "God of our silent tears." In a real sense, Black Religion [is] grounded in the belief in a supernatural power outside of human history yet uniquely focuses on that power's manifesting itself in the form of interventions into the crucible of American race relations.[8]

The social upheaval and trauma of the Great Migration, in which nearly five million blacks, mostly Christians, moved from the slavery-tainted South to the industrial, urban centers of the North beginning in the 1920s, was deepened by a simultaneous crisis of religious authority within the Black Church, which had conspicuously fallen out of step with the rhythm and logic of the subversive, resistant, protest spirit of Black Religion. In this context, thousands of blacks, displaced from the South and disaffected with the church, converted to Islam in part because its message appealed to their religious and political sensibilities.

During this period in American history, the lay understanding of Islam was that it was a racially egalitarian, monotheistic religion.

Popular cultural references, such as Shriners parades, conflated Islam, African wisdom, Eastern luxury, and magic in both black and white social worlds.[9] Interest in Islam among blacks was primed by blacks' earlier investments in other transnational moral geographies, whether the rise of political and cultural pan-Asianism at the turn of the century, the biblical lost tribes of Ethiopia and the growth of communities of Black Hebrews before World War I, and most importantly, Marcus Garvey's influential Back to Africa movement in the twenties.[10] Alongside Garveyites, Black Hebrews, and others agitating for black liberation, Muslim leaders made the lives of suffering blacks in northern cities intelligible through their radical Islamic critiques of the material and psychological effects of American racism and through transnational moral geographies in which the Muslim world was not only a homeland but also a utopic, moral countercategory to the racist dystopia of the US.

This chapter juxtaposes Omar's journey and studies with accounts of an earlier generation of Muslim American religious leaders and seekers who endured police harassment, state surveillance, and even imprisonment because of the political stands they took and their Islamic critiques of the status quo. Like Omar, they grappled with questions of identity and social justice, questions that are both religious and political. By examining three of the most important Muslim communities in the first half of the twentieth century—the Moorish Science Temple, the Ahmadis, and the Nation of Islam—we see the ways their articulations of countercitizenship and ambivalence toward the American mainstream emerge through their different moral geographies, moral geographies that Malcolm X inherited and amended at the end of his life and that continue to echo in Omar's account of his journey and studies in Egypt.

Transcending Race through Moorish Roots: Moorish Science Temple of America

Born in 1886, Noble Drew Ali's early life remains a source of debate among historians. One account suggests he was the son of a Cherokee woman and a Moroccan immigrant, another that his parents were ex-slaves living among the Cherokee. According to some accounts, as a teenager, he traveled to Egypt, where he may have been initiated into a mystical sufi order; scholars also trace his religious movement to involvement with the Shriners and a Canaanite temple in Newark, New Jersey. Historians agree that Ali arrived in Chicago in 1919 as a preacher and developed a modest following. He founded the Moorish Holy Temple of Science in 1926, although the name was changed to Moorish Science Temple of America (MSTA) in 1928. Ali attracted followers by emphasizing that Islam was the "natural" and "original" religion of blacks and emphasizing Islam's amenability to the terms, logic, and aesthetics of Black Religion. Combining a valorization of a utopic homeland of the Muslim world with a practical vision of challenging white racism, the MSTA received a great deal of attention in the poor, black enclaves of northern cities. Within a few years, Ali established satellite temples in fifteen cities, including Milwaukee, Detroit, Philadelphia, Newark, Cleveland, and Baltimore, which served as many as ten thousand worshipers and had a much broader black audience of attentive sympathizers.[11]

The MSTA was one of the first of a long line of Muslim communities in the US that struggled to be recognized as dignified and legitimate religious communities and that fought against virulent forms of American racism and nativism. Moore argues that American religious minorities have defined what it meant for them to be American "by turning aspects of a carefully nurtured sense of separate identity against a vaguely defined concept of mainstream or dominant culture," rather than by merely embracing the American mainstream outright.[12] Historically, the ambivalence produced by outsiderhood, often expressed as a rejection of the US, has operated as a way of imagining one's community into the nation, although these minorities' countercitizenship was first and foremost a critique of the enduring inequalities in American politics and society. Ali framed claims for recognition from the US government through oppositional claims of belonging to a transnational, imagined Muslim community. Ali's invocation of Moorish roots involved a complex double move that affirmed the categories of nation and citizen and simultaneously refused and transcended them, through identifications with a global Muslim community. By identifying as Moors, who he claimed were the descendants of Canaanites and Moabites in the Holy Land, Ali referenced the respected African polity of the Kingdom of Morocco and the sacred moral geography of the biblical Middle East in the same breath, places that had positive associations for most Americans.

Until Ali's mysterious and untimely death in 1929, the MSTA commanded a great deal of positive attention from the large, diverse crowds (including local politicians) that gathered to witness its public parades and celebrations, in which members wore black fezzes, white turbans, and long robes and waved crescent-and-star-adorned flags. The MSTA also reached wide reading publics through regular, sympathetic newspaper coverage in periodicals such as the *Chicago Defender*. In addition to the wearing of fezzes and exotic robes, Ali's reclamation project centered on accessing an intellectual heritage, the Islamic knowledge ("Moorish science") that signified the promise and possibilities of the authentic, meaningful, morally rectified life that the MSTA offered. The term *science* itself connoted progress, upward mobility, healing, and novelty, but Ali claimed that his teachings were ancient truths kept secret by the Muslims of the utopic East (in India, Egypt, Arabia, and Palestine), knowledge mediated through his prophecy. In one legend, Ali received his name and a charter to teach Islam in America from shaykhs in Morocco and the Sultan Abdul Ibn Said in Mecca, Saudi Arabia.[13] The signs of this recovered knowledge were not only material but also bodily and linguistic. Ali developed a social program of daily prayers facing eastward, vegetarianism, and abstinence from alcohol and licentious entertainment. The MSTA fostered economic institutions and preached financial independence, establishing successful businesses, such as the Moorish Manufacturing Company's popular line of oils, incense, and soap. Members also asserted their political voice by publishing their own newspaper, lobbying for political candidates, and in some cases openly challenging racial segregation, which they held did not apply to them since they were Moors and not "so-called Negroes."[14] Ali was sensitive to the power of language and in 1927 replaced all the references to God with "Allah" in his scripture the *Holy Koran of the Moorish Science Temple*, a text that was plagiarized from apocryphal, Christian-based scriptures and that has no relationship to the Quran. He also is reported to have said, "The name means everything," and had his followers change their surnames to Muslim titles that he believed connoted regality, such as El or Bey. For MSTA members, the adoption of new names and dress and their distinctive food and healing practices were religious acts, reflecting a spiritual and sensory reorientation to the black body that transcended race and that paralleled their reorientation to the Muslim world.[15] The Moorish religious practices and assertion of a transnational religious identity made them more spiritually and physically resilient in the face of the harsh and humiliating realities of everyday life in American ghettos.

The inverse to the MSTA's exotic material representations of an Islamic utopia was its construction of the US as a racist dystopia. Members carried nationality cards that asserted their true nationality as Moors, an implicit rejection of being identified as "Negroes" and treated as racial inferiors by whites. Below the person's adopted Moorish name, the card read,

> This is your Nationality and Identification Card for the Moorish Science Temple of America and Birthrights for the Moorish Americans. We honor all the divine prophets, Jesus, Mohammad, Buddha, Confucius, and Jonah. . . . [You] are a Moslem under the divine laws of the Holy Koran of Mecca. Love, Truth, Peace, Freedom, and Justice. "I am a citizen of the U.S.A."[16]

The Moors' nationality cards are a material assertion of their countercitizenship, encompassing their contradictory desire for inclusion and their embrace of their difference. As religious and (usually) racial minorities in the US, Muslim Americans have invariably been embedded in the discourse of identity politics and, more specifically, what Charles Taylor has called "the politics of recognition," a form of identity politics particular to modern liberal-democratic polities whereby marginalized groups make rights claims on the state on the basis ultimately of an equal right to difference. The desire of marginalized groups to be recognized by the state and the dominant culture is premised on the threat of others' failure to recognize that identity. Such invisibility is a denial of social citizenship, marginalized groups claim, and is oppressive because they suffer real damage when they are defined in confining or demeaning terms that reduce them to false distortions, to mere stereotypes and undignified modes of being.[17] Ali's claim to rights of recognition as Moors and protection from the state was based on such a

Fig. 2.1. The Moors drew the attention of crowds, the press, and politicians with exotic dress, parades, and healing self-care products. (From the Digital Collection of the Schomburg Center for Research in Black Culture, New York Public Library)

conception of a right to difference *and* belonging. The nationality cards appealed to the state for the recognition of their rights and simultaneously condemned the racially exclusionary policies of the state.

The MSTA provided an alternative, transnational, religious vision of the world that challenged American racism and appealed to the nation-state through a radical, religious politics of recognition. In its religious narrative, whites imposed the (racial) marks of the "colored" through slavery, making race a human rather than divine construction. In Ali's version of the boyhood legend of George Washington, the cherry tree was not a tree but the red banner of the Moors that Washington cut down in order to strip them of their heritage and their rights. Ali argued that as Moors they should have been exempt from slavery by the 1682 "Black Laws of Virginia," which distinguished Moroccan nationals from American blacks. According to Ali's legend, George Washington

was aware of this exemption but wanted to make their Moorish ancestors forget their true identity in order to enslave them.[18] By injecting the
simultaneously ethnic and religious category of Moorish American into
the raging debate at the time among blacks over whether they should
be called "Negro," "black," "colored," or "Ethiopian," Ali modeled a way
for his followers to resist the constraints of American racial categories,
to proudly identify with the Asiatic Muslim world even while asserting
their rights as Americans. The nationality cards that members flashed
when stopped by police fused a politics of recognition and an assertion
of American citizenship with a rejection of the American mainstream
and the racial status quo. Similarly, in draft-registration cards and cen-
sus forms, MSTA members challenged the conventional racial taxon-
omy by fusing their politics of recognition and their theology of skin
color; they refused to check the "Negro" box and insisted state officials
recognize their skin as olive, their identity as Moors.[19]

Importantly, Ali's counterclaims to Moorish roots, Islamic religious
heritage, and civilizational progress deflected but did not undermine
the dominant biological claims of the racial inferiority of blacks. The
appeal of Moorish identity was also informed by the benefits, protec-
tions, and exceptional treatment the MSTA believed ethnic immigrants
received from their home countries' embassies as well as the ways not-
quite-white immigrants crossed race lines and were allowed to trespass
into segregated, white-only spaces.[20] The public assertion of difference,
articulated through Eastern dress and names, ultimately made the
MSTA politically suspect and frequently the subjects of police harassment and surveillance. In the 1940s, MSTA members opposed the draft
for World War II because they did not want to fight the Japanese, a
fellow "colored" nation. The FBI launched a decade-long program in
which the MSTA was classified as a threat to national security because
it was linked to Japan, and the FBI imposed an extensive surveillance
program which included undercover informants, intimidation, and
even mass arrests of members.[21] The MSTA survived this political scrutiny, but the movement never fully recovered or thrived as it had in the
twenties and thirties, with many founding members joining the Nation
of Islam or converting to Sunni Islam. Ali, like his contemporary Garvey, was opposed to integration. In 1938, in West Valley, New York, a
community of former Moors who had converted to Sunni Islam bought

a sizable portion of land and established a utopic Muslim village named "Jabul Arabiyya" (Arabian Hills), and they became known in the area as the "Black Arabs." The Philadelphia community later established the "Ezaldeen Village" in New Jersey.[22]

Ali's followers rejected the constraints of American racial categories through assertions of Moorish roots, a global religious community, and a noble intellectual heritage. Despite the allusions to Eastern origins and divine Eastern routes of religious study that peppered MSTA mythology—including Jesus's mystical travels to India, Tibet, and Egypt and a Moroccan empire that ruled Africa, the Americas, and even the Atlantis islands—the MSTA was a decidedly American, and Americanizing, religious phenomenon. If the name means everything, the name of the organization, the Moorish Science Temple of *America*, is itself significant.[23] When Ali referenced Canaan, he did so with the knowledge that displaced southern blacks used it to mean both heaven and Chicago.[24] In short, the transnational moral geography of the MSTA did not simply challenge the racism of the US but challenged the category of nation itself, remapping Morocco and the US.

India's Black Religion Mission: The Ahmadis

In 1920, Mufti Muhammad Sadiq, an Ahmadi immigrant from India, opened a mosque and a small newspaper on the south side of Chicago. The Ahmadis are a sect originating in northern India, followers of a charismatic preacher, Mirza Ghulam Ahmad, who in 1876 claimed to receive divine directions to bring Indian Muslims, Christians, and Hindus together; Ahmad claimed to be the awaited messiah (and, by some reports, a prophet) shared by Christians and Muslims and the incarnation of the Hindu god Krishna.[25] Although he and his followers insisted they were Sunnis, the sect was labeled heterodox by Sunni and Shia Muslims in India, for whom the finality of Muhammad's prophecy in the seventh century is an essential feature of the Islamic creed. At the turn of the century, the combination of persecution from other Muslims as well as from Hindus in India's nationalist Hindu-only movement and conflicts with British Christian missionaries over defaming the Prophet Muhammad led the Ahmadis to organize formal missions beyond India to Europe, West Africa, Australia, and the

US. The Ahmadis named their missionaries "Pioneers in the Spiritual Colonization of the Western World." Although they appropriated the Orientalist division between the spiritual East and the Western expansionist tropes of the pioneer and the New World frontier, the Ahmadis reversed this imperial mythology. Like the symbolic reversals of the Moors, the Ahmadis addressed non-Muslims worldwide as a colonized people who had been misled about the Prophet Muhammad, and they promoted Islam as an emancipative, politically dissident religion with a transnational moral geography that challenged the purpose and foundation of the nation-state.[26] The dissemination of their English translation of the Quran alongside their literature and periodicals reflected their energetic efforts to root Islam in the US.

The missionary to the US, Mufti Muhammad Sadiq, was remarkably successful in drawing a diverse set of converts. On the ship to New York alone, he converted "four Chinese men, one American, one Syrian, and one Yugoslavian to Islam."[27] During a seven-week sentence in a Philadelphia detention house, where immigration authorities transferred him upon docking, Sadiq attracted nineteen other converts from a dozen different countries. Although his Islamic vision was ecumenical and panethnic, Sadiq found that his message was especially attractive to American blacks. The Ahmadi missionaries' success in the US in this period was arguably due to their ability to translate the egalitarian ethos of Islam to the terms of Black Religion. The Ahmadis not only incorporated the recovery of origins and Islamic roots (in part, like the MSTA, through name changes and exotic dress), the revalorization of African and Indian roots, and challenges to white supremacy into their American missionary work; these formal elements of Black Religion came to define the movement in the US. Sadiq and his converts walked the streets dressed in robes and turbans, reinforcing Americans' clichéd images of Muslims, the mystical Orient, and its grand civilization. They took out ads in a Chicago paper's religion and spirituality page encouraging blacks to come to their Sunday services to learn about the religion of their forefathers and the racial utopia of the Muslim world.[28] In Sadiq's view, Islam was a universal truth that would emancipate Americans from the falsehood of Christianity and a narrow nationalism.

For the Ahmadis, Islam was not a religion for blacks so much as a religion that allowed American blacks to inherit a broader, alternative

Fig. 2.2. Mufti Muhammad Sadiq, pictured here in a 1921 edition of the *Moslem Sunrise*, was one of the most successful Ahmadi missionaries, attracting a diverse set of American converts.

history, one more universal and less constraining than the bitter legacy of American slavery. In their periodical, the *Moslem Sunrise*, Sadiq regularly made trenchant, religious critiques of American racism and the US government. In an article titled "If Jesus Comes to America," Sadiq argued that the messiah would be turned away at the US border, first because immigration from his country of origin was barred by the Asian Exclusion Act but also because he would be penniless and barefooted, a disorderly act. Among other criminal acts in the eyes of US government officials, Sadiq imagined Jesus would get into trouble with the law because of his inclination to make his own wine and to preach without proper credentials. Sadiq was sure that Jesus would dodge the draft as well, as many blacks who did not want to fight a "white man's war" were doing in this period.[29] In addition, the newspaper often featured maps of the US superimposed with a rising sun, with Chicago renamed "Zion city" at the sun's center as well as maps of a then-undivided India, indicating holy sites where Jesus and Saint Thomas the apostle were buried and areas of Muslim rule such as the province of Hyderabad and the neighboring kingdom of Afghanistan.

In 1923, Sadiq returned to India after converting more than seven hundred Americans; for decades, the Ahmadi movement continued to grow and thrive in northern cities beyond Chicago, including Cleveland, Kansas City, and Washington, DC. Like the New York and Philadelphia Sunni communities that had once been part of the MSTA, Ahmadis in Detroit, Syracuse, and Newark also aspired to establish intentional communities in the US, but their poverty prevented them from realizing their own dreams of self-sufficient utopic Islamic villages in the US. Although they successfully established large, multiracial communities that numbered over ten thousand converts by 1940, debates over religious authority and charges of ethnic chauvinism ultimately fractured Ahmadi communities. Under the leadership of early Ahmadi missionaries such as Sadiq, blacks achieved titles of Islamic authority through religious study (shaykh and shaykha diplomas for male and female students, respectively); however, over time, the Indian teachers began to develop increasingly hierarchical relationships to their American converts and students.[30] In later decades, the ultimate authority to teach, missionize, or lead in the Ahmadi community became tightly guarded as the exclusive realm of Indians and Indian Americans, which led to accusations of bigotry. Exposure to Sunni Muslims also raised questions about the Ahmadi notion of prophethood for many members of Ahmadi congregations, prompting many Ahmadi converts to become Sunni or to leave Islam altogether; as a result, Ahmadi communities dramatically shrank in the second half of the twentieth century.

Typically, scholars divide the histories of African American Muslims between the racial-separatist communities, such as the MSTA, and universalist, multiracial communities, such as the Ahmadis; however, such schemas fail to account for the ways a wide spectrum of blacks drew on Islam to challenge American racism, including many who did not formally convert. In the period before World War II, Americans, primarily African Americans, were converting to Islam through contact with either Muslim immigrant missionaries such as Sadiq or African American Muslim preachers such as Ali. Both the Ahmadis and the MSTA presented Islam as a way to transcend American systems of racism both spiritually and politically. Both groups preached an Islamic message that cohered with the ethos of Black Religion, which anchored the project of divine justice in this world, in the here and now.

With the exception of Malcolm X, historical figures such as Noble Drew Ali and Mufti Sadiq are rarely recognized as important antecedents by contemporary Sunni student-travelers such as Omar because they are not recognized as "authentic" or "orthodox" Muslims and legitimate predecessors. Unfortunately, historians often implicitly (and sometimes explicitly) reproduce the same normative exclusionary practices, dismissing the religious claims of those whom they characterize as "heterodox Muslims," "proto-Muslims," or "racial-separatist Muslims" and casting the groups as sociopolitical movements in the guise of Islam; this scholarly impulse to debunk claims of authenticity extends to the racial claims of these Muslims as well, treating their alternative constructions of difference primarily as a performance.[31] When scholars characterize Ali and Sadiq as charlatans and opportunists rather than "genuine" religious leaders, the men and women of these communities are rendered either as failed Christians, failed Muslims, or failed blacks because of their desire to transcend the constraints of American racial categories through Islamic material forms and cosmologies. Even Moore's framing, with all its nuance, ultimately falls into the pattern of constructing religion as a kind of political means to a political end (i.e., recognition as Americans), reducing black Muslims to a black nationalist movement beyond the pale of genuine religious experience.

Rather than reducing these adherents' understanding of Islam to a kind of means to the end of political recognition as Americans, I reverse this analytical move by placing the accent on their desire to become more vigorously Muslim rather than their desire to become American. I am interested in the ways different Islamic narratives of countercitizenship, each invoking the Muslim world as a countercategory to the US, have been a religious means to a religious end for a diverse set of American Muslims over time. Historians too often divide the histories of Muslim immigrants and blacks in this period, excluding immigrant Muslims as participants in Black Religion communities. In fact, the Ahmadis were not the only Muslim immigrants with an active interest in missionary work in the US and with a radical, Islamic critique of American racism. Sunni immigrants had similar success in finding converts by fusing radical, Islamic commitments to social justice, transnational moral geographies, and Black Religion.[32] For example, in the twenties, the Sudanese immigrant and Sunni revivalist Satti Majid drew large numbers of black converts in northern cities, as well as Arab and Caribbean immigrants, by linking the antiracist message of the Quran and the anticolonial movements in the Muslim world to black liberation. He fused Sunni learning with the ethos of Black Religion, inspiring some African American seekers to follow him to Egypt in the thirties.[33] Like the Ahmadi communities after him, Majid emphasized the convergences between Islam and Black Religion and nurtured religious learning and leadership among his black followers. Highlighting the Black Religion roots of these early Muslim American communities does not negate their Islamic sincerity or imply false consciousness or thinly guised political motivations on their part. Rather, treating Black Religion as a discursive tradition in its own right helps us make sense of the ways Islam came to be seen as an authentic medium of religious authority in communities already entrenched in a religious tradition.

These Muslim communities were grappling with double consciousness, the racial and spiritual condition that Du Bois argued robs a people of a true, unified sense of self because of the perpetual burden of seeing themselves "through the eyes of others, of measuring one's soul by the tape of a world that looks on in amused contempt and pity."[34] They were also double in their attachments to Islam; Islam became a way for them to resist the ways they were interpolated by whites, even though their Islamic practices and claims were articulated in part through the register of American Orientalism. The Ahmadis and the MSTA creatively appropriated Orientalist exotica in service of transnational moral geographies that posited the Muslim world as a utopic countercategory to the West; Islamic places and peoples were not only racially egalitarian but also rich in knowledge and dignity. Scholars who emphasize the performative qualities of the MSTA's and the Ahmadis' use of Orientalist tropes often betray a territorial bias in their accounts of the processes of cultural appropriation, neglecting the fact that racial imaginaries are also often profoundly religious. Scholars often compare Ali's use of Eastern symbols and invocation of Moorish origins and a utopic, Eastern homeland to the popular white lodges in the same period, such as the Shriners, which also appropriated Islamic symbols but to very different ends. While white Shriners used these symbols ironically, black participation in such lodges and parades and appropriations of Oriental signs was neither playful nor politically neutral. Islamic rituals and articles of clothing were treated as religious survivals of a distant, utopic past, forceful reminders of the violent erasures perpetrated by slavery and racism that haunted northern American ghettos. The turbans, crescents and stars, and exotic robes worn by MSTA members and the Ahmadis were far more than exotic fashion and performance; they symbolized a historical and divine recovery of knowledge lost in the tragic upheaval of American slavery that had wrenched Islam from African slaves, akin to the quotidian objects that archeologists use to provisionally reconstruct history.

The same scholarly misapprehension of borrowings of Eastern material forms as merely Orientalist theater that characterizes scholarship on the MSTA and the Ahmadis is also found in some scholarship on contemporary African American Sunnis, particularly Salafis. Today the Salafi movement is among the most popular strains of the worldwide Islamic Revival, including in the US, in part through an extensive missionary campaign of Saudi-based revivalists tailored to American Muslims that began in the sixties and was most powerfully felt in US mosques in the eighties and nineties. This revivalist movement has made powerful inroads in African American communities in particular. Salafism is a modern, Protestant-styled theological reform movement that is iconoclastic and scripturalist and that venerates the beliefs and practices of the earliest generations of Muslims. Like the term *Protestant*, the term *Salafi* is an umbrella term, as Salafis vary widely in their beliefs about politics and the status of other Muslims and non-Muslims; however, the term *Salafi* is often used interchangeably with the term *Wahhabi*. The Saudi-based Wahhabi movement is one of many Salafi strains and tends to be sectarian, insular, and socially conservative; the Saudi monarchy made it the state religion and supported its missionary outreach including to the US. In the eighties and nineties, few American Muslims identified directly with the Wahhabi movement, but a general Salafi revival was felt in many US mosques in this period, attracting many African American Sunnis, inspired by the promise of a pure, authentic Islam.[35]

Scholars often represent non-Arab Muslims in global Muslim piety movements originating in the Arab world as culturally inauthentic, and we see this troubling trend to reify the "real" in research on African American Salafis who adopt the distinctive dress and behaviors associated with the movement as well. In these cases, "local" Islam becomes an academic salvage project, with scholars reterritorializing Islam and hardening and fixing the categories of "local" and "authentic." They bemoan the embrace of what they term "Arab" or "Saudi" interpretations or religious practices outside these "culture zones" in the same way scholars of globalization might bemoan the consumption of McDonald's hamburgers outside of the US. Such works treat orthodoxy as a blunt coercive instrument rather than a relationship of power between Muslims, in this case, the power to missionize around the world. Although some Salafi missionary work is sustained by Saudi petrodollars, the oil wealth of missionaries is not enough to explain the global appeal of this modern, reform movement.[36] Yet the troubling, territorializing framework which maps particular islams as belonging to particular countries or "cultural zones" continues to be employed regularly, including in scholarly accounts of African American Salafis.[37] These scholars explain blacks' appropriations of Arab cultural forms solely in terms of an Arab hegemony, an impact-response model of cultural encounters that flattens the religious lives of African Americans to mere (racial) identity politics. Salafis' appropriations of Arab cultural forms are treated as suspect, as a capitulation to Arab supremacy and black self-denial; thus African American Salafis are reduced to failed blacks, just as an earlier generation of scholars reduced the Moors to failed blacks because they identified as olive-skinned Asiatics. The Muslims of the MSTA and Ahmadi communities believed their religious and racial identities were co-constituted, and the move on the part of some historians to reduce their ideas about who they were to invented traditions and ideological denials of their "real" race betrays these scholars' own commitments to dominant American racial taxonomies and mappings of the Muslim World; the same is true for scholars who work on contemporary black Salafis. Rather than assuming that black Salafis' attractions to Arab cultural forms as "pure" and "original" is merely evidence of the success of Saudi Salafi missionaries imposing an Arab hegemony, we ought to investigate the multiple layers of meanings these cultural forms have for African Americans who incorporate them into their Islamic bodily practices. As scholars, we ought to focus on *how* black Muslims, like all

Muslims, argue over the definition of authentic blackness and orthodox Islam, rather than starting from the assumption that certain forms of Islam are compatible or incompatible with what we presume is authentic black culture.

ABU FUBU

Cairo was growing on Omar thanks to the hospitality of some young men he met on the street trying to sell him a desert tour. The young men work in a papyrus shop and they are his adopted older brothers in Cairo, his guides to the beguiling city. Omar enjoys watching them lure in tourists and charm them with their carefully rehearsed jokes delivered in perfect English, complete with American slang. They taught him how to understand the curses cab drivers exchanged with one another in a Morse code of fierce honks. He wasn't learning Arabic as quickly as he wanted to, but he is now fluent in the language of Cairene honks.

His Egyptian tutor, Ahmad, is growing on Omar too. Omar is disappointed to find that even religious men in Egypt, such as Ahmad, are clean-shaven and wear Western clothes. Omar teases Ahmad about how he wears the same worn corduroy jacket with elbow patches to every lesson. Ahmad disapproves of how Omar dresses too, usually in long white robes and sandals. Even when Omar does wear jeans and a shirt, he rolls up his pants well above his ankles.

"I tell [Omar he will] give the American people a fundamentalist impression," Ahmad complains to me. "The blacks think [exact] copying of [the way] the Prophet [lived] is Islam, [using] a *miswak* [stick as a toothbrush] and [wearing] a *thawb* [robe], like Omar. It is true that at the time of the Prophet there were arrogant people who had servants carry the [trains of their robes] behind them and the Prophet [rebuked] them, but Salafis take it [too literally when they insist] we must reveal our ankles. If you dress and act like [Americans] and befriend them, your da'wa [missionizing and representing Islam in the US] will be more effective."

Omar resents Ahmad's unsolicited advice and ignores Ahmad's pointed comments, focusing instead on persuading me that Islam is a better religious fit for blacks in the US. "Black people have more respect for Islam than anybody else, than a lot of foreign Muslims. [Ahmad] knows it. That's why he risked his life for them." The previous summer a black family from Philadelphia had inadvertently gotten Ahmad into trouble. Ahmad was so impressed that the family sold all their worldly belongings in the US in order to move to Egypt to study Islam that he offered to tutor the couple's three young boys in Quranic recitation for free. The boys were homesick for America and often acted out, and one July afternoon, Ahmad decided it was too hot to concentrate and took them to the beach. Unfortunately, at the beach, they attracted the attention of the police. Ahmad was arrested and questioned for hours: Did he have a permit to teach the Quran? Who were these Americans? How did he know them? The Americans were released, but the police detained Ahmad, delivering him to another facility in the middle of the night where he spent the most horrific two weeks of his life. "Ahmad knows those black kids are the future of Islam—ask him yourself."

Ahmad recounted his two weeks of imprisonment in painful and explicit detail: how he was denied food and a toilet for twenty-eight hours, how he laid on the cement floor weeping inconsolably in a rancid, dark cell which he shared with seventeen bearded men whose only crime as far as he could tell was being religious. Ahmad was interrogated and beaten daily, spared only one night, when the police brought in three Moroccan prostitutes for their own entertainment. After thirteen days, Ahmad was escorted to his village in a police car and released and uncuffed before his tearful, shaken family. The pain of his ordeal only multiplied when he learned of the police searches and verbal abuse his relatives suffered in those two weeks when they feared he was dead.

"And [the police] are all Muslims!" Omar shakes his head in disgust and wonders aloud if he would have been happier studying in a less Westernized Arab country such as Saudi Arabia instead of Egypt.

Ahmad assures Omar that Saudi Arabia is worse than Egypt, with an even more corrupt police force and fast-food restaurants encroaching as much as a stone's throw away from Islam's holiest site. Smiling sadly, he jokes, "You can order a Big Mac as you circle the kaaba [in prayer]."

Omar's adopted brothers are not particularly religious, but they share Ahmad's suspicions of Saudis and their Islam. They tease Omar about his youthful inexperience and his piety: his scraggly, uncut goatee and boyish, hairless cheeks, the way he turns his back to the belly dancer when she begins her act at their favorite local cafe, or his idealized view of Saudi tourists, who they insist are all hypocrites and homosexuals. Salafis, with their Saudi Islam, are ruining Islam in Egypt, they insist. They warn him about those who wear their religion on the outside, reminding him that appearances can be deceiving.

A clipped newspaper comic hangs above the stove in the back room of their papyrus shop: a Ramadan merchant, selling stickers to the faithful, a fake callous that could be worn on your forehead, an imitation of the callous formed from repeated prostrations in prayer. Omar often studies the comic while his friends cook dinner for him; he wonders about the people he sees on the street and in his study circles, their foreheads blackened, bruised, calloused.

Omar's friends in the shop ask him questions about Islam, questions about American music and movies. They love Tupac and Jay-Z, and when Omar tries to explain why they should not use the n-word, they protest that they are niggers, too. Like Ahmad, they tease him about his clothes, his rolled-up jeans, his long robes, and his FUBU jerseys. When he explained that FUBU stands for For Us, By Us, they roared with laughter. His nickname was born: Abu FUBU.

White Signs, Black Divinity: The Nation of Islam

In 1931, Elijah Poole, son of a black Baptist preacher, was in the throes of the particular kind of doubt and sadness that come with personal religious crisis. It was during this period of his intense disenchantment with the Black Church that he encountered an enigmatic immigrant silk peddler while sitting in his parked car outside Detroit. Initially, Poole believed that this enigmatic man, W. D. Fard, was an Arab from Mecca, Saudi Arabia, but ultimately he would teach his followers that Fard was God incarnate. Together, in 1932, they combined the sensibilities of Black Religion with Islamic signs and practices to create the Lost-Found Nation of Islam (NOI) in Detroit. The NOI's aim was simple: to "mentally resurrect" the "so-called Negro" from the self-deception and false-consciousness of American racism, what Poole called the "tricknology" of whites, by returning blacks to Islam, their "original religion."[38] By 1934, Fard had mysteriously disappeared, and at the time his prophet, known as the Honorable Elijah Muhammad, led between five to eight thousand Muslims in Detroit and Chicago. During World War

II, Muhammad and several of his followers served federal prison terms for failing to register for the draft. The failure of the state to recognize their principled opposition to the war only strengthened Muhammad's resolve to grow the NOI once he was released from prison in 1946; he drew new converts with steady success and by the late fifties had thousands of card-carrying members congregating weekly in dozens of temples in twenty-eight cities.[39]

In the NOI's foundational myth, whites abused, betrayed, or, ironically, fulfilled the American dream and the promise of modern science, creating tragic consequences for humanity. In contrast to the MSTA's replacement of race as a worldly construction with the potentially empowering language of ethnicity and religion, NOI theology defined race as divine creation. Muhammad and Fard reversed the categories, however, by making whites rather than blacks the racially marked group. In the NOI's alternate creation myth, a black scientist created the monster of whiteness and unleashed this evil on earth. The myth reconceptualized blacks as superior, explained how they were overtaken, and described the practical conditions necessary for the restoration of their dignity and power. Muhammad rejected the Black Church's standard interpretation of the New Testament, the stories of forgiveness and suffering as a path to redemption; quite the opposite, he argued, these stories of endless patience, of long suffering, were enslavement narratives. Muhammad instead emphasized the logic of Old Testament justice to map out a moral geography that was simultaneously racial, political, and divine. It divided the world and its history into a war between good (black, Islam, Asia-Africa) and evil (white, Christianity, Europe-America). In *The Supreme Wisdom*, Muhammad posited a utopic image of the Muslim world, an Islamic Afro-Asia as a beautiful place without slavery, where Muslims enjoyed peace and material wealth.[40] In 1959, Malcolm X's field report from Arabia confirmed Elijah Muhammad's vision of a global, racially egalitarian umma of Asiatic black people, noting that Arabs ranged "from regal black to rich brown, but none are white," and assuring him that he found "no color prejudice among the Moslems."[41]

Muhammad affirmed the significance of NOI's connection to global Muslim communities and nations, and in contrast to Drew Ali, he challenged the assumption that blacks were simply a subset of Americans. Asserting and denying a black connection with the territory of the US in the same breath, Muhammad appropriated the myth of the American frontier: "[Allah] has declared that we are descendants of the Asian black nation and the tribe of Shabazz, . . . the first to discover the best part of our planet to live on."[42] The "discovered" land alternated between the rich Nile valley, Mecca, and even an ambiguous set of states in the black belt of the American South (reversing the patterns and pains of displacement of the Middle Passage and the Great Migration). Muhammad's religious vision contained both this-worldly and otherworldly aspects, although he located heaven and hell in the earthly realm. The NOI's moral geography of the Muslim world expanded beyond Muslim Africa to include Egypt, Asia, Arabia, the American South, and even outer space in his apocalyptic prophecy of a "Mothership" or "Motherplane," "a human-built planet measuring one-half mile by one-half mile 'squared'" that would bomb the Earth.[43] Yet the Mothership myth is not strictly escapist since heaven is a state on Earth achieved through divinely ordained black liberation. True to the ethos of Black Religion, Muhammad's mystical world always interpenetrated the material world.

The NOI cultivated a strong ethos of self-improvement and learning. Before disappearing, Fard established a school in Detroit, named the University of Islam, in the home of Muhammad. In 1934, the Detroit Board of Education tried unsuccessfully to close the school; as the NOI grew, it opened satellite schools throughout the urban centers of the Northeast and the Midwest. The NOI, true to its motto, "Do for self," successfully developed economically autonomous black communities, promoting economic separatism, enforced far more extensively than the MSTA did, in order to cultivate black self-sufficiency in the American marketplace. The NOI's radical economic program included the boycott of white businesses; the development of a black nationwide bank, black hospitals, black factories; and the purchase of farmland for raw materials. Through its extremely successful and empowering model of black intellectual, economic, and cultural self-sufficiency, the NOI imbued the quotidian realities of everyday black life with divine purpose, despite persecution and surveillance from the government.

The NOI moral geographies reoriented blacks to the Muslim world and the imminence of a global power shift, but it also mapped black transcendence "beyond time and space, positing a primordial origin for the black man, who had no beginning and has no end."[44] As with the

Fig. 2.3. Elijah Muhammad, pictured here in 1962, inspired thousands with his vision of self-transformation, such as his young protégé Malcolm X. (Courtesy of Eve Arnold / Magnum Photos)

MSTA, esoteric knowledge lost, secretly concealed, or willfully with-held looms large in NOI cosmology, particularly arithmetic. The NOI also transformed its followers' knowledge of the Bible. Old Testament stories and stray Quranic verses alike were prophecies, not histories, for the NOI and thus spoke to the black experience of slavery and racism in the US. Rather than identifying with Jews as a prototype for black liberation (as Christian civil rights leaders such as Martin Luther King Jr. were doing), Muhammad blamed the Jews for usurping the place of blacks as God's chosen people. In addition to theology, the NOI taught practical skills and bodies of knowledge to improve people's day-to-day lives in urban ghettos, from how to cook and eat healthy foods to start-ing and growing a small business. Muhammad stressed a need for "clean living" that consisted of a complex set of bodily rituals.[45] He sought to change the way people spoke, dressed, and ate, banning "slave" foods such as pork and cabbage. He also prohibited straightened hairstyles that imitated whites and a long list of vices, including gambling, drinking, and smoking. NOI members changed their last names to "X" to signify the unknown, their lost intellectual and spiritual heritage, but also to highlight the moral uplift of the NOI that transformed a convert into an ex-thief, ex-prostitute, ex-smoker, and so on.

While Muhammad rejected what he saw as blacks' blind and degrading imitation of whites, he consciously appropriated cultural forms from the dominant white culture as a strategy of racial uplift: black bowties, two-piece suits, erect postures, polished speech. This was a significant departure from the Ahmadis and the Moors, who appropriated exotic, Eastern cultural forms as symbols of Islam. Ironically, as Sherman Jackson points out, Muhammad's appropriations of white "high" or mainstream culture forged "a new, alternative modality of blackness that was both identifiably 'Islamic' *and* American, . . . a deeply-felt and publicly recognized 'Muslim' identity without importing any of its material features."[46] Perhaps the NOI's most popular product, the "bean pie," is most emblematic of this cultural blending; the recipe is made up of primarily American ingredients, with only a touch of the exotic, Eastern spices that came to characterize the cuisines of African American Ahmadis and Sunnis who adopted the cuisines of Muslim immigrants. Embracing and reversing elements of "high" white culture to define both authentic blackness and authentic Islam, Muhammad's countercitizenship also appropriated and inverted the notion of Manifest Destiny at the heart of American exceptionalism, which sanctioned the US's expansion of its territory and extension of its political, social, and economic influence as the inevitable unfolding of divine will.

Despite the NOI's nationalistic signs—from its flag featuring crescent moons and stars to its small, unarmed, but effective military wing, the Fruit of Islam (FOI)—Muhammad's program of racial separatism did not translate into a concrete plan for the establishment of a modern nation-state or for emigration east. Muhammad often made vague assertions about blacks having some "land of their own"; however, he was not taking practical steps to develop an intentional, utopic Islamic community as some Ahmadis and Sunnis in this period aspired to do. This "land of their own" ranged in geographic region (Africa, Asia, or southern states), and there was little concrete discussion of a specific form of governance (democratic, authoritarian, etc.). The NOI's focus and energies were directed to its pragmatic strategy of economic separatism within the US economy rather than the ideal of establishing a contiguous black state. Sometimes dismissed by historians as evidence of Muhammad's muddled nationalistic vision, the NOI's ambiguity about land and nation had a powerful religious resonance; the ambiguity is in fact part of its religious outsiderhood and its transnational critique of the nation-state.[47]

By the 1950s, the NOI had grown to include dozens of temples in twenty-eight cities, with thousands of card-carrying members. Although the NOI is often referred to as an exemplar case of the black nationalism of this period, its discourse of countercitizenship cannot be divorced from either its explicitly religious content or its insistently transnational dimensions. Muhammad predicted that the fifties was the turning of the tide, with people of color everywhere rejecting the global domination of whites as colonial powers and as Cold War superpowers. Muhammad was inspired by the anticolonial movements in Africa, India, Asia, and the Middle East. Along with such figures as Fidel Castro in Cuba, Kwame Nkrumah in Ghana, and Jawaharlal Nehru in India, Egypt's Gamal Abdel Nasser represented heroic, anticolonial defiance to this Muslim community, particularly in the wake of the 1956 Suez Crisis, which drew the admiration of Muhammad. In Muhammad's eyes, Nasser fused the spirit of Arab and African racial and anticolonial struggle; Muhammad exchanged correspondence with Nasser, and Nasser's picture hung in some NOI homes.[48] Muhammad refused to participate in the civil rights movement at a time when his African American Christian rivals, such as Martin Luther King Jr., framed the moral imperative for civil rights in terms of mainstream nativism and American exceptionalism; that is, the "benevolent supremacy" of the US as the moral Leader of the Free World required the US government to grant blacks their freedom, establishing the US's legitimacy as a superpower. With the Truman Doctrine reframing communism as a greater threat than colonialism in the Third World, the US state justified its aggressive foreign policies, including military interventions, suppression of democracy, and support for colonial and authoritarian rulers because of the "greater good" of fighting communism and capturing hearts and minds.[49] While King and other liberals accepted this Cold War logic of American exceptionalism, the domesticated struggle for black liberation was too narrow for Muhammad's vision.

Although Muhammad and Fard authored the NOI's utopic Islamic moral geography, its dark, dystopic imagery of the US was most memorably elaborated by Brother Malcolm X, a young prison convert who quickly rose in the ranks of the NOI to become Muhammad's star minister. In a nationally broadcast television series in 1959, *The Hate That Hate Produced*, Malcolm X brought the NOI to the stage of national and international politics. Malcolm X had a keen understanding of the ways place constitutes the idea of the self, of the ways that making an alternative, imaginative place is essential for making the self. Through his evocative descriptions, he defamiliarized the violent, terrifying, but all-too-familiar landscapes in which police dogs tore into black flesh; black bodies were beaten, lynched, and discarded; and black babies and children were blown up in churches.[50] Malcolm X's terse and visceral descriptions represented blacks' segregated and squalid living conditions as unnatural, not inevitable. Malcolm X most clearly articulated the NOI's countercitizenship: "We didn't land on Plymouth Rock. The rock was landed on us!" Malcolm X painted the US as a dystopia, "one of the rottenest countries that has ever existed on this earth. It's the system that is rotten; we have a rotten system. It's a system of exploitation, a political and economic system of exploitation, of outright humiliation, degradation, discrimination."[51] His critique of capitalism and mapping of a dystopic America questioned the where of blackness:

> Negro doesn't tell you anything. I mean nothing, absolutely nothing. . . . It's completely in the middle of nowhere. . . . [It] doesn't give you a language [or culture] because there is no such thing as a Negro language [or culture]. . . . The land doesn't exist, the culture doesn't exist, the language doesn't exist, and the man doesn't exist. They take you out of your existence when they call you a Negro.[52]

In contrast, Malcolm X embraced the NOI's alternative, Islamic moral geography and its inclusive transnational imagined community. In Malcolm X's registration for the Korean War (coerced under pressure from the FBI), he filled in the blank under "I am a citizen of" with "Asia," and under reasons for his conscientious objection he wrote, "Allah is God, not of one particular people or race, but of All the Worlds, thus forming All

Peoples into One Universal Brotherhood." Under religious guide, Malcolm X wrote, "Allah the Divine Supreme Being, who resides at the Holy City of Mecca, in Arabia."[53] In 1955, Malcolm X represented the NOI at the African Freedom Day Rally and called for a Harlem conference modeled on the Afro-Asian Conference of nonaligned countries in Bandung, Indonesia, which rejected both US and Soviet dogma. He told black leaders that "the dark world" was the global majority, that its political solidarity would undermine racism and neocolonial rule and also liberate it from a colonized consciousness, an internalized inferiority complex.[54]

Ironically, as Elijah Muhammad's political interest increased in the postcolonial Muslim world, especially in the Middle East and North Africa (particularly with the creation of Israel in 1948 and the ensuing war and the territorial struggle in 1956 over the Suez Canal), his relationship with his coreligionists outside the NOI in the US became more and more strained. With the growth in immigration in the postwar period and a new politicization of Islam in the Middle East, the number of immigrant Muslims hounding the NOI leadership with challenging questions after lectures became increasingly hard to ignore. NOI leaders such as Malcolm X struggled to justify the ritual practices and theology of the NOI on the basis of the Quran, the scripture they shared with Sunnis, Shias, and Ahmadis, and leaders from each of these groups, both immigrants and blacks, accused the NOI of heterodoxy. For example, Taleb Dawud (the black Sunni husband of jazz singer Dakota Stanton) publicly accused the NOI of being an illegitimate Islamic sect. Dawud attacked Muhammad's denial of an otherworldly resurrection and the omission of the five daily ritual prayers, and he also accused Muhammad of being banned from Mecca by the Saudi government and its pilgrimage committee for his doctrinal innovations. Importantly, in addition to Dawud's theological critiques, he published a picture of Fard with the caption, "White Man is God for Cult of Islam."[55] It is revealing that Dawud's attack on Muhammad's authority is couched not only in terms of his doctrinal inconsistency with Dawud's definition of Islamic orthodoxy but, just as important, as a deviation from Black Religion. Dawud questioned the authenticity of the NOI's black origins and its critique of white supremacy by accusing the group of having a "white" and even a Nazi leader (most historians believe Fard was either Arab or South Asian, and he was not a Nazi) rather than simply making theological objections to the NOI's anthropomorphism of Allah or its omission of prayers facing Mecca (the NOI faced Chicago during ritual prayer in this period).

In 1959, Muhammad, partly as a response to Dawud's public challenge to his religious authority, made a pilgrimage to Mecca and a short tour of a few other Muslim-majority countries. Privately, he was disappointed when he did not find the utopic Muslim world he expected but poverty-stricken and largely illiterate populations in Saudi Arabia, Pakistan, Egypt, and Sudan.[56] However, the coverage of the trip in NOI's paper, *Muhammad Speaks*, made no hint of Muhammad's disappointment or ambivalence and focused on his political solidarity with Arabs in the Middle East, describing the "black hills" of Mecca's desert landscape in racially evocative terms.[57] Muhammad renamed NOI temples "mosques" after the trip. Upon his return, Muhammad responded to Dawud's criticism with a counterattack on Dawud's black authenticity and religious authority, accusing him of being a sellout to the "pale Arab." This was one of the first public indications of Muhammad's changing views on the Muslim Middle East, which was rife with a powerful rivalry between pan-Arab socialism (sometimes with a nod to Islam) as embodied by Egypt's Nasser and a counter, pan-Islamist movement being nurtured by the Saudi monarchy, which supported Islamist movements that challenged the hegemony of Arab nationalism.

The NOI continued to define itself in terms of a global Muslim majority, but Muhammad paid increasingly less attention to the questions raised about his Islamic authority and legitimacy by Muslims. He refused numerous invitations to debate rival Muslim leaders because he knew he would have been entirely outmatched if the terms of the debate were based on knowledge of the Quran. In contrast, Muhammad's sons were developing deep attachments to the Middle East and Sunni Islam. Throughout the fifties, there was an on-and-off split between Elijah Muhammad and his adult son Wallace, who became Sunni; Wallace was periodically censured by his father for his Sunni teachings in the Philadelphia mosque. Muhammad's son Akbar moved to Egypt in the sixties and studied at the famed AlAzhar University, one of the premier Sunni institutions of learning in the world. In return trips to the US as a new convert to Sunni Islam, Akbar decried the NOI theology as "homemade"; his father, in turn, cast him out of the NOI and labeled him a heretic.[58]

Yet these charges of Islamic heterodoxy against Muhammad did not necessarily diminish his authority in the eyes of most of his followers. Even after Malcolm X's famous defection, NOI mosques continued to grow in number into the seventies, with new converts replacing those who became Sunni or left Islam altogether.[59] When other Muslims attacked him, Muhammad did not abandon Islam; he merely abandoned those Muslim critics. As historian Edward Curtis notes, it was the Honorable Elijah Muhammad's "Islam of self-reliance, black chosenness, and divine retribution that many saw as their pathway to liberation from oppression, self-hatred, and hopelessness. It was his Islam rather than the Islam of his critics that made their lives new."[60] Nevertheless, Malcolm X's conversion to Sunni Islam, the NOI's implicit role in his assassination, and resultant internal fracturing of the Nation of Islam all led to a shrinking of the Nation, first in the late sixties and, more significantly, in the eighties. Many who left the NOI became Sunni. The NOI's authority crisis in the late sixties foretold the diminishing importance of Black Religion as a discourse of Islamic authority for Muslim Americans, embodied in the career of their star minister, Malcolm X, who faced the brunt of the challenges from other Muslim Americans as the NOI's primary spokesman.

Malcolm X, Mecca, and the Black Atlantic

In November 1964, Malcolm X was suspended from the NOI for disobeying Elijah Muhammad by referring to the assassination of President Kennedy as the "chickens coming home to roost." This was a stray, insensitive, and egregious comment that eclipsed the central message of Malcolm X's statement, which was an otherwise powerful critique of the Kennedy administration's troubling foreign policies in Africa. Muhammad instituted a gag order; Malcolm X feared it was the first step in the NOI's broader program of isolating and possibly even assassinating him.[61] When Malcolm X left the NOI shortly thereafter, he insisted that he would always be a Muslim, that he still upheld Islam as the spiritual force necessary to restore the moral fiber of American blacks. He formed his own organizations, Muslim Mosque

Incorporated in Harlem's Hotel Theresa and the Organization of Afro-American Unity, the latter imagined as a secular umbrella organization for activists to develop and coordinate their efforts toward black liberation.

His *Autobiography*, published posthumously, presents an overly simplified picture of ideological rupture, of Malcolm X's embrace of Sunni Islam as a reaction to Muhammad's 1964 sex scandal. Longstanding religious and political differences between him and his mentor, not the allegations of sexual indiscretions, led to the split. For example, Malcolm X's relationship to Ahmadi Islam is documented as early as during his prison sentence from 1946 to 1952, when he was under the tutelage of an Ahmadi inmate named Abdul Hameed. At the time, he even memorized Arabic prayers phonetically. In one of his last interviews, in the magazine *Minbar al-Islam*, Malcolm X noted that in prison he was most impressed reading about Muslims' political victories, whether the seventh-century founding of Islam or the military successes of Muslim forces against European crusaders.[62] Sunni Muslim challenges to the NOI that Malcolm X regularly encountered as an NOI minister but did not have the intellectual resources to defend first began to take a serious toll on his faith in Muhammad as early as the late fifties. In 1960, Malcolm X took Mahmoud Shawarbi, a Sunni Egyptian professor at Fordham University and a United Nations adviser, as a religious tutor. He also had a number of other important Sunni influences: his sister Ella, who established an Arabic school in Boston and financed his hajj trip; Wallace Muhammad (Elijah Muhammad's son); and Sunni university students from North Africa and the Middle East who attended his speeches, in particular a Sudanese Dartmouth student named Ahmed Osman.

Whenever Malcolm X's first private doubts in the NOI's theology or its political disengagement from the civil rights movement took hold, he did not publicly voice his changing views until 1963. On a television show in Los Angeles, Malcolm X declared, "One becomes a Muslim only by accepting the religion of Islam, which means belief in one God, Allah. Christians call him Christ, Jews call him Jehovah. Many people have different names but He is the creator of the universe." He went on to include submitting to the one God, praying, fasting, charity, brotherhood, and respect as characteristics of the Muslim—almost

the "five pillars" of Islam.[63] By this time, Malcolm X was regularly making the argument that whites could be defined as devils on the basis of
their racist behavior, not their biological makeup, contradicting what
Muhammad established as NOI orthodoxy. Malcolm X was growing distant from the vision of the NOI theologically and intellectually
but also politically, invoking human rights and calling for the "ballot
or the bullet." Even as an NOI member, Malcolm X insisted international bodies were the best resource for American blacks to appeal to
for human rights rather than appeals to the US government for civil
rights. Remarking on the unity among millions of Muslims from
China to West Africa to a crowd of two thousand in Harlem, Malcolm
X proclaimed, "Islam is the greatest unifying force in the Dark World
today, . . . a force and a factor that has long been recognized by the
major powers of the world."[64]

On April 13, 1964, Malcolm X left for the hajj, the Islamic ritual most
emblematic of the ideal of the umma, unity in religious fellowship. The
narrative template of the *Autobiography* punctuates various points in
the book as conversion moments when Malcolm adopts a new identity
and name, such as in the pilgrimage chapter, titled "El-Hajj Malik El-
Shabazz," which is used to dramatize and legitimate political and religious views that he had long held and that had been suppressed by the
NOI, but it also dramatizes Malcolm X's emergent moral geography of
the Dark World, which drew on the geography of the postcolonial Muslim Afro-Asia in order to remap America as a social justice project.

In contrast to the utopic imagery of a Muslim Afro-Asia or a futuristic
outer-space vision that characterized NOI theology, Malcolm X's emergent moral geography of the rising Dark World as elaborated in the *Autobiography* and his final writings and speeches is oriented to the immediate future and to a coterminous Islamic civilization that could inspire
and align the dispossessed around the world, Muslims and non-Muslims
alike, in the fight for global racial justice. In the *Autobiography*, Malcolm
X describes his plane on the way to Saudi Arabia; it was not only piloted by
a black man (to his astonishment) but packed with "white, black, brown,
red, and yellow people, blue eyes and blond hair, and [Malcolm X's]
kinky red hair—all together, brothers! All honoring the same God Allah,
all in turn giving equal honor to each other."[65] Before arriving in Saudi
Arabia, Malcolm X spent a few days sightseeing in Cairo, where he was

impressed not only with the genius of the pyramids but with the industriousness of the bustling metropolis's modern schools, massive highways, and skyscrapers; he marveled at Egypt as a leading African nation, even manufacturing its own cars and buses. In his travel diary, Malcolm X noted that European tourists ignored the signs of a modernizing Middle East; they were interested only in the "architectural wonders (scientific achievements) of ancient Egypt"; he suspected that the industrialization and modernization efforts of Nasser aroused fears in the former colonizers.[66] In the *Autobiography*, Malcolm X draws on exotic imagery, describing his Saudi dorm as a scene out of the pages of *National Geographic* magazine and Mecca as a city "as ancient as time itself, . . . surrounded by the crudest-looking mountains [that] seem to be made of the slag from a blast furnace." He describes the Kaaba as a huge, black stone house in the middle "being circumambulated by thousands and thousands of praying pilgrims, both sexes, and every size, shape, color, and race in the world."[67] Importantly, this exotic imagery is combined with descriptions of being thrilled by the new construction around the Kaaba, which he believed would surpass the Taj Mahal as an architectural feat.

In the *Autobiography*, Malcolm X diverges from the moral geography of the US as a dystopia through aspirational language and nostalgic longing for home. The hajj ritual serves as an illustration of the utopic possibility of human communion, a pivot point in Malcolm's new political vision, one that could recuperate and redeem the US. Malcolm X consistently marks himself as a foreigner in the Middle East and Africa, through his clumsy encounters with other pilgrims, his struggles to assume "Eastern" postures for ritual prayers, postures that his Western limbs were untrained for, and as he mumbles through unfamiliar Arabic prayers after his religious guide the way a child might. Malcolm X writes, "A part of me, I left behind in the Holy City of Mecca. And, in turn, I took away with me—forever—a part of Mecca."[68] He also took the US to Mecca. Malcolm X recounts in detail how he took every opportunity to explain America's "race problem" to other pilgrims. In his letter from Mecca, Malcolm X writes, "What I have seen and experienced on this pilgrimage has forced me to . . . toss aside some of my previous conclusions. . . . [If] white Americans could accept Islam, the Oneness of God (Allah) [they] too would then accept in reality the Oneness of Man."[69]

Just as Elijah Muhammad's moral geography reversed the Great Migration, the account of Malcolm X's travels in the *Autobiography* represents the hajj trip as his first outside the US, dramatically opening a space for the development of his own moral geography. Malcolm X swaps out the NOI's esoteric knowledge or "science" for the political savvy and industriousness of Arab political leaders he discovers abroad, what he terms the "worldly knowledge" of contemporary, "civilized" Arabs and Africans. Consider this passage from the *Autobiography* in which he describes his Saudi host:

> Dr. Azzam [was] a highly skilled diplomat, with a broad range of mind. His knowledge was so worldly. . . . He spoke of the racial lineage of the descendants of Muhammad the Prophet, and he showed how they were both black and white. He also pointed out how color, the complexities of color, and the problems of color which exist in the Muslim world, exist only where, and to the extent that, that area of the Muslim world has been influenced by the West. . . . [Any] differences based on attitude toward color . . . directly reflected the degree of Western influence.[70]

In addition to instructing him in the basic elements of Sunni theology and ritual practice and warning him that he might encounter Arabs with a sense of ethnic and religious superiority, Shawarbi prepared Malcolm X for his hajj trip by giving him a copy of *The Eternal Message of Muhammad*, written by the pan-Islamist AbdAlRahman Azzam, the uncle of Malcolm X's host.[71] Like Elijah Muhammad's strategic silence about his disappointment in finding rampant illiteracy and poverty abroad, Malcolm X's selective attention to constructions of difference and ethnic and social stratifications within Muslim-majority societies was also in service of his own emergent moral geography. Malcolm X did not represent the contemporary Middle East as a racial utopia; rather, racial harmony and black roots are embodied in the Prophet's bloodline. Similarly, Malcolm X invokes the hajj ritual to inspire people working for racial justice in the US. Indeed, poet Cheryl Clarke notes that Malcolm X's hajj to Mecca became a guiding trope of deliverance from oppression for black-consciousness movements in the sixties and seventies; like Martin Luther King Jr.'s mountaintop, Malcolm's hajj fused Mecca as utopic inspiration and destination, such that "one is always getting there."[72] Malcolm X's impressions of Azzam might also be read as a narrative reversal: the egalitarian ethos of Islam can be a cure to the kind of American racism described in his *Autobiography*. That is, the egalitarian ethos of Islam, and its ability to counteract racism, is the inverse of the racism seeping into Muslim societies through encounters with European colonialists.[73] At a press conference in New York on Malcolm X's return, he specified his new "spiritual insights," describing the intimate sharing of drinking cups with Muslims whom he would have once considered white, explaining that Islam had seemingly removed racism in Muslim societies and that it had the potential to do the same in the US. Malcolm X's account of his pilgrimage in the international press reclaimed the US as a place where social justice and racial equality might be realized. Malcolm, now El-Hajj Malik El-Shabazz, called Americans to believe in the oneness of God in order to replicate Islamic racial harmony in the US. However, this iconic press conference was the last time Malcolm directly promoted Islam as the vehicle of change in the fight against US racism.

Contrary to historical narratives that use the hajj as the turning point toward Malcolm X's embrace of integration and the civil rights movement or to a color-blind Islam, a closer look reveals that the choice for Malcolm X was not between integration and separation but between integration and internationalism. Malcolm X grappled, however, with the question of which internationalism. Curtis argues that in a moment when Islam was becoming increasingly politicized in the Middle East, Malcolm X was taught (and believed) that religion and politics were in some sense fundamentally contradictory; he "ceded the authority to define the meaning of Islam (and hence, the authority to decide what was legitimately Islamic) to his [Arab] missionary sponsors."[74] When we consider Malcolm X's interviews, speeches, and letters beyond the *Autobiography*, it is evident that he did not cede Islam to his Arab sponsors; Malcolm X simply did not embrace the transnational pan-Islamist vision or the moral geography of his hosts in Saudi Arabia. He aimed only to inspire Americans with the racially egalitarian symbology of Islam.[75] Pan-Africanism, and the transnational moral geography of the Dark World which enveloped but was not restricted to the postcolonial Muslim world, became his preferred strategy for awakening the revolutionary consciousness of blacks, as opposed to mass conversion to

Islam in the US which seemed increasingly impractical. In Lagos, Nigeria, on the last leg of his trip, students in the Muslim Students Association gave Malcolm X a blue robe, an orange turban, and the name "Omowale," meaning "the son who has come home." In Accra, Ghana, Malcolm X met with black American expatriates who tried to persuade him to also relocate to Ghana, but he remained unwavering in his commitment to return to the US, while remaining oriented to Africa politically and emotionally.[76] "[Physically] we Afro-Americans might remain in America, fighting for our Constitutional rights, but . . . we must 'return' to Africa philosophically and culturally and develop a working unity in the framework of Pan-Africanism."[77] Malcolm X also visited Liberia, Senegal, and Morocco, where he made sure to see the Casbah ghetto created by the French; he dubbed Harlem "America's Casbah." Finally, he traveled to Algiers, Algeria, where the revolutionaries made a profound impact on him.

Malcolm X's moral geography unmapped the Muslim World as a discrete and distant geography for his American audiences; his transnational moral geography of the Dark World connected sites of oppression abroad to US ghettos and connected the American fight for racial justice to human rights and anticolonial struggles around the world, to Africa, Asia, Europe, and Latin America. His moral geography also challenged his Arab sponsors and hosts to recognize American Muslims as part of the umma, to reject the borders that separated the Muslim World from the West, to reorient their politics toward approximating justice here on earth. Malcolm X did not seriously engage the religious debates that were burning issues of the day in the Middle East, although he did have some sympathies for the grassroots activists of the Muslim Brotherhood whom he encountered in Lebanon and Algeria, sympathies he diplomatically concealed from his Egyptian sponsors, who considered the Muslim Brotherhood a political threat.[78] His primary engagement with his Sunni hosts overseas was to persuade them that American Muslims deserved their political and financial support as coreligionists, and that they ought to broaden their political investments. Although Malcolm X valorized the worldliness of Arab elites, perhaps for narrative effect, in the *Autobiography*, Malcolm X's private writings reveal that he did not idealize Arabs as possessors of Islamic knowledge. In a letter he never lived to send to Islamist revivalist Said Ramadan, an Egyptian leader of the Muslim Brother-hood exiled in Europe, Malcolm X wrote, "Much to my dismay, until now the Muslim World has seemed to ignore the problem of the Black American, and most Muslims who come here from the Muslim World have concentrated more effort in trying to convert white Americans than Black Americans."[79] He goes on to argue that Arabs were too pas-sive in their missionary efforts in the US, that they were too parochial; they failed to understand the universality of the Quranic injunction to justice, "non-Arab" psychology, and the cultural and political contexts outside the Middle East. He added that blacks were a more "fertile soil" for Islam than whites were, and he lamented that he was not getting enough financial support from overseas Islamic institutions. Upon his return from the hajj, Malcolm X installed Shaykh Ahmad Hassoun, a Sudanese scholar he met in Saudi Arabia, as a teacher of theology, law, and Arabic in his New York community; Hassoun's salary was provided by the Saudi-based Muslim World League.

When Malcolm X returned to Cairo later in 1964 for a conference sponsored by the Organization of African Unity, he told an audience of Egyptian students that the black struggle was not only a concern for Africans but, in Quranic principle, "must also be the concern and moral responsibility of the entire Muslim world."[80] When he got to Saudi Ara-bia as a pilgrim to perform the *umra*, Malcolm X purposely downplayed the Cairo speech and his racial and pan-Africanist politics to his Islamist hosts for fear of losing them as allies. He underwent a brief training in Sunni law and theology as a *da'iy* (revivalist) under the auspices of the Muslim World League and focused on his ambition to provide an Institute for Islamic Studies in the US within his Muslim Mosque. Perhaps as a way of assuaging the fears of his Arab hosts about the strength of his Sunni commitments, he named the NOI and American Zionists as obstacles to missionizing as a Sunni in America. His hosts in Egypt and Saudi Arabia each attempted to bring Malcolm X into their own rival political move-ments; however, they were unsuccessful because Malcolm X's humanist political vision for the Dark World was more global than the umma.

As Malcolm X forged ahead with his pan-Africanist political agenda, he simultaneously continued his private religious studies in Islam. Mal-colm X spent eighteen weeks in the Middle East in 1964, a period of time that is omitted from the *Autobiography* and largely overlooked

Fig. 2.4. In Egypt, Malcolm X met with Islamic scholars of the famed Sunni institution of higher learning, AlAzhar University. (Courtesy of Corbis)

in the dominant American historical memory of his life, a Malcolm X mythology dubbed "Malcolmology." In contrast to the general public memory, which overlooks his religious studies abroad, his Islamic studies in the Middle East loom large and are greatly exaggerated in the Malcolmology of American Sunnis (although his studies are often fused with the hajj trip).[81] He spent several weeks studying at the Muslim World League and extended his trip until October with funds from the Supreme Council of Muslim Affairs (SCMA) in Cairo. Malcolm X faced a final exam before the rector of Cairo's AlAzhar University under the supreme imam, Shaykh Hassan Maa'moun, who also gave him credentials as a *da'iy*, or Muslim missionary and revivalist, in the US. Importantly, with two rival Islamic institutions in Saudi Arabia and Egypt recognizing him as a *da'iy*, Malcolm X became the conduit for a number of global pedagogical networks that connected Muslim American student-travelers to teachers and institutions in the Middle East. Rival pedagogical institutions in the Middle East offered Malcolm X expense-free scholarships for black Muslims studying at the Muslim Mosque. Twenty scholarships to Egypt's AlAzhar University were underwritten by the Cairo-based SCMA, and in Saudi Arabia, Malcolm X was offered fifteen scholarships for his American Muslim followers to study at the University of Medina.[82] Malcolm X's mainstreaming of (Sunni) Islam had a lasting influence on American Muslims; however, his radical, pan-Africanist political legacy was largely lost in US Sunni mosques after his death. As we will see in the next chapter, the moral geography of the Dark World that he promoted at the end of his life was ultimately eclipsed by the transnational moral geographies of newly arrived revivalist immigrants. As a Sunni, Malcolm X continued to echo the pragmatic and political ethos of Black Religion, even arguing that Sunni Islam was a better fit for blacks than the NOI because it nurtured an engagement with politics: "I believe in religion, but a religion that includes political, economic, and social action designed to eliminate [injustice], and make a paradise here on earth while we're waiting for the other."[83] In his private writings, it is clear that Malcolm X saw Islamic symbols and scriptures as a source of inspiration for his political vision; he looked to Islam's rituals, its ethos, its language (Arabic) but not to Arab states or peoples. To his coreligionists who feared that his racial politics belied his recent conversion to Sunni Islam, Malcolm X countered that the Quran "compels the Muslim world to take a stand on the side of those whose human rights are being violated no matter what the religious persuasion of the victims is."[84]

As a Sunni leader, Malcolm X never arrived at a way to animate his vision for global racial justice with the social justice vision of the Islamist activists in the Middle East, whose popularity was growing not only throughout postcolonial Muslim societies but also in US mosques, and he was killed before he could resolve this dilemma for himself or his followers. In one of his last interviews, he complained, "For the Muslims, I'm too worldly, for other groups, I'm too religious, for militants I'm too moderate, for moderates, I'm too militant. I feel like I'm on a tightrope."[85] Ultimately, Malcolm X's pan-Africanism animated his countercitizenship and radical humanism, but Islam remained a source of personal inspiration for social justice. His murder in 1965 cut short his development of a comprehensive religio-political vision as a Sunni comparable to the one he developed as an NOI minister. Other black Sunnis inspired by Malcolm X, such as Max Stanford (later Muhammad Ahmad) of the Revolutionary Action Movement and H.

Fig. 2.5. American Muslims celebrated the US postal stamp honoring Malcolm X; however, in US mosques, Malcolm's legacy of private spirituality looms larger than his radical political commitment to social justice.

Rap Brown (later Jamil al-Amin) of the Student Nonviolent Coordinating Committee, contributed to black radical thought and led the fight against racism in the US, but their religio-political vision of social justice never became dominant in US mosques.[86] In the decades following Malcolm X's death, his legacy as a Sunni leader has been one of private spirituality.

BLOOD IN THE STREETS

The stone mosque is crushingly full. The imam details the test communicated in a dream, the unwavering faith of the Prophet and his family, and the miracle: a son replaced with a lamb by the hands of an angel before the blade of sacrifice; after the blindfold is removed, the grateful tears of a father. Omar swells with a mixture of joy and awe as he makes his way out of the crowd, between strangers' embraces and exchanges of fistfuls of candy and dates, searching for his sandals in the circles of greetings and well-wishes.

The quiet, wealthy, tree-lined neighborhood Omar knows so well is bustling with people who obviously do not live there. Small, excited crowds gather at the gates of houses where lambs are being slaughtered in the yard. The fresh meat is sliced and packed and quickly passes from hand to hand in plastic grocery bags. Tree branches bend slightly with the weight of colorful lanterns. Omar watches a little boy run clumsily down the street barefoot with two yellow balloons and two heavy bags of raw meat. The bags knock against his shins, and the strings of the balloons tug at his fingers with the breeze.

Omar marvels at the tables in the street spread with white sheets covered in the same uniform geometric pattern of orange, blue, and red, interrupted by plate after plate of food for strangers. He stops next to a small group of cab drivers who are not quite home. Over powdery sugar cookies filled with crushed walnuts, they fight over who will take their new friend home for lunch as an Eid guest. Omar laughs and disappoints all three. His friends from the papyrus shop are already waiting to whisk him out of Cairo for a Bedouin feast in the desert.

"*Sharafuna* [honor us with a visit], Abu FUBU." They invited him to their homes outside Cairo in Giza dozens of times. He promised he would spend this Eid with them.

As he walks to meet his friends, past the holiday crowds, the tables and scents and celebratory cheers, Omar's eyes fix on the ground, on the little rivers of blood that trickled into the street. This is the anniversary blood of lambs, of sacrifice.

This is the story of Abraham and his son.

Omar's thoughts wander to his own father, who left a son and young mother without a reason, without a penny, without looking back. "But Allah *Al-Razzaq*. We did OK. Allah provides," he assures his perplexed Egyptian friends who adore their fathers. His mother made sacrifices of her own blood, sweat, and tears, all for her only son.

Omar pauses to look back at the trail of bloodied footprints behind him. Blood and cement, families and sacrifice, distance and time, desert dust and miracles. For the first time in a long, long time, a single tear escapes, trickling down Omar's cheek.

The Diminishing Authority of Black Religion in US Mosques

By looking at how Muslim Americans have variously mapped the Muslim world in their religious imaginaries, we bring into focus the religious charge of their American identities and also the shifting criteria used to decide what constitutes Islamic authority in US mosques. Specifically, we see how shifts in the construction of Islamic authority parallel shifts in Muslim Americans' claims on and critiques of the nation. For the MSTA, the Ahmadis, the NOI, and Malcolm X, Islamic justice was synonymous with the social and spiritual project of demonstrating the divine illegitimacy of white supremacy. The potency and power of the narratives of countercitizenship of the MSTA, the Ahmadis, and the NOI confirmed that Islam was their authentic, "original" religion and challenged the state, but it also confirmed that blacks were Americans and that Islam was an American religion. For the Moors, their imaginary homeland of Morocco and the identification cards documenting their "real" citizenship were symbolic rejections of American racism but also appeals to a more just social order in the US. The Ahmadis' missionary efforts produced diverse congregations and utopic, intentional communities in which Islamic racial egalitarian principles could be lived and practiced in the US. The origin myths of the Nation of Islam pivoted on Eastern homelands, but its religious energies were directed to the local fight against American racism. Malcolm X's transgressive pan-Africanism and use of Islamic symbols sustained a moral geography of the Dark World which was both a critique of US foreign and domestic policies as well as a recuperative, domestic and international social justice project; he also made a religious and political critique of his coreligionists in the Middle East as an American Sunni.

In the first half of the twentieth century, the simultaneous moves for political recognition and the (often radical) religious challenges to the very notions of the nation-state and race were articulated by many Muslim Americans in terms of blackness and across a range of Islamic and mythical horizons (Mecca, Mauritania, Morocco, Israel/Palestine, Egypt, Ethiopia, India, Tibet, Africa, Asia, Atlantis, outer space). Although the countercitizenship of these Muslim communities centered on issues of displacement and their Eastern origins, they constructed Islam as an *American* religion. Ali and Sadiq employed imported, exotic cultural materials to construct a religious narrative of ethnic difference, but they did not reject racial categories outright. The NOI developed and articulated religious authority in local, black American terms, simultaneously referencing a remote but glorious heritage and creatively appropriating elements of "high" white culture. The bowties and suits that became trademarks of the NOI and the robes and turbans of its predecessors, the MSTA and the Ahmadis, demonstrate the imaginative ways American Muslims appropriated and reconfigured the material culture of whites, Africans, and Asians as local, American symbols of their transnational Islamic roots and routes. These signs simultaneously indexed national and transnational belonging, but they were also critiques of the state and American racism. The geographies of Africa, Asia, and beyond were charged Islamic symbols but not destinations even for those who traveled abroad, such as Elijah Muhammad and Malcolm X. Distant places, whether Morocco in particular or Islamic Africa and Asia and the Muslim world in general, acted as moral, utopic contrasts to an American racial dystopia, but not literal homelands. Malcolm's identification as "Asiatic" and his distaste for the term "Black Muslim" do not reflect a racial false consciousness or ambivalence about blackness; rather, these are assertions of the "particular universal of Islam" and its alternative moral geographies. Like the MSTA and the Ahmadis, Malcolm X and the NOI articulated an alternative, radical ontology of the self through Islam; by reorienting their bodies toward the Orient, they refused "to engage with the first principles of white America's definitions of blackness."[87] While the appropriation of exotic cultural forms from the Muslim world punctuated the moral geographies of the MSTA and the Ahmadis, the NOI rejected the American mainstream and challenged the nation through its imaginative deployment of cultural forms appropriated from "high," white culture. Through Muslims' ambivalent and contradictory identifications as both American and not American, they fused signs from the mythical landscape of the utopic Muslim world as well as American fantasies of manifest destiny and the frontier. These competing moral geographies fueled their religious imaginations and shaped their constructions of Islamic religious authority.

Transnational imagined communities are not necessarily more benign than national ones; both create horizontal comradeship through exclusions and constructions of difference and by imagining away the persistence of real social inequalities that are never shared evenly and equally. After all, the Moors of the MSTA made their rights claims by distinguishing themselves from blacks. Among the Ahmadis, India and Indianness retained a religious primacy in tension with the egalitarian ethos of these communities. The countercitizenship of the NOI was built on appropriating and excluding Jews from the Bible and was limited to people of color. By the end of the sixties, most Muslim Americans no longer defined Islamic religious authority in terms of Black Religion. In the next chapter, we will see how new transnational moral geographies invoking the umma, with its global, horizontal religious kinship, conceal different sets of inequities among Muslim Americans, amplifying the importance and religious value of some members of the umma while excluding and suppressing others. After 1965, the dominant narratives of countercitizenship in US mosques and the growing popularity of the Islamists moved the focus away from domestic racial justice toward a far less radical Muslim outsiderhood than what was espoused by figures such as Drew Ali, Muhammad Sadiq, Elijah Muhammad, and Malcolm X.

3

Imaginary Homelands, American Dreams

Sunni Moral Geographies after 1965

THE HOOPS

Usman remembers his arrival to Damascus—on a one-way ticket, with only his ambitions, a small suitcase of books and clothes, and a list of classical books he wanted to study—with some embarrassment. "In college, you read, say, five books in a course in any given semester. So I thought I'd get through six books of *fiqh* [law] and get a basis in *usul* [legal theory], you know. I thought it would take a year or so. Of course, I was completely wrong."

It was seven years ago when Usman, still sleepy with jet lag, presented his list of books to the teacher he had traveled across the world to study with. The shaykh, he remembers, was taken aback. He asked Usman if he understood that there was a prescribed order in which books were mastered. He found Usman's self-selected list cocky for a beginner. As a way of humbling Usman, the shaykh ordered him to begin working on his Quranic recitation with another shaykh, who lived in a remote village well over an hour outside Damascus. The class was held every morning immediately after *fajr* prayer. Usman began his hour commute at four in the morning, a trip involving three bus changes and poor roads that made sleep impossible.

The mosque was small and poorly lit, indistinguishable from other buildings in the moonlight. After the prayer, the shaykh sat with a small circle of students and began giving a lesson. Usman sensed that he should not approach them and sat along the mud wall with a throng of other students who were practicing their recitation with one another or reading silently. The shaykh's class went on for almost an hour and a half. Then he began calling students from the wall over one at a time to recite to him. He spent close to half an hour for some, and he would spend five minutes with others. Usman tried to catch the shaykh's eye, but each time he looked back at him blankly and motioned to someone else. Usman tried to contain his nervous restlessness, determined not to make another bad first impression. It was almost ten o'clock before the shaykh finally invited him to approach. Usman introduced himself and thanked the shaykh for seeing him. He then hurriedly explained that he was from America and had ambitions to study and that he wanted to get the most out of his limited time in Damascus and asked if the shaykh would honor him by teaching him. The shaykh's facial expression remained unchanged even as Usman, who knew he was talking too much and too fast, became impassioned about the urgent needs of Muslim Americans and the crisis of Islam.

When the shaykh finally spoke, he asked Usman to read the opening chapter of the Quran. Usman recited the verses slowly, his voice shaking slightly as he scanned the shaykh's face. The shaykh did not correct him but said that he needed to work on his pronunciation of a number of the letters. He recited the verses properly for him and told him to return the next day at dawn. Usman was confused. Did this mean he was invited to join the Islamic law class he taught after the prayer? No. It meant that somewhere between the dawn prayer and the late morning the shaykh would spend five minutes listening to him recite. Usman was stunned. Between the commute and the line to see the shaykh, Usman had spent seven hours for five minutes with the teacher. He was afraid to protest but gingerly asked if he could make an appointment. As soon as the words left his lips, he knew he had asked the wrong question.

For months, Usman endured the long commute and unpredictable wait for the shaykh's time. Sometimes, after Usman had waited four or five hours, the shaykh would announce he had plans—a picnic, a guest, an errand—and Usman would return home, dejected that he did not get even five minutes. Usman remembers those first few months in Syria with laughter now, so many years later. He admits that the long waits, the difficult phonetic drills, and the chasing after disinterested teachers humbled him.

"It is all on purpose. They make you jump through hoops to see if you have the resilience and the patience that you are gonna need. It's a test and a lesson at the same time because traditional education is a hard, long process, and it's not just about abstract knowledge but also character building."

Usman has proven himself to his teachers. In fact, Usman's teachers take his studies even more seriously than he does. They insist that given his circumstances and his abilities, his studies are a personal religious obligation. "My teachers said, 'You have the ability to stay, you have the intellectual interest, and you have the diligence, so it's become a *fard 'ayn* [an individual religious obligation] on you. It's not that there aren't people that are more intelligent than you or more diligent than you, but considering the state of Muslims back in the US—the lack of scholars, imams that are engineers, the crisis ...'—so they convinced me."

Usman's goals have become less ambitious over the years. He takes classes in a state-sanctioned religious institute, but he laughs and says this is only to appease his father and Assad, the Syrian president. Throughout his time in Damascus, he has vigorously pursued private traditional study circles on the side. He embraces his identity as a "student for life" and quotes the Prophetic hadith: "Learning is from the cradle to the grave." He aims to develop a level of mastery of law and Islamic jurisprudence such that once he returns to the US he will be able to conduct independent research with only an occasional reference to his teachers.

"The goal [before returning to America] is to get to the level where no book is intimidating, no tool is too difficult to access, and the ability to discuss intelligently with someone from another *madhab* [school of Islamic law]. Spiritually, I want to feel that any book I pick up on *tasawwaf* [spiritual self-improvement] I can read and say, 'Yes, I am working on that. I am actively trying to become a better man on that and not to be a hypocrite.' I won't go back until I am a different person."

US Mosques and the Global Islamic Revival

Since the first decades of the twentieth century, Muslim Americans have subverted the nativist construction of America as a Christian and then Judeo-Christian nation through alternative transnational moral geographies that tie them to the global umma. Muslims' transnational moral geographies not only oppose dominant constructions of the US as a nation and the official mappings of the country's domestic and foreign policy; they challenge the very meaning of citizenship and national belonging. American Muslims simultaneously reject the American mainstream and make claims to be recognized as Americans, but like religious outsiders before them, this contradictory process ultimately Americanizes them. The dominance of one moral geography over another in US mosques is not clean or absolute; Muslim Americans' moral geographies are overlapping and in perpetual competition, but it is revealing to see how, when, and why one becomes more compelling and popular than another. Although I represent a range of moral geographies quasi-chronologically in this chapter, as in the previous one, the history I weave together is not a linear, continuous, or strictly chronological narrative but a fragmentary and allegorical one.

This allegorical history offers a framework for analyzing Muslim debates over religious authority from the early twentieth century to today, by mapping the competing modalities of authority that employ different moral geographies into three "periods"; although I represent them chronologically, the dominance of one modality over others is not clean or absolute, as they are overlapping and in perpetual competition. The previous chapter focused on the first period (roughly from the interwar period to the sixties), when Muslim Americans defined religious authority primarily (but not exclusively) in terms of Black Religion by invoking a transnational black (and brown) umma and utopia as a countercategory to the US. Our second period begins with the dramatic reshuffling of Muslim American religious leadership and with the changing criteria of religious authority after 1965, propelled by three key factors: (1) large-scale demographic shifts which made new (Sunni) immigrants the majority and Sunni Islam the most populous form of Islam in the US; (2) the reordering of Sunni leadership along class lines such that professional expertise in prestigious technical fields (particularly medicine and engineering) augmented claims to Islamic authority; and (3) the slippery and shifting constructions of race amid a post-civil-rights ethnic revival in the US, which marked some Muslim converts and some Muslim immigrants as brown and/or black and others as white or not quite white.[1]

As new, well-educated immigrants, primarily from South Asia, the Middle East, and North Africa, immigrated and eventually assumed leadership of American Muslim mosques after 1965, they also developed a different transnational moral geography: the Muslim third world as diasporic homeland. Muslim homelands, particularly Arab ones, figure not as racial utopias but as the umma's moral and political core. This transnational moral geography appealed to many American Muslims— new and old immigrants alike, as well as African Americans—because it made the seismic shifts happening in US mosques intelligible. This nostalgic, diasporic outsiderhood soon became the primary form of countercitizenship espoused by new, nationally recognized immigrant leaders such as Dr. Ismail Al-Faruqi but also for African American Sunni leaders such as Elijah Muhammad's Sunni son Imam Warith Deen (né Wallace) Mohammed. Their diasporic outsiderhood simultaneously produced ambivalence about the American mainstream while embracing the American Dream, a dramatic departure from the fierce protest spirit of Black Religion which lay at the heart of the dominant form of countercitizenship of so many American Muslim communities in the first half of the twentieth century.

Over time, however, the authority of nostalgia for diasporic homelands lost its salience. In the third (contemporary) period, roughly since the nineties, unofficial training abroad in the classical Islamic disciplines, what Usman seeks in Syria, has replaced diasporic nostalgia as the dominant modality of Islamic religious authority. A transnational moral geography of the Islamic East—as an archive of Islamic knowledge and a pedagogical destination—was popularized in the nineties by Shaykh Hamza Yusuf, a leading Sunni public intellectual who, like Malcolm X, is an iconic Muslim American student-traveler. By juxtaposing the journeys and studies of Usman with an account of the rise and fall of other transnational moral geographies, espoused by an earlier generation of student-travelers and Muslim American leaders such as Ismail Al-Faruqi, Warith Deen Mohammed, and Hamza Yusuf, the contemporary phenomenon of Muslim American youth studying abroad in underground pedagogical networks emerges not only as part of a continuous history of Muslim seekers partaking in the ritual of the *rihla*, traveling to seek knowledge, but also as the result of a specific set of historical ruptures.

The Rise of Sunni Authority in American Mosques

Before 1965, most Muslims in the US were African Americans, and only a small fraction were African American Sunnis. The majority of Muslim immigrants before 1965 were Shias and Ahmadis. The new dominance of Sunni Islam in US mosques after 1965 did not mean that American Muslims simply imported an expansive Sunni intellectual tradition to the US. Instead, the shifts in the US were a part of a global fragmentation of Sunni religious authority, itself linked to the modern collapse of historic Islamic pedagogical systems. Parallel to the sudden growth and popularity of new revivalist voices in the public sphere of Muslim societies, state-enforced reform policies intent on the "modernization of Islamic knowledge" restructured the historic Islamic universities and madrasas and their classical Islamic disciplines. These shifts are critical to understanding how and why American Muslims in the post-'65 period, both immigrants and American converts to Sunni Islam, conflated the prestige of the professional knowledge of new Muslim immigrants with Islamic knowledge.

Throughout South and Southeast Asia, Africa, the Balkans, and the Middle East, the contemporary crisis over Sunni authority emerges as a result of historical reconfigurations within postcolonial Muslim societies, including the development and secular reform of public education in Muslim societies, which led to the matriculation of far more professionals in technical fields than classically trained Islamic scholars; a related decline in the political and social status (and religious credibility) of historic Islamic universities and their classically trained alumni; and the emergence of new literate audiences produced by print and media technologies (and, later, the Internet). By the sixties, across Muslim societies, conscientious men and women without formal seminary educations had inundated bookstores, newsstands, and kiosks with Islamic magazines, newspapers, pamphlets, books, and even fatwas expressing their personal religious views, the latter genre previously penned exclusively by the classically trained scholars associated with Islamic universities and madrasas.[2] The new breed of revivalist authors filled the vacuum left by historic institutions of religious authority as they were co-opted and absorbed by colonial and later newly independent postcolonial states such as Syria and Egypt.

Most of the widely read authors associated with the Islamic Revival do not meet older, premodern criteria of Sunni religious authority: neither are they trained in the classical disciplines nor is their authority derived from pious reputations cultivated among those who know them personally. Today one simply has to become a popular and persuasive author in order to command a religious following that could stretch around the world. In other words, not only have the historic Islamic pedagogical institutions and their alumni been eclipsed by the revivalists, even the informal institutions of authority, such as word-of-mouth reputations of piety based on proximate, intimate, face-to-face encounters, are transformed such that local saints and religious leaders compete with the popular revivalist writers and preachers for the attention of devout Muslims. Today revivalists in the US transmit their teachings through pulp religious literature and pamphlets, cassette tapes, CDs, DVDs and video tapes, and more recently, new media including YouTube videos, podcasts, blogs, and Internet streams of sermons, public debates, and online classes. In the late sixties and throughout the seventies, many college-educated revivalists immigrated to the US, and they dramatically reconfigured Islamic authority and American Muslim institutions.

Professional Islam and the Authority of Diaspora

Muslim immigrants to the US in the late sixties and seventies were primarily skilled professionals, more upwardly mobile than African American Muslims and the country's existing, established immigrant communities. In addition to boosting the economy, the Cold War technology and arms race created a need for scientific and technical labor that American college graduates could not fill. These new immigrants came to the US en masse because the 1965 Hart-Cellar Immigration Act abolished quotas restricting immigration from Asia and increased the number of visas for professional immigrants in order to boost the faltering US economy. Rolling back racist immigration restrictions was one of the victories of the broader civil rights movement, itself a result of the politics of the Cold War in which domestic racial inequities became increasingly embarrassing as the US championed itself as the defender of the Free World. During the Cold War, the Middle East was of growing political and strategic concern to average Americans. As news coverage of the Middle East increased in the US, so too did the prominence of the Middle East increase in US mosques.

As skilled professionals, Muslim immigrants to the US in this era were rarely trained in classical religious studies, and they brought with them what one scholar calls the "professional Islam" of the global Islamic Revival and what another decries as "pamphlet Islam."[3] The revivalists posit that educated lay publics are better suited to interpreting and implementing Islamic scripture than are the out-of-touch, classically trained elite scholars in Islamic "ivory towers." Of course, not all Muslims who are active in the Islamic Revival around the world are college-educated professionals. However, the fact that Muslim leadership in the US was and continues to be dominated by individuals with college degrees from secular universities rather than Islamic madrasas and seminaries profoundly shapes contemporary debates about Islamic authority. After 1965, it became common for the imam (prayer leader) of a US mosque to be a professional immigrant, often a bearded engineer or physician with no formal religious education. As the number of these revivalists with professional pedigrees grew in the US (colloquially termed the "brain-drain" immigrants), so too did the country's mosques, and Muslim congregations increasingly organized themselves along class, linguistic, and ethnic (and sometimes national) lines.[4] Although blacks remained the largest single ethnoracial bloc of American Muslims, they were by the late eighties an overall minority in US mosques.

As a result, new criteria of religious authority became ascendant in Muslim counterpublics, criteria based in part on a personal, recent, and nostalgic connection to the Muslim world and a professional education, rather than classical religious training or cultural intimacy with the American mainstream. The more recently arrived and more upwardly mobile immigrants commanded greater authority than did American, English-speaking blacks as well as earlier "Americanized" generations of English-speaking immigrants who were often working class. The years of college education and the associated social prestige of professional careers augmented the religious authority of the new "brain-drain" immigrants. For many converts to Sunni Islam, the vast majority of whom were African Americans, even something as basic as the ability to write Arabic letters endowed a teacher with Islamic authority. Thus, the demographic shift, coupled with the conflation of both immigrants' professional expertise and their social status with religious expertise and, often, a presumed religious literacy in Arabic cost blacks in many Sunni mosques their leadership roles and voices in setting religious and political priorities. The religious institutions and interpretations of the (often multisectarian) older, and typically working-class, mosque communities of "Americanized," English-speaking immigrants were also overtaken, abandoned, or displaced by the new professional immigrants, at a smaller scale.[5]

In the professional immigrants' efforts to simulate their homelands, they introduced new transnational moral geographies of the Muslim world as Diasporic Homeland that became dominant in Sunni mosques in the US. Rather than a mythical utopia and a symbolic resource in service of an American religious and political project, as it had been for many of the most important Muslim leaders in the first half of the twentieth century (even Sunni leaders such as Malcolm X), the Muslim world became an imaginary homeland in a diasporic sense: a nostalgic object, a political focal point. Returning "home" was a dream capturing immigrants' imaginations but very rarely something they took practical steps to achieve. Mirroring patterns of earlier Christian and Jewish immigrant communities, Muslim preachers had more authority if they came from "back home," from the immigrants' country of origin. Just as early Irish immigrants to the US preferred Irish priests or early German Lutherans insisted that US church services be in German, Muslim immigrants attempted to re-create their distant homelands in the spaces of American mosques by having services in their native tongue, even at the expense of other congregants not being able to follow the sermons. America's early mosques were usually repurposed houses and storefronts and blended into urban landscapes; after 1965, more and more mosques were purpose-built, and mosque architecture interrupted urban and suburban landscapes, simulating the skylines of the Muslim World with each dome and minaret.[6] In diaspora, immigrants' dress, food, and etiquette acted as shards of memory, acquiring not only greater emotional significance but religious authority.[7] Interestingly, immigrants' cultural fragments carried a religious charge even for many black and white Muslim converts who donned ethnic clothes and cooked "Islamic" foods from recipes shared by Middle Eastern or South Asian immigrants; some even developed overnight Arab or South Asian "accents" in their speech. For earlier generations of American Jewish immigrants, the lines between secular and sacred were often blurry, and as such, religious habits maintained a decisive influence on behavior that was no longer primarily religious; but this was the inverse phenomenon. Muslim immigrants' cultural practices that were not sacred in their countries of origin became "Islamic" in American mosques because they carried a nostalgic value.

THE IMPORTED IMAM

Usman's parents are of that generation of Egyptians who came of age with Nasser's promise of pan-Arabism and socialist justice, who saw the brief unification of Syria and Egypt and dreamt of a lasting change in the region, in the world. His father's bitter disappointment in Nasser and in Egypt spurred his immigration to the US. Usman's father finds it hard to be an Arab nationalist so far from Egypt, especially living in a house with teenagers who speak Arabic begrudgingly.

Despite the family battles over Arabic, Usman remembers looking forward to going to his local, suburban mosque with his family on the weekends, to basketball games in the parking lot, to the big, noisy holiday parties with tables overflowing with trays of lamb and rice and baklava prepared by his mother and her friends. Malcolm X's *Autobiography* awoke something in him. Usman loved history even then, and the Sunday-school lessons on the Prophet's biography captured his adolescent imagination, especially the military battles. Usman thrilled at the stories of the fledgling band of Muslim soldiers prevailing over the massive pagan armies in sword-clanging, man-to-man combat, overcoming their enemies by the sheer force of their courage and faith and the brilliance of their innovative military strategy.

What Usman dreaded was the sermons. Their mosque had what Usman calls an "imported imam," an electrical engineer with a heavy Arabic accent and a gift for screaming through the entire delivery of his sermons. His topics alternated between the depravity of the political leaders in the Middle East (Egyptian presidents Nasser, Sadat, and Mubarak were favorite moral counterexamples) or the backwardness and spiritual heedlessness of his own hell-bound congregation. Sometimes, Usman remembers, he would accuse them of deserving the humiliations of history: European colonization, US foreign policies, their own corrupt dictators, all proof of their ineptitude and backwardness.

In Syria, it is Usman that is the imported student, an experience that has softened him toward his hometown imam. "As a society, Syria really is oppressive. It does kind of get to you, things here, the poverty, being on the losing end of a battle. You feel so sad when you see things and are helpless, and it's relentless and frustrating—just day after day, thoughts: 'Why don't these people have food? Why can't this kid get medicine?' It can become despair, and you start to hate [Syria's] upper class. And that's wrong because Allah is clear. Wealth is a test and poverty is a test. You are not what you own any more than the poor are better than the rich. The only difference between people that matters is *taqwa* [God consciousness]."

Usman's first two years in Damascus were his hardest. He avoided the upscale Damascene neighborhoods that attract Western tourists, and he moved into a humble apartment in a friend's neighborhood. Taking odd jobs between classes, he lived on next to nothing to prove to himself that material things did not define him, that he was more. When the window fell out of the decaying wall in their first apartment, Usman was relieved by his wife's reaction. "She said, 'I prefer not to live like this, but [now] I know I can live with [money] and live without it.'"

Those years of weeks without meat and winters without heat were more than a test and more than a lesson. It was what Usman unlearned then that he values most. "American Muslims are very high-strung about [Islam], about getting money and making it. I learned how not to be [high-strung] here. I know a shaykh, and in his thirties and forties, they were revolutionaries: they started unions in Syria. And at the same time, he was writing sufi poetry in the middle of all this brutal [political] violence. So he is working for social justice but still finds beauty in life. And no matter what happens, his faith is unshaken. The unions were a means, not an end. So if it succeeds, it's from God; if not, it's from God. Some of these individuals, it's like nothing can penetrate them. You tell them so many thousand people were killed, and they think it's terrible, but nothing really [devastates] them. I used to read about these people, and they are few, but now I've actually met some. You know, their house burns down, someone's father dies, or they lose a child, and they're sad, yet they go on. They obviously mourn, they have emotions, but their perspective allows them to cope with things without losing hope, without becoming ugly, jaded, angry. They say, 'This is all from Allah,' and mean it. They see everything as directly from their Lord, and that's a strength. In the West, we see everything as causal, but they see things as causal, and then they see beyond that. So it's not like their lives are stress-free or that it's fun to be poor, but there's this sense of understanding, of coping, of contentment [that Americans] are missing."

Now Usman lives in a pretty, middle-class neighborhood on the outskirts of Damascus and devotes as much time to his job in a boutique bookstore as he does to his classical studies. His wife and sons enjoy small luxuries afforded by his steady work, material things that his friends in his old neighborhood will probably never see—"in this life, at least," he adds, ruefully.

Leaders of the Free Umma

Like the racial utopia of an Islamic Afro-Asia of previous generations of American Muslim leaders, the invocation of the global Muslim umma constituted the core of the countercitizenship of a new generation of Muslim American leaders who defined themselves against the American mainstream. Paradoxically, the immigrant revivalists' oppositional rhetoric had a mainstreaming effect; however, their politics of recognition was also a means to creating a cohesive and transnational *religious* community in their new country. In the US, new immigrants shared their memories of colonialism, political mobilization, national independence, war, and activism as religious revivalists. Concern over politics in the Muslim third world, and particularly its Arab core, couched in a narrative of transnational religious belonging—that is, stressing one's obligation to the umma—became a dominant mode of Islamic authentication. The new centrality of the Muslim third world, and particularly the Middle East, for American Muslims paralleled the US government's increasing political interests in the region. Major international events such as the 1967 Arab-Israeli war, the oil crisis of the seventies, and the Iranian Revolution and hostage crisis all increased Muslim Americans' global religious consciousness. From the realms of government policy to popular culture, representatives of the Middle East made the region interesting to ordinary Americans through a moral geography in which the US, as the Leader of the Free World, competed with the Soviet Union for the hearts and minds of people in the third world.[8] While making trenchant critiques of US foreign policies, American Muslims' discourse echoed the nationalist vision of American exceptionalism and an American global primacy as the Leader of the Free World but with an Islamic twist: American Muslims as the leaders of the umma because they enjoyed American freedoms.

Though the new immigrants' diasporic homelands inspired nostalgia and preoccupied them politically, their daily efforts were geared toward life in their adopted country. As more and more revivalist Muslim international students settled in the US, these immigrants developed Islamic institutions locally and nationally on a much wider scale compared to previous generations of Muslim leaders, and consequentially, they shifted the primary focus of religious discourse in mosques from local social justice concerns to global political events in the Muslim third world. Many Muslim international students were affiliated with or sympathetic to the Muslim Brotherhood, the popular Islamist movement, and they had seen its intellectual leader, Sayyid Qutb, jailed and executed by Egypt's Nasser for his political beliefs. Similarly, South Asians linked to the Islamist Jamati Islami movement had seen Maududi, Qutb's South Asian intellectual counterpart, sentenced to death; like Qutb, Maududi's untimely death made his books into bestsellers. In the context of the periodic brutal crackdowns on Islamic revivalists by secular autocrat regimes, political dissent against these regimes, often paired with criticism of Western imperialism, became a mark of a preacher's religious integrity, particularly in the Middle East. This pattern of conflating religious authority and political legitimacy was replicated throughout US mosques. Critiques of corrupt puppet regimes in Muslim countries and foreign occupation of Muslim lands, especially in the Middle East, and the decadence of the imperial West became popular and regular themes in Friday sermons in US mosques. Despite the comparatively minimal risk of criticizing distant tyrants in the Muslim third world from American pulpits, dissent-at-a-distance became a salient mode of religious legitimacy for revivalist immigrant preachers as well as American converts; speaking truth to power (even an absent one) became a key sign of religious integrity. For the vast majority of post-'65 immigrants who founded, led, and participated in these umma institutions, the debate was not about whether to stay on and become American citizens but rather about how (and how not) to become American, albeit with a wistful nostalgia for their homelands.

The continuous arrival of new immigrants throughout the later decades of the twentieth century revived the nostalgic sense of attachment to immigrants' countries of origins and the exaggerated political importance of the Middle East, again not only for immigrants and their children but for many white and black converts and their children as well.

The most important and influential umma institution developed by Muslim immigrants was the Muslim Students Association (MSA). Devout revivalists (primarily students in technical and scientific fields via Cold War university programs) founded it at the University of Illinois at Urbana-Champaign in 1963. Although the MSA had Islamist (but not militant) roots, the campus chapters attracted an incredibly diverse spectrum of Muslim Americans and very quickly evolved into an umbrella institution, not reflective of any one specific strain of Islam or even of Islamist political ideology (although the Muslim Brotherhood remained the most dominant revivalist influence until the nineties).[9] With a diverse membership from over thirty-five countries, from Albania to South Africa and from Morocco to China, the MSA nurtured a global Islamic political and religious consciousness, maintaining the

Fig. 3.1. University of Michigan members of the Muslim Students Association, pictured here in 1968, hosted a national MSA conference at their campus in 1967. (Courtesy of Nisar Grewal)

Middle East as its political focal point. In the words of one leader of the organization, the MSA's purpose was to "leverage for the best interests of the Muslim Ummah across the world."[10] The midseventies oil boom helped the MSA's dramatic growth, and by 1983 there were 310 chapters in North America with more than forty-five thousand members.[11] Although it was conceived as a student organization, from its inception, nonstudents participated. Of course, not all or even most immigrants and international students studying to become professionals in US universities developed and nurtured such politically conscious attachments to the global umma. Many had (and have) only diasporic attachments to their nation of origin, a kind of national bilocalism (attachment to two places, here and there) that does not challenge the conceptual underpinnings of the nation-state the way transnational moral geographies of the umma do. But these bilocal, diasporic moral geographies never became dominant religious modalities across ethnic and racial lines for Muslim American counterpublics the way transnational, Islamic ones did.[12] In other words, the Islamic idiom of the umma, with Arab immigrants as the presumed guardians of the faith (as the native speakers of the language of the Quran), drove the new Arab primacy in US mosques after 1965, not the parallel iterations of Arab nationalisms, as evinced by the career of one of the most influential revivalists in this period, Dr. Ismail Al-Faruqi.

Al-Faruqi's American Medina

In 1921, Ismail Al-Faruqi was born to affluent parents in British-controlled Palestine. After studying in a madrasa as a child, Al-Faruqi attended a French Catholic school and went on to earn a degree in philosophy from the American University in Beirut. In 1945, British colonial officers appointed him as the governor of Galilee; however, his political career was cut short with the creation of Israel in 1948. As a political refugee, Al-Faruqi was a fierce anticolonial critic of the Israeli occupation of his homeland. Al-Faruqi traveled to the US to pursue graduate studies at Harvard and the University of Indiana. His studies in the US sparked a new interest in Islam and inspired him to become a student-traveler to the Middle East. He traveled to Cairo and from 1954 to 1958 studied theology at AlAzhar University where he was profoundly influenced by revivalists who dominated the Islamic public sphere and who were increasingly influencing reform-minded scholars within AlAzhar.[13] These intellectuals emphasized the Islamic roots of all modern sciences and rationality and inspired Al-Faruqi to consider questions of epistemology that were to define his career as an intellectual and an activist in the US.

After visiting fellowships at McGill University in Canada and the Central Institute of Islamic Research in Pakistan, Al-Faruqi returned to the US in 1963 to pursue a career as an academic and as a Muslim activist. He worked at the University of Chicago and at Syracuse University, before taking a position at Temple University in 1968. At Temple, Al-Faruqi's encounters with students from the MSA had a transformative effect on his identity and his politics; he saw the organization as an embodiment of the umma concept: "more than a body, it was the spirit of the Muslims."[14] He confessed to one of the members, "Until a few months ago, I was a Palestinian, an Arab, and a Muslim. Now I am a Muslim who happens to be an Arab from Palestine."[15] Al-Faruqi was deeply invested in the primacy of the Arabic language and Arabic ways of knowing the world for all Muslims, a concept he grappled with and revised in light of pan-Arab nationalism throughout his life, but his "Muslim-first" identity politics became a definitive feature of the MSA. Al-Faruqi's particular vision of the umma did not celebrate the diversity of Muslims but advocated Islam (like America) as an ideal "melting pot"; in fact, echoing Salafi revivalists and the Saudi reformer Muhammad ibn Abd Al-Wahhab, Al-Faruqi was profoundly suspicious of culture as a source of impurity in religion. He saw Muslims' cultural particularities as residual and inessential diasporic forms that retreated into the background in the US, with American college campuses as a kind of umma laboratory. In fact, he railed against Malaysian and Arab coeds who organized student groups that were both ethnic and Islamic as undermining the principle of unity at the heart of the race-blind, culture-blind umma concept. Their view of the umma was of cultural harmonization, not homogenization, but it was Al-Faruqi's vision that became dominant. Al-Faruqi believed the MSA chapters in the US, as a pure umma institution, allowed Muslims to "transcend their cultures and history and construct a universal homogeneous Muslimhood."[16] He likened American Muslims to American Pilgrims, writing that Muslim immigrant revivalists were "a God-sent gift [to North America]. . . . [Their] spirit is nearly identical with that of the early founders of the New World, who ran away from oppression and tyranny seeking a [religious] haven."[17] In this way, Al-Faruqi argued that the US was a "land of opportunity" but that the opportunity was religious, not material, the opportunity for Muslims from all walks of life to create a community away from the cultural and political baggage of the Muslim World. Al-Faruqi became one of the MSA's most energetic advocates and leaders, as well as one of the most popular reform-minded revivalists in the US.

Another umma institution, the Islamic Society of North America (ISNA), grew out of the MSA in 1981, targeting the worship-related needs of Muslim American counterpublics. ISNA organized major national and regional conferences and published religious periodicals, inheriting the MSA's monthly magazine, *Horizons*. ISNA afforded the intellectually curious American Muslim an opportunity to hear and interact with eminent scholars from overseas and to network with American Muslim activists across the US.[18] With the help of a few charismatic speakers such as Al-Faruqi who developed national followings, ISNA quickly outgrew its mother organization, the MSA. With tables upon tables offering clothes, religious paraphernalia, housewares, charity collections, artwork, Islamic books, and video- and audiotaped lectures, the ISNA bazaar became the proverbial marketplace of ideas for Muslim Americans, attracting tens of thousands of Muslims each year and representing the ethnic, racial, sectarian, and ideological diversity (and social hierarchies) of American mosques. The leaders of the umma institutions such as the MSA and ISNA in the seventies and eighties primarily looked to public intellectuals and revivalists in the Middle East for political and religious advice, such as the Egyptian Shaykh Yusuf Al-Qardawi, who, in an open letter to American Muslims, cautioned them against the dangers of assimilation, urging them to missionize and "build a society within a society to ensure [the next generation's] Muslim identity."[19] Even as immigrant revivalists such as Al-Faruqi worked toward the goal of American social citizenship, they maintained a belief that their deepest religious attachments lay elsewhere, in their diasporic homelands. These professional immigrants constructed Islam as an Eastern religion that existed in the US as a result of immigrants' routes and their genealogical roots.

Fig. 3.2. Ismail Al-Faruqi's vision of a race-blind umma was the ethical foundation for local and national emerging Muslim American institutions. (Courtesy of International Institute of Islamic Thought)

Although Al-Faruqi supported ISNA as an umbrella institution that served American Muslims' immediate devotional needs, he and his long-time Saudi collaborator, political scientist AbdulHamid Abu Sulayman, wanted to develop an umma institution that served the intellectual needs of the umma around the world.[20] They linked what they saw as the civilizational decline of Muslim societies to a crisis of Islamic knowledge and authority that was the result of an ethical and conceptual gap between Western social and natural sciences and Islamic values and intellectual traditions. The enormously influential pedagogical vision of Al-Faruqi and AbuSulayman was simultaneously an antiestablishment critique of secular academia and a conciliatory intellectual project. They developed a programmatic approach to reclaiming the Islamic intellectual tradition usurped by the West and resolving what they called the "crisis of the Muslim mind."[21] Their reform project was named the "Islamization of Knowledge," an intellectual revolution that they claimed would restore the postcolonial Muslim world and make it a thriving civilization once again. The first step required Muslim intellectuals to labor toward the harmonization of Islamic scholarly traditions and values with the secular academic social and physical sciences. In other words, by bringing Islamic scholarly traditions to bear on disciplines such as anthropology, sociology, and political science, Muslim scholars could "Islamicize" the disciplines, producing knowledge recognizable as conceptually linked to a reformed Islamic scholarly tradition but also recognizable as intellectually sound in theory and method by secular academics.[22]

The "Islamization of Knowledge" project is premised on the Islamic roots of the Enlightenment and echoes the religious imaginaries of the NOI, the Ahmadis, and the MSTA by invoking a stolen intellectual heritage that must be recovered. Al-Faruqi and AbuSulayman posited that premodern Europeans' borrowed the principles of rational and scientific inquiry from Muslims, and in secularizing these bodies of knowledge, they distorted them. Muslims were thus obligated to reclaim and reappropriate this knowledge by restoring its Islamic roots, and American Muslims were the ideal agents for the development of an Islamic, alternative modernity because they would eventually transfer this paradigm to their home countries after graduating from college in the US. However, Al-Faruqi came to the bittersweet realization that most of the international students were not returning "home," that the US was becoming their home. This realization precipitated the formation of two other US-based umma institutions devoted to the "Islamization of Knowledge": a Muslim think tank based outside Washington, DC, the International Institute of Islamic Thought (IIIT); and the first Islamic college in Chicago, the American Islamic College (AIC), financed by AbuSulayman's patrons in Saudi Arabia and later by the governments of Pakistan and Malaysia.[23] IIIT hosted dozens of conferences around the world, attracting hundreds of Muslim intellectuals.

The primacy of the emigration in the prophetic biography made it a fertile metaphor that Muslim American immigrants, particularly revivalists such as Al-Faruqi, drew on to talk about the post-'65 immigration of a critical mass of upwardly mobile Muslims to the US. The Islamic calendar begins with the Prophet Muhammad's emigration from Mecca to Medina in 622. The hostile persecution faced by his small community of followers in Mecca had led Muhammad to leave the city he loved and to establish a Muslim polity in Medina. For Al-Faruqi, the post-'65 immigration to America was analogous to this first Islamic migration, the *hijra*. In his writings and speeches, Al-Faruqi compared American Muslim immigrants to the Prophet's companions from Mecca who followed him to Medina; he proclaimed, "[America] is our Madinah, we have arrived, we are here."[24] Accounts of the Prophet's life often emphasize the dangers and possibilities of his clandestine journey to Medina and the Prophet's struggle with his sense of displacement, which, although painful for him and his followers, secured the future of Islam, and American Muslim immigrants made parallels between their own senses of exclusion, crisis, loss, desire, and displacement in the US. Immigrants such as Al-Faruqi inscribed the Prophet's nostalgia for Mecca onto their nostalgia for their homelands, just as Muhammad's political successes after fleeing Mecca became a model for them to aspire to in their American Medina.

Al-Faruqi's moral geography of the American Medina expresses Muslims' acute sense of displacement as religious outsiders in the US and political victims of the antirevivalist, secular regimes in the Muslim World. It simultaneously confirms and rejects Muslims' identifications with America by producing ambivalence toward the Muslim World and the US in complementary ways. Ironically, the new immigrants' invocations of the racially, ethnically egalitarian umma emphasize Muslims' moral high ground without necessarily nurturing a politically engaged race-consciousness. After all, for Al-Faruqi, cultural diversity was a residue from the immigrants' points of origin, to be transcended in the US with a race-blind Islam just as the different, hierarchical tribal affiliations were undermined by the Prophet's tribe-blind Islam, which created a more egalitarian social order in seventh-century Medina. In this sense, the US-based umma institutions had a utopic potential in Al-Faruqi's view, offering the possibility of a kind of intentional community in part due to its safe distance from the messy social realities of the postcolonial Muslim World.

When Al-Faruqi was brutally murdered in his Philadelphia home in 1986, his death galvanized and mainstreamed the Muslim American counterpublics in ways he would never have imagined. In response to the attention from the media and the local government, some leaders of the umma institutions began to argue for active participation in US electoral politics as a way to protect Muslims as a vulnerable minority in the US but also as a way to further the cause of the global umma by affecting US foreign policies. Although leaders of the umma institutions received resistance from Muslim revivalists who feared such political mobilization would result in cultural assimilation and become a distraction from religious piety, most of them did not question the legitimacy and fairness of the American political system. While they recognized a bias against Islam in the media, they operated under the assumption that the sheer force of their votes could change US foreign policies. In addition to new efforts at political organizing, a new generation of umma institutions emerged from the MSA, including an organization called the Fiqh Council, charged with handling worship-related issues, specifically the growing number of questions in Muslim communities in North America related to the implementation of Islamic law (*sharia/fiqh*) in their daily lives.[25] The council of religious scholars offers legal and policy recommendations, arbitration, and conflict-resolution services to American Muslims on a wide range of topics, from funerary rites to stem-cell research; the council presents itself as sensitive to the local needs of American Muslims in ways Muslim scholars issuing their religious opinions overseas cannot be. The council has established working relationships with Islamic legal experts (academics and muftis) worldwide and conducts research in order to develop an Islamic religious law for Muslims living in North America as minorities.[26] It is in these ways that Al-Faruqi's moral geography mainstreamed Muslim Americans even as it nurtured global attachments to an umma that superseded any national ties, whether to the US or to immigrants' countries of origin. Sunni constructions of authority and the new meanings of the American mainstream and the Muslim world became ascendant even in predominantly black communities, such as the American Medina moral geography that Wallace Muhammad developed to transition the NOI first into Sunni Islam and ultimately into the American mainstream.

The First Emancipated Slave: Mainstreaming and Reinventing the Nation of Islam

Elijah and Clara Muhammad's son Wallace broke with his father's Nation of Islam several times over his embrace of Sunni Islam. In 1974, he reconciled with his father. After inheriting the heavily contested leadership of the NOI (in place of Louis Farrakhan) in 1975 after his father's death, Wallace Muhammad led the movement through a remarkable transformation to Sunni Islam and an equally remarkable divorce from the radical protest spirit of Black Religion. (Louis Farrakhan later broke away in reaction against Wallace Muhammad's Sunni reforms and his political deradicalization, recommitting to the original NOI theology and to the ethos of Black Religion.) As a Sunni, Wallace Muhammad developed an alternative narrative of countercitizenship, appropriating the figure of Islam's first (black) emancipated slave, Bilal al-Habashi, or "Master Bilal," but within a decade he abandoned countercitizenship narratives altogether, embracing American citizenship.

Wallace Muhammad renamed the Sunni Muslims of the Nation of Islam "Bilalians" and renamed himself Imam (rather than Minister) Warith Deen (Inheritor of the Faith), also known as Imam W. D. Mohammed. He also referred to himself as a *mujaddid*, or renewer of the faith, a title that did not violate Sunni doctrine regarding the finality of Muhammed's prophethood, a heterodoxy that Sunni critics charged against both the NOI and the Ahmadis. In one of the stories of the first Muslim community, the Ethiopian slave Bilal bravely refused to reject Islamic monotheism even while being tortured by his Meccan slave master. He repeatedly called out "the oneness of One," as he was nearly crushed under a boulder. Freed with the aid of a fellow convert, Bilal migrated to Medina, and his melodic voice earned him the position of the official prayer caller in the Prophet's mosque. The figure of "Master Bilal" embodied a triumphant quality and became a point of pride for American Muslims, proof of Islam's core commitment to racial justice and an antislavery ethos even at the religion's dawn, in contrast to the dark legacy of slavery that marks the founding of the United States. For black Sunnis in particular, Warith Deen Mohammed's invocation of the foundational period of Islam, and particularly Bilal's story, infused Islam with a (racial) triumphalism that contrasted the utopia of the first Muslim community and the dystopic conditions of America's black slaves. Such references to the racial legacies of Islam and the US's founding are less about the past than they are about the future of Islam in the post-civil-rights US.

The figure of the emancipated slave in the Bilal myth created the space for alternative national (as well as transnational) moral geographies, including an African American diasporic nostalgia that did not contradict but highlighted the empowering, emancipative qualities of Islam. During the 1976 celebration of the NOI holiday Savior's

Day, Muhammad flew the American flag and called for Muslims to involve themselves in American politics.[27] In a poster created for the event, Muhammad's face is superimposed over a map of the US, a symbolic rejection of black separatism. In 1978, he renamed the Fourth of July "New World Patriotism Day." In speech after speech, Muhammad stressed that Islam was compatible with American values such as personal freedom, individualism, and even secular democracy, a consistent message over his thirty-four-year career as Imam.[28] In addition, Muhammad successfully reincorporated elements of mainstream black culture into his community and made them "authentic" Muslim practices. Just as new immigrants sought to simulate the East in new mosques and to set new political priorities, Muhammad cultivated his own nostalgic simulations of mainstream African American culture, including cultural forms his father had scorned. Soul food, the traditional southern dishes that his father had expressly forbidden as "slave foods," became staples at his followers' events across the country, with substitutes for the pork in accordance with Islamic law.[29] Muhammad's use of the figure of Bilal, as the emancipated Muslim slave, softened the shame and stigma his father had attached to legacies of American slavery, including "slave foods."

At each step in the former NOI community's transition to Sunni Islam, however, Muhammad encountered fierce criticism and suspicion from Sunni immigrants (suspicious of his racial politics) as well as from other African American Muslims, both Sunnis and those in Farrakhan's breakaway sect of the Nation of Islam, who were disillusioned with his abandonment of the radical, oppositional spirit of Black Religion. In response, Muhammad developed a narrative of religious evolution, adopting his father's language of the "Second Resurrection." He claimed that Fard intended eventually to move the NOI to "orthodox" or "Sunni" Islam, recounting how Fard had given to Elijah Muhammad an Arabic Quran wrapped in green cloth that was being saved until the right time. The Imam incorporated "the Nation of Islam's mythology but at the same time [rejected] it . . . as a [mere] prerequisite stage."[30] Muhammad embraced the professional Islam of the Sunni revivalists and in 1977 began replacing Sunni black leaders in his mosques around the country with immigrant preachers, often doctors and engineers with no formal religious training. In an important symbolic gesture, Muhammad, with the assistance of the MSA and the Saudi-based

Fig. 3.3. Wallace Muhammad replaced the NOI holiday Savior's Day with Ethnic Survival Week, a heritage celebration. (Courtesy of Islam in America collection, DePaul University)

Muslim World League, hired an Islamist Sudanese shaykh trained in Medina and appointed him imam of his mosque in Chicago in 1978. Muhammad even abandoned the name "Bilalism" in the early 1980s, just a few years after adopting it, in order to prove his integrity as a Sunni Islamic reformer.[31]

But by the mideighties, Muhammad became disaffected with his immigrant coreligionists and even began holding his own national conference in Chicago parallel to ISNA; he also began promoting an independent interpretation of the Quran, even applying a verse about duplicitous allies to other Muslims who "represent foreign concerns."[32] Although Muhammad created opportunities for his followers to formally study Islam with classically trained scholars from overseas in his mosques and even abroad in Syria, Muhammad vigorously asserted his own authority to interpret the Quran despite being primarily self-taught, itself a mark of the Salafi revivalists' influence on his thinking.

"It is not enough for God to tell us through another race, we still feel insecure. We feel unapproved that we still have not been validated as a man. [Immigrants] are the master, and we are the boys."[33]

Although Muhammad maintained intellectual, financial, and diplomatic ties to the Muslim world, he moved away from a transnational moral geography to a national moral geography. Over the years, through his own highly original Quranic exegesis, Muhammad fused the biblical exodus with both the foundational mythology of the United States (he often remarked on the beautiful, divine language of the Constitution) and a narrative of American exceptionalism, first through the figure of Bilal and later through the trope of umma as (American) nation, such as in this 1987 speech:

> One community under God. Isn't that what we are? *Ummatun wahidatun* under God, responsible to Allah? You've heard that same language, haven't you? One nation under God. Now that language from the Constitution of the United States, or its introduction, or preamble to the Constitution of the United States—one nation under God is not new. Fourteen hundred years ago, that's more than 1000 years before that language was formed—same language, one community, responsible to Allah. And we may say one nation under God, because umma can be translated as nation sometimes. *Ummatun wahida*, one united people . . . responsible to God.[34]

By anticipating the language of the Constitution (just as the figure of Bilal prefigured the emancipation of American slaves), Islam made Muslims more American than Americans. In this speech, Muhammad reinterprets Quranic verses about the obligations to be moral exemplars (applying them to Muslims' special role in the US) while also reformulating the story of Exodus as a rejection of transnational Muslim and transnational black outsiderhood. Instead, he emphasizes the national connotations and (divine) obligations of the umma concept in order to lead his followers into the American mainstream and into an unambivalent embrace of American citizenship.

> The real meaning of Exodus is not as much in leaving a place as in moving to the condition promised by God. And this African Americans have

not yet done—they have not yet accepted that we are a legitimate part of this country entitled to a share of it like everyone else. . . . After I became a leader I lifted the flag in respect, the American flag. . . . Most of my own people didn't like it. . . . Why? Because most [blacks] feel like they are on the outside too. . . . We're a minority in this country with a double job of establishing ourselves. . . . As a minority in America we have to start with a double concern . . . to establish ourselves, and . . . to complement America, to be a beautifying addition, a healthy addition . . . in this plural society we call America.[35]

Like his criticisms of his coreligionists, Muhammad's critiques of American racism were relatively mild; with the law on the side of African Americans after the passing if the Civil Rights Act, Muhammad insisted that the primary obstacle in their fight against racism was no longer structural inequality but the psychological effects of false consciousness.[36] Muhammad's mainstreaming efforts dramatically reoriented his African American Sunni community's attention from the Muslim world to the US.

Rather than the transnational moral geography of the Muslim world as homeland, in the late eighties, Muhammad began to promote a nationalistic embrace of American citizenship, recasting the American Medina as home rather than a diasporic community. Unlike the revivalist immigrants of the umma institutions, Muhammad's moral geography of the American Medina made an additional analogy between American Muslims and the Jews and Christians who lived under Muslim rule, religious minorities who were as invested in the success of the polity as the Muslim majority was, just as Muslims had to fully invest in America. In this vein, Mohammed took a number of unpopular stances, encouraging Muslims to join the US armed forces and supporting the US, Saudi Arabia, and Kuwait against Iraq in the Persian Gulf War in the nineties. Although his community continues to be the largest black Sunni community in the US, Mohammed's mainstreaming efforts drew the ire of Sunni immigrants and the majority of Sunni African Americans who remain far more ambivalent about the US and who continue to be deeply invested in transnational moral geographies. In contrast to their transnational countercitizenship and black outsiderhood, Mohammed modeled Sunni patriotism. It was not until after

Fig. 3.4. Warith Deen Mohammed speaks to reporters. Upon his death in 2008, he was memorialized as a leader who brought African Americans not only to embrace Sunni Islam but also to embrace their American identities. (Courtesy of *Horizons*)

September 11th that umma institutions led primarily by professional immigrants, such as ISNA, began to replicate the same kind of explicitly patriotic religious rhetoric, abandoning countercitizenship narratives and their ambivalence about the American mainstream in order to promote a national rather than transnational moral geography. As one revivalist Egyptian American preacher admonished the predominantly immigrant audience at an ISNA conference in 2009: "Home is not where your grandparents are buried; home is where your grandchildren will be buried!"[37] Such calls to reject diasporic nostalgia and embrace the US as home is a far cry from the original religious vision and ambivalent countercitizenship of the founders of umma institutions such as ISNA.

From Racial Dystopia to (Muslim) American Dream

In the seventies, eighties, and nineties, professional immigrants' critiques—of Muslim rulers and autocrats in the third world, of US foreign policy, of American racism—were framed as quintessentially Islamic critiques. Despite their nostalgic longing for their homelands, the positive religious valences of the US in the moral geographies of the professional revivalist Muslims created the conditions for a religiously charged political opposition to "the West" in general and the US government in particular that coexisted alongside their mainstreaming efforts. Their belief in the Islamic potential within the West converged with Malcolm X's political vision, which he developed at the end of his life, in which the US was a project, a laboratory for social justice, but the revivalists articulated it through the rhetoric of Islamic revivalists of the postcolonial Muslim world, not primarily through the radical humanism and antiracism of Malcolm X. The Egyptian intellectual Muhammad Abduh, one of the most widely renowned religious reformers of the early twentieth century, upon his return from Europe was reputed to have said, "I went to the West and saw Islam, but no Muslims; I got back to the East and saw Muslims, but not Islam."[38] In the moral geography of the American Medina, the American Dream is itself Islamic. To this day, immigrant revivalist preachers frequently reference the Islamic possibilities and promise that life in the US offers devout Muslims, for example, the ability to earn a *halal,* or licit, income, unpolluted by the oppressive conditions of third-world economies in which one is forced to give, and even receive, (sinful) bribes just to survive. Their American Medina is exceptional as the (Islamic) Land of Opportunity.

The revivalist immigrants' diasporic outsiderhood produced new narratives of countercitizenship, although in far less radical terms than the MSTA, the Ahmadis, and the NOI. This nostalgic modality of transnational, Islamic countercitizenship Americanizes Muslims even as it places them outside and in opposition to the American mainstream by wrapping the US into the foundational mythology of Islam. In the context of a post-civil-rights US, claims that Muslims are more American than other Americans fuse assertions of religious outsiderhood with claims for political recognition. The emblematic Quranic verse associated with the umma countercitizenship narrative reads as follows: "O people! We created you from the same male and female and made you distinct peoples and tribes so that you may know one another, not to despise one another. The most honored of you in the sight of God is the one who is most righteous." This thirteenth verse from the Quran's forty-ninth chapter became a rallying cry for American Muslims, and it has been and remains one of the most frequently cited verses in speeches and sermons in US mosques to this day. A line from the Prophet Muhammad's final sermon is along the same themes and is also among the most frequently cited Prophetic traditions in American Muslim counterpublics: "All mankind is from Adam and Eve; an Arab has no superiority over a non-Arab, nor does a non-Arab have any superiority over an Arab; a white has no superiority over a black, nor does a black have any superiority over a white except by piety and good deeds. Understand that every Muslim is kin to every other Muslim and that the Muslims constitute one community." American Muslim revivalist writers and preachers, through their invocation of these scriptural passages, recognize racial and national tensions but also assert Islam as a moral countercategory to the US by claiming that in Islam's foundational period, the religion offered a solution to racism that continues to plague the US even after the passing of the Civil Rights Act.

As the moral geography of the American Medina became dominant among American Muslim counterpublics, the West remained an important moral countercategory. Many black Sunnis mistook immigrant revivalists' resentment and disdain for the West that permeated their sermons and writings as a common opposition to white supremacy; after all, the (white) West had operated as a countercategory in the Black Religion moral geographies. However, the economic promise that brought many immigrants to the US in this period and that allowed them to achieve upward class mobility led them to distinguish whiteness from Westernness. Brain-drain immigrants enjoyed particular economic and political privileges as American citizens (some even as marginalized, racialized ones), but they often vehemently opposed US foreign policy in their home countries. And thus the anti-Western sentiments that immigrant revivalists expressed in impassioned Friday sermons rarely addressed domestic social justice and political issues or explicitly critiqued American racial or class injustice. One prominent

African American Muslim scholar-activist, Aminah McCloud, frames her critique of these revivalist immigrants in terms of the American Medina moral geography, claiming that revivalist immigrants take non-Muslim American whites rather than their African American coreligionists as the "Ansar," the Medinan locals who supported and helped the Prophet and the immigrants from Mecca adjust to their new home.[39] Her allusion to immigrants' alliances with whites is in reference not only to their participation in the post-civil-rights white flight from the cities to the suburbs but also to their failure to challenge domestic state policies that collectively punish blacks by constructing them as a criminal population.

We can better understand the ambivalent position of post-'65 immigrants within the context of the white ethnic revival in the US since the civil rights movement, in which the pilgrims at Plymouth Rock lost their prominence in the national myth to the hardworking, industrious immigrants who came later through Ellis Island. Or, to use historian Matthew Jacobson's formulation, in our post-civil-rights hyphennation, white ethnics have become more quintessentially American than WASPs. Their ethnic self-distancing from white privilege, with claims that *their* grandparents never killed an Indian or owned a slave, reduced racism to a dark and distant chapter of American history, allowing them to gloss over the persistence of racial discrimination in housing and hiring from which they directly benefit. Some white ethnics appropriate the language and logics of civil rights, pitting their political grievances against "unfair" black privilege in national debates over affirmative action and welfare reform.[40] Although brain-drain immigrants are not up-from-their-bootstraps Ellis Island immigrants, in the seventies, eighties, and nineties, they could easily imagine themselves realizing the American Dream alongside white ethnics without acquiescing to white supremacy. In the context of the white ethnic revival, diasporic outsiderhood allowed professional Muslim immigrants to carve out a space for themselves at the margins of the American mainstream; they could invest in the American Dream and enjoy not-quite-white privilege without embracing white guilt or white supremacy.

Professional immigrants' assumption of leadership and transformations of religious authority involve a discursive sleight of hand in which "the West" replaces white supremacy as the oppositional category that

American Islam is primarily defined against.[41] In contrast to the domestic, explicitly racial politics of an earlier generation of urban, immigrant preachers in tune with the protest spirit of Black Religion, the professional immigrant preachers who settled primarily in the suburbs rarely focus on issues such as police brutality, unemployment, and drugs. The economic promise that brought these immigrants to the US and that sustains their moral geography of the US as an (Islamic) Land of Opportunity cannot be reconciled with the pervasive suffering in American inner cities; from their new position in America's middle and upper middle class, professional revivalist immigrants became complicit in making the suffering of Americans (but not Muslims abroad) invisible and tolerable in order to sustain the myth of the (Muslim) American Dream. Although in the sixties and seventies umma institutions actively participated in charitable works that served the needy in the US as well as Muslims abroad, the growing diversity among revivalists made the issue of charitable giving, like the question of participating in electoral politics and the nature of gender segregation in mosques, a divisive issue. In the eighties and nineties, as the influence of immigrant Salafi preachers with an insular and sectarian tendency grew, there was a significant increase in the number of gender partitions erected in US mosques and a corresponding decrease in immigrant Muslim participation in local charitable efforts. Immigrant Salafi preachers often balked at contributing charity to inner-city soup kitchens that would presumably serve sinners, alcoholics, drug addicts, and prostitutes. Suffering Muslims overseas, by contrast, they insisted were more deserving of charity because they were both poorer and presumably more virtuous than America's downtrodden.[42] Interestingly, African American Muslim leaders, even Salafi leaders, were largely undeterred in their local charitable efforts, with a few prominent Sunni preachers repeating the NOI's success, leading efforts in American cities to rehabilitate addicts, gang members, and former inmates and to revitalize ghetto economies with Muslim businesses. Yet a cursory review of articles in ISNA's *Horizons* magazine from the eighties and nineties reveals that the plight of those in the inner city, even Muslim coreligionists, paled as social justice concerns compared to oppressive Western foreign policy in the Muslim world. Although *Horizons* did begin to feature domestic issues in the nineties, it is only since September 11th that the overwhelming majority of ISNA's *Horizons* issues feature front-page stories about Muslim American communities and domestic social justice issues rather than suffering Muslim populations abroad.[43]

Although mosque congregations remain among the most diverse in the US, they are not always racially and ethnically egalitarian, despite the enormous focus on social justice and unity in sermons.[44] While antiblack bigotry is often an unspoken element of American social citizenship, the majority of professional immigrants were not and are not interested in simple assimilation, nor is it accurate to characterize these mosqued immigrants as "nouveau whites."[45] In US mosques, it is precisely professional immigrants' desire to maintain close ties with their particular ethnoreligious community (not whites), and their belief in the legitimacy and superiority of their own cultural-religious norms (not those of whites), that in many cases facilitates the marginalization of their black and working-class coreligionists. In the American Medina moral geography, as we have seen, the American mainstream figures simultaneously as an object of desire and disdain. It is precisely this ambivalence toward the American mainstream, and the strong identification with those who are not white, that undergirds these revivalists' countercitizenship and provides the moral scaffolding for the prioritization of the political and social needs of Muslims overseas (coded as the umma) over those of local, American Muslims, particularly those in the inner city. Thus, the countercitizenship narrative of the utopic (Muslim) American Dream depends on erasing the reality of economic and racial exploitation in the US and then fusing nostalgic longings for diasporic homelands, transnational politics, and utopic projections onto the American economy.

Similarly, Imam Warith Deen Muhammad's use of the figure of Bilal weds his vision for Muslim Americans to the foundational period of Islam, and therefore, Bilal acts as a mainstreaming conduit just as America's economic promise does for many professional immigrants. The triumphalism behind Muslims' narratives of countercitizenship— the notion that Muslim Americans are more American than Americans—drives mainstreaming processes for many American Muslims across ethnic and racial lines; conversely, the notion that Americans are more Muslim than Muslims themselves also mainstreams immigrants (and some black Sunnis) while rejecting the coercive quality of assimilation or the guilt of coveting whiteness and "selling out." It is revealing that Muslim immigrants arriving since the eighties have not replaced the professional immigrants of the post-'65 era as community leaders, despite a "fresher" connection to diasporic homelands. The moral geography of the American Medina allows Muslims (both blacks and immigrants) to move toward the American mainstream with their heads held high, content in the belief that America's egalitarian ideals only confirm the original vision of Islam.

Other leaders have popularized narratives of countercitizenship that vehemently reject the American mainstream and espouse religious isolation, built on analogies that construct the US as a dystopic Mecca rather than a promising American Medina; these transnational moral geographies of the umma have been attractive to American converts as well, but they have not become dominant. Like working-class African American and Latino Muslims, the social and political needs and religious priorities of many recent immigrants from South Asia, the Middle East, and Africa remain peripheral to the professional immigrants at the helm of umma institutions. These recent immigrants from the Middle East, South Asia, and Africa (particularly those who are working class and who are not part of the chain migration through the family reunification sponsorship of professional immigrants) aspire to American citizenship as a form of class mobility even as they often describe the American Dream as a mirage.[46] Most have menial jobs, including those who are college educated but unable to find work in their fields in the US.[47]

The political critiques of some Muslims and the economic and social frustrations of others have morphed among the fringes of American Muslim counterpublics into even more radical narratives of countercitizenship. Umma institutions such as the MSA established a Jihad Fund for material and financial support for the "freedom fighters" in Afghanistan in 1981, parallel to the investments of many white ethnics in overseas causes in this period. Like the thousands of American Jews who volunteered for Israeli military service after the Six-Day War, radical narratives of countercitizenship and transnational moral geographies inspired some Muslims to commit more than a donation. In some cases, American Muslim men traveled to fight (and a few died) in military jihads around the world in the eighties and nineties, in Afghanistan against the Russians and in Bosnia against the Serbs. Importantly, in those conflicts, American Muslim jihadists were fighting alongside US soldiers, not against them—perhaps the most extreme example of how Muslims' countercitizenship narratives, even in their most radical forms, actually Americanized Muslims in the period before September 11th.[48]

Desert as Archive: From Hijra to Rihla

The nineties were a particularly divisive decade for mosqued Muslims, as communities fractured along sectarian and ideological differences and split across growing ethnic and racial and class conflicts. In the context of fierce and often hostile religious debates in US mosques, American Muslim revivalist leaders increasingly depicted the demographic diversity of US mosques as a religious problem. Persistent conflicts over race, ethnicity, and class differences, and persistent hierarchies that emerged along these same fault lines, fostered a pervasive sense of religious crisis over the inability to define Sunni authority in particular. Many Sunni American communities remain split over the question of who should run their mosque: A recent immigrant imam educated in Islamic pedagogical institutions abroad but possibly out of touch with mainstream American culture and the pressing needs of American Muslims? An executive board composed of highly educated professional immigrants who are financial sponsors of the mosque? Or a black American convert without formal religious training but with cultural sensitivity and an intimate understanding of American society? The fault lines, as we have seen, are not only those of class and racial difference but are generational as well. The question, however, remains the same as it has for nearly a century: who speaks for Islam in America?

In the nineties, a new modality of religious authority began to dislodge the conflation of professional and religious bodies of knowledge and social prestige. The Islamic quest for knowledge (*rihla*), rather than Islamic migration (*hijra*), seized the popular religious imagination of Muslim Americans. As a result, Muslim leaders energized a range of efforts within various contemporary US mosque communities to push the debate about the nature of religious authority beyond identity politics of ethnic, racial, and class identity. History, accessed through traditional training in the classical Islamic sciences, was one solution to the growing crisis of authority as a potentially universally acceptable criterion of religious authority. Rather than identity, knowledge would transcend the structures of power and equalize the field of religious discourse since, in theory, no one ethnic or racial group, no one socio-economic class—or even, a growing number of American Muslim revivalists argue, neither gender—would be especially privy to sacred knowledge, even with Arabic as the Islamic lingua franca.

In the early nineties, a young white American convert to Islam elaborated on the traditional notion of the *rihla* and popularized a new moral geography, the Islamic East as Archive, as a pedagogical destination. His vision, as we have seen, caught fire across the US, particularly with first- and second-generation Muslim immigrants from South Asia and the Middle East. In 1988, Shaykh Hamza Yusuf (born Mark Hanson) returned to the US after ten years of what he called "traditional" Islamic training (what I call *classical* for the sake of clarity), most famously in the deserts of Mauritania. When he returned to and resettled in San Francisco's Bay Area, he quickly developed a national reputation in Muslim circles as a powerful and learned orator. Draped in regal robes and sporting a turban, Yusuf seemed at first glance to be a simple and unselfconscious embodiment of the white sheik in old Hollywood films, the Orientalist cliché of the white man gone "native" in the deserts of Arabia. But while dramatic, his life story is far from a Hollywood cliché.

Like the Malcolmology of American Muslims, in which Malcolm X was ardently studying Sunni Islam in the last year of his life, Yusuf's conversion narrative and studies overseas have a mythic status in US mosques. He is another iconic model of the American Muslim student-traveler abroad—he is not well known to most Americans the way Malcolm X is, but he has powerfully influenced the shape of contemporary Islam in US mosques. The Hamza Yusuf myth begins with a near-death experience in a car accident that inspires both his conversion to Islam and his journey across the world to study at the knee of a Mauritanian shaykh in the western Sahara. Of course, like Muslims' Malcolmology, the Yusuf legend contains far fewer details and far more exaggerations than his biography. Looking beneath the hagiography, we can uncover his particular pedagogical philosophy, which popularized transnational Islamic pedagogical networks abroad as a source of "traditional" Islamic knowledge.

Born in Walla Walla, Washington, in 1958, Hanson was raised in Marin County in Northern California. His father, a humanities professor, and his mother, an activist in the civil rights movement, the antiwar movement, and the nascent environmentalist movement, exposed him to political organizing. In 1977, in the aftermath of a near-fatal car accident, he found an English translation of the Quran on the bottom shelf of a used bookstore and revisited Shakespeare's *Midsummer's Night Dream*; the two texts set him on a new and difficult path of considering the possibility of powers in the world that were beyond human perception and his own mortality. Hanson's girlfriend at the time convinced him to visit a Muslim acquaintance of hers from Mecca living in Santa Barbara; the man and his wife were part of a Shadhili sufi order, devotees of a white convert to Islam in the UK, Shaykh Abd AlQadir as-Sufi, a man who was to play a pivotal role in Hanson's life.[49] After a few visits with the sufi devotees, Hanson, then eighteen, converted to Islam and dropped out of junior college to learn basic Muslim rites. Though some of as-Sufi's followers had established a community in Berkeley, Hanson decided to emigrate to the UK and live with the shaykh and his sufi community. In addition to the time he spent in Norwich as a devotee, Hanson traveled sporadically to Islamic intellectual centers in India, the Middle East, and Africa, where he was hosted by As-Sufi's followers. He quickly developed a reputation as a prodigy and rose in the ranks of the order. In 1979 an Emirati scholar named Abdullah Ali Mahmood persuaded Hanson to move to the Emirates and pursue Islamic studies at the Islamic Institute. Hanson recalls that he was "shattered" by the pervasive poor quality of instruction, which he characterized as "a pale imitation of the West."[50]

Over the course of the four years Hanson lived in the Emirates and took classes at the Islamic Institute, he met a number of West African students who impressed upon him the importance of studying with prominent, classically trained teachers. By then completely fluent in Arabic, Hanson had studied Quranic recitation, rhetoric, poetry, law, and theology, among other classical Islamic disciplines, but most of his studies were informal, one-on-one tutoring with esteemed scholars, supplementing the classroom instruction he was getting from the Institute.[51] Alongside his studies, Hanson worked first as a muezzin, climbing the minaret to call the prayer, and later as an imam for a mosque congregation made up mostly of Afghani laborers supporting their families and the war efforts against

Fig. 3.5. Hamza Hanson was photographed by a Moroccan journalist while attending a conference of Muslim scholars in 1983.

the USSR. Over the years, his relationship with as-Sufi became increasingly strained as Hanson's scholarly reputation ultimately eclipsed that of his mercurial teacher. Hanson's formal and public break with As-Sufi in 1984 was painful but he had already been moving in a different intellectual direction. In the Emirates, Hanson met several prominent Mauritanian scholars who dramatically changed his course of study once again, impressing upon him that without rote memorization one could not truly possess knowledge. The Mauritanians he met distinguished "between daylight scholars and nighttime scholars. A daytime scholar needs light to read books to access knowledge, but a nighttime scholar can access that knowledge when the lights are out, through the strength of his memory and the retention of knowledge."[52] Hanson moved to North Africa in 1984, studying in Algeria and Morocco, as well as Spain and Mauritania. In Mauritania, he developed his most lasting and powerful relationship with a teacher, Shaykh "Murabit Al-Hajj" Muhammad Fahfu, whom he studied with in the desert for several months. It is his relationship with Al-Hajj that becomes paradigmatic for Hanson; he rarely mentions As-Sufi publicly. Hanson came back to the US from Mauritania in 1988 to become a nurse in order to serve the sick and indigent once he returned to Mauritania. Ultimately, however, he remained in the US, and after earning his nursing degree alongside a study of homeopathic medicine, he also earned a bachelor's degree in comparative religion.

During this period, Hanson, then known as Imam Hamza Yusuf, served as the imam of the Santa Clara Mosque, and he became part of the Muslim American speaking circuit, offering lectures and sermons in mosques and Islamic centers across Northern California. One of his earliest educational projects was initiating small religious retreats called "Islamic Pow-Wows," where he and a few other like-minded Muslim American preachers would counsel new converts as well as Muslim youth seeking to renew their commitment to a devout Islamic lifestyle.[53] Gradually, he was invited by Muslim student groups and national Muslim organizations to deliver talks on college campuses and Islamic conferences throughout the US. Yusuf developed a national reputation in Muslim American counterpublics as a gifted orator with flawless Arabic and a sharp wit. His striking command of Western philosophy and the classical Islamic sciences, punctuated by pop-culture references and his pitch-perfect recitation of Arabic scripture became his signature, earning him a reputation as a speaker that could draw thousands in any city he traveled to in North America and western Europe.

Yusuf's speeches to American Muslim audiences, which he delivers in English, are peppered with his own highly original explanations of Islamic scripture, a combination of etymological analyses of Arabic words and references to Western anthropology, history, linguistics, and natural and health sciences (albeit with simplified representations of them). Yusuf speaks at an accessible register, appealing to Muslims across the spectrum of religious practice. In other words, although Yusuf skillfully displays the depth and breadth of his "traditional" training, one does not need to know much about Islam or history or linguistics or politics to follow his arguments. His speeches blend references to great thinkers of the past (from Plato to Ibn Rushd to Einstein), history lessons about the glorious past of the premodern umma (contrasted with bloody episodes in the Christian past and the modern West), his own scathing critiques of consumerism (usually in the form of sarcastic jokes about American popular culture), and moral outrage directed at politicians and political movements (in the US and the Muslim world alike) and at his Muslim audiences for knowing so little about their own religious heritage. By the early nineties, Yusuf was established as a leading public intellectual for Muslims in America, and he remains the main attraction at the annual ISNA conference, speaking to tens of thousands each year.

Part of Yusuf's broad appeal lies in the way he brands himself and the Islamic pedagogical project he promotes as "traditional." In contrast to the revivalists such as Al-Faruqi who advocated for Islamic reform and progress and the recuperation of rational, academic disciplines, Yusuf insists that the key to the future of Islam is in the past. In his lectures and published pamphlets, Yusuf stresses the glorious premodern history and traditional pedagogical systems, marginalized in most of the world's modernizing Muslim-majority states. The tapes and CDs of Yusuf's lectures consistently outsold any of his peers in this era. His biting political commentaries reflect his intimate knowledge of history, politics, and culture—both of the US and of the postcolonial Arab and African worlds—equipping him to articulate the frustrations, fears, and ambivalence of immigrant Muslims in a way they themselves struggle to express in English and to communicate to their American-born children.

Yusuf transcends many of the religious differences that divide US mosque congregations, in part because he never commits himself in public to anything more than "traditional" Sunni Islam or a vague, unspecified sufi spirituality, sustaining his wide appeal among a diverse range of mosqued Muslims (in contrast, for example, to his private allegiance to particular sufi orders and shaykhs). Despite his consistent and trenchant critiques of an equally vague "political Islam" of the revivalists, some of his most ardent supporters and largest venues for speaking, such as ISNA, were founded by and continue to be dominated by Muslim Americans directly and indirectly tied to the global Islamic Revival. Yusuf's Muslim rivals and critics challenge his claim to represent "traditional" Islam, particularly those critics from reformist movements such as the Salafis, reformists who experienced a dramatic rise in their popularity in the nineties and who are hostile to many sufi practices on theological grounds. However, since Yusuf has never been recognized as publicly endorsing a particular sufi order or a particular sufi practice, these theologically based critiques have done little to diminish his popularity, even among Muslims who are swayed by Salafi critiques of the "superstitious" elements of sufism.[54]

Although Yusuf has avoided divisive legal and theological issues as well as a narrow categorization, he has taken a very specific and aggressive stand on one of the global debates in contemporary Islam: traditional higher learning as the new universal criterion of Sunni authority. Yusuf argues that a classical Islamic education is a true liberal arts education that nurtures free-thinking in the Aristotelian sense because it is based on the mastery of the trivium (grammar, rhetoric, and logic) and then the quadrivium (arithmetic, geometry, music, and astronomy). The modern educational system, in contrast, is a utilitarian, "illiberal form of education designed to create functioning illiterate people who could service society."[55] In 1996, Yusuf cofounded, with a local immigrant philanthropist, the Zaytuna Institute in Hayward, California, named after the historic Islamic madrasa-university in Tunisia. The Institute offered on-site courses and programs at its campus, and weekend intensive courses across the US and in historic Islamic intellectual centers in the Muslim world, featuring Yusuf's own teachers and peers from his time studying Islam abroad. More importantly, he inspired a new generation of Muslim American youth to follow his example and study "traditionally" overseas.

Hamza Yusuf's dramatic life story, his white skin, and his signature turbans and robes (adopted in US mosques by many converts to Islam in the eighties and nineties) are frequently the source of comment and marvel in Muslim American counterpublics. Many Muslim critics of Yusuf dismiss his enormous popularity as a function of the drama of his "Eastern costumes" and oral performances, the spell of his charisma. A more serious criticism of Yusuf's marked appeal to Muslim immigrants (one often leveled by African American Muslim critics) is made in psychological and racial terms: Yusuf's status—white, male, American— and his embrace of not only the religion of Islam but the cultures of the Middle East and Africa (and "traditional societies" in general, as he often calls them) affirm the value of Islam and restore the dignity and sense of self-worth of the postcolonial immigrants who have internalized white supremacy.

While Yusuf's whiteness has certainly been fetishized by some immigrant Muslims, a phenomenon Yusuf himself acknowledges and condemns, it is his demonstrable intellectual skills that have been the primary focus of his Muslim admirers in the US and worldwide. His reputation as a learned and inspirational public orator have set him apart from other convert preachers who were part of the American mosque speaking circuit in the nineties. Yusuf's construction of religious authority replaces immigrants' experience of diaspora and nostalgia for their homelands with his references to deep history, such as the glories of Islamic Spain. He recuperates marginal sites in Spain and in the Middle East and Africa by hosting retreats for American Muslims there, presenting these locations as destinations for the recovery of an intellectual heritage that would restore a universal criterion of religious authority. Yusuf's lectures emphasize the glories of Islamic history and the importance of the preservation of classical Islamic sciences. It is not simply Yusuf's fluency in Arabic and English, in classical Islam and Western philosophy, but his ability to bring his classical Islamic education to bear on American life that Muslim Americans find incredibly compelling. Hamza Yusuf commands authority by making the deep history of Islam relevant to Muslim Americans, reinvigorating their sense of a binding connection to their intellectual tradition and precolonial history.

Hamza Yusuf single-handedly altered the religious imagination of thousands of mosqued Americans by shifting attention away from the postcolonial Arab states toward the little-known African country of Mauritania, which he constructs as a utopia. Echoing the tropes of lost knowledge and the radical countercitizenship of Elijah Muhammad and others, Mauritania is Yusuf's utopic counterpoint to the US, a modern dystopia. Echoing his contemporaries, the revivalist immigrants, Yusuf describes postcolonial Muslim societies, particularly those in the Middle East, as dystopias as well. In US mosques in the nineties, Yusuf's personal transformation in Mauritania inspired a new vocabulary of authenticity based on the past and charged by the symbol-laden desert. Yusuf explains: "Mauritanians—really, West Africans—still have an incredible pride of culture, of language, of religion, whereas most of the Arabs have had their pride taken away from them, because they are a defeated people. They co-opted the conquerors' culture."[56] Yusuf's explicit, if standard, critique of Arab governments is fused with his simultaneous representation of Mauritania in ahistorical, apolitical, and highly exoticized terms, akin to Noble Drew Ali's construction of Morocco.

Yusuf's simple embrace of the romance of travel reproduces the Eurocentric imagery of discovery, including the anthropological trope of the noble savage. Consider Yusuf's description of meeting the son of his future Mauritanian teacher as an encounter with a "living fossil."

> Looking at this man for me was like looking at someone coming out of the seventh or eighth century. . . . The desert people of Mauritania, they are almost halfway in the unseen world. Their dreams are so extraordinary. I mean, we notice about the aboriginal people, they are very connected to the dream world, the *alim al-khayyal* its called in Arabic, the imaginal world. And I'm seeing this in these people. You think of water, and suddenly someone is handing you a bowl of water. I ended up spending seven years with the Mauritanian people. . . . One of the things many Muslims forget is that our own Prophet Muhammad . . . was in a sense this bridge between the ancient and the young culture because he was raised among the Bedouin and yet he was a city dweller. He was a merchant, and yet his roots were rooted in this ancient culture. [We moderns] talk about values, we don't talk about virtues, because values are relative. What is expensive in one place is cheap in another place, whereas . . . honesty, . . . courage, . . . [and] generosity [are virtues] in every culture on this planet.[57]

Yusuf defines Mauritanians (and aboriginals) in terms of cultural essences, as only quasi-human, half living in an unearthly realm. He refers to them as premoderns, residual traces of ancient, vanishing, and utopic cultures that have miraculously survived into the dystopic modern world, just as in the seventh century Muhammad was sent to a Bedouin community that raised the orphan in a desert environment to protect him from the increasingly urbanizing Mecca in seventh-century Arabia. When Yusuf describes the Prophet as a bridge between cultures, between the past and the future, between rural and urban, he is implicitly constructing himself (and other American student-travelers) as bridges as well. Like Malcolm's invocation of the hajj as a mobile and generative Islamic symbol for Americans, Yusuf invokes the Islamic quest for knowledge (*rihla*) as a mobile, generative, cultural bridge to (American) modernity. In other words, by imbibing the essence of Mauritanians, one can access the universal truths—honesty, courage, and generosity—and mobilize them in a critique of modernity. He describes Mauritanian culture in terms of universal virtues, in terms of abstractions, a place and a people outside time. It is, therefore, not surprising that while Mauritania looms large in American Muslims' religious imaginations as a result of Yusuf's mythmaking, most Muslim Americans know little of the history or politics of this fabled country; many might be surprised to learn it is the poorest in the Arab League or that it has been ruled primarily by a series of brutal military juntas since independence from France.[58]

Alongside Yusuf's occasional invocations of troubling Orientalist tropes, his rhetoric about traveling for Islamic knowledge in the Middle East powerfully links his studies abroad with a centuries-long, global phenomenon of Muslim seekers traveling to seek knowledge, the *rihla*. Yusuf describes Mauritanian culture as a pedagogical one, as an archive of traditional knowledge mediated by individual learned teachers and spiritual models, distinguished by their teaching abilities and trained minds.

What struck me about the West Africans is this presence. They actually walk upright. They were walking with dignity. . . . They were proud that they were Muslims. Then I found out that these people grew up in

Fig. 3.6. Hamza Yusuf talks about his studies in Mauritania in the 1999 documentary *Faces of Islam*. (Courtesy of the BBC)

tents in the middle of the Sahara desert with goats and sheep and camels, and I am listening to them talk about fine points of grammar and
the subtleties of the Quran and points of jurisprudence of Islam and history. . . . The word *darasa* in Arabic means "to study"; it also means "to
become effaced," it means "to lose all traces"; and obviously one meaning is the traces of ignorance but also just losing this personality, this
ego, this desire for me, that the world is for me. And we've got a planet
filled with people saying "me, me, me." And the world is not me. The
world is us. . . . That is what Islam is teaching us. Islamic education is to
teach these tools to people so that they can move in the world as trained
minds. There is spirituality rooted in this training. It is not simply the
abstraction, . . . but it is sitting with people who are not only transmitters
of this knowledge but also spiritually transformed individuals, people
who have gone into the depths of their souls and have moved internally,
have trained their souls at the hands of those who trained their souls,
[teachers going all the way] back to the Messenger of God. . . . And these
people have unfortunately become anomalies now in the Muslim world,
but [they] still exist. . . . In learning this knowledge from them, another
kind of knowledge is being transmitted: the knowledge of humility, the
knowledge of purity, the knowledge of not having an ulterior motive.
And this is hard for people to understand who have spent their entire
lives in the world of ulterior motives! It's hard to imagine that there's
actually people who might not have an ulterior motive in wanting to be
good to you, in wanting to help you. It's really the purification of the self
from cynicism, right? And its something deeply rooted in our—in our
worldview, cynicism, a peculiar Anglo-Saxon characteristic.[59]

In his transnational moral geography, Yusuf reconstructs the deserts
of West Africa first and then the rest of the Islamic East as Archives
of tradition in two senses: first, as the repositories of the knowledge of
tradition embodied by scholars who are talented and learned teachers
and, second, as archives of spiritual knowledge, peopled with teachers who can guide and teach a seeker to become sincere, to forgo the
Anglo-Saxon cynicism that pervades American culture. Both the
modern West, populated by cynics and consumers, and the postcolonial Muslim world, populated by defeated Muslims aping the West, are
dystopic, while the deserts of Mauritania figure as utopic margins of

the postcolonial Muslim world. "Traditional" scholars, Yusuf argues, are marginalized in their own societies, like archival documents whose importance and significance must be sought out and pieced together. He constructs these marginalized, pedagogical spaces in the Islamic East as utopic places that invite scholarly and existential inquiry, that hold a space for hard questions, contemplation, and truths which can be discovered and which can be transformative not only intellectually but spiritually. In other words, Yusuf's moral geography is not primarily about ancients and moderns but sincere seekers and cynics.

THE WHITE SHAYKH

When Usman was eighteen, he finally found an imam who inspired him. "Shaykh Hamza, he's the first imam who I thought knew what he was talking about and could get that across to an audience. I was really impressed. The first time I saw him was at a MAYA [Muslim Arab Youth Association] convention in Ohio or Chicago or someplace, something my parents had kind of dragged me to, and I remember right after I heard him give the talk I immediately bought the lecture I had just heard. They were dubbing it right there, and so I bought a copy to take home." Usman's parents were impressed by Hamza Yusuf's flawless Arabic, but Usman was impressed by the way he "dropped quotes" in his speeches: Quranic verses, historical facts, pop-song lyrics.

"When I first heard him, I just thought Hamza Yusuf was living it. Imam AlGhazzali has a famous quote in his book: *"alim bila 'amalan junun wa 'amalan bila 'ilman la yakun."* 'Knowledge without action is insanity, and action without knowledge is [vanity] and cannot be.' And in Shaykh Hamza I saw someone who had the *'ilm* [knowledge] and the *'amal* [put it into action], like how he handled questions, how he was able to take what is in the books and apply it to American society and how he was able to relate the *din* [Islam] to the *dunya* [world]. That was something that really impressed me, making Islam real, not just a story about a long time ago."

Initially, Usman's parents were pleased by his renewed interest in Arabic and the increased time he spent praying and reading about Islam, especially since their own efforts—a steady stream of private after-school tutors—had been so ineffective. His father jokes that after all his efforts to teach his children the Egyptian dialect of Arabic, a white American inspired his son to want to learn and speak Arabic like a Syrian. Usman's father notes sarcastically that at least Hamza Yusuf does not have a Syrian accent.

Seekers are in search of better answers, but Usman came to Damascus looking for better questions. The problem for Usman was not that he feared a lack of answers. If anything, when he was in America, Usman feared there were too many answers and too few questions. "I just felt there was too much argument and not enough knowledge in America. We would go around in circles, and no one really knows anything. And I would see that in myself—you know, coffee in hand arguing with my friends into the middle of the night—and I hated the façade of it. So I decided, no, I would come here and just reground myself. I mean, at first I thought I would be here for a year and do Arabic and kind of soak up some quote-unquote spirituality, go back and do graduate school or something research oriented in the States. And I wouldn't go back 'til I had a handle on it, not necessarily like I'll solve all the problems of the world but just feel that there was substance to what came out of my mouth.

"[Shaykh Hamza] was my first exposure to this idea, al-'ilm fi'l-sudur laysa fi'l-sutur [knowledge lies in human hearts, not in the lines of a book]. With Shaykh Hamza, it was inspiration. The next level was real, serious scholarship, not just a lecture but a book in English, and that opened the door to thinking, what if I could read, I mean really read, books in Arabic?"

Now Usman can read centuries-old books in Arabic: philosophy, theology, law, even poetry. When Usman calls home, he spends most of his time talking to his mother, though he knows his father is hovering nearby. When his father does finally get on the phone, tension tends to dry up the conversation. His father's first question is always the same: "Are your studies finished, or will you finish me first?"

"[My father] can't understand. My mom is not thrilled about me being here, but she's glad that I am not somewhere doing drugs, which I could have easily slipped into at one stage between high school and college. When my dad wanted to cut me off—see, my mom is more spiritual and romantic than my dad anyway. She used to play the guitar. She tries to pacify my dad, who has gone from enraged to just irritated with me. My dad's thing is being a professional, financial security. At one point he wanted me to do an Islamic university program, Islamic studies either at an Islamic university in the Middle East or back in the US, but I'm not interested in the Islamization of knowledge or something too postmodern. In a university, you know, it's very intellectual. Islamically, the learning process is not only intellectual. You can have someone who is a PhD and a feminist and whatever, and then he's convicted of date rape or of having child porn on his computer. I mean, what's the point of these intellectual peaks if there isn't an equally strong development of character? [In Islam,] there's the spiritual element, the social element, the family element, the physical element of teaching your body things, and none overtake the other."

I recite the first half of the same rhyming couplet: "Knowledge lies in human hearts." Usman nods.

Imagining the Place of Islam from America

Through Yusuf's rise to prominence in US mosque communities in the nineties, he popularized a nostalgic vocabulary with a triumphant Islamic twist, referencing a deep and glorious Islamic history and intellectual criterion that could be universally accepted by Sunnis as a solution to their divisive and incoherent religious debates. Not surprisingly, his moral geography of the Islamic East as Archive is one that Muslim American youth find broadly appealing. He has introduced Islamic intellectual canons and pedagogy to American Muslims at a scale unparalleled by any other Muslim American leader. Of course, Yusuf had many important predecessors and peers, Americans who traveled to Muslim societies for religious training in order to preserve Islam in the US, including Malcolm X. Like Yusuf, Warith Deen Mohammed created opportunities for his followers to travel and study overseas; he modeled how the study of scripture and Arabic can create space for independent exegesis and religious expertise while still allowing an embrace of the American mainstream. However, Yusuf's narrative of transformation through travel popularized the notion of an explicitly antiestablishment and enticingly "traditional" education at a much larger scale in US mosques than Malcolm X, Warith Deen Mohammed, or anyone else has, thus altering the parameters of the debate about

Islamic religious authority. His countercitizenship pivots on the history of a glorious civilization—transethnic, translinguistic, and transnational—with contemporary Muslims in the US and around the world as its rightful heirs. To this day, Yusuf is an icon for many Muslim American youth who, inspired by him, make their own pedagogical journeys east in order to lead more authentic Muslim lives and to alleviate Islam's crisis.

My quasi-chronological schema of the dominant modalities of Islamic authority links them to shifting, competing moral geographies of the Muslim world: first, an Islamic Afro-Asia as a racial utopia; second, the Muslim world as Diasporic Homeland, as a nostalgic and political focus; and, finally, the Islamic East as an Archive of tradition and a pedagogical destination. This fragmentary, allegorical history of American Muslim religious imaginaries reveals both the continuities and differences between a wide range of constructions of Islamic authority in American mosques in ways a more conventional history cannot, such as the striking parallels across various transnational moral geographies, between the dystopic and utopic rhetoric of Elijah Muhammad, Ismail Al-Faruqi, and Hamza Yusuf; the mainstreaming power of nostalgia for both immigrants and African Americans such as Warith Deen Mohammed's community; and the contradictions and elisions and exclusions built into the universalist ideal of the global umma such that only some parts can stand for the whole.

American student-travelers such as Usman may not recognize the cultural, political, and religious genealogies of their studies abroad running any deeper than Hamza Yusuf's conversion—especially not to historical figures who they consider "heterodox" Muslims. Whether Muslim Americans recognize them or not, there are ambivalent orientations toward the US that have been formulated, reformulated, and revised by American Muslims over the course of the twentieth century and the first decades of the twenty-first century, and, paradoxically, they have often brought Muslims closer to the American mainstream. These older debates about American citizenship, nostalgic longings for glorious pasts, mappings of utopias and dystopias, and radical, transnational attachments to political and religious communities echo in contemporary Muslim Americans' relationships to the umma and the Islamic East. The desire to resolve crises of authority in US mosques motivates Muslim American youth to travel abroad for Islamic study, to seek out the utopic margins of the dystopic, postcolonial Muslim world as a *destination*. Their journeys index their psychological dislocations as religious and often racial minorities in the US, propelled by fears and anxieties that everything authentically Islamic is under attack, endangered, that their sacred tradition is in crisis. With the hope that they will raise the moral consciousness of their US communities and resolve the authority crisis on their return, their journeys eastward are, to borrow Gilroy's phrasing, "rooted in and routed through the special stress that grows with the effort involved in trying to face (at least) two ways at once."[60] It is to these journeys abroad, to the student-travelers who face away from America even as they hope to return to root Islam in the US, that we now turn.

PART II

Tradition Bound

4

Retrieving Tradition

Pedagogical Forms and Secular Reforms

KHIDR ON FRIDAYS

After a long semester in Jordan, Richard's tutor, Amin, announces that he has to return home to Damascus before his wife has their baby. Richard likes Amin, and since he already has a tourist visa, he decides to follow him to Syria. Richard finds the ugly beauty of Damascus's dusty, winding roads and aged, crumbling buildings far more appealing than Amman's expansive highways and sparkling neighborhoods of newly constructed white apartment complexes. Damascus looks the part of a historic Islamic city better than Amman does, but Richard remains unsettled by the gaps between his expectations for his studies abroad and what he is learning.

"My problem was I thought coming to the Middle East would be like an ISNA conference, getting spiritually reenergized. But this experience is nothing like ISNA. ISNA lectures are kind of passively absorbing information, and so you can just sit there and feel inspired, let Hamza Yusuf just blow your mind open. Here, to be a student, to learn anything, you have to work. It's not a passive learning experience at all."

Amin takes a special interest in Richard, with daily lessons in the mornings and visits and suppers most evenings. Amin acts as Richard's guide in Damascus, taking him to museums and ancient ruins and offering impromptu history lessons. Richard notices how Amin quietly curses the ubiquitous effigies of Presidents Bashar and Hafiz Assad as they drive through Damascus. Once when Richard commented that he felt sorry for the young men in fatigues, armed and stationed throughout the city, Amin warned him not to be taken by their youth. Only God knew what kinds of acts of torture they commit behind closed doors.

[handwritten margin note: Goes to middle east to be "spiritually re-energized." exoticized]

"For me, I thought in the East, they get it, they feel it, and actually, for some, it's the opposite. You find all kinds of Muslims here. Its not that Syria is more spiritual per se, but you *are* more conscious of the possibilities for becoming spiritual. You hear Quran tapes in the taxis, the [call to prayer]; it's a Muslim country. We are all trying to figure out how to please Allah. How do we make our [prayers] not just actions?"

Night and sleep and heat and limbs have all become heavier in Damascus. Still, when the voice of the muezzin at dawn nudges through Richard's open window and into his dreams, calling, "Prayer is better than sleep," he cannot ignore him. Richard's prayer life has become richer in Damascus now that he is out of the rat race, out of his cubicle, out of that world where money chased its own tail in the name of industry, a world where he had not been unhappy, just unsatisfied.

Along with Richard's private tutoring in Arabic and Islamic studies with Amin, he studies with a calligraphy teacher in Damascus. Shaykh Waleed is a small man with piercing eyes and a sensitive face softened by his white beard. He speaks no English except for "yes" and "wow." During their lessons, he selects verses from the Quran and models the formation of the Arabic letters in the different scripts for Richard. The muscles of his hand move gracefully. He has the patience of a saint, and Richard believes he is one, insisting that Shaykh Waleed is the most extraordinary man he has ever met.

"I love the idea of the *'arba'in* [the Forty Saints], these secret masters in Damascus. And I really believe Shaykh Waleed is one of those people. I have never met anyone like him. He pours water for people at the mosque. He's not an imam or a famous scholar. He's just, basically, an anonymous peasant pouring water in the mosque, but to me he's just very, very religious, just a paradigm of what a Muslim should be: no hypocrisy, actions better than words, just making *dhikr* [supplications] constantly, just trying to please Allah. That's something to take back [to the US] with me."

Richard prays *juma'* in the Umayyad mosque. The rhythm of life on Damascene sidewalks is perceptibly altered on Friday afternoons: people walk with a brisk excitement, at once solemn and upbeat. Richard always arrives early, making his way to the front entrance through the crowds of black-haired men. He leaves his shoes on the same wooden shelf each week, against the same marble column, under the same stained-glass window, and watches the red and blue carpets fill with bodies, freshly showered and scented for the prayer.

Every time the scratch of the imam's voice first comes over the battered speakers, Richard is reminded of the history of the ancient mosque, the people that have prayed there, burying their faces in prostration in his same spot. Not always, but sometimes, in the unison of standing, bowing, prostrating, and sitting, the moment swells and shivers through his body. With his eyes closed, he takes in the heavy scent of musk and sweat, the thick brush of the rug against his skin, the sounds of thousands of bodies rising and falling, babies crying, chandeliers tinkling in the breeze, and the throaty recitation of eternal verses.

"The building has changed, rebuilt and rebuilt on the same land . . . and before that, a temple and a church [in that same location]. But if you think about it, the smells and sounds in that mosque are the same now as they always have been—well, except for the fans and speaker feedback. But that's really powerful for me because that takes you out of your time. You feel like you're in this ocean of people, one single drop, but not just the people with you now but all the people that have ever prayed there, and it makes you feel so insignificant. We take these false positions, we think our life is so valuable or we're so irreplaceable, and then you realize, no, I'm nothing, I'm just a drop in time, but at the same time, you feel God's attention is on you."

As Richard makes his way out of the mosque, he always scans the crowd, but he is not looking for his friends or his teachers. He searches profiles, studies the smiles and eyes of strangers, hoping to recognize a light in a glimpse of a face he has never seen before. "Shaykh Waleed told me that Khidr [Moses's spirit guide] prays here every Friday. *Allahu 'alam* [only God knows] in what shape, in what form, but I imagine that I would be able to tell if I saw Khidr even from far away. Maybe that's not the point, *Allahu 'alam*."

Destination Tradition

As we will see again and again, Muslim Americans' travels abroad for Islamic knowledge are preeminently acts of the religious imagination. As they traverse the urban centers of the Middle East, studying Islam in unofficial study circles in cafes, classrooms, and on the floors of mosques, American student-travelers such as Richard long for the impossible: for a place where they can experience an Islamic past that is already gone, already lost. What is in the dust that settles in a thin film on any- and everything in the Middle East? Is it a defiant reminder that what they came for is lost yet its remains are everywhere around them? Or is it a teasing hint that the past is almost within their grasp, omnipresent, waiting to be found and brought back to life in the present? Michel de Certeau invokes the metaphor of birds that lay their eggs in others species' nests to describe the nature of historical memory, for a past produced in the present, "in a place that does not belong to it." The inscriptions of the past remain invisible and elusive, yet perpetually possible, reborn through the touch of new circumstances located in the present.[1]

For American student-travelers in the Middle East, the new circumstances that bring the tradition to life in the here and now are the heated debates about Islamic education that dominate the public sphere in the Middle East. Religious intellectual centers in the Middle East, such as Amman, Damascus, and Cairo, attract American students because they offer a rich and diverse pedagogical landscape where they can learn about their tradition. However, before they can pursue serious study, American student-travelers must first make sense of the dizzying public debates about Islamic education and its reform.

Across pedagogical networks in the Middle East, just as in US mosques, the crisis of Islam is usually narrated as a simple conflict: as the breakdown of the classically trained scholars' religious authority and political credibility, facilitated by the onset of colonial rule and the emergence of new literate counterpublics that are part of a global Islamic Revival. For thousands of years, the story goes, an Islamic education was a sign of prestige for the wealthy and politically powerful. Such an education was only possible through classical Islamic pedagogical institutions such as Islamic primary schools and Islamic universities and seminaries. Various colonial regimes (British, French, Dutch, and Italian) and postcolonial modernizers after them have all vigorously sought to circumscribe the influence and curtail the financial support for these historic institutions of Islamic learning around the world— testament to the perceived religious influence and political power of the classically trained religious scholars and teachers running these institutions at the time. In Syria, as in most Muslim societies, nation-alization programs have since subsumed Islamic educational systems, and today most classically trained Islamic scholars are government employees, dismissed by many Muslims as the illegitimate mouthpieces of brutal regimes. Colonial and postcolonial educational reforms also successfully shifted the perceived hierarchy of education, so that West-ern-style, secular, public education is now widely considered a better road to upward mobility. Whether in Egypt, Jordan, or Syria, madrasa education has ceased to be seen as an effective means of social advance-ment; today the middle and upper classes in Muslim societies around the world learn about Islam in schools run by the state or by reform-minded Muslim educators. The consequence of this elite defection is that the historic institutions of Islamic learning, both primary and secondary schools as well as Islamic universities, are left primarily to poor students from rural regions, madrasa-educated "peasants" such as Richard's calligraphy teacher, Shaykh Waleed, or to mediocre students from middle-class families.[2]

Clearly, despite the sweeping secular reforms, Islam has hardly eroded from public life in cities such as Damascus.[3] An ironic and unintended consequence of secular educational reforms was the dra-matic reconfiguration of the scope of religious authority, the creation of a political and religious vacuum that was filled by Muslim men and women such as Richard's tutor, Amin, individuals with secular educa-tions and a commitment to reviving their tradition through their grass-roots charitable and educational efforts. With the press as their new pulpit, a new breed of revivalist intellectuals (writers, editors, and pub-lishers trained as lawyers, doctors, engineers, economists, and journal-ists) have demonstrated that they do not need the scholarly credentials of a classical pedigree in order to command an audience and compete with the declining historic pedagogical institutions.

Consider Amr Khaled, a wildly popular celebrity-televangelist whose stylish suits and self-help-themed sermons, peppered with Egyptian and American slang, have earned him the moniker "the Arab Oprah"; although he has an accounting degree, his emotive preaching and facil-ity with the Quranic verses and hadith he has committed to memory have made him one of the most influential religious authorities today, not just in the Middle East but worldwide, with a following of millions

Fig. 4.1. Televangelist Amr Khaled's self-help talk show has earned him a rock-star following among Muslim youth in Arab countries and diasporas. (Courtesy of Olaf Blecker)

of devoted Muslim youth.[4] Revivalists such as Khaled want to radically alter the contours of their societies and states through a public implementation of norms they take as "truly" Islamic. The efficacy of their writings and speeches depends on their ability to inspire and persuade their audiences, not on carefully cultivated reputations of scholasticism or piety.

Today the revivalists in the Middle East compete with the classically trained scholars not only for the local Muslim masses but for American student-travelers such as Richard who must learn the local nuances of global debates about Islamic authority in order to navigate the pedagogical networks abroad. For example, in the US, rather than competitors, classically trained scholars such as Hamza Yusuf are central to the American da'wa movement alongside the revivalists who typically lead mosque communities and umma institutions. Put simply, the revivalist (*da'iy*) and the scholar (*'alim*, plural *'ulama*) are overlapping types in the Islamic Revival in the US and often (but not always) competing types in the Middle East.

While the different relationships and degrees of tension between the revivalists and the 'ulama are important for understanding how debates about Islamic learning play out on the ground in the US and the Middle East, it is equally important to see that the differences between the revivalists and the classically trained scholars are more often a matter of degree than kind. Whether in the US or the Middle East, revivalists and classically trained scholars are deeply invested in resolving the crisis of authority and protecting Islamic education from the censure of governments suspicious of the unofficial study of Islam. As a result, they have produced flourishing and diverse networks of unofficial Islamic learning as a way to keep their tradition alive. As they compete in the Islamic public sphere, they aggressively define themselves against one another and against the state's program of secularization. Rather than adopting their simplified usage of opposing terms such as *secular* and *religious* or *traditional* and *reformist*, I provide an alternative, more complex and less bifurcated mapping of these debates about Islamic learning and the transmission of knowledge on a spectrum. We will see that despite the different methods and philosophies of the classically trained scholars and the revivalists, they are equally invested in the transmission of tradition, and despite their protests, both the revivalists and the 'ulama have acquiesced in fundamental ways to secular reforms and secular definitions of Islamic expertise.

Importantly, debates about Islamic education and its reform are not new. In fact, the purpose of Islamic pedagogy—particularly in the context of growing global literacy—and the question of how it should be organized and reformed, has been a recurring public debate under way for two centuries in Egypt, Turkey, Iran, and India and for over a century in the Muslim societies of Southeast Asia and West Africa. Whether in Islamic pedagogical institutions for young children that are centered on memorization of the Quran or Islamic institutions of higher learning such as seminaries and universities, the questions of what the study of Islam should look like and what, if any, role the state should play in introducing and carrying out educational reforms remain some of the most hotly debated political issues in Muslim societies. These debates run hot because they take us to the heart of political and cultural struggles: struggles that are rife in nearly every Muslim society today, struggles that emerge from a modern history of dramatic shifts in power between Islamic pedagogical institutions, colonial rulers, and the governments of modern, postcolonial nation-states. Debates about Islamic pedagogy are also central to the aims of Americans such as Richard who want to resolve the crisis of authority that grips Muslim counterpublics in the US. Each iteration of these pedagogical debates over generations and to this day is driven by the question of how Islamic knowledge is transmitted over time; in other words, they are essentially debates over which pedagogical model is the best engine to sustain tradition into the future.

A core set of questions drive contemporary, global debates about Islamic learning and Islamic religious authority. First, is the nature of the Islamic canon, organized into disciplines such as Islamic law, theology, rhetoric, philosophy, and even calligraphy, each with its own methodology, fixed or amorphous? Second, is the Islamic canon and its methodologies the focus of inquiry (that is, the means to the end), or is it only the basis for Islamic intellectual inquiry (that is, the means to the means to the end)? In other words, is the purpose of Islamic higher learning to teach fidelity to a fixed and finished canon and set of methodologies and to simply apply them to new contexts and new questions in order to assimilate them? Or should Islamic education cultivate an ethical sensibility, as a mode of scholarly inquiry focused outward that continuously expands the canon, that embraces a plurality of methods and disciplines in order to engage creation and revelation?[5] More specifically, is the value of the canon and its methodologies in the knowledge it contains, or is there also value in the form in which canonical knowledge is received? This chapter examines the contested category of the correct, or authentic, pedagogical model for transmitting Islamic knowledge to the next generation of Muslims and how that model emerges from the considerations of American student-travelers, who often study with both revivalists and classically trained scholars in the Middle East. Amid the fierce pitch of Islamic debates in the public sphere in cities such as Damascus, American Muslims such as Richard identify and pursue what they call "traditional" religious studies and in the process exclude other forms of Islamic learning as not sufficiently "traditional."

The pedagogical perspectives on Islamic learning and the transmission of tradition are fluid and fall along a spectrum; I have identified the three most prominent orientations, what I will call *formalist, pragmatist*, and *reformist*. For formalists, the pedagogical form is as important to the transmission of the tradition as the subject material being taught. For pragmatists, their aim is to preserve the core curricular content, but they are open to reforms that are pedagogically efficacious. Reformists see historical Islamic educational systems as in need of serious reforms because they are morally compromised, not just ineffective or outdated as the pragmatists do. These orientations—formalist, pragmatist, and reformist—index three palpably different visions of Islamic education, visions that do not fit well into the spectrums of conservative to liberal and secular to religious that are typically used by Western observers to describe debates about Islamic education in the Muslim World.

READING IN A SOFT VOICE

Cairo is dotted with small language institutes aimed at foreigners, students who are learning Arabic as a second language. The unassuming buildings are kept meticulously clean, staffed with cheerful men and women accustomed to playing camp counselor to students who are often homesick and bewildered by Cairo. These teachers and tutors are typically devout Muslims, and the institutes develop quiet reputations based on the religious leanings of their employees, at least among the more discerning foreign students. One center is reputed to be filled with sufis, another with Salafis. I learn which centers offer Quranic Arabic, which centers have gender-segregated classes, and which centers attract the most non-Muslims.

Of all the teachers and tutors I encounter in Cairo, I like Um Ali best. She is only a few years older than I am, a patient teacher, and a natural storyteller. She comes to my apartment twice a week for private lessons. Women with veiled faces rarely come to my neighborhood; our doorman often calls to tell me that he has spotted her long before she enters the building. Then I start boiling the water for the tea.

We have settled into a comfortable routine. Together on my living-room sofa, we read books and articles that I select, our heads bent over women's hagiographies, popular religious pamphlets and booklets on controversial religious questions, and published fatwas. She brings her chubby, smiling baby daughter along and nurses her during our sessions. Um Ali's daughter falls asleep to the sound of my voice and the constant, hollow roar of the street traffic below; her mother translates difficult sections and corrects my guesses at invisible vowels. We speak in soft voices so as not to disturb the baby. And when the baby naps longer than usual, we have another cup of tea.

Although our political views often overlap, we rarely see eye to eye on religious issues. Our debates are spirited and open but always friendly. It is the pulp religious literature that sparks most of our arguments: the cheaply published pamphlets and booklets found in tiny kiosks all over the city, usually written by no-name authors with crude, shaky arguments constructed on a few, stray Quranic verses or Prophetic hadith. An American friend introduced me to the genre, a dramatic departure from my carefully selected readings of scholarly books and fatwas penned by classically trained scholars. I always grab the booklets and pamphlets I find most disturbing and wrongheaded, the ones with the most distasteful covers.

One in particular is so bad that it makes Um Ali laugh out loud, although it gives me a headache. It is titled *Women Make Up Most of the Population of Hell*. On the cover, a green, long-lashed, cartoon snake wears glossy, red lipstick and oversized, pink, dangling earrings. This, I try to convince Um Ali, is the problem with the revivalist movement: everyone is an expert, and the most asinine arguments share the shelf with real scholarship, and not everyone knows the difference.

Um Ali is active in Egypt's Islamic Revival. While a college student at Cairo University, she became an Islamic political activist, a fierce advocate for social and environmental justice, for women's rights, for the poor, risking imprisonment countless times by participating in student protests. Over time, she took less and less interest in political change, which seems hopeless; she is sure Mubarak will be replaced by his son. She has redirected her energies to changing ordinary people around her by calling them to the faith.

Still, she curses Mubarak because her talented husband is chronically underemployed. Most men in her neighborhood are. She is the reluctant breadwinner for her growing family; she worries that her husband's frustration and pride will drive him to leave Egypt and to take a job in an oil-rich Gulf country. She marvels at how I live in Cairo alone for so many months, seeing my husband only every few weeks in short visits to Amman, all for research, all for a book yet to be written. If I write a pamphlet instead, she teases me, I will probably have a bigger audience.

The Secular Roots of the Islamic Revival: The Authority of the Revivalists

The mass secular educational systems implemented throughout the Middle East in the twentieth century did successfully transmit modern science. But these societies did not develop a philosophy of liberal education that is key to such education in the West, nor were they able to compete with the abstract inquiry that was an integral part of the classical Islamic religious disciplines taught in madrasas and seminaries. As a result, the first few generations of students graduated by these secular educational systems were intellectually and politically docile, trained to serve as military officers or government officials. As the twentieth century progressed, however, the national education systems expanded to include thousands of young men and women from more humble social origins, such as Um Ali; these literate and politically disaffected graduates joined the growing ranks of the unemployed and underemployed. Rather than harboring hostility or suspicion toward religion, these reform-minded graduates of secular universities were much more inclined to follow those who "could credibly cite Muhammad as their inspiration for political reform over those who took their cues from Voltaire, or Thomas Jefferson or Karl Marx."[6] Ironically, the secular educations of these young people prepared them to labor toward an Islamic Revival and to recalibrate Islam as a political idiom, filling the political vacuum created as states assumed control of Islamic institutions and silenced or co-opted the voices of religious scholars (the 'ulama).

Perhaps the clearest case of new religious authorities eclipsing the 'ulama is the history of Egypt's "modernization" of AlAzhar. The historic AlAzhar University in Cairo, among the premier scholarly Islamic institutions for centuries, underwent spasmodic educational reforms under both French and British colonial rule as well as a slow but steady "modernization" program initiated by Egyptian officials and reformist 'ulama within AlAzhar under King Farouk.[7] For example, when the

British took control of Egypt in 1882, their ambitions for pedagogical reform were relatively modest; they made use of a small number of elementary Quran schools (only forty-six out of the more than five thousand) for the instruction of writing, reading, and arithmetic. In fact, they were ambivalent about educating the Egyptians at all, as their experience in India had convinced them that any education beyond elementary school only increased "native restlessness."[8] "A little learning is a dangerous thing" was a colonial motto.[9] Indeed, in July 1952, Gamal Abdul Nasser rose to power with the Young Officers' coup d'etat.

By 1961, Nasser had implemented a powerful series of curricular and systemic reforms that culminated in the nationalization of AlAzhar. This created two tracks of public education, one run by the Ministry of Education and the other, AlAzhar's Islamic schools and its university, run by the Ministry of Endowments. As a result, Azhari scholars became government employees and were expected to promote Nasser's vision of secular pan-Arab socialism. Nasser envisaged AlAzhar producing a new kind of 'ulama, scholars well versed in both religious learning and the modern secular disciplines. It was in this period of reform and transition that the Palestinian American revivalist Al-Faruqi came from the US and studied at AlAzhar; as he grappled with reconciling his madrasa education and his Western liberal arts education in philosophy, Al-Faruqi was profoundly inspired by the revivalists in the public sphere and the reform-minded 'ulama within AlAzhar. Nasser was remarkably successful in warming Azhari 'ulama to a reconciliatory intellectual project and to integrating the Azhari 'ulama into the educational mainstream, at least in the short term.

In newly independent Egypt, Nasser's reforms were the "final blows" of a slow series of colonial reforms that brought AlAzhar into the fold of the state and, ultimately, compromised its intellectual and religious reputation. By linking the reformed AlAzhar too directly to his increasingly brutal regime, Nasser deprived the institution of credibility.[10] The reformed institution has trained competent and often apolitical religious intellectuals over the past half century, but with graduates' government affiliation, they lack the social respect and the intellectual freedom to compete with the much more popular and outspoken revivalist authors graduating from secular public schools and universities. As a result, throughout the Middle East and beyond, revivalists, such as

Al-Faruqi in the US, were increasingly dominating the Islamic public sphere.

In contrast to the 'ulama subsumed by Nasser's government, the revivalists claim that it is their political credibility and political autonomy as well as their intellectual dynamism that differentiate them from the politically and intellectually compromised 'ulama, making the revivalists the true representatives of the tradition. While the 'ulama identify with earlier generations of pious Muslim scholars through intellectual genealogies, the revivalists suture themselves to the exemplary past primarily through their identifications with the political and intellectual autonomy of Sunni scholars in the past. Prior to colonial reforms, the community of religious scholars that made up the state's lawmaking arm generally maintained their independence from the state's political actors and thus acted as a balance against abuses of state power. In fact, the figure of the dissenting scholar looms large in the religious imaginations of the students and teachers in these global networks. Most of the popular heroes and heroines memorialized are brave and pious intellectuals who suffered for their unwavering convictions at the hands of often unjust and brutal rulers—as several American student-travelers reminded me, all four of the eminent scholars for whom the four Sunni schools of law are named were imprisoned or tortured. The autonomy of classically trained scholars (and local saints) from premodern rulers and their governments granted the community of religious scholars a kind of credibility; they were seen in the premodern era as guardians of justice, as the official and impartial administers of a stable and consistent body of law and ethics that laypeople could appeal to for protection or legal redress.[11] In other words, Sunni Islam has its own tradition of separating "religion" (or at least religious authority) and the state, so to speak, although for most of Islamic history the separation was not a secular one.

The process of secularization in the West is typically understood as an expansion of the distance between politics and religion. However, the opposite has happened in Muslim societies across the Middle East: as countries have secularized and modernized, the distance between religious scholars and the state has actually narrowed. That narrowing has diminished the roles, social prestige, intellectual credibility, and political power of the scholarly class of the 'ulama. Revivalists in the da'wa movement, such as Um Ali, maintain a distinction between their unblemished ethical motivations, on the one hand, and the state's co-opted Islamic institutions, such as AlAzhar, that churn out classically trained, politically docile 'ulama, on the other. In the Middle East, the agency and authority of the revivalist (*da'iy*) derives not from the state-administered religious bureaucracies but from the alternative revivalist institutions that produce "unofficial" Islamic knowledge. Revivalists generally see themselves as part of a moral revival that is in tension with official state policy and state institutions such as AlAzhar.

Undoubtedly the revivalists effectively articulate programs of social justice and question the state in the name of Islam, and some, such as Amr Khaled, are popular public intellectuals with rock-star followings. In the Middle East, da'wa movements have decentered (but not eliminated) the authority of the 'ulama; however, narratives of the devastating decline of the classically trained 'ulama are often overstated.[12] The 'ulama have responded to the modern fragmentation of Islamic authority (not always enthusiastically), and some have embraced the revivalists and have been able to enhance their influence, broadening their audiences, contributing and even setting the terms of national and global religious debates.[13] Egypt's curricular reforms of the sixties were supposed to blur the distinctions between religious and secular knowledge, but these "modernization of knowledge" reforms also had the unintended consequence of blurring the distinctions between public opinion, social scientists, the new religious authorities, and, specifically, the Azhari 'ulama, ultimately bringing these intellectuals into conversation with one another over their common dissatisfaction with the state.

In a political climate hostile to Muslim counterpublics, Islamic authority is also buttressed and protected through political autonomy and political legitimacy. Like the popular revivalist preachers, the periodic jailings (or, occasionally, national expulsions) of classically trained 'ulama by the state are frequently referenced as a sign of their religious legitimacy by their students.[14] Some of the most high-profile and active classically trained scholars in the contemporary da'wa movement in the Middle East distinguish themselves among the 'ulama as politically legitimate despite being affiliated with state institutions, what historian Malika Zeghal terms "peripheral scholars."[15] Shaykh Yusuf AlQardawi, the Azhari scholar whom the leaders of umma institutions in the US often turn to is one such example.

In Egypt, the government reacted to instances of unintended alliances between a few politically conscious 'ulama, often peripheral scholars such as AlQardawi, and the populist revivalist opposition to the regime by taking up a range of aggressive programs to regulate the Islamic studies curriculum of the public educational system and to keep Islamic spaces and discourses under tight state surveillance. In 1996, new legislation in Egypt required imams to obtain licenses from the state in order to give sermons, and the state began stationing censors, spies, and police in most mosques. Rather than warming observant Muslim Egyptians to state projects, such policies engendered a growing pessimism about the legitimacy of the state-licensed imams and even about the potential of their sermons for religious enlightenment.[16] The Egyptian government's censoring of neighborhood mosques resulted in a diffuse network of Islamic counterpublics establishing alternative pedagogical sites in the social margins, where teachers could share Islamic knowledge with students without the pressures of having to bend Islamic teachings to the will and whims of the government. Students organize study circles in homes, mosques, or shops under the auspices of a master teacher, and although less systematized than a madrasa, advanced instruction in Islamic disciplines could be pursued through this technically illegal but vast network. The informal study circle is the most prominent form of religious learning for revivalists in the piety movements, such as Um Ali, and for American student-travelers such as Richard. In other words, in the context of the global Islamic Revival, the unofficial study circle is the contemporary Islamic pedagogical form par excellence.

In addition to the peripheral 'ulama such as AlQardawi who now lead the Islamic Revival, other classically trained 'ulama have also witnessed their own resurgence in popularity distinct from the revivalists. In rare cases, they too are products of the secular track, such as Shaykh Ali Gomaa. Unlike most Azhari faculty, Gomaa came out of the secular track of education, earning a bachelor's degree in commerce at Ain Shams University in 1973. Although the strict separation of the two educational tracks, secular state-run schools and the state-run Azhari schools, now extends through college, it was still possible for graduates of the public educational system to enroll in AlAzhar University as freshmen in the seventies. Gomaa earned a BA in Islamic studies in 1979, followed by a master's and a PhD in Islamic jurisprudence.

More importantly, he developed a reputation as a prodigy, and under the direction of a number of esteemed scholars, he pursued unofficial Islamic studies in study circles, memorizing the Quran and a number of classical texts and earning a long list of *ijazas*. *Ijazas* are licenses (but not diplomas) from teachers that formally recognize their student's proficiency in the material, qualifying them to teach others. In addition to certifying the mastery of a specific canonical text, the *ijaza* is first and foremost an emblem of a bond to a shaykh who follows in a line of teachers and students that, invariably, goes back to Prophet Muhammad himself. In 1988, Gomaa became an instructor at AlAzhar, and although he never developed the rock-star-like following of many popular revivalist preachers such as Amr Khaled and peripheral 'ulama such as the far more famous Al-Qardawi, Gomaa built a devoted and sizable following of students within AlAzhar and beyond through his cassette-tape and CD lectures, open study circles, and popular sermons. Gomaa also developed a reputation for being at least mildly critical of the government, an unusual quality among the Azhari faculty. Gomaa's colleagues, fellow senior Azhari professors, both admired and resented the fact that Gomaa could criticize Mubarak's regime seemingly without consequence because of his personal, political, and social connections.

When Gomaa was appointed as the regular Friday preacher at the famed Sultan Hassan mosque, he began to attract a much wider following among the Egypt's devout middle-class, college-educated men and women. As the Mubarak regime commenced a series of neoliberal reforms in the nineties that opened Egyptian markets to foreign investors, Gomaa became a critic of Western cultural (but not economic) domination. In religious terms, Gomaa was a firm critic of the wide spectrum of revivalists, both the "westoxified" reformists and the Salafi reformists of the da'wa movement such as Um Ali. Gomaa's own pious reputation and conservative social values made him a difficult target for his revivalist critics, and despite his mild criticisms of the state, Mubarak's regime viewed him as a potential ally. Once he became Grand Mufti in 2004, Gomaa rose to international prominence, particularly in the US, where he regularly contributes op-eds in the *Washington Post*.[17] As Gomaa's example shows, the 'ulama can compete for a popular audience with new, revivalist preachers in the Middle East, and they also successfully attract American student-travelers.

A PUBLIC SECRET

Shaykh Ali Gomaa leads a popular, not-so-secret study circle after the dawn prayer in the Turkish corner of the AlAzhar mosque, drawing an eclectic range of students: Azhari undergraduate and graduate students, ordinary devout Egyptians introduced to the shaykh through his cassette-tape sermons, student-travelers from all over the world, and surely a government spy or two. Shaykh Ali's male students stand as he enters the room, kissing his hand in greeting, arranging the pillows on his low chair. In his regal robes and fez, the shaykh reads from texts perched on small wooden stands, as rows of men and women sit on the floor before him, hunched over their own copies of the books, following line by line, making tiny notes in the margins. The classes contract and expand with the seasons; sometimes more than a hundred students listen intently to the shaykh into the late morning, other times only a few dozen. It is an impressive, animated class; often a tourist or two is taken in by the sight, lingering in the doorway to watch.

One of Shaykh Ali's devotees, a graduate student in AlAzhar's Sharia college, first urged me to attend, promising that Shaykh Ali's class would be an unparalleled experience. Not all of the shaykh's students sit at his knee the way the ones at the mosque do. At AlAzhar's University campus, Shaykh Ali addresses large, modern auditoriums filled with students chewing gum and rifling through the morning paper, and often the shaykh himself seems bored as he moves through dry and mechanical lectures. But at AlAzhar mosque, the students sit in rapt attention, and Shaykh Ali comes alive, reading and spontaneously elaborating the intricacies of a legal manual or of the famous sufi text *The Aphorisms of Ibn Ata'Allah*. He makes centuries-old texts exciting and timely, tying them to burning issues of the moment: current events, political rumors, Western stereotypes about Islam and Muslims. He regularly reminds his students that the purpose in reading medieval legal texts is to learn how to think from the great classical scholars: "You must stand where they stood and think and reflect."

It seems everyone wants something from Shaykh Ali, a little time and a little attention, a confidence or a compliment. He creates a sense of intimacy in his classes, but he also has a keen sense of how to protect the boundaries between himself and his students without seeming cold or unavailable. As Shaykh Ali leans over to answer a student's question about the text in a whisper, an American student in the back of the room raises her hand and asks for the question and answer to be repeated. The shaykh smiles wryly and, in a mild reprimand, tells her, "Perhaps you are not meant to hear what you cannot hear."

The shaykh sees his class at the mosque as an introduction to and a preservation of a kind of literacy that is being lost, one that books alone cannot keep alive. "Our intellectual heritage is written with a specific nomenclature, a specific terminology, and the modern educational process is about to lose this terminology. The [classical tradition] has an outer shell, its terminology, and if we lose that terminology, we lose its meaning. The modern educational [system] has nearly lost its connection to the [classical tradition]. I reestablished the [open, classical] Azhar lessons in order to protect the language of the [classical

Fig. 4.2. An article on Shaykh Ali Gomaa's study circle in AlAzhar Mosque was featured in the Muslim American magazine *Islamica*, with this photo of him in his office. (Courtesy of Shams Friedlander)

tradition] so that there will remain people who can understand [its particular, technical terminology]. I am worried that some day the *turath* [Islamic classical tradition and its terminology] will become like the hieroglyphics, understood by no one. . . . I want people to continue in the tradition of knowledge reading the classical texts the way they were written, not the way people [today] want to understand them."

Um Ali warns me, again and again, to be suspicious of sufi shaykhs, of their misguided theology, of their mystique, manufactured in all kinds of ways: an aloof distance, an electric charisma, an ambiguous biography, strict codes of deference and respect. A chorus of admiring laughter follows Shaykh Ali's backhanded compliments and quick-witted insults often directed at his peers at AlAzhar ("country bumpkins") and at Muslim scholars in the West ("intellectual lightweights"). As we walk into the noisy bazaar, I confess to one of his American students that I find the shaykh has a cocky air, the kind popular professors often have. With a smile, he shakes his head and tells me, "No, no, you're taking it the wrong way. That's just his Muhammad Ali."

New Forms of Literacy, New Forms of Expertise

Modern state reforms of Islamic education, whether initiated by colonial or postcolonial rulers of Muslim societies or by reformist 'ulama, are often cast as a simple process of "secularization," presumed to be both desirable and inevitable cultural changes which come from above, pounding on the religious living in enclaves below, like a hurricane eliminating obstructions in its path. Such a crude but enduring construction of secularization as the simple erasure of religion fails to account for the complex political backdrop that profoundly shapes systems of Islam education and debates about its reform to this day. If we understand secularization not as the elimination of Islam but, rather, as various ways of containing Islam, abstracting Islam, dividing Islam from other parts of the social landscape, societies such as Egypt, Syria, and Jordan are thoroughly secularized.[18] Modern Muslim conceptions of Islamic expertise contain, abstract, and divide Islam from other bodies of knowledge in ways distinct from premodern conceptions of intellectual mastery of Islamic disciplines. For example, the great eleventh-century philosopher, theologian, jurist, and sufi AlGhazzali is often held up as morally exemplary by both revivalists and the 'ulama who often invoke his famous quote, "Whoever supposes that knowledge is realized through speculative theology, abstract proofs, or academic divisions is an innovator. On the contrary, knowledge is a light that God casts into hearts." AlGhazzali's conception of knowledge was *not* of mastery of a discrete field of Islamic information but of the internalization of knowledge through embodied practices of piety; the light of guidance was the key to all modes of cognition. Although this view of Islamic knowledge is widely held up as an ideal, in practice, both the 'ulama and the revivalists talk about Islamic expertise in secular terms, as a jurisdiction of knowledge to which they lay claim.[19]

In this sense, the 'ulama and the revivalists are both thoroughly modern and secular; again, their differences over how to define Islamic expertise and authority are differences in degree, not in kind. The 'ulama and the revivalists share a conception of Islamic bodies of knowledge as an academic discipline. By looking at secularism as a presence rather than an erasure—in this case the presence of a new conception of expertise—we see that the standard questions, of where secularism ends and Islam begins or whether (or to what degree) Muslim societies have "secularized," do not take us very far in understanding contemporary Muslim debates about Islamic education and its reform. The more fitting question is, how is religious authority recalibrated by Muslims, both the revivalists and the 'ulama, in modern, secular terms?

The increased participation of ordinary Muslim revivalists such as Um Ali in Islamic intellectual debates is often mischaracterized as the "fragmentation" and "democratization" of older, hierarchical, and less egalitarian configurations of Islamic religious authority.[20] Modern mass literacy has undoubtedly vastly increased lay readership of scripture, Quran and hadith, and spurred the emergence of new Islamic genres of pamphlets and fatwa blogs. However, the metaphor of democracy is a misnomer because it implies that the power to interpret religious sources has moved from a small elite to the masses. Although the vast growth in *who* reads is one of the biggest changes between the premodern and modern intellectual worlds of Islamic scholars, the more critical difference in the reshaping of religious debates is *what* does and does not get read. The emergence of new Islamic print and cyber cultures is not primarily the result of an expanded literacy but of a new *kind* of literacy. In other words, the contemporary crisis of Sunni authority pivots not on the question of who is literate but on what kinds of literacy count as authoritative.

The adaptations and successes of scholars such as Gomaa in the context of the modern fragmentation of authority are much more than the results of the successful branding and packaging of their speeches, writings, and fatwas to the new Islamic counterpublics that consume the revivalists' literature and media. Rather, the 'ulama's new success reflects their own adaptations to and interventions in modern secular epistemic shifts and secular educational reforms. Both the revivalists and the 'ulama consider themselves the true representatives of the tradition because they claim their vision of tradition most closely resembles the original intent of prophet Muhammad. The revivalists are not indebted to the 'ulama for their own understanding of Islam and often do not even recognize the 'ulama as having any expertise at all, dismissing them as uneducated government puppets. The 'ulama's particular perspective on the crisis of authority emerges out of this sense that they are no longer widely recognized as experts. The 'ulama maintain their claims to religious authority through their continuous intellectual genealogies, in part by making their own acquiescence to secular norms invisible.

Classically trained 'ulama and the revivalists are thoroughly modern and secular not simply because they use modern technology or because they criticize modernity but because their respective conceptions (and objectifications) of Islamic knowledge as a field in which they claim expertise is thoroughly modern and secular. As graduates of the secular track who learned about Islam in the relatively depersonalized settings of classrooms, the revivalists developed a secular conception of Islamic knowledge as an abstract, disciplinary object, as "a subject that must be 'explained' and 'understood.'"[21] In other words, the state's promotion of a modular, regime-friendly Islam inspired Muslim counterpublics to think of Islam in a similarly disembedded and formulaic way.[22] As a result, the revivalists developed their own academic approach to the study of Islam, what I refer to in chapter 3 as the "professional Islam" that came to the US with the "brain-drain" immigrant revivalists such as Al-Faruqi, an approach that abstracts religious thought from classical pedagogical forms and practices by first reclaiming rational empiricism as originally Islamic.

Like the revivalists, the 'ulama have adopted secular conceptions of Islamic knowledge in order to reestablish their diminished religious authority. In general, the 'ulama do not see the secular codification of Islamic law in modern states and the reenergizing of innovative interpretation of Islamic law (*ijtihad*) as threats to their authority. As historian Muhammad Qasim Zaman observes, on these issues the 'ulama simply insist that "just as things would go dangerously awry in any area of life unless the 'experts' in the relevant field would handle it, so too is codification [of Islamic law] flawed and ijtihad [legal innovations] perilous in their view, unless performed by" them.[23] The contemporary 'ulama also adopt a secular view of Islam as a field of which they claim true and exclusive expertise.

Gomaa illustrates this shared secular conception of Islam as an academic field as he makes a distinction between the expertise of the classically trained scholars and the revivalists whose ideas about Islam pervade the Internet.

> Knowledge has its sources, methodology, and tools by which it can be passed on to others through the educational process. Cultural awareness, however, does not. One can learn something, while remaining ignorant of other things; one can become proficient in one thing while lacking proficiency in other things, because the logical sequence of sources, methodologies, tools, and goals have not been completed to their proper end. There is a big difference between knowledge and [cultural awareness]. The difference is comparing a doctor to someone who has some medical awareness with regard to their personal hygiene, protection from disease, their dealings with over the counter medications. If they get a headache or become nauseous they can medicate themselves without recourse to a doctor since these are every day occurrences which do not fall into the category of things that require the consultation of a specialist. . . . [A man deludes himself when he] tries to turn cultural awareness into knowledge so that he becomes a doctor as a result of having some information about medicine. This [problem] is very widespread among those who want to set themselves up as teachers without first having been educated.[24]

Scholars such as Gomaa have come to understand themselves and the knowledge they produce in fundamentally different—that is, modern and secular—ways than the premodern 'ulama did, because they understand religious knowledge to be a particular kind of discrete body of knowledge, a scholarly area, a field in which one might be an expert, comparable to the expertise in the field of medicine.[25] But the 'ulama do not acknowledge this as a secular and modern break from the premodern pedagogical culture they claim to inherit and represent.

Both classically trained teachers and students in these networks reproduce a narrative of historical continuities and survivals, of Islamic civilizational highs and lows, of Islam's "golden age" and centuries of "decline" that correspond to the social prominence of the 'ulama themselves. Historians have widely discredited such baseless and sweeping dismissals of Muslim societies after the thirteenth century, a period that saw the rise of the Ottoman, Safavid, and Mughal empires. In fact, the appropriation of such narratives of civilizational high and lows (both premodern and modern) are what postcolonial scholar Partha Chatterjee calls a "derivative discourse"; like Arab nationalists who construct the flourishing of non-Arab Muslim empires in this period as a hiccup in the "normal" evolution of Islamic history, the 'ulama also adopt the Orientalist historical narratives of decline and stagnation of the Muslim World after 1300 that Europeans used to justify the cultural and intellectual need for their colonial interventions in Muslim societies.[26] In other words, just as American student-travelers draw on Orientalist tropes which function as productive mistranslations, so too do the 'ulama in the Middle East invoke abridgements of history and Orientalist narratives of civilizational decline in order to bolster their own claims to authority and to their proper place in history.

Both the tradition claims of the 'ulama and the revivalists elide the ways each set of religious intellectuals has acquiesced to a secular conception of Islamic knowledge that would be unrecognizable to the premodern 'ulama they claim as precursors. Clearly, the real divide is not between secular revivalists and traditional 'ulama or between those who want pedagogical reform and those who do not. Rather this is a contest between different kinds of reform of Islamic education—each side claims that its vision for reform is genuine and legitimate because it is anchored in the tradition, while the other reformers are insidious and will disfigure the tradition in the name of reform.[27]

The Heart of the Debate: Pedagogical Forms, Content, Context

Tradition is a process of debate over what links past, present, and future in a continuity that is meaningful and authoritative. In our commonsense understanding of tradition as a discrete body of ideas and practices, the transmission of tradition is imagined as a simple act of preservation: elements from the past survive into the present and persist into the future. The more open-ended and complex conception of tradition that I develop here allows for a more nuanced way to imagine how tradition moves over time, not as a simple preservation of a closed set of past elements but as a mediation process that is reflexive and selective. Elements of the past are mediated into the present by custodians, individuals in the present who decide which aspects of the past are nonessential to the tradition's future and, therefore, may be deleted or deemphasized. Custodians also decide which elements should be emphasized, highlighted, even added in order to ensure the tradition's survival in the future; both the 'ulama and the revivalists, whether they admit it or not, have embraced secular conceptions of expertise and assimilated it into the tradition.

The critical evaluation and selective endorsement of elements of the past and the present does not tarnish the authority of tradition. As long as no essential elements are deemed to have been erased or muted in this mediation process, the tradition, while only a semblance of what it was in the past, is vested with the authority of being equivalent to its totality in the past. Equally constitutive of the selective process of the preservation of tradition is the cultural process by which people in the present identify elements of their own necessarily localized, social realities that are consistent with the past, that cohere with the tradition, and that are made eligible for assimilation into the corpus of tradition, such as modern pedagogical forms like classroom instruction and modern textbooks as well as secular constructions of expertise. In other words, custodians of tradition engage in the process of defining what counts as tradition in the present; they do not simply hand off what they received from the generation before them to the one that will follow them. In the case of debates about education, the question is what elements of Islamic education can be subtracted and what elements from modern education can be added while ensuring that Islamic education remains recognizably traditional and relevant. In the following sections, we will examine how the three different orientations to Islamic education—*formalist, pragmatist,* and *reformist*— emerge in encounters between teachers and students in these transnational networks.

THE PROVOCATIVE STUDENT

Even though Maryam hasn't been a student at the Nile Center for Arabic in years, she is still something of a legend there. Eight hours of intensive private Arabic lessons six days out of the week, and one year later, she completed all ten levels. She remains friends with her former teacher, Um Ali. Um Ali is working toward a religious studies certificate at a women's Islamic institute in the evenings, and she attends a study circle with several other women at the institute, all alumni of Cairo University. She persuaded the group that Maryam was a sincere convert and not a CIA agent, and before long Maryam began leading their discussions. Um Ali insists that Maryam is the most promising American student she has met yet.

Maryam converted to Islam almost ten years ago, but she accepts the fact that she will always be considered a *muslima gadeeda*, a new Muslim, in Cairo and probably even once she returns to the US. Before becoming Muslim, she had always imagined she would live and die where she had been born and raised. She is no longer sure if she could live in Ohio ever again.

"People always describe becoming Muslim as a journey, but for me being Muslim has been journey after journey," Maryam explains, laughing lightly. She stretches her palms before me so I can read her cinnamon-colored travel lines for myself. She has lived in Cairo for years, but her studies have taken her to smaller, quieter parts of the world as well, dusty villages in Pakistan and Turkey. She asks to see my travel lines, deeper and darker than her own. She points out that I have better love lines, too.

Maryam is pleased that I know how to read a palm and to steam rice the right way, like a Pakistani woman, not like most of the American daughters of immigrants she knows. "My first taste of the Muslim world was village life in Pakistan. It was a culture shock, but more shocking to me was the fact that these women, who were very culturally traditional, would miss prayers. The same thing happened when I first came to Egypt. Here I am killing myself to learn Arabic, and these [Arab] women already know it but they don't want to learn and to read the way I do."

After graduating from the Nile Center, Maryam took AlAzhar's high school exam in order to eventually be tracked into AlAzhar's university system. She placed as a second-year student and decided against telling her parents that she was staying on in Cairo to start high school. The class had several international students, but she was the only Westerner. Most of the girls were nineteen, and even though she was a few years older than they were, or perhaps because she was, Maryam felt overwhelmed and anxious.

She found the classical texts taught at AlAzhar more difficult to navigate than the campus was. "I came in late, and, for example, in *fiqh* [law] my class was already at transactions. Well, I knew the Arabic, but I couldn't follow. You have to learn the [technical] vocabulary, and I remember they kept talking about the *'ayn*, this basic term in almost every sentence, and I couldn't figure it out. I knew it could mean 'eye' or 'a spring.' It was weeks before I figured out the *'ayn* is the object being bought or sold. So when I started a private *halaqa* [study circle] on the side, that taught me *how* to read [classical texts]."

At AlAzhar, Maryam is not a legend the way she is at the Nile Center, but she has a reputation for working hard and causing trouble. "Azhar was a disappointment: it's not that clean; the students talk; the teachers are late, and they inject their own personal opinions into the lessons [about Islamic law]. Azhar has a crisis of sincerity. Cheating is rampant. Some teachers give out the answers. And I have a strong personality, so I'd stand up in class, I'd go to the head *madira*, whoever: 'It's wrong.' And they will [recite the verse] to me: '*Wa'l-fitnatu ashaddu min al-qatl.*' ['Provocation is worse than murder.'] And I am creating *fitna* [being provocative]."

Months of Cairo's ceaseless noise and the screeches and tremors of the train made Maryam yearn for the silences of open, flat fields, the music of crickets. "I had heard of a Quran school in Turkish countryside. They have traditional [Quran schools] in Turkey, the way Egypt used to have. So one day I just suddenly decided to take a year off from Cairo."

At the Turkish Quran school tucked away in the mountains, Maryam fought off more rumors that she was a spy. "I lived in this school near the border of Georgia. I don't know what kind of intelligence they thought I was getting in the tea fields, but they're not used to foreign [white] women." She describes the drills the teachers and students conducted in case they were ever visited by the police: where to hide their books and blankets and bodies. Maryam patiently answers my questions even though she rarely talks about the practice drills and the surveillance. She doesn't like talking about it. But her green eyes light up when she describes what she studied and how.

"This was a very traditional form of education, what I was really looking for. It was divided into three programs: Arabic, Sharia, or Quran memorization. Since my Arabic was strong, I decided to memorize Quran. They have a special way of structuring the memorization. So, if you do a page of memorization a day, the first day you do the last page of the first *juz'* [book], then the [last page of the] second *juz'*, then the third. So after a month you have memorized the last page of [all thirty books of the Quran], and so the next month you move to the second-to-last page. The girls memorize from back to front and then front to back, and they have to recite the whole thing. They do everything that way. I've memorized both ways, the conventional way and their method, [which] is easier. I actually did a *ruba'* [a fourth of each book] each day, which was hard. By the time I came back to Cairo, I had memorized half the Quran, *alhamdulillah* [all praise is due to God].

"We all sat on the ground and put our books on wooden [stands], the *adab* [etiquette] with the teachers, the way it should be. They say '*ustadhatuna*' [our teacher], not '*ustadha flan*' [teacher so-and-so] because they understand that the amount you can learn from the teachers is directly proportional to your respect for the teachers. It's sad because ever since the government raised the minimum public education [in Turkey], these schools suffer. They are kind of underground, under the government radar, and they can't produce students to replace the teachers because by the time the girls have been through the secular schools and traded their *hijabs* [scarves] for miniskirts, it's too late. And so this beautiful system dies a little more."

A government raid spurred her return to Egypt, to AlAzhar. Although her Azhari curriculum includes many classical texts, and her private studies have always paralleled her classes, Maryam became increasingly frustrated with her inability to immerse herself in traditional pedagogy. "Traditional education means you study books, not subjects. You are mastering books. It's not academic, general, gist learning."

Maryam's private study circles are her lifeline to the traditional education she craves. Over the past few months, Maryam has been combing a theology text with a shaykh over the telephone. He makes minor corrections to her careful reading and elaborates the finer nuances of the work in response to her sharp questions. They get through three pages an hour. Two weeks ago, though, she found him waiting for her on the corner across from her neighborhood mosque. He had had a visit from three American men, clearly spies, and they asked about her, his American student. How did he know her? What was she studying? What did they talk about? He was a simple man and had four mouths to feed. He did not want any trouble. He asked Maryam not to call again.

As the shaykh walked away too briskly, she watched him with feelings of disappointment and frustration but not fear. If it came to an interrogation, God forbid, she is determined to be brave and stoic, as silent as her silk bookmark halted on page 141.

Formalists

One of the key ways formalists construct the pedagogical continuities to the premodern intellectual worlds of Islam is through the licensing of expertise. Advanced formalist students (known as "students of knowledge") devote several years to consecutive study in the hopes of mastering specific canons, and in the course of their studies, they develop fluency in classical and colloquial Arabic, spiritual training, and legal and theological expertise. Study often culminates in an *ijaza*. This image of the initiatic student-teacher relationship (sometimes exaggerated, sometimes romanticized, sometimes anachronistic) shapes how many American Muslim formalists such as Maryam search out teachers as intellectual and moral models in the social margins of cities such as Cairo, Amman, and Damascus or occasionally in rural villages and desert camps. Turkey's underground madrasa network is attractive to

American Muslim student-travelers such as Maryam who have a formalist orientation because it promises access to an Islamic pedagogical system untouched by modern state reforms and thus a particular, more "traditional" kind of Islamic literacy.

Formalists see an intrinsic value in what they define as "traditional" pedagogical forms, and their pedagogical vision is holistic and initiatic, with the teacher-student relationship at the center. For formalists, initiatic learning imparts more than curricular content from teacher to student, which is why Maryam emphasizes that not only the method of memorization but the student-teacher relationship is what constitutes what she calls "traditional learning." Ideally, the teacher is a model of Muslim behavior and character and, therefore, tailors the curriculum to the particular intellectual and spiritual needs of the student. Although informal and unofficial, the formalists' educational system is very hierarchical and accompanied by detailed intellectual genealogies and strict codes of respect and deference toward teachers and peers. Many of the student-travelers seek out the deferential training as much as the rigor of academic religious studies. Gomaa's resistance to share a private explanation to one student with the entire class, as described earlier, reflects his commitment to this individually tailored spiritual education. As he made explicit, although his students read the text together, he considers them to be at different levels of intellectual and spiritual maturity and believes that the knowledge that might benefit one could confuse or trouble another at a different level. Importantly, his students believe that he, as the teacher and spiritual guide, is a far better judge of their needs and abilities than they are themselves.

Formalists focus an enormous amount of energy on pedagogical etiquette as an endangered pedagogical form, part and parcel of the initiatic learning process. Male students often scramble to stand and kiss the teacher's hand in greeting as he enters, setting up his seat cushions and, in some cases, the speakers and microphone. These are not merely helpful gestures. Rather, part of these students' character training is to develop humility by learning to give due respect. When female students have male teachers, they are not able to express their reverence in such physical ways. (Male students rarely have female teachers.) Female students are, however, very creative in finding indirect ways to express the strength of their feelings for their male teachers. One striking example is a young Indian American woman in Amman, Jordan, who purposely rented an apartment next to Shaykh Nuh Keller's house and befriended his wife. She explained to me that over time she earned the privilege of washing the dishes every night at the shaykh's house. Although she is a sufi devotee and a student of Arabic, she sees the practice of washing her shaykh's dishes as among her most important work of the day. I asked her if she thought the shaykh was aware of her routine. She was slightly startled, as if my question had never occurred to her. She explained that she had never asked if his wife had mentioned it to him and that what mattered was that God knew. The purpose and pleasure for her was in the fact that in this small (even secret) way she gave a small service to her teacher and his family, for he had made such a profound impact on her.

For advanced formalist students such as Maryam, their ambitions to become religious scholars in their own right leads them to search out the forms of classical Islamic pedagogy which cultivates the mind and the soul, something that Maryam finds neither with her revivalist teachers at the Nile Center nor at AlAzhar. Despite AlAzhar's curriculum, which includes classical texts, the university has embraced a pragmatist orientation to Islamic learning that is focused on content, what Maryam disparages as "gist learning." But "gist learning" is precisely what student-travelers such as Richard are looking for.

BOOKSTORE ISLAM

Richard is guarded about his conversion story in Damascus, but he admits to his tutor, Amin, that he is an ex-boyfriend convert. One of his college girlfriends was an Iranian American art student. She wasn't religious, but she piqued a cultural interest in the Middle East. It was a general interest: light, roving, and, he had believed, aimless. Persian art, Moroccan music, a few semesters of Arabic—"nothing systematic," he says: "But then I started reading more about Islam then, and I started to realize I liked it. It was all very clear: the oneness of God, human prophets, a thinking man's religion, which I liked, but it had a spiritual side, too, and this whole cultural thing. And for some reason, I never really connected it to the Taliban." September 11th was the turning point, forcing Richard into the finality of his own mortality and into the realization that his interest in Islam had grown into something more than casual.

"As a white convert, I really did not want to learn Islam in English. I didn't want to just understand what it meant, have everything translated to me. I wanted more than just Borders [Bookstore] Islam, reading whatever someone happens to translate or whatever some [American] bookstore happens to have in stock. So when I came across Shaykh Nuh's [translation of the medieval legal text] *Reliance of the Traveler*, that changed my whole thinking. Here was this white convert, a sufi shaykh in Jordan [who] had made this huge intellectual contribution. He wasn't just sitting on the sidelines [of Islamic debates]; he's got the Arabic, and he's an authority."

[handwritten margin note: to read text in its own language = real Islam]

When Richard came upon Shaykh Nuh's community in Amman, he was quickly turned off by its social conservatism, specifically their rigid gender segregation. Richard feels that Shaykh Nuh lacks vision and that his small world in Amman makes Islam seem "depressing," especially "the ninjas," Richard's irreverent nickname for the shaykh's black-burqa-clad devotees. But Richard still has a reluctant reverence for Shaykh Nuh.

"The thing about Shaykh Nuh is he is just so pious. This guy is in the mosque praying all the time. You never just run into him in the street. He spends most of his life in worship, no question about that. It's hard to argue with that. How do you argue against a guy who makes *tahajjad* [prayers] every night? Even if he's wrong?" But Richard does have an argument with Shaykh Nuh's vision, about its inapplicability outside the few streets in a small neighborhood in Amman that he had made into his own island, constantly repopulated with fresh devotees from all over the world. What did they take away? What could they take away?

"[Shaykh Nuh's philosophy] goes against our liberal arts educational model, the marketplace of ideas. For sufis, they think certain thoughts are bad for you. You know, 'don't read the paper, don't watch TV,' or 'you can't understand [this or] that' or say anything about *x* until you've done twelve years of studies.' But in your mind, you have thoughts and questions, and I am not trying to become shaykh of the world, but I do want to feel like I have some level of access to my own religion. I also realized being here that there are things they can't teach me. Not everything translates, culturally. I am not into these kiss-the-hand social hierarchies. I'm not. And a lot of the gender stuff here, there's no future for it in the US."

In Damascus, Richard continues his studies of Arabic and Islamic law that he began in Amman, and while less "depressing," they remain difficult for him. "I still think Muslims are overly legalistic, and law is not the answer to the problems in most Muslims lives. But I am studying *fiqh 'ibadat* [ritual law] because I realized that it's not just pick and choose your favorite classes. I mean, I do have to learn how to make and keep *wudu* [ablutions for prayer] even though it's not really fun or even interesting. It's not exciting in terms of new information. It's a lot of effort to get anything at all, and a lot of times it's very frustrating because most of the time, you don't feel inspired. So the last few months has been about me turning down the volume on my life a little. At first I was bored out of my mind, but part of it is working through your boredom. Now I realize that I have limits with how good my Arabic could get and also that getting access to Islamic literature takes more than vocab cards. I also realized it can't all be inspiration; it has to also be challenging. That's why I love doing my [calligraphy] with Shaykh Waleed, to remind myself that the beauty of *Al-Jamal* [God] is what guided me to [Islam] in the first place."

Pragmatists

Most American student-travelers espouse a pragmatist view of Islamic learning, although they see at least some value in classical pedagogical forms such as memorizing poems and intimate one-on-one relationships with teachers. Reformed pedagogical institutions such as AlAzhar have taken a similarly pragmatic approach: the classical pedagogical content is most critical and must be preserved, retrieved, and transmitted. In other words, the pedagogical forms, such as the strict sequence in which formalists teach books or even the ways Islamic knowledge has been organized into disciplines themselves, are essentially historical accidents with no value aside from being well tested and effective. For the pragmatists, such as Amin and Richard and many of the reform-minded teachers and students at AlAzhar University, the preservation of tradition is neither dependent nor necessarily enhanced by preserving particular historic pedagogical forms. Rather, if they study the classical texts (usually out of the classical order that the formalists such as Gomaa want to preserve), they do so with the intent of learning a classical vocabulary and concepts, which can be abstracted and applied beyond the domain the formalists define.

The debate about Islamic learning is at its core a debate about how tradition ought to be transmitted over time. Muslims in the present mediate tradition by redefining what counts as tradition in the here and now by adding, subtracting, and recasting tradition. Formalists may claim they are simply passing down what came before even as they quietly subtract elements of what they received as the tradition, such as Keller's choice to leave the presumably obsolete chapter on slavery out of his translation of the classical legal text *Reliance of the Traveler*. Pragmatists are much more explicit than formalists about their own role in shaping—and not just passing along—tradition. The authority that is derived from engaging rather than necessarily replicating the past might be illuminated by a consideration of the parallel ways precedent works in systems of law. In law, we begin with the assumption that two cases, one in the past and one in the present, are never exactly the same. However, this lack of identicalness does not preclude the possibility of precedent because there may be a condition of similarity and, therefore, relevance between the past and present cases. Whether one interprets the present case as similar enough or different enough from the past is not the litmus test of what is within or outside the law (or tradition). Simply engaging the past establishes a meaningful and creative relationship to the past, whether one follows the precedent or not, and it is this process of engagement, not preservation, that is the foundation of traditional authority.[28] For both the formalists and the pragmatists, the selective process by which they determine what past pedagogical forms ought to be preserved and passed on intact, which ones can be modified, and which ones can be eliminated because they are unnecessary to preserve tradition into the future is a process of careful consideration. Custodians, in their capacity as receivers of tradition in the present, do the intellectual labor of reconciling the elements that will be abandoned, modified, and added by developing narratives about the transmission process and either establishing or maintaining the structures and methodologies that sustain the transmission process. Frederick Schauer, in his thoughtful reflection on the nature of precedent, remarks, "We never decide not to follow a precedent just because we do not feel like following it, but because something about the instant case is different from the precedent case. And if this is so, then the burden-creating conditions and the burden-satisfying conditions are measured along the same plane—similarity and difference."[29] The point to stress is that continuity does not require identical replication of the past, that it is the very process of reflection and reference that constitutes tradition, not the production of identical replications or the movement of a static set of ideas and practices over time.

As teachers and students make decisions about what to study and teach and how, they all recognize that the factors that make past pedagogical forms and methods relevant is contingent on time and place. Formalists such as Gomaa and Maryam express resignation over the growing popularity of the revivalists' pragmatic and reformist approaches in the Middle East. Furthermore, they are suspicious of what American student-travelers with a pragmatic orientation, such as Richard, think they are carrying back. They believe that American student-travelers with a pragmatic orientation simply cannot develop the depth of knowledge required to constitute true Islamic expertise. Although less wedded to the pedagogical forms of the past, pragmatists such as Richard are just as invested in the preservation of their tradition as the formalists are. The difference is in what they define as the essential elements of tradition; in other words, the pragmatists are traditionalists even though they do not assign the same significance to particular pedagogical forms and they have a less rigorous and fixed definition of Islamic expertise. For Richard, Damascus is a place where he can retrieve the bodies of traditional knowledge he believes are essential for Islam's survival in the US and leave off other practices for the same reason. He hopes he can attain enough of a mastery of Islamic disciplines to contribute meaningfully to the discourse in US mosques, to be a leader with some degree of authority. As we will see, reformists too are just as invested in being custodians of tradition as are pragmatists and formalists.

THE DANGERS OF A LITTLE KNOWLEDGE

Together, Omar and I help Ahmad with his fellowship and student-visa applications to the US, and I try to dissuade Ahmad from writing a theological refutation of the Nation of Islam as his dissertation. Hoping to reassure him, I explain that today most African Americans are Sunnis anyway.

Ahmad has tutored dozens of African Americans in Egypt; the problem for Ahmad is that too many of them are the wrong kind of Sunnis. "Black Muslims are all Salafis! The [Salafi] blacks only want theology, not law, and a little recitation. I tell them, 'You have to learn Arabic, positive law, and exegesis, not only theology!' The Salafi, whatever bit of knowledge he came with, he won't change it here," Ahmad exclaims, laughing and gesturing at Omar, who ignores him and continues typing on the keyboard. Frowning, Ahmad tells Omar sternly in English, "If you [blacks] do not know how much you do not know, how little your knowledge is—power, prestige, fame, these desires poison you. In Islam, a little bit of knowledge can be very dangerous. You [Americans] may leave Egypt with a turban, may be considered 'ulama [scholars] in the States, but you are only students of Islam, not [scholars]. Not everyone can be an *alim*, but at least some Americans must be. Otherwise, how will you have Islam in the States? How will you do da'wa?"

Omar and Ahmad have had this argument before, and Omar does not hide his irritation with his teacher from me. "I tell [Ahmad], 'I know. I've given da'wa.' Most white people don't want to hear about Islam. Our duty is to tell them, but Prophet was with the downtrodden, the oppressed. And who's most oppressed in American society? Think about it. Segregation still exists, and, you know, more black people will listen to Islam." Omar grows more and more impassioned. "The Quraysh [Pagan Arabs] tortured the Sahaba [the Prophet's Companions], but the Muslims weren't playing games, just drinking *shai* [tea] and riding camels around! They had to establish monotheism or else. Life or death! If you look at the *sunna* [the Prophet's example], I mean, really look at it as your model— no fear; stand up for what you believe in—I mean, Muhammad—that's my homeboy!" Omar catches himself and with reddened cheeks quietly adds, "*Salla Allahu 'alayhi wa sallam* [Peace be upon him]."

As a way of illustrating Omar's irreverence, Ahmad turns to me and blurts, "Omar thinks Azhar is a *batil* [illegitimate] institution."

Omar looks up from the computer screen, a smile playing on his lips. He likes to get a rise out of his Azhari teacher. "It is a *batil* institution."

I feel for Ahmad. "A lot of Muslims call it the Harvard of the East," I tell Omar.

Omar laughs. "Well, if it makes you feel any better, the Harvard of the West is a *batil* institution, too."

Ahmad looks pained. This is also an argument they have had many times before. "*La, la akhi* [No, no my brother]. AlAzhar is a historical institution; even the tourists respect it and visit and benefit. The reality is there is good and bad at AlAzhar but—"

"The tourists?" Omar interrupts him. "You go off of what tourists think?" Omar rolls his eyes and turns to me. "That's their ghetto mentality, see? That's why he don't like my clothes. You go off the *sunna*: Don't assimilate. It's good to be different. Like the hadith: 'Islam began as a stranger and will return as a stranger. So glad tidings to the estranged.'"

"*Ya Rab!*" Ahmad slaps his forehead in exasperation. "[The Prophet's cousin] Ali, *radiyallahu 'anhu* [may God be pleased with him], said every pot gets smaller as you pour something in except for *'ilm* [knowledge], which makes it wider. Azhar does not force you to take one opinion. You learn it all and pick your own. He does not even understand and respect that there are four *madhahib* [legal schools]."

"That's the whole problem, right there. What was the Prophet's *madhab*?" Omar throws up his hands. "He doesn't get it. One time, you know, me and him, we got into it, and as he's leavin', he goes to me as he's leavin', 'One of these days, I'll figure you niggers out.' I blew—"

"*Ya akhi*, I apologized a thousand times."

"I blew. I mean, do you think I came to Africa to be called a 'nigger'? They don't get it. They don't get us. This guy in my mosque back home, *that's* dangerous."

Reformists

Muslim intellectuals must determine how to apply standards of relevance from the pedagogical systems and curricula of the past to the pedagogical needs of the present. Only that squaring of past with present will ensure that tradition can survive with its authority intact. For Ahmad, as a graduate student at AlAzhar and, therefore, a pragmatist, the authority of the revelatory event of Prophet Muhammad's life—the receipt of divine scripture through Gabriel—merges with the authority of the "modernized" pedagogical system of AlAzhar because he sees those changes as cosmetic, not affecting the content of Islamic disciplines. He objects to the possibility that Omar may be granted a religious authority in the US that, by Ahmad's standards, Omar has not earned; such objections echo the anxiety of Gomaa and other formalists, although they have an even more narrow definition of Islamic expertise which even Ahmad, as a student trained at the reformed Al-Azhar, fails to meet. As a pragmatist, Ahmad sees the intellectual content taught at AlAzhar as continuous and sufficient to constitute tradition.

By contrast, Salafis, as reformists, assert a narrative of the past that is defined by rupture; they believe that since there is not a well-established foundation in the recent past, we cannot presume continuity with the remote, sacred (deep) past of the tradition's foundation. As a Salafi, Omar believes Muslims today must seek independent knowledge of the revelatory event, outside the disciplines and through direct (often but not always literal) readings of scripture. The reformist narrative of rupture depicts tradition in the recent past as a moral departure or degeneration from its own beginnings; they define their authority in the present as a recurrence, but not a continuation, of the raw potential of Islam's foundation.[30]

This may seem like a sweeping claim to authority, but as John Pocock notes, the special appeal of unselfconsciousness of those who lived in a tradition's foundational period looms large in debates about tradition's transmission in many religious traditions:

> Because the intellect cannot grasp the full meaning of any act in the sequence of a tradition, it cannot grasp the whole meaning of the tradition; and consequently it is very easy to think of action as the carrying on of a style, the continuation of a mode of behaviour whose character can be apprehended but never analysed, and which in turn is realized in action rather than in conceptualisation, . . . [like the] stories of craftsmen who could perform their tasks perfectly because they did not consider how to do them, who were perfect in their style because they did not conceive of it as a style.[31]

This is why the unselfconsciousness of the founding generation is so often celebrated across many traditions; the Prophet's community and the first few successive generations are perfect in the unselfconsciousness of their Islam, like Pocock's craftsmen. Perhaps more than any other strain of Islam, Salafis lionize the unselfconsciousness of the founding generation, and they deny their own process of investigating the past in order to determine which elements ought to be preserved intact, which ones modified, and which ones deleted, as well as which other elements might be added to tradition.[32]

For example, Omar counters Ahmad's challenges about the depth of his religious knowledge by challenging Ahmad's lack of knowledge about American culture and specifically the politics of race in the US, including what Omar sees as the racial limits of educating American whites about Islam in the hope that they might convert. Omar argues that Ahmad's ignorance of race is more dangerous in the context of US mosques than are his own deficiencies of academic religious knowledge, such as what he sees as the largely irrelevant differences in the legal methodologies of the four Sunni legal schools. In other words, Omar comes to recognize the *religious* value of his own intimate (cultural) knowledge of the racial climate of the US and the racial politics of US mosques. However, his narrative about how tradition is transmitted conceals his own engagement with tradition, his own assessment that American racial politics are necessary for the tradition to be "relevant," as he puts it, in US mosques.

Ahmad's and Omar's competing narratives of the history of tradition's transmission—Ahmad's is continuous; Omar's is one of continuity, discontinuity, and then continuity again—highlight the ways that historical consciousness and reflexivity in the transmission process is subjective.[33] Like Omar, Um Ali is a Salafi. She believes one should approach revelation directly, disregarding the ancillary Islamic canons, particularly when they deviate from the Quran and hadith scriptures themselves. She holds that Islamic pedagogy must be reformed and reimagined in order to properly preserve and transmit tradition to future generations. She believes the methods and content of the classical Islamic disciplines are rife with elements that contradict the original message of Islam, such as hierarchical teacher-student relationships, particularly in sufi orders, which she considers theologically deviant. In contrast, Richard's objections to "kiss-the-hand" social hierarchies of sufi orders are made in pragmatic rather than moral terms, as difficult to translate cross-culturally, not as ethically wrong.

Beyond Secular/Religious

Clearly, devout teachers and students on all sides of these debates about pedagogy are invested in the transmission of tradition. The competing narratives offered by formalists, pragmatists, and reformists over the proper transmission of tradition lie at the heart of debates about pedagogical forms and genealogies. Their arguments about *how* Muslims must learn are also linked to *what* Muslims must learn.

Pragmatists and reformists often accuse formalists of simply desiring to know a fossilized canon, one assumed to be definitive not because it is persuasive or compelling but simply because of its historical origins. Formalists, in turn, charge pragmatists and reformists with uncritically exalting the modern university. Even when formalists, pragmatists, and reformists are not directly engaged in debate, proponents of each of these positions are acutely aware of the other positions and develop their own positions in contradistinction to them. Although I never encountered a feminist reformer among the formalist student-travelers in Shaykh Nuh's enclave in Amman, Jordan, I was struck by how much time and effort these American student-travelers spent discussing and critiquing feminist reformist positions, in particular, the inordinate amount of energies spent analyzing the footnotes in the writings of Professor Khaled Abou ElFadl, a feminist, Egyptian American law professor at UCLA. In his writings, Abou ElFadl offers an account of tradition animated by an ethical humanism and a critique of pervasive, sexist interpretations of revelation and the reactionary posture of some revivalists that presumes that the most strident and conservative position on any issue related to women must be the most Islamic one.[34] Interestingly, the sufi students' criticisms of ElFadl were less focused on the details of his arguments and primarily concerned with what he lacks in pedagogical pedigree—despite, they sarcastically noted, assuming the title of "Mufti of America" for himself.

Such acute awareness of other perspectives is evident across the pedagogical spectrum. In the pragmatists' view, some past pedagogical forms are mere relics, weighing down Islamic learning, while others are valuable and worth preserving. For the reformists, past practices are not only no longer relevant today, but some institutionalized practices actually contradict the true message of revelation: in the eyes of Salafis such as Um Ali or Omar, through theological and ritual deviances; and through the sexist distortions of earlier generations of custodians, for feminist reformists such as Abou ElFadl.

The spectrum I offer here allows us to see deeper layers of these debates, beyond the very real, but often exaggerated, rivalries of the ʿulama and the revivalists and beyond nominalist constructions of these orientations as simply different, sui generis "islams." By focusing on genealogies, forms, and narratives of transmission, a clearer picture of these pedagogical landscapes in the Middle East emerges than the one that newly arrived American student-travelers struggle to navigate.

It is common in the Middle East, as a guest in someone's home, for hosts to have their children recite verses of the Quran for you. Still, I was stunned when the five-year-old son of an American student in Cairo recited the grammatical poem the *Ajrumiyya* from memory. The *Ajrumiyya* is one of the most popular Arabic grammar books to study in these transnational networks, as the fourteenth-century poem contains all the foundational rules of Arabic grammar. Hamza Yusuf recommends the text to American Muslims as the ideal way to learn Arabic. Lines divide the pages of the book between the verses of the poem (in bold script) and, in boxes that curve around the poem, the commentary (and sometimes a commenting on the commentary); the boxed text expands on the concise, precise, and metered verse, the way hypertext operates on websites. The American, a formalist, had spent countless hours earning an *ijaza* to teach the *Ajrumiyya* and then overseeing his son's memorization of it.

In contrast, the revivalist teachers who usually interact with beginner and intermediate American student-travelers (often teaching them Arabic and the positive law of ritual worship) are puzzled and even exasperated by the American "demand" for—and, from their perspective, fetishization of—texts such as the *Ajrumiyya*, texts that are essentially indecipherable to most ordinary Arabs, even highly educated ones. These revivalist instructors frequently asked me to explain why certain American student-travelers insist on learning grammar rules from a fourteenth-century poem rather than from a textbook. One instructor in a revivalist institute swore by the *al-Nahu al-Wadih* series, standard grammar textbooks taught in Egyptian schools, but he confessed that it was often difficult to persuade American students to study these books in lieu of classical texts such as *Ajrumiyya*. In revivalist centers, teachers were eager to show me the stacks of shiny textbooks written for students learning Arabic as a second language, packages of professionally printed flashcards and laminated posters, folders of bright, perforated worksheets, and tidy audio labs equipped with players, tapes, headphones, and sometimes even computers.

As we have seen, these debates are not about whether the 'ulama and the revivalists embrace new media and technology; many of the formalist 'ulama, such as Gomaa, do. The debate is over the nature of tradition, whether its canon is fixed or amorphous. Formalists such as Gomaa hold that pedagogical forms are as much a part of tradition as pedagogical content, and therefore they have a relatively fixed view of the Islamic canon and its methodologies, although it is one in which new questions and contexts can be absorbed and assimilated. Gomaa is deeply concerned that the technical languages of the classical canon will become incoherent if they are not taught in the proper way, through an initiatic transmission of Islamic knowledge from classically trained teacher to student. Even when secular, modern universities in the Middle East, such as Um Ali's alma mater, Cairo University, teach the classical canon, they do not use what Gomaa considers "traditional" pedagogical methods and forms. The highly technical canons of Islamic law, theology, and exegesis—with their discipline-specific terminology and conventions of argumentation, citation, and style—remain inaccessible to most Muslims, even college-educated ones. The pragmatists, such as Richard, Ahmad, and Maryam's professors at AlAzhar University, see Islamic pedagogical forms as a means to an end. Although they may or may not have attachments to historical pedagogical forms, they do not see those forms as having an intrinsic value for the tradition in and of themselves. Therefore, the pragmatists' definition of the boundaries of the Islamic canon is far more amorphous than the formalists'. Finally, Salafi reformists, such as Um Ali and Omar, see the canon as fixed but polluted, while feminist reformists see the canon as open but polluted. As American student-travelers engage in debates about Islamic education, their pedagogical choices reflect their own, particularly American perspectives on the charged global debates about the nature and purpose of Islamic education, shaped by the dictates and constraints—both political and intellectual—of studying Islam unofficially in the social margins of the Middle East.

We have seen the way the traces of secular reforms pervade these debates about tradition and even get incorporated into tradition, but it is important to remember that religious traces also constitute the secular. In political climates hostile to the unofficial study of Islam, the culture of deference that many American student-travelers are learning through these underground networks is not simply pomp and circumstance; some see it as a strategy for coping with state surveillance. Both the students and the teachers refer to the development of an Islamic comportment as particularly useful in the context of various political pressures. One American student-traveler explained that for him learning to operate under the cloud of surveillance of a politically repressive regime such as the Syrian government was a key part of his spiritual training, since controlling the tongue (avoiding gossip, backbiting, lying, and even excessive talking) is a virtue that he is being trained to cultivate. Practical skills for coping with police states are transformed into pious skills for coping with base desires and impulses. Just as the governments in Egypt, Syria and Jordan absorb, assimilate, and even eliminate Islamic pedagogical institutions and practices, devout Muslim teachers and students also absorb and assimilate the state's regulatory and policing practices into their own Islamic pedagogies of piety.

5

Choosing Tradition

Women Student-Travelers between Resistance and Submission

DREAM WITNESS

Maryam and I make our way across the cool marble courtyard of Al-Azhar Mosque, passing young boys from all over the world reciting Quran in small circles and older students frowning into thick manuals. We enter the room marked "The Turkish Corner" and approach Maryam's Malaysian girlfriends, books tucked under their arms, sharing stories and flaky pastries in whispers and small bites by the shoe rack. As we wait for Shaykh Ali Gomaa to arrive, one of the girls asks Maryam to tell them the story of her conversion dream.

In Cairo, just like in the villages in Pakistan and Turkey and even back in Cleveland, no one tires of the story of how Mary became Maryam. It seemed someone asked her to tell the story nearly once a week. Converts, and especially white women converts, are novelties everywhere Maryam goes, back in the US but also here in Egypt. Cairene cab drivers offer her elementary lessons in Islamic law: "Pork is forbidden." Others are immediately convinced she is a religious authority: "For an American woman to become Muslim, you are truly guided by God." They press to hear about how she came to see the lie of the Trinity: the absurdity of God as three, a family, a father and a ghost with a son. Truth be told, the Trinity never bothered her, though she rarely shares this in Cairo. The Trinity made sense to her then, the way nursery rhymes make sense without needing to make sense. It was something else, or a million little things, washing over her in slow waves.

She knows her friends, with bated breath, with Muslim childhoods and little exposure to Westerners, expect a story about a moment. She obliges them even though she is not sure that guidance can be distilled into an event, the workings of the heart and soul into a beginning, a middle, and an end. A story about a moment promised that things could change, that the future could be different from now.

Even now, Maryam's friend Noor reminds us, weren't the Americans about to pounce on Iraq? Remember, Iraq had seen worse. The shaykh said the Mongol invasion of Baghdad was the deepest cut into the Islamic tradition, threatening its very existence, bleeding rivers black from the ink of destroyed libraries. And in a generation, they were guided, they became Muslim. Things could change in one generation, people could change in a generation. Or in a moment.

And maybe it was a moment—or a dream.

She is standing on a hill in a desert. She is alone. She feels thirsty and tired from walking. So she stands still in the warmth of the sun. And then a shadow passes over her, and she is suddenly, impossibly cold. She thinks it is a cloud at first and looks up. It is the shadow of a great bird, mighty and strong. The shadow slides off her, slides off the hill. And she watches this bird. The bird grows smaller and smaller in the sky until she is staring into blue emptiness. And then it is not even blue anymore.

"I think I was eight. I've never forgotten that dream," she tells them.

Maryam means she was eight the first time. The dream has come to her again and again over the years. Whenever she has that dream now, she begins a complete reading of the Quran first thing the following morning. She reads every spare moment, her eyes running over the peaks and valleys of Arabic letters, racing to finish the book so that she might sleep well again. And, yes, she had that dream the night before she took her *shahada*, uttering the words that made her Muslim, made her soul new. "There is no god but God, and Muhammad is God's Messenger."

Guidance in a moment, like a dream shrunk into the blink of an eye. But it was true, and it makes for a great story in English or in Arabic. The Malaysian girls crowded around us have lips parted in awe and open smiles, exhaling divine praises. Yes, it was definitely a great story. What does it mean? Maryam shrugs and says what she always says: "*Allahu 'alam* [only God knows]."

Noor agrees and references a hadith. "*Allahu 'alam*. But you could ask Shaykh Ali. After all, there are true dreams. True dreams are one-fortieth of prophethood."

Maryam shakes her head. She had asked a sufi in Pakistan once, but she did not understand much of the interpretation translated back to her. That was back when she was in the Tablighi Jama'at. They were the ones who first introduced her to Islam in Cleveland. They were the ones who taught her how to pray. In fact, it was an Indian woman, Auntie Pakeeza, who urged her to pray on whether she should become Muslim; she taught her how and sent her to sleep and see. That same night, she had the dream and bore witness to the truth of Islam the next day.

"Why?"

She had had that dream so many times, and she always thought it was an eagle. But that night she was sure it was a vulture.

So, in the morning, Maryam bore witness.

Choosing Tradition, Resolving the Crisis

In the context of the discourse of the crisis of Islam, converts, but particularly white women converts from the West, have a particular cachet in postcolonial, Muslim-majority societies such as Egypt. On the one hand, the white Western woman convert is the token victory for Muslims who identify with being on the losing end of the so-called clash of civilizations, the West versus Islam. She is presumed proof that family, community, and tradition (Islam) will triumph over individualism, agnosticism, and moral decadence (the West). She affirms and confirms who and what is right and wrong in a global culture war and the military proxy wars throughout the Middle East between "us" and "them." After all, she was one of "them" and chose to become one of "us." The notion of Westerners choosing to convert to Islam inspires a special puzzlement for many Americans, who find it perplexing that someone, and especially a woman, could be one of "us" and then choose to become one of "them."

In the book *Muslim Women in America*, authors Yvonne Haddad, Jane Smith, and Kathleen Moore write, "Why any Western woman would choose to become a Muslim is quite beyond the comprehension of most Americans."[1] Arguably, when they write "Western woman," they refer to the white Western woman. The image of a black, Latina, Asian, or another woman of color donning a hair wrap, performing bodily religious rituals, even embracing patriarchal family structures is not nearly as jarring to most Americans as a white Muslim woman doing so, because religion is assumed to come "naturally" to the poor and to people of color. The white woman, rights endowed, of questioning mind, and most importantly, free, figures as the antithesis of the rights-deprived Muslim woman draped in heavy fabric. What appeal could a religion so profoundly patriarchal and restrictive such as Islam possibly have for her?

Although most women who convert to Islam in the US are not white, a considerable amount of academic attention and energy has been directed at explaining the appeal of Islam to white women. Scholars tend to presume that women of color who become Muslim (usually in reference to black women) identify the appeal of Islam in terms of the same racial, political, and social factors as their male counterparts, such as Islam's historical relationship to social justice movements in the US, its racially egalitarian ethos, the emphasis on spirituality and personal discipline, the fostering of community, respect for elders, and traditional values.[2] Haddad, Smith, and Moore argue that in the case of African Americans, "Latino/Latinas, Native Americans, and other minority groups, one of the initially compelling attractions of Islam has been [its] challenge . . . [to] white racism and economic exploitation, and the exclusion of people of color from the upper strata of American society."[3] In contrast, when these authors turn to explaining Islam's appeal to white Americans in the same text, they offer a gender-specific, spiritual explanation, suggesting that the mystical sufi strain of Islam "has served to attract the most Anglo women converts," although they concede that the estimates are shaky and that this explanation might only apply to a subset of "flower children" spiritual seekers who were part of the sixties counterculture.[4] In the absence of a total explanation, such as the ones routinely used in reference to the large communities of black and Latino converts to Islam in the US, scholars fall back on a specific set of hypotheses to explain why Islam appeals to some white American women. Most of these arguments construct the dominant culture and religion in the US as one that lacks spirituality, community, and moral cohesion in contrast to the particularly attractive features at the "heart" of Islam (including justice, rituals, a "simple," "clear," or "logical" theology). In other words, whatever the dominant culture lacks, Islam provides in abundance (homosociality is a common example). Another common narrative (and, again, one that is rarely invoked in scholarship on black converts) is the story of the white American woman who falls in love with a (brown) Muslim man. The woman's commitment to Islam often surpasses that of the Muslim man she loves and (usually) marries and sometimes outlives her commitment to the relationship.

Arguably, the efforts of scholars to explain white American women's conversions to Islam emerge out of a statistically significant demographic difference between the numbers of white women and white men in American Muslim communities. Demographic studies on Muslim Americans consistently show that white women converts outnumber white men, although the fact that Latina converts outnumber their male counterparts does not inspire the same investigation.[5] In other words, the energetic efforts to explain Islam's appeal to white American women reflect more than a statistical anomaly; in fact, the analytical strategies of scholars who write about American Muslim women mirror more general trends in historical and anthropological feminist scholarship on Arab Muslim women and Muslim women generally. Whether looking at white American female converts or Muslim women generally, most scholars continue to be preoccupied with the same core questions that puzzle lay publics in the US as well. Why do women choose Islam? Why do they choose patriarchy?

In the context of Muslims' own debates about the crisis of Islam, the exclusion of women is a key fault line, taken as evidence that their tradition is doomed if the problem cannot be fixed. In this context, Muslim women carry a double burden of both proving that their religious choices make sense and also reforming the intellectual worlds of Islam in order for their tradition to survive into the future. For many Muslim women, including the scholars and student-travelers in the pedagogical networks examined here, the primary object of resistance or obstacle to their religious goals is not male power or patriarchy but the *nafs*, the temptations and weaknesses of their own souls. Yet Muslim women scholars and students in these networks are deeply invested in demonstrating that their religious lives emerge from free choice; they want to redeem Islam from its image in the West as an excessively patriarchal tradition but also to resolve the crisis of Islam by reestablishing space for female religious authorities, an index of their profound double consciousness. Again and again, I was struck that American women

student-travelers, far more often than their male counterparts, presumed that I would be interested in their stories of conversion or reversion, stories that emphasized their autonomy, their questioning minds.
In fact, I spent a good portion of my time in the Middle East recording
these kinds of accounts. In this chapter, I juxtapose two different sets
of questions about religious authority as a way of illuminating the ways
in which the crisis of Islam discourse is gendered. The first set focuses
on Muslim American women's efforts to bend to a transcendent will,
a will that did not necessarily accord with what might appear at the
surface to be their own self-interest. Rather than looking at the ways
patriarchal articulations of Islam constrain the lives of female student-
travelers or the ways the women triumph against them, I focus on the
ways the "strong language" of choice and (religious) freedom constrains
the women's representations of their devotional practices.[6] The second
set of questions about religious authority takes up the ways women student-travelers both challenge and acquiesce to the limitations imposed
on them in the worlds of Islamic higher learning in a context in which
the very presence of Muslim women intellectuals is posed as a way of
resolving the crisis of authority. As we will see, American women student-travelers are often put in a difficult double bind of denying their
exclusion in the name of tradition while simultaneously struggling to
be included in male-dominated intellectual circles, ultimately muting
the reality of their actual pedagogical experiences in defense of the
Islamic ideal of learned female authorities.

Importantly, the strong language of choice is not simply an external
(Western) frame that is imposed on these Muslim student-travelers, a
frame that they are unable to resist; Muslims themselves, both in the US
and in the Middle East, are often deeply invested in the idea of choosing Islam in the context of the discourse of crisis. As discussed earlier,
Maryam's conversion story has an incredibly rich life in places such as
Cairo; it is not only part of her personal past but immediately becomes
recursive, abstracted into broader historical and anticipatory narratives
about the crisis (or crises) of Islam, not only for students of knowledge
such as her Malaysian friend Noor but also for ordinary people she
encounters in her day-to-day life who marvel at her story and draw all
kinds of political and religious implications from the idea that Maryam
chose Islam over her all-American life. In Cairo, Maryam's conversion

story functions as a way for her and her peers to talk about the danger of the extinction of their tradition, the (then impending) US-led war in Iraq, the escalating political tensions in Egypt and throughout the region, and the dark chapter of Islamic history that was the Mongol invasion. Yet by virtue of her identity as an American and, most importantly, as a (white) woman, Maryam's conversion story also articulates hope for the preservation of the tradition and the future resolution of the crisis of Islam, a worry that consumes her community of students of knowledge and scholars in Cairo as they pursue the intensive study of the sciences of Islamic law, theology, and philosophy.

In addition to giving us insights into the broader debates about the crisis of Islam, the ways the strong language of choice constrains female student-travelers' narratives about their studies also deepens our understanding of the ways the crisis of Islam discourse is profoundly gendered. In the course of studying American Muslim female student-travelers, and studying with them in the Middle East, I became less interested in what these American women often insisted I represent—their free choice as devout women—and more intrigued by what I found hardest to represent, their cultivation of various forms of submission to the divine through religious practices and the ways the trope of crisis both motivated and undermined their claims to Islamic authority.

Recognizing Our Protocols of Recognition

Conversion and reversion narratives are not structured by a simple, linear temporality in which we embrace a new framework and reject an old one. Rather, conversion narratives require seeing the old framework with new eyes, thus converting the future and the past together. They are built on the slow discovery of clues leading to the inevitable climax of conversion (or reversion). In Maryam's conversion narrative, her questions and doubts and her repeated dreams fuse the pre- and postconversion periods of her life. In my private conversations with Maryam, she, like many converts, both men and women, often identified becoming Muslim as a process, not as an event, and yet she routinely tells a conversion story that climaxes in a single, repeated dream. The contradictory ways in which Muslim women student-travelers such as Maryam talk about religious authority (as choice and not quite choice) indexes what we might call a *protocol of recognition* of freedom and resistance. This protocol of recognition determines what is legible to us by shaping our modes of perception, establishing not only what can be perceived but how perceived things such as religious authority and religious practices—and their antecedents, such as obligation and duty—are to be understood or categorized.[7] Maryam narrates her conversion in contradictory ways: as a passive process, which emphasizes being chosen by God for divine guidance through signs such as true dreams, but also as an active, decisive event in which her questioning mind led her to choose and publicly profess Islam as her religion. Maryam's dream is a sign and an event, something she receives but also something she creates through her conversion act and later through a reaffirmation of her conversion in the form of a complete reading of the Quran. The narratives of female American student-travelers, both converts and reverts, who navigate female networks of learning in Egypt and in Syria, expand our ability to recognize the devotional practices of these Muslim women as complex cultural forms that cannot be reduced to acts that are either free or coerced, chosen or imposed, genuine or mechanical.

Hannah Arendt's essay "What Is Authority?" offers an exploration of the links between tradition, religion, and authority that help us see the complexity of women student-travelers' attachments and pedagogical practices.[8] Authority and religion are etymologically associated with binding, or obligation to the past. *Religion* is derived from the Latin *religare*, "to bind," and *authority* from *augere*, "to augment." Arendt defines *authority* both as a concept, based on common reference points of experience and authenticity, and as an event, the unfolding of tradition's sacred founding. Drawing on Plato, Arendt differentiates between authority and authoritarian forms of power, such as coercion or violence; she argues that in contrast to mere power, genuine political authority must compel obedience without force. Although violence and coercion might serve the same function as authority (compelling the obedience of people), these different forms achieve these ends in distinct ways and are not interchangeable.[9] Authority requires standards of truth or rightness that simultaneously transcend and refer to the present social context. In the previous chapter, I described the transmission process by which people in the present (custodians) mediate (rather than simply preserve) tradition by deciding which aspects of the past are nonessential and, therefore, may be deleted or muted as well as deciding which elements should be emphasized, amplified, even added in order to ensure tradition's survival in the future. Of course, the custodian's selections are always subjective, but this does not mean that they are "free" choices, opportunities to invent tradition through a "religious opportunism" (i.e., knowing the answer they want to get before bringing the question to bear on tradition). For people in the present receiving tradition, the authority of tradition is constituted by expectations, demands, pressures, and limits that exert a pull on them and even restrict their freedom or ability to act in self-interest, but in a way that feels natural, authentic, authoritative.

We might make an analogy between Arendt's notion of authority and the experience of love.[10] Love feels both internal and external to the self, something from within us but also something that happens to us, just as the sense of being bound to an authority is located within and outside the self simultaneously. Recognizing authority, like recognizing feelings of love, implies a level of self-consciousness, an organic development, but not necessarily choice. Love's binding quality is naturalized in hierarchical and egalitarian relationships, whether between parents and children, lovers, or friends; the bond of love is something we are acutely conscious of without exactly choosing it. Both relationships of authority and love are conceived of as spontaneous and genuine, but they are also strong, with their own inertia. Authority, like love, exerts clear demands on the individual and even restricts his or her freedom or ability to act in self-interest, but in a way that feels natural or authentic to the self. Like love, authority is not easily investigated or verified; it is, as philosopher Ludwig Wittgenstein said of mythology, groundless, so stable.[11] We can be confident that someone loves us without being able to prove it, without needing to prove it. Arendt's reflections on authority provide us with a way of thinking about the workings of authority internal to the self for the student-travelers, workings that are distinct from the religious debates that animate these networks.

FOUR WALLS AND A PRAYER RUG

"This might be the happiest time in my life, even though I'm homesick," Leila muses while penciling a heart above the small block letters she has drawn on the back of her notebook. I-S-L-A-M. For someone so deliberate in her speech and movements, she is surprisingly unselfconscious. She recounts how she came home from her community college class one day armed with a plan.

She began her case to her father with a Prophetic hadith. "Pursue knowledge even if it takes you to China." Or Syria. Alone.

Her father grew up in a small Lebanese village where daughters left home when they got married, so it was no surprise that he was completely against it. He broke a dish against the table to make his point. A few weeks later, she presented to him a yellow folder of research, and a few months later, she was pricing plane tickets. Now, almost a year later in Damascus, she proudly presents the same folder to me. It reads like a corporate business report, with a budget in an Excel spreadsheet and colorful pie charts and diagrams, comparing different cities that offer classical Islamic studies: Cairo, Egypt; Fez, Morocco; Hadramawt, Yemen; and Damascus, Syria.

Of course, Leila misses her family and thinks about them every day. This is her first time away from home. A year is a long time. Still, in Damascus, she can just be Leila, nobody's daughter, nobody's sister, and nobody's almost-wife.

Leila has been feeling old ever since she turned twenty-one. She does not know how many proposals her father has rejected on her behalf since her broken engagement two years ago. Her ex-fiancé surprised them all, but he bruised her father's ego the most. Their phone began to ring again a few months later and then less and less frequently.

In Damascus, for the first time in a long time, Leila does not feel old. "Here it is just you, four walls, and your *sajjada* [prayer rug]."

Prayers in Damascus are different, and that makes the sacrifice of a year more than worth it. Leila finds silences and a peace she has never known before, five times a day. And she has a focus that feels like freedom, or like a distance and nearness at the same time: distance from worries and high expectations and nearness to the only Judgment that matters. She shuts the French doors to block the soft voices of her roommates, unfolds her sage-green prayer rug, and spreads it out like a banquet for her new concentration.

Leila memorizes the Quran between her prayers throughout the day. In the afternoons, she walks across town to recite to her teacher,

Reem. "It is hard to work [on recitation] with tapes. You're listening to someone and trying to mimic him, and then you're recording your own voice and playing it back. It's like when I call my parents in Florida, sometimes there's an echo on the line, and it breaks your concentration in the conversation, on what you're saying. When you're practicing your *tajwid* to a tape, it's the same. It's hard to hear your own timing. There are certain sounds in your head, and you're trying to make those sounds in your head before you make them with your voice, but you're hearing this other voice plus your own voice. So it is harder because after a certain point, the Quran starts to become part of you, inside of you. You're programmed to it, like there's always a tape running inside of you. It's more than just the feeling of memorizing. So for me, the tapes kind of push the *qira'a* [recitation] outside of me, which I don't like. But Reem just listens, and then she goes over my mistakes; so it's tuned to me, and that is much better."

Reem does more than help Leila with her recitation skills. She guides her in nurturing an intimacy with God, a kind of dialogue. She tells Leila that whenever she wants to speak to God she should make *dua*, expressing her innermost desires and requests in spontaneous prayer. In the ritual prayer, God answers through the recitation of verses committed to heart. Every word of the Quran written onto Leila's heart is a message and a reminder from God to her.

Locked away in her room, in prayer, there is only Leila, four walls, and a prayer rug that caresses her face with each prostration. The walls are smooth with corners like neat slices in creamy white, meeting the curve of the ceiling's crown molding in a string of pearls, like a wedding cake turned upside down.

Ritual as Manual

Leila's story, at its surface, fits easily in our protocol of recognition: she is striking out on her own, traveling in search of truth in a strange country (rather than just visiting her relatives in Lebanon), carving out time for herself to be alone in order to get over her broken engagement. Leila is an agent, an American young woman who has sought out the comforts of a nurturing set of fun girlfriends (she once described her Qubaysi-yat community in Damascus as a "nonstop slumber party"). In other moments, it is clear Leila wants much more than to get away from her father and his high expectations, her gossipy community, the pressures of the Muslim "marriage market" as she calls it. Her compulsion to learn is strikingly strong. She has spent a considerable amount of time, energy, and money to learn and study the Quran, and she is driven by a compulsion that is not quite chosen. For many American student-travelers, the ability to experience deep concentration is itself seen as a retrieval of tradition. Ritual worship works on the aspects of the self that are simultaneously there (from before worldly time) and not there (yet), complicating our notions of the here and now as well as our notions of an autonomous will. Leila's account is not only the details of her curriculum and her view of her pedagogical pursuits but also the limits of our own protocol of recognition, which makes her report to her father far more legible than her desire to internalize the Quran by committing large amounts of it to memory or to "program," as she puts it, her body to pray.

In the West, it was as recent as the turn of the twentieth century when the dominant meaning of ritual went from "a *script* for regulating practice" (ritual as manual) to a symbolic, communicative type of practice, and this change coincided with an increasingly interiorized construction of the self as having an essential, private core where authentic emotions reside.[12] In the Islamic cosmology, the core (but not private) self is the *fitra*, one's natural faculty for recognizing the human's true relationship and cosmic debt (due in worship) to God, which becomes muted and suppressed in the world through deviance and forgetfulness. Ritual is seen as a means to correct the human propensity for misrecognition and forgetfulness. In a context where ritual is still manual for devout Muslims such as Leila, prayer is both a pious means (developing an appetite or desire for worship) and a pious end in itself (fulfilling a divine requirement). The discipline of ritual prayer (*salat*) is seen as instructive (manual) in ways that unstructured, spontaneous prayer requests (*dua*) are not, as Leila's teacher points out to her. Through ritual prayer, *salat*, and Quranic memorization, Leila recites and further internalizes God's speech, which reminds her of her true identity and relationship (of cosmic debt) to God. Rituals fuse transmission and creation in the space of actions and practices in which correctness is taken for granted. Traditions are made up of shared and acknowledged ritualized practices that assume the necessity of the subject's participation.

Subjects engaging in rituals may be notably self-conscious and deliberate, evidence that rituals are much more than arbitrary habits. There is a creative element in ritual practice even if one does not feel "free" to alter the form of the ritual.[13] Rather, the mimicry in ritual is itself best understood as a creative act of transmission. Ritual elements highlight the way time moves in tradition and fixes (but does not eliminate) creativity.

American student-travelers attempt to reshape themselves in accordance with the scripts of rituals of worship (which, as manual, are also rituals of pedagogy, as we saw with the formalists in the previous chapter) as well as rituals of pedagogy (which, as a religious means, are also rituals of worship). Ritual worship such as prayer or Quranic memorization does not require the suspension of spontaneous emotion and individual intention, nor is it necessarily a space of cathartic release the way Leila describes her *dua*, a pious form that we might more easily recognize as sincere because it is unstructured and spontaneous. What is harder for us to recognize is that for Leila, her authentic self is not located in the core of private emotions expressed in *dua*. She believes her authentic core is something she must labor to uncover or, more precisely, recover and reinvigorate. Leila attempts to transcend her anxiety about not being married, "running out of time," and the judgment of her American mosque community. In prayer, Leila sets her familial and social relationships and anxieties about being judged in relation to God and the final, divine judgment, but she also transcends her identity in those relationships by recovering her relationship of submission to the divine will.

The illegibility of the creative dimension of ritual practice is due, in part, to the philosophical problem posed by the category of freedom. Anthropologist Saba Mahmood provides a nuanced account of the ways the philosophically unwieldy category of freedom structures scholarship on Muslim women's religious practice. In her insightful review of the historical and anthropological literature on Muslim women, she demonstrates how the philosophical conundrum of freedom maps in two analytical directions as scholars attempt to understand Muslim women's religious lives and motivations. She shows how the prevalent, although not always useful, philosophical distinction between negative and positive freedom produces these two separate bodies of analysis. Positive freedom refers to one's capacity to realize an autonomous will, unencumbered by the weight of custom, transcendental will, or tradition, and, under such conditions, one's autonomous will presumably express itself in predictable ways, in accordance with the presumably self-evident categories of "universal reason" and "self-interest." Negative freedom refers to one's capacity to make self-guided choices in the absence of external obstacles, whether imposed by the state, corporations, or other people. Negative freedom prevails in scholarship that explores the dimensions of women's lives that are independent of men, and this scholarship characterizes these spaces as endowed with more expansive potential for women's fulfillment or self-realization. Mahmood argues that the idea that individual autonomy is connected to the ability to realize the desire of one's "true will" so overdetermines feminist scholarship that it essentially functions as a guiding principle.[14]

Leila's desire to memorize and study can be subsumed under the rubric of free (if illiberal) choice. The problem is that such a reading runs the risk of projecting an autonomous will on a religious subject who experiences the compulsion to learn as something that happened to her, not something she chose. Mahmood, rather than taking resistance and the desire for freedom as her guiding frame, excavates an alternative genealogy of Muslim women's pious desire for religious submission. She insists we cannot assume "that all human beings have an innate desire for freedom, that we all somehow seek to assert our autonomy when allowed to do so, that human agency primarily consists of acts that challenge social norms and not those that uphold them, and so on."[15] Driven by the religious obligation to learn and nurture pious habits, women in the Qubaysiyat networks create intellectually and spiritually stimulating communities, warm, nurturing, and relatively egalitarian homosocial spaces and support networks, where social distinctions such as marital status, physical beauty, national origin, and to some extent even socioeconomic class are suppressed and even transcended. Religious devotion and pious achievement is the only distinction among these women that is expressly identified and enforced.

THE SECRET MEETING PLACE

Leila, her friends, and I wait and try to look like we are not waiting. This is the secret meeting place that is not very secret, in front of this particular florist, across from that bus stop, and down the street from the new mosque, on this bright and busy street. The girls recount stories about how they communicated locations and times for their classes over ice-cream cones. We try to not check our watches.

"When his father was still alive, they used to be very careful on the phone, very, very careful. You would just call and say, 'Oh, how about tea on Thursday at So-and-So's place?' and never say anything more than that. But now, with the son, everyone is less careful. A girl I have never even met called me yesterday and just said, 'Are the classes still at seven?' Everything is looser now with the son," Leila explains in a voice just above a whisper.

You never use his name in the street or even in the privacy of your apartment, though his face is plastered everywhere. Bashar al-Assad inherited his father's brutal regime in 2000. Both father and son tolerated the Qubaysiyat, ignoring their activities and classes, because the women are steadfastly silent on the topic of the Syrian government—and, it is rumored, due to the movement's success in attracting the wives and daughters of some of the wealthiest and most powerful businessmen and religious scholars in Syria. Still, Leila and her friends are vigilant about being watched, listened to, or followed by a government spy. Before I can ask Leila any more coded questions, a young white woman in a pink scarf and a white dress approaches. She is the British stranger Leila has been asked to wait for. We start down the street toward a sparkling apartment complex. "I've just arrived this morning, so I'm really tired," she tells me. "I just came from the hotel."

"How did you know to find us here?" I ask her.

"I knew the name of this neighborhood from a friend in London, but I didn't quite know exactly where you'd be waiting. It was quite hysterical with the taxi driver because I don't really speak Arabic; all I know how to say is *"ala yamin'* [to the right] and *"ala shimal'* [to the left], so we were [circling] around for a while. But when I saw you, I knew. *Subhanallah*, it's a miracle I got here! I really need a roommate that speaks Arabic."

"We'll find someone for you," one of Leila's friends assures her. Laughing lightly, she adds, "But even if you just speak to them in English in a FOB [fresh off the boat] accent, they'll kind of understand you."

"We are the ones with the broken accents here, remember?" Leila reminds them softly, but with a trace of irritation in her voice, as we climb the stairs to the apartment.

"We Are Not Political": The Case of the Qubaysiyat

Shaykha Munira Qubaysi, a charismatic seventy-three-year-old woman, is indisputably one of the most influential religious authorities in contemporary Syria, although most of her followers have never seen her or heard her speak. The shaykha, who lives in hiding, is estimated to have at least seventy-five thousand followers in the movement named after her (the Qubaysiyat) in Syria itself and thousands in diaspora, primarily in the neighboring countries of Jordan and Lebanon but also significant numbers in Syrian enclaves throughout the world, including the US. The Qubaysiyat attract many Muslim American student-travelers who are not Syrian American, such as Leila, or even Arab American, such as Fawzia. Some student-travelers become part of these networks in the US, but many find them upon arriving in Damascus and are attracted to them because of their accessibility. Two white American scholars based in Damascus are in charge of the Western student-travelers in the order; they teach weekly classes in English and arrange for their private (but free) tutoring with Syrian teachers (usually one-on-one but sometimes in small groups), and they also directly supervise the studies of a small but growing group of advanced students of knowledge. The bulk of their teaching is related to memorization and recitation of the Quran, but a significant amount of time is also devoted to Islamic law and theology and spiritual disciplines. The private teachers, usually local Syrian women assigned to the student-travelers by one of the American ansas, tailor the lessons to the specific levels of American student-travelers such as Leila.

In Syria, the Qubaysiyat are largely credited with the surge in women's interest in religious education as a part of the Islamic Revival; there is now a greater number of girls' religious schools than boys' schools in the country. The total number of such schools is estimated to be around seven hundred. There are about eighty such schools in Damascus serving about seventy-five thousand women and girls, and the Qubaysiyat operate at least half of these schools in addition to the study circles

Fig. 5.1. In Syria, the Qubaysiyat have been incredibly successful in reinvigorating the tradition of female scholarly leadership and in claiming a space for devout Muslim women in the public sphere. (Courtesy of Jeroen Kramer / *New York Times* / Redux)

and private sessions for adults. This is extraordinary given the fact that under Assad's regime in Syria, as in many countries in the Middle East, any religious activity that is not formally sanctioned by the state is illegal. In a surprising move in 2006, the government began allowing the Qubaysiyat to teach public classes in mosques and schools. After 2006, the Qubaysiyat began to do so tentatively, for the most part, continuing to operate in secret.

Just as in Egypt, the Muslim Brotherhood was (and remains) an enormously popular grassroots Islamist movement in Syria (although it has gone through a range of significant transformations in the past few decades). In the eighties, this grassroots Islamist movement attempted a coup against President Hafiz Al-Assad and his socialist Ba'ath regime, which culminated in the crushing government seizure of Hama (a town north of Homs) and the massacre of, by the official reports, about thirty thousand people, most of whom were civilians. The massacre was followed by a massive government crackdown on observant Muslim Syrians generally (not only those associated with the Brotherhood or with political subversion), which included mass jailings and disappearances,

rampant abuse and torture of civilians rumored to have Islamist leanings, heavy surveillance, and the clamping down on all mosques and
religious activity. In this volatile period in the years after the massacre, Assad developed a programmatic reform of Islam designed to win
over the religious Syrian masses and instill in them a strong national
and civic identity. To this end, he built a number of mosques and religious schools and developed training programs so that preachers would
propagate an Islam that was devoid of domestic political concerns, one
that was sanctioned by the government and that sanctioned all government action. Just as in Egypt, the Syrian government's persecution of
men suspected of Islamist activity through frequent and brutal interrogations and jailings since the eighties had the unexpected consequence
of creating a flourishing underground religious world where women,
such as Shaykha Munira Qubaysi, were able to resurrect the centuries-
old tradition of study circles led by shaykhas (called *ansas* in this community), female religious scholars. Subjecting women to mass jailings
and torture would have resulted in a public outcry that the government
could not risk, and the regime essentially tolerated the religious activity
of women revivalists by turning a blind eye. Since the Qubaysiyat and
other such underground religious networks of women do not talk about
domestic politics or critique the Syrian government, they are essentially
left in peace, although they presumably continue to be monitored quite
closely and they still meet clandestinely. Under both Assad regimes,
Syrian women have taken advantage of their relatively greater freedom
to pursue religious activity by forming underground pedagogical networks, reinvigorating classical Islamic disciplines such as recitation,
memorization, Islamic law, theology, and ethics, all elements of Islamic
pedagogy that are watered down in the government-monitored public
Islamic spaces of Syria. It is this increasingly prominent role of female
revivalists in the public sphere that is a key characteristic of the Islamic
Revival, not just in Syria or the Middle East but around the world.

The Qubaysiyat are a derivative of a global Sunni sufi order, the
Naqshabandi. Despite their populist valences and the large numbers of
participants (all women), the Qubaysiyat maintain an air of exclusivity
and a strict formalist hierarchy structured in concentric circles, with
Shaykha Munira Qubaysi at the center and chains of female teachers
linking students back to her and, as they claim, through the shaykha's

own shaykh back to a chain of students and teachers which originates with the Prophet Muhammad. For most of the women who attend their classes with varying degrees of regularity and fluid membership (i.e., the outermost concentric circle, many of whom may never formally become devotees), the Qubaysiyat are more of a sufi-inflected, revivalist network than a formal sufi order. However, more advanced students do identify as formal sufi devotees of a shaykha. The colors of students' overcoats and headscarves (wrapped and folded with the distinctive Qubaysi puff under the chin) correspond to their pedagogical level and proximity to the center. Leila wears a white scarf with a long, khaki-colored overcoat; more advanced devotees wear navy-blue scarves and navy-blue coats; and those few who reach the highest levels of achievement intellectually and spiritually are permitted to wear all black and a face veil.

THE ANSA

We enter the elegant, familiar flat and slip off our shoes in the marble foyer. There are about twenty young women present, all Westerners, chatting with one another in quiet voices. When the ansa, or teacher, arrives, a hush falls over the room. The women immediately assume a spot on the floor in front of an ornate and overstuffed armchair.

Ansa Tamara, a white, American expat, is infectiously amicable. Her presence is commanding and yet also unassuming. Age has softened the geometry of her face, but she has a youthful radiance with the lilting, laughing way she tells stories, the room hanging on her every word. She begins the class with religious songs in English and then launches into a stirring talk on the upcoming lunar month of Rajab, the month of forgiveness, and the importance of increasing repentant supplications. At the end of the class, she gives the students a spiritual exercise. "If you make twenty-five hundred *astighfar* [daily repentant supplications], take it to twenty-five thousand in Rajab. That's only five thousand with each prayer. You will see you can do it. This is the month of forgiveness. We can't forgive ourselves and Allah forgives us. Let's be nervous for a few weeks and examine every move we make. Let's mean each and every *astighfar* we make."

As the students trail out of the apartment, a small group of newcomers, hoping to be assigned a recitation teacher, join me around

Ansa Tamara's armchair. Ansa Tamara begins with the new British girl and asks her to read from the longest chapter, *Al-Baqara*. After a few stilted lines, the ansa stops her and asks about the length of her stay. She explains that she plans to stay for three months. The ansa instructs her to read as many pages as she can a day, accompanied by a CD of a professional reciter, throughout the months of Rajab and Ramadan. Once she has been through the Quran from cover to cover a few times, the ansa will hear her again and find her an appropriate teacher.

"No, I don't think you understand. I'm only here for a few months. I don't want to waste any of my time," she protests, clearly embarrassed. "I spent a lot of money to come here," she adds, tiny tears trembling in the corners of her eyes.

"Of course not. We'll listen to you after Eid." Ansa Tamara's smile conveys the finality of her decision. Leila wraps an arm around the British girl and reassures her that the ansa will find her the perfect teacher after Eid. Then she pulls her to the other side of the room to introduce her to a potential roommate and to go over the different denominations of Syrian currency.

Ansa Tamara turns her attention to me. She always politely refuses my requests for a formal interview, but she does not mind entertaining a few of my questions about her American students after classes. I try to tune out the British girl's loud whispers from across the room: "I can read to tapes back home. I am willing to pay. She didn't even let me explain."

Ansa Tamara seems unfazed by the girl's insistent complaints, absorbed and amused by her own description of her Western students. "We get so many students; *fa* [so], for some it's like a drive-through order. There's this Western arrogance of what Islam is, that they come already knowing what they need to know: read this book and this book. 'I read this book.'" The ansa mimics a high-pitched voice. A few of the girls giggle, but the ansa's real joke was next: a self-described American feminist who showed up looking for an Arabic tutor. She had no interest in studying Islam with the ansa because she found her too conservative. "She had nails out to here, makeup, layers and layers of makeup, and she wanted a [free] teacher. But she tells me she's just here to learn Arabic, only Arabic. I even gave her a teacher and—it's so funny, you know—she didn't come back because she felt she was 'above the level.'"

Ansa Tamara laughs with her students for a moment, her clear, blue eyes studying my face. "*Ilm* [Knowledge] with *taqwa* [God-consciousness] is the base of Muslim life: learn it and teach it. That's not an -ism; that's our *din* [religion]."

Piety and Feminism

Feminist scholars of religion were taken unaware by the global resurgence of Islam in the last few decades of the twentieth century (alongside other global religious revivals), and its widespread popularity among middle-class women in Muslim societies parallels the particular puzzlement around white women converts in the US. Just as religion is assumed to come more "naturally" to women of color in the US, so is it presumed to come naturally to the poor. At a historical moment when women in Muslim societies such as Syria had more material and social possibilities available to them, feminist scholars and lay critics were perplexed to find many middle- and upper-class Muslim women actively support a movement that seems inimical to women's presumably self-evident "interests and agendas." One type of scholarly explanation is simply that these Muslim women suffer from false consciousness, that they are pawns in a grand patriarchal order, simply managing their images to get by (thereby dismissing women's own understanding of their lives). In Syria, such cynical readings of the Qubaysiyat abound among their lay critics. It is rumored that the Qubaysiyat safeguard their networks from government policing through the "targeted" recruiting of important women who either belong to influential families or are becoming educated professionals and high-profile leaders in their local communities. This has given the Qubaysiyat a reputation as a kind of boutique Islamic network in Syria, with meetings often taking place in posh apartments with a line of black Mercedes sedans picking up and dropping off devotees for evening classes. In these analyses, the popularity of the Qubaysiyat is a function of their branding, such that being a recruit is itself a sign of social status for Syrian women.

Rather than reducing Muslim women to cynical manipulators trying to accumulate social capital in a man's world, some feminist scholars focus on religious women's small and local forms of resistance and subversion in unlikely Islamic spaces. Rather than asking why women choose Islamic patriarchy instead of feminism, they pursue other questions: how do women contribute to reproducing their own domination, but also how do they resist and subvert male dominance? In this analytical mode, Islam is a potential resource for women, although not the only one, which can provide the conceptual tools and practices to challenge male power and to redirect or recode tradition in accord with women's "own interest and agendas." Anthropologist Lila Abu-Lughod, in her essay "The Romance of Resistance," questions the extent to which she and other feminist scholars working in this mode wrongly project resistance to male power on Muslim women as a kind of pre-political feminist consciousness, one the female subjects of these studies would not recognize. In reviewing her own previous research of a marginalized community of Egyptian Bedouin women, Abu-Lughod highlights how women both embrace and resist patriarchal prohibitions and restrictions, as she explores women's opposition to particular arranged marriages (but not the institution of arranged marriage itself), their sexually irreverent private jokes and poems in which women both exalt and make fun of men, and finally, women's own enforcement of gender segregation, their fierce protection of female-only spaces where they enact a range of minor defiances of male kin by using secrets and silences to their advantage.[16] When Muslim women's actions seem to reinscribe patriarchy, feminist analysts working in this mode search out moments of disruption and opposition to male authority—the nascent feminist consciousness.

The Qubaysiyat lend themselves to such readings of protofeminist resistance. The physical and social mobility that the underground Qubaysiyat network offers challenges the dominance of husbands and parents. For example, Muslim American student-travelers such as Leila are often able to delay marriage or to get the social and psychological space they need to heal from a relationship gone wrong. Although the movement's rhetoric about the religiously sanctioned patriarchal gender roles appears relatively rigid, the fact remains that this women's movement has reconfigured the gendered spaces of Islamic pedagogy and ritual practice, and it cannot be dismissed as merely reinscribing traditional gender roles. For example, the intense homosocial bonding between students and the ansa and between peers often competes with the obligations to family in general and to male kin specifically.

Teachers remind (and reprimand) recent brides and women who are engaged to be married about the dangerous, consuming qualities of romantic love, which might distract a devotee from her obligations of religious study (and her obligations to her ansa). Along the same lines, the ansa frequently reminds her students about the importance of revering one's parents in Islam, yet students' devotion to the ansa sometimes competes or even eclipses their devotion to parents and husbands, particularly those who are not observant. In fact, a recent, popular Syrian soap opera satirized a Qubaysi devotee who abruptly leaves family functions at inopportune times to visit her ansa.[17] Pious Muslim critics of the Qubaysiyat in Damascus often invoke extreme examples as evidence that the ansas are too intrusive in family matters. There have been several rumored cases of the Qubaysiyat using methods of vigilante justice, taking devotees who were being abused by a husband or father into hiding in the network.

Although societies such as Egypt and Syria had and have significant feminist movements with deep histories that have won on key issues of gender equality, feminism continues to be dismissed as a Western political ideology, and (white) Western feminists are routinely caricatured and ridiculed in networks such as the Qubaysiyat.[18] As an underground Islamic revivalist movement in Syria, the Qubaysiyat are by definition rebellious and antiestablishment, and they often make fun of the male government spies whom they defy but also fear. Husbands are also a frequent aim of jokes for having fragile egos or for being easily manipulated. These jokes are often directly tied to serious intellectual and moral challenges against the excesses of male power, framed as lessons on Islamic law, exegesis, or theology. In one lecture on the husband's obligations to his wife in Islamic law and the illusion of power that husbands wrongfully believe God grants them, Ansa Tamara Gray ended the talk with a personal story. She described how her husband had been rude to her, taking out his frustrations from work. Rather than engaging him, she endured his harsh words with patience, with the conviction that the prayers of the patient are granted. Later that evening, her husband found her in intense prayer, and afterward he apologized to her profusely and asked her nervously if she had prayed against him (of course, she had not). The ansa reenacted the scene in a comedic manner, standing in prayer, murmuring feverishly into cupped hands with a smile playing on her lips, sending the students into peals of laughter. The pursuit of religious knowledge places these women in conflict with several structures of authority, including but not limited to Western cultural domination (and Western feminism), the Syrian government, the male-dominated world of imams and muftis, and the authority of parents, siblings, and husbands. Yet the rationale behind their teasing, critiques, and rebellions against these different social authorities is not predicated on gender equality and, therefore, often escapes our protocol of recognition.

Abu-Lughod worries that feminist scholars' triumphal readings of Muslim women's small defiances fail to capture the larger constellations of (patriarchal) power that structure them. Abu-Lughod draws on another ethnographic example from her work with Egyptian Bedouin women: a generational conflict over lingerie, which young brides covet and their maternal elders find distasteful. Reading young Bedouin women's desire for lingerie as a simple defiance of elders and the community's gender norms elides the ways in which young women's forms of rebellion "back them into wider and different sets of authority structures, or the ways in which their desires for commodities and for separation from kin and gender groups might be producing a kind of conformity" to the political and economic demands of a Westernized, Cairene elite, tied to a global, neoliberal, and patriarchal economy.[19] In the same way, Leila's campaign to convince her father to let her go to Syria to study for a year is not only a small rebellion; it is also a capitulation to the dominant American values of individualism and independence from extended family obligations, precisely the kinds of "American influences" that Leila's parents worry will distance her from them. Rather than admire resistance in and of itself and search out cases of the (partial) failure of systems of patriarchy, Abu-Lughod urges scholars to complicate our analyses of resistance as diagnostics of power and to expand our definition of what counts as resistance. Mahmood extends Abu-Lughod's argument farther, arguing for the uncoupling of religious subjects' desires for self-realization and salvation from the Enlightenment notion of an autonomous will. For Mahmood, *resistance* itself is problematic as an analytical point of departure for understanding the religious lives of the devout Muslim women in these kinds of networks. She asks whether the term *resistance* can be used to describe human actions "which may be socially, ethically, or politically indifferent to the goal of opposing hegemonic norms. . . . [Is it] even possible to identify a universal category of acts—such as those of resistance—outside of ethical and political conditions within which such acts require their particular meaning?"[20]

BOUNDARIES

Sometimes in the Middle East, everyone was a "student of knowledge." Other times, only the advanced students were "students of knowledge." It was a slippery, rubber-band title, defined by firm but elastic boundaries, simultaneously inclusive and exclusive, humble and elitist, the way "believers" could mean all of us sometimes and only the best of us at others.

I had met several American women who were students of knowledge in Damascus and Cairo before I met Maryam. They fought so much harder than the men to prove themselves to their teachers as smart and hardworking students; yet too often, it seemed to me, their modesty stood between them and their ambitions. Maryam's eyes light up with a distant memory. "Do you remember that movie *Yentl*? Barbra Streisand was in it. I think about that movie sometimes when I get frustrated with the glass ceiling. It's about traditional learning systems, Jewish, and in it she dresses up like a boy to study the Torah. My favorite part is when she asks her father why they have to hide her studying from the neighbors when they can't hide it from God, and he says, 'God will understand. I'm not so sure about the neighbors.'"

Maryam's neighbor brings her sweet tea and warm bread every morning. She marvels at her spunk and intelligence and drive but worries about Maryam and her roommates living alone the way they do. She teases Maryam about her bookishness and urges her to forget becoming a scholar, to get married and start her own family.

Maryam and her two Turkish roommates are the only foreigners in her working-class Cairene neighborhood next to the train tracks. Whenever I visit Maryam at her spare, boxy apartment, her two Turkish roommates linger in the room, silently listening to us talk, even though they are both always very shy around me. She met them in the madrasa in the Turkish countryside. They want to learn English, especially the younger one, Fatima, but Maryam is resolute in her refusal to teach them. "Not until your Arabic improves!" she scolds them when they beg her to teach them a few words.

They are much younger than she is, teenagers, and although they have similar, delicate features, I learn they are only friends, not sisters. Maryam befriended their families in Turkey, and the girls' parents entrusted her to take them with her back to Egypt, to watch over them and see that they complete their Islamic studies. When I protest that she is too harsh with them, she insists that she takes the responsibility of watching over their studies as seriously as her own. At first, for Maryam, it was almost an accident, what to study and where, but now she knows why.

"They are doing pretty well in the Azhari system," she admits," but I want them to work harder. They are not hungry enough for the knowledge." She finds their interest in English and their disinterest in Arabic frustrating. "I want to inspire other girls to study. These girls are special and have a lot of potential, but . . . " Her voice trails off.

I try to soften her frustration with the girls. After all, they might have dreams and ambitions different from her own—not everyone wants to be a student of knowledge, I remind Maryam; it is not the only path to being a seeker.

Maryam smiles with resignation. We have had this argument many times. She cannot imagine a better life than the life of religious study, and she cannot seem to muster up the anger over the little indignities she suffers as a student that come so easily to me. Maryam is passionate about her desire to be part of a chain of teachers and students that stretches back to the time of the Prophet, a chain that she has every intention of stretching over the Atlantic, once she returns back to the US. "The secret of our tradition is the *isnad* [chain of transmission]. That's where the *baraka* [blessedness] is." In Turkey, Maryam read books with her teacher with the confidence that she was a part of generations and generations of teachers and students uninterrupted, a cycle of teaching and learning, memorizing and mastering. Maryam believes in the power of the chain, in its blessings, and she never tires of trying to convince her young roommates and me of its power. It is not the chalkboards and bells ringing in AlAzhar's classrooms that bother her. As much as she loves the madrasa system, she is resigned to the fact that it is a dead system in Egypt, a dying system in Pakistan and Turkey, and that she will never be able to fully resuscitate it once she returns to the US. "We've lost the system, but as long as we don't lose the traditional knowledge . . . "

Maryam still hopes to go back to America as a scholar, to teach, but she is always vague about when and how. A paper degree from a university under state control means little to her. "In Azhar, it's just about the *shahada* [degree]. PhDs mean nothing to me. Once I finish my BA, I'd like another BA from Azhar, maybe in hadith. The word *'alim* [scholar] has become a joke; it's tragic. Other women are not able to study, [so] I am obligated to teach back in America, but I haven't given a lot of thought to how. I know my knowledge is an *amana* [responsibility]," Maryam explains. "It's not a museum piece to store in my brain cells. I have to put it to use. [Knowledge] wasn't just poured into my head, to be poured out again." Maryam unscrews an imaginary cap on the top of her head. Fatima, her roommate, giggles softly. "Knowledge is a *fard kifaya* [collective religious obligation] for women. I've learned Arabic, I've sat, *alhamdulillah* [all praise is due to God], with people in *fiqh* [law], in *tajwid* [Quranic recitation], in hadith, in *tafsir* [exegesis], but I haven't been able to finish, which is agonizing but, *insha' Allah*, I will."

"Why has it been so hard to finish books?" I ask her.

"My being a woman is a big problem for me. It limits what I can see. I had a *fiqh* teacher who wouldn't let me study with him until I went through a whole book with his daughter. I hated it because I came so far and everything, for second best? Why? And the male *tullab al-'ilm* [advanced students of knowledge] have such easy access, and we work just as hard or harder. Some *shuyukh* don't teach girls, even in groups. They say, 'To not open the door to things.' They think to study is not as important for women and that we have so many male scholars, so it's not a necessity for girls to learn. But we are Americans, and we want to be part of society. We want to be seen as authorities."

The Low Ceilings of Higher Learning

In theory, Muslim women can reach the highest intellectual positions in Islam, but in practice, there are multiple gender barriers that prevent female students of knowledge from navigating the peaks of the Islamic intellectual world and reaching high levels of scholarly mastery and religious authority. Although female student-travelers who are either beginners or intermediate students have little trouble finding female teachers or group classes, at the highest levels of the Islamic disciplines, which in unofficial settings typically require one-on-one tutoring, there are few female teachers and few male teachers willing to take on female students. The restrictions on female students—Maryam invokes the feminist trope of the glass ceiling to describe them—are couched in terms of the norms of modesty that treat women's pursuit of knowledge as an optional luxury rather than a pressing need. At other times, I found male scholars describing the paucity of women authorities as a symptom of the crisis of Islam, a problem that must be solved in order for the tradition to survive into the future.

Interestingly, despite Maryam's frustrations, she does not articulate a clear vision for how she might challenge the gendered system of hierarchy, as she does when she is talking about the corruptions of Al-Azhar or even the need to raise the intellectual bar in American mosques. Instead, she resigns herself to the limits of the system and accepts them as subjective human flaws that do not reflect the divine design, as her reference to the film *Yentl* makes clear. It makes little sense to describe this as a protofeminist consciousness since it is not articulated in terms of feminism but in terms of the discourse of crisis. What is important and difficult to see is how the gendered crisis of Islam discourse is simultaneously a defensive and creative reaction to the construction of Islam as an excessively patriarchal tradition by feminist critics. The invocation of crisis both creates and eliminates discursive space for debates about the ideals of Islamic scholarship with regard to women intellectuals and the realities female students and scholars face in their day-to-day learning and teaching. It is in this sense that Mahmood's focus on pious subject formation fails to account for the double consciousness of female revivalists in Egypt and elsewhere; while Mahmood is right to recuperate their cultivation of piety from mere identity politics, the homosocial spaces of female revivalists in places such as Egypt are never isolated from the broader discourse of the crisis of Islam, which renders Islam pathological because it is "excessively patriarchal," because that double consciousness also constitutes Muslim female subjectivity.[21]

Female American Muslim student-travelers, like the Muslim women in contemporary piety movements in the Middle East, are asserting their presence in previously male-defined spheres, but the very idioms they use to enter those male-dominated spaces are ones that subordinate them to the authority of men. Purportedly "feminine" virtues such as shyness, modesty, quietness, and humility are often the necessary condition for their enhanced public role as religious leaders. Ironically, it is far more common to find female religious leaders and teachers in Syria, where gender boundaries between teachers and students tend to be stricter, than in Egypt, where mixed-gender study circles are common but usually led by a male teacher. This is partly what motivated Maryam to leave AlAzhar and Egypt for the women's madrasa in the Turkish countryside.

A HUSBAND MADE OF BOOKS

"It's funny what [my parents] tell their friends: that I'm a Muslim lawyer, that I'm learning Arabic, that I'm becoming a Muslim minister, Islamic graduate school. They don't understand or want to understand. I know they worry that I'm OK, but I'm tired of 'When'll you come home?'"

Maryam's parents thought that she was hiding from her old life, or running, or pushing something away, and that someday she would grow tired and lonely in the desert and see the error of her ways—and come home to Ohio, maybe even to church.

"Ever since I turned thirty, my mother has been on me to get married, you know, grandchildren. When the John Walker Lindh thing broke, I called her. 'Finally, the man I've been waiting for!' She didn't laugh, though. She has no sense of humor about things like that. Believe me, that lost boy has made everything harder for all of us."

Over the years, Maryam has struggled with restlessness and with those sharp stabs of joy and pain that are love. In Cleveland, it was flushed cheeks and a student visa about to expire, but something inexplicable happened, and then nothing happened. In Pakistan, a crush almost turned into an arranged marriage but was cut short before the engagement because she got malaria and nearly died. Her parents had to fly to Pakistan to collect her, sick and lovesick, from a clinic so dingy that her mother has nightmares about it to this day. Years later, in Turkey, Maryam's friend introduced her to her handsome and bright brother, but he was too young by a year, and his mother was too old to bear disappointment.

In Cairo, Maryam has learned the jealousy of wives and the bitter taste of divorce. He was fifty-five, and her friends did not approve. Maryam insisted that he had a sweet gentleness about him. He believed in her and supported her studies, and she still felt an affectionate gratitude for him. She forgave him for the painful night when he tried to explain that his wife might have been able to get over a second wife who was Egyptian but not a *khawagiya*, not an American, never. Maryam was a humiliation his wife swore she would not bear any longer, and she was the mother of his four children, after all. Maryam listened to his explanation and nodded, dry eyed, pretending to understand, pretending she had braced herself.

"How did you come to be OK with being a second wife?" I ask her again.

"*Ya Ustadha* [oh, Professor], are you going to teach me how to think like a good feminist? Or like a girl in an Indian movie?" To tease me a bit more, she sings an off-key and mispronounced Bollywood lyric. "You know, everyone tells me to get married, and I am open to it, but he's got to understand my priorities. I need a man, if there's such a creature, who would be happy that his wife studies and either won't get jealous that studying is my first obligation or bothered by the ways teachers affect students. You can't help but be affected by your teachers because *'ilm* [knowledge] transforms your personality, and the teacher is the means. For the Eastern mentality, I know, it's hard on the husband's ego. So I'm absolutely willing to be a second, third, fourth wife. No problem. But he's also going to be a second husband, *ya'ni* [meaning] my first obligation is to my books; my studies come first. So if I never get married, no problem. Really. I'll still have my library. But if you do come across some tall, dark, handsome [student of knowledge] as you're doing your interviews," her voice trails off. She smiles even though she is serious.

If I do, I will. I will tell him that she is not like the women he knows. She will not mind when he needs some time on his own. She will not tie questions to his silences or absences. Her world of books has trained her to bide loneliness with patience, especially the loneliness that can creep into marriage.

"I know I can't become an *'alima* [female scholar] because how would I live my whole life in the company of 'ulama [male scholars]? It's impossible unless I marry someone who is a great *'alim* himself." A husband who is also a colleague will allow Maryam the freedom to navigate the scholarly spaces she longs for without the risk of impropriety or immodesty. "I studied with a blind shaykh once, and we went through several books. And he decided either I'm going to marry him, or we're not going to continue the lessons. He wasn't what I was looking for in a husband, so that was the end of that."

Lying in her bed, Maryam studies in the swirl of cotton bed sheets and loose paper. Sometimes, she is startled awake to find words on dry lips, an open book across her chest, dry pages pressed to her skin with the sweat of sleep.

Breaking Old New Ground

The seismic growth in the number and the scale of influence of female scholars widely recognized as religious authorities is part and parcel of the modern, global Islamic Revival's transformations of Islamic learning and authority; however, this is not a simple story of the progressive growth of women's authority and freedom. On November 2, 2009, the Grand Mufti of United Arab Emirates, Ahmed Al-Haddad, announced that in 2010 the Emirates would appoint the world's first state-sanctioned female mufti, noting that six Emirati women were under consideration as potential candidates for a program of several months in one of the Sunni schools of law (the Maliki school) and Islamic legal theory. In a fatwa he authored in February 2009, Shaykh Al-Haddad sanctioned women's roles as muftis and confirmed that their religious opinions applied to both men and women. Although Shaykh Al-Haddad concurred with AlAzhar's position that female muftis could not occupy the political office of Grand Mufti, he insisted that women muftis' religious authority was in no way limited by gender. As evidence in support of official or quasi-official state-sponsored programmatic reforms of Islam, such claims about the newness and firstness of Muslim women's religious authority are made regularly, contrasted with the historical reality of the near monopoly of Islamic higher learning by men. Interestingly, despite getting a fair amount of media coverage in the Arab press as a radical innovation, Al-Haddad's fatwa itself cites many historical precedents for female muftis, including female contemporaries of the Prophet. In other words, upon closer examination, what Al-Haddad actually claims is new is the sanctioning of female muftis by a modern nation-state. Ultimately, even this claim does not hold up under scrutiny. More than half a dozen other governments beat the UAE to the punch with government-funded training programs for Muslim women religious scholars in the past few decades: Egypt, Iran, Turkey, Morocco, Malaysia—each claims to be first, and several have matriculated graduates. For example, in 1961, the same year the Egyptian government assumed control of AlAzhar University, a women's theological graduate college was founded which today graduates thousands of female students in Islamic law (including an "imam" track launched in 1999 with an incoming class of fifty-two). AlAzhar regularly publishes the fatwas of female muftis on its website as well as in its literature. And, since the nineties, the Egyptian government has been underwriting and licensing women "dai'yat," or preachers. In contrast to the Egyptian government and AlAzhar, the Turkish government officially recognizes women as muftis and as representatives of the state. The Turkish program was launched in the eighties, with twenty-nine women graduates in 1990, and it has grown exponentially since 2000. In 2008, more than four hundred women were employed by the state as muftis and preachers in Turkey, and half were tenured.[22] The Turkish government trains women in Islamic law as rigorously as their male peers (in contrast to the "semester" program the UAE has developed); however, the state designates the women graduates as "assistant muftis," even though their religious opinions carry the same weight as those of male muftis for the lay Muslim men and women who appeal to them.

By focusing exclusively on the question of formal power and institutions, states, state projects, and state subjects, we miss the richness, complexity, and messiness of the negotiations of authority on the ground. A crisis of legitimacy plagues the female preachers and assistant muftis in Turkey, who, as state employees, are often viewed as aligned with a corrupt government hostile to Islam (and, ironically, a state apparatus which reinscribes the very gendered hierarchy the religious training of women is supposed to dislodge). Importantly, Turkish government-trained women muftis are competing with unofficial, female religious authorities with different, older pedagogical pedigrees, such as the underground madrasa networks that Maryam participates in as well as other unofficial religious networks such as sufi orders which attract American Muslim student-travelers. The excessive and triumphant focus on the novelty of these state-initiated, programmatic reforms belies the complex negotiations of women's religious authority in the Middle East through the sloppy conflation of religious authority and institutional power endowed by governments.[23] For example, one of AlAzhar's deans, Suad Saleh, although not officially recognized as a muftiyya by AlAzhar or the Egyptian government, has had an enormously popular call-in fatwa show in Egypt since the early nineties in which both male and female callers seek her expert religious opinions. Ironically, the Grand Mufti of Syria, Shaykh Ahmad Hassoun, in his announcement of the launching of the training program for women muftis, added the caveat that women's fatwas will only apply to women. In this regard, the novel program does break with centuries of the Islamic legal tradition; it is innovative and original in its gendered restriction.

The fanfare over the "new" female authorities in the Middle East indexes the ways in which the crisis of Islam discourse is profoundly gendered; "new" female authorities are proof that the tradition is being reformed and becoming more gender inclusive. Women represent the possibility of resolving the crisis of authority, but their very presence sometimes masks the very exclusions that generate a sense of crisis. Ironically, as we have seen, all the energetic efforts from state actors, religious officials, and even student-travelers themselves to prove that women do have Islamic authority can undermine the efforts to make the highest levels of Islamic learning more inclusive. In my own case, as an affiliated scholar at AlAzhar, I was enthusiastically received at the men's college, frequently meeting with high-level male faculty and advising male graduate students. When I expressed interest in the activities at AlAzhar's women's campus, it was clear that the female scholars and students were perceived as doing less rigorous work. Several of my male Azhari colleagues dissuaded me from visiting the women's campus precisely because they felt my research was too important and too serious to be sidelined at the women's campus, although in my view the female scholars and students matched their male peers in academic rigor and knowledge. Despite this pervasive acknowledgment of the lack of parity between the two campuses, the ability to talk about the exclusion

Fig. 5.2. On a fatwa call-in TV show, Suad Saleh listens intently to a caller who seeks her advice and her religious opinions (fatwas). (Still from documentary film *Veiled Voices*; courtesy of Brigid Maher)

of women at the highest levels is consistently muted by the inclusion of token female intellectuals such as myself. While the young Azhari men I mentored were reverent, always referring to me as "Doctora," I often caught glimpses of their gender biases and prejudices. The first time one of them met my husband in an elevator, he excitedly pumped his hand and exclaimed, "Sir, you must be a genius!" In response to my husband's surprise, the young man explained to him, "Well, your wife is very smart, so, of course, you must be much, much smarter than her."

6

Transmitting Tradition

The Constraints of Crisis

THE ROPE AND THE ANCHOR

The familiar flat is noisier and more crowded than usual because today is a party, celebrating Fawzia's successful recitation exam and her receipt of an *ijaza*. A large sheet cake congratulates her in pink icing on the dining-room table. Cold drinks are passed from hand to hand, and the young children, usually restricted to a bedroom and a babysitter, are running around in their socks between the small circles of students. The ansa's own son, a long-legged boy with freckles and messy red hair, is wearing a Spiderman costume two sizes too big, hanging from the stair railing, showing off his superpowers to his mother's students. The ansas have brought a folk singer, an old woman with a soaring voice. She sings songs in praise of the Prophet, accompanied by a drum and the faint and uncertain voices of American girls unfamiliar with the Arabic lyrics.

Fawzia showed me the *ijaza* that morning in her apartment, in between impromptu dance lessons from her Arab American roommates in preparation for the party. The document lists the names that link Fawzia to an *isnad*, like an invisible thread of names interlocking, braiding, and knotted at each generation, linked and double looped all the way back to the Prophet in a smooth, unbroken line. Now Fawzia's name is a knot, and now this thread will travel back to California.

Fawzia makes a grand entrance, adorned with a silver, plastic tiara pinned over her white scarf and a white, sequined apron dress with princess sleeves slipped over her clothes and tied in the back. We circle around her, cheering and clapping and dancing, as she moves her hips and arms to the rhythm of the drum.

"Is that the bride?" the young daughter of one of the Syrian *tajwid* teachers asks.

"She thinks anyone in a white dress is a bride," her mother explains. "Yes, that's the bride. Isn't she beautiful?"

As Fawzia's roommates tease her, saying her moves are more Bollywood than bellydancing, Ansa Tamara signals for the singers to stop. Once things quiet down, she assumes her seat and the students settle on the cleared silk rugs at her feet. She begins by explaining in a quiet and pleased voice how important Fawzia's achievement is, what it means to be part of the chain, its permanence.

Then Ansa Tamara becomes more solemn and turns to the crisis. "Our *din* [tradition] is organized into generations, and each generation had its challenges. Islam is never threatened. Even the Crusades, they threatened Muslims, not Islam. American ideas, Western ideas, these are not challenges to Islam. Don't forget America is a baby, only two hundred years old. Spain was a Muslim country for eight hundred years. And each generation, there is a *mujaddid*, who renews and revives the *din*. And Allah says '*man mujaddid*' [the one who renews] and '*man*' [who] is a neutral term, not masculine or feminine, so a woman could be a *mujaddid*. A *mujaddida*."

The student seated in front of me nudges her friend, as if to suggest she might be the one. They both suppress giggles.

"And our generation, our time, we feel we are in a crisis, and we will have our *mujaddidin*, too, to renew Islam for this generation—not in the sense that they add new, American things to Islam but in the sense that they reconnect us to Allah. When you disconnect from Islam, you disconnect from Allah. When Allah is not pleased with you, people are not pleased with you, but, sometimes, people are displeased because Allah is pleased. When you go back, Fawzia, people might tell you that you changed too much in Syria. People want to change things to make Islam fit America, so Americans will like Islam or even convert.

"Allah has no need for wimpy Muslims. The state of Islam is because of the Muslims; we are all part of the problem. You have to remember that your *ijaza* is an anchor to the Quran; the Quran is your anchor in this life. This is the rope of Allah, Allah's speech. Cling to the rope, or at least cling to someone you think is clinging to that rope and follow her. For me, sometimes I see someone after years, after she's been with us, and she's trying to be more Western. She's stopped wearing her *manteau* [overcoat]. And you don't feel that same love. The bond is broken. But others, you see someone after years, and she's still connected. It's like you never left; we'll just pick up where we left off. You girls can send your shaykha an email. For me, when I was in the US, I could not communicate with my teacher or see her for years, but I held tight to my Islam, my Quran. There won't be that distance unless you choose it."

Ansa Tamara pauses and smiles at the silent students before her, a few faces wet with tears. She raises her hands in a simple prayer. "Allah choose for us to be able to choose you. *Ya Allah,* let us be from those ones. Put Islam in front of us in a beautiful way."

Strangers Traveling

Does Islam have a home, a land, a place with borders? If, as the American student-travelers I encountered in the Middle East believe, Islam is a universal tradition and not an "Eastern religion," why did they call their journeys to the Middle East a "return"? A "return" to what, exactly? A "return" to where, exactly? After all, most of them are "returning" to cities in the Middle East they have never been to before. When I would bring up the contradiction between the idea of an Islamic homeland, their language of "return," and the universality of Islam, they would often answer me with a Prophetic hadith: "Be in this world as though you were a stranger traveling a path." Life in this world, they would remind me, is a transitory and fleeting journey. Home for the believer is in the next life. While American student-travelers do, of course, believe that this world is temporary and that the afterlife is eternal and, therefore, their real home, this answer elides the fact that the overwhelming majority of the American student-travelers come to the Middle East with the intention to return to the US. Their commitments of enormous amounts of time, resources, energy, and effort in working toward a future for their tradition in the here and now belies their desire for a home for Islam in the US.

As archives of tradition, the intellectual centers of the Middle East are imagined as a temporary stop for American student-travelers, who believe their journeys must eventually lead them back to their US mosque communities. They are explicit that their travels are a means and not an end; they are in the Middle East to retrieve tools to ensure the future of

Islam back in the US. The Middle East is a detour, not a destination. In this chapter, we will see how the debates over the nature of the transmission of tradition across time (between then and now, as we saw in chapter 4) and across cultural difference (from the Middle East back to the US) generate different moral geographies: some student-travelers embrace the US as home, as a future site of their tradition's growth, while others are far more ambivalent about the US as a destination.

Religious intellectual centers in the Middle East, such as Amman, Damascus, and Cairo, attract American students because these cities act as nodes in their moral geography of the Islamic East as Archive. The authority of these landscapes is contingent on a temporal relationship to the Islamic past and an Islamic future in the US; Muslim Americans experience the sense of feeling bound to tradition in ways that simultaneously transcend and link them to the present, past, and future. The narrative of the transmission of tradition over time and space is always told from the perspective of someone located in the present; from the vantage point of the custodians in the present, the links between tradition's past and tradition's future are imagined.

The Qubaysiyat, for example, produce a narrative of continuous, initiatic transmission of tradition which is manifest in the relationships of students to their teachers and in the possibility of students such as Fawzia earning an *ijaza*, earning her place in a long, continuous pedagogical genealogy that will stretch into the future and, in this case, from Syria to the US. While the formalist conception of the *ijaza* pivots on a narrative of the continuous, uninterrupted transmission of tradition over time, as we saw in the previous two chapters, the Qubaysiyat's narrative of the transmission of tradition across culture (expressed in territorial, spatial terms) is not always continuous, as Ansa Tamara Gray's warnings about returning student-travelers conveys. To be sure, the Qubaysiyat's narrative of the transmission of tradition is one of many produced by devout Muslims in these pedagogical networks. Muslims are perpetually debating the exact nature of Islam's transmission process, the extent of their tradition's fluidity and fixity over time and space. After all, Muslims with a pragmatist orientation might challenge the importance of the *ijaza* to tradition's future, questioning whether it is a pedagogical form worth preserving into the future; those with a reformist bent will take issue with the Qubaysiyat's claims of uninterrupted continuity to the Prophet's practice and method that Fawzia believes her *ijaza* embodies. As we have seen, more often than not, in these global pedagogical networks, Muslims' differences over the transmission of tradition over time are a matter of degree. They all see the transmission process as a collective effort but not necessarily a uniform one. The transmission of tradition happens not only over time but also over cultural boundaries that are imagined in spatial terms. This chapter takes up those debates about the transmission of tradition over time that were introduced in chapter 4 but examines them alongside related debates of transmission over space and across culture, which reveal the competing visions within these global networks of the future of Islam in the US.

CARRYING ISLAM

"Cairo is the Muslim Paris!" Sakeena says softly, as she leans over toward me.

We are sipping cold drinks on a shady spot of grass in the courtyard of the American University of Cairo, where Sakeena is spending her junior year abroad and where I sometimes shop for books in English. Her attention is happily fixed on a small group of co-eds flirting with each other on the other side of the courtyard. A young couple walks in front of us, hand in hand. Like Sakeena, the young woman wears a simple white scarf over her hair, although tied and pinned differently. "See? I might actually meet a Muslim man here and fall in love!" Sakeena smiles. "I always thought I would marry a born Muslim, a black born Muslim, like me, but now I am not sure it matters any more."

Sakeena hates when Egyptians mistake her for a convert. "Some people [in Egypt] think I'm a convert because I'm black. I get that all the time [at AUC]. And then I tell them that my grandmother is even Muslim, and they're like, 'Oh, really?' She even met Malcolm [X] once. Did I tell you that story?" she asks, turning to face me. I nod; she has told me the story twice. "That's one thing I've been trying to figure out: the racism in Egypt. It is constantly in the back of my mind, and I look for racism. Sometimes I'm like, 'OK, I see how it is,' like when I remind them Egypt is in Africa. But then I can't always see the racism because I'm not obviously black to some of them. Some people actually think

I'm Egyptian." She is light skinned, but Americans could always make her out. "It makes me sad in a way: that they don't see me as black or that I can't say much about it, if there is racism here or not." Sakeena is quiet for a moment.

"All I know is just because you grew up in a Muslim country does not mean you know your Islam." This is an observation I have heard from Sakeena many times. Sakeena describes her visit to the famous mosque and mausoleum of the esteemed eighth-century jurist Imam Muhammad ibn Idris al-Shafi'i: "You see people do all kinds of crazy things [at tombs]. The women drop money in it 'cause they think because Imam al-Shafi'i was a doctor that being near his grave is gonna heal them. Spooky stuff."

I tell her to look for the little copper boat on the main dome at the mosque the next time she goes. Since most domes of mosques have a crescent on top, Sakeena asks me to explain the significance of the vessel. "It's supposed to symbolize his knowledge, that Imam al-Shafi'i had this vast sea of knowledge. They fill the boat with water and seeds as a birdfeeder."

Sakeena is more impressed by the mosque's location than its architectural elements. Its home is one of Cairo's most infamous neighborhoods, the City of the Dead, a massive graveyard where it is said a million homeless people live in tombs. No matter how many times she walks through it, the place leaves Sakeena in terrible awe. "You never get used to it," she shakes her head. "It is so depressing, but at the same time it's like the poor people here are different or being poor here is different."

I wonder what she means, wonder if she means the scale of Egypt's poverty or just the way Egyptians talk about poverty, without confusing its causes and consequences, without assigning blame in small, looping circles. Before I can ask her to explain, she says something that surprises me even more.

"Honestly, though, I feel like Islam has to survive in America for it to survive in the rest of the world, because on some of these big issues we [Muslim Americans] are the only ones keepin' it real."

"What makes you say that?" I ask her.

"So my Quran teacher, she's *hafiza*, memorized [the entire Quran] as a young kid, really smart. But Egyptians like her, regular Egyptians, you know, they don't wanna admit that, yes, a Muslim killed all of those

innocent people [on September 11th]. They are like, 'It was too organized to be Arabs, too professional. Arabs are too backwards to have
done it by themselves.' They have all of these crazy conspiracy theories. And we keep arguing, like back and forth. We keep trying to convince each other. Like one day, she brings me pictures of the towers, the
holes. I started to understand that basically they need to believe this for
themselves, and I need to believe what I believe for me, as an American.
And I told her that. 'Haqiqatkum mukhtalif min haqiqatna' [your reality
is different from our reality]. And she hasn't brought it up since. Carrying this din [tradition in America], we need our own leaders and our
own scholars; otherwise we'll be stuck with their baggage, and we don't
need it. That's what our Imam [Warith Deen Mohammed] always says.
We have our own problems. And that's the thing about Imam al-Shafi'i.
When he moved from Iraq to Egypt, he changed all of his fatwas 'cause
he saw that the situation was different, the cultures were totally different, the people were totally different. So if that was Iraq and Egypt then,
then what about Egypt to America [today]?"

Destination Tradition

Tradition, like culture, is passed on within a particular perspective, a
particular narrative that links the past, present, and future. As we have
seen, tradition is never an independent entity moving through time and
space; rather, tradition is dynamic, and it derives part of its dynamism
from the transmission process. This transmission process is also subjective and shaped by the needs and assessments of people in the present.
As Walter Benjamin put it, "every image of the past that is not recognized by the present as one of its own concerns threatens to disappear
irretrievably."[1] Tradition is built on the past, and yet its relationship to
the past is not natural but discursive, constituted by discontinuities as
much as by its continuities. The analogy of a river changing its water
captures the way the past operates in a tradition, as "a continuity of
adaptation," both "unlike the present and yet continuous with it."[2]

As we saw in chapter 4, the selective process by which custodians
determine what elements of tradition ought to be preserved and passed
on intact, which ones can be modified, and which ones can be eliminated because they are unnecessary to preserve tradition into the future

is a process of careful consideration. Custodians, in their capacity as receivers of tradition in the present, do the intellectual labor of reconciling the elements that will be abandoned, modified, and added by developing narratives about the transmission process. The critical evaluation and selective endorsement of elements of the past by Muslims in the present is not controversial in and of itself. As long as no essential elements are deemed to have been erased or muted in this reception process, the tradition, while only a semblance of what it was in the past, is vested with the authority of being equivalent to its totality in the past, just as the water moves but the river remains the river. Those elements that get picked up in the river are made eligible for assimilation into the corpus of tradition without disfiguring it or tarnishing its authority, as we saw in chapter 4 with the secular conceptions of Islamic expertise. If custodians recognize a set of ideas or practices as part of the tradition, it is vested with full Islamic authority, regardless of its actual origins or the fact that it would have been unknown to the founding generation. Likewise, the transmission of tradition always involves excising parts of tradition that are received and deemed no longer relevant or unimportant. This reflexive view of the transmission of tradition as expanding and contracting over time, with deletions and additions, is not only a scholarly one but also a normative one. In a narrative of the transmission of tradition, the great eighth-century jurist and founder of one of the Sunni schools of law Muhammad ibn Idris al-Shafiʻi not only documented the process of selective transmission at work in Islamic law between the founding generation of the Prophet and the next several generations of Muslims following him, he argued for a new, alternative selection criterion based exclusively on hadith. In other words, although Muslims treat the transmission process as a natural, simple act of passing an untouched tradition through time, they understand that transmission is a process of synthesis; the perpetual debate among Muslims is over the criteria by which custodians operate.[3]

Student-travelers receive tradition from their teachers and peers, who mediate tradition by expanding and contracting what counts as tradition in the here and now, but the Americans also want to participate in the mediation process. Mediating tradition requires people in the present to decide which aspects of the past, or of the present in a different cultural context may be allowed to drop off or at least be deemphasized in the present—in Sakeena's words, the "baggage" of those from whom she receives the tradition. Mediating tradition also requires deciding which elements should be emphasized, highlighted, even added in order to ensure tradition's survival in the future; in Sakeena's case, the pressing realities of her US mosque community shape the criteria by which she identifies elements as traditional or not. Sakeena recognizes that part of the mediation process is the recognition of local needs, and she references al-Shafi'i's example of tailoring his legal rulings to the different cultural contexts of eighth-century Cairo and eighth-century Baghdad. She considers herself an active participant in the transmission process, a custodian filtering what is and is not authentic and essential to her tradition in order to ensure its survival in the future as relevant and meaningful for the American umma.

FAILURE

The desert that is Jordan has had a blizzard: eight heavy inches of a national emergency that has halted the city for five days. As Jawad makes his way out of Shaykh Nuh's neighborhood and down the steep hills, he imagines the remaining puddles in the soggy earth as a blanket of white snow. Most of it has melted away; few signs remain: a few stubborn, molten snowmen, black slush in the gutters, the trees with black, brittle traces of death on their green leaves, like children growing gray.

Jawad is on his way to buy an airline ticket. Jawad's mother called from the emergency room. His father had had a small heart attack, but, thank God, they caught it in time. It is time to go home. That is the right thing to do. Jawad is packing his things. He is not ready to go back. Yet he is excited to go back, dreaming of his mother's curries. And he is mad at himself for it.

"I want to be someone who practices everything he knows. But I know that even if everyone I loved came to Jordan, I would still miss America. That's why I feel like I failed. Shaykh Nuh says that 'The tree planted on a toxic waste dump without being rerooted in new, good soil will produce poisonous fruit.'" This has been another failed attempt to reroot himself. Each time, Jawad's life in Jersey City draws him back.

I tell him that its perfectly natural that he wants to go back home. He bristles: "Why would I want to go back to a place filled with billboards?"

"But Amman is filled with billboards," I respond, baffled. "Actually, a lot of the same billboards."

Jawad is quiet for a moment and then answers slowly, "Yeah, but [Shaykh Nuh's neighborhood] Hay Kherabashah isn't. I am just glad I have a light to follow. Shaykh Nuh always says, 'Eat righteous food because restaurant food is prepared by heedlessness. Food matters. Who prepares it matters.' He says, 'Murids get tripped up by food without knowing it. Salty and fried foods angry up the blood.' And this is one thing I can take back to my dad, to help him with a new diet. Even in my *jahiliyya* [ignorant adolescence], I always ate halal [meat]. That was one thing I always did, even in high school, even when I was messing up."

Jawad worries that Shaykh Nuh is disappointed in him. "I don't bother him with the details about my mistakes, but I know I'm not where I need to be. So I am just embarrassed about saying goodbye to him, 'cause he can see those kinds of things. I have changed some but not enough. You have to change a lot, especially if you expect to change the conditions back home or here. These Arab countries, they are all so close together, like states in America, but the borders here are a nightmare, even with an American passport. Shaykh Nuh was arrested and thrown in jail because they accused him of smuggling books on *tasawwaf* [sufism] into Syria. All of these countries—America, Israel, Jordan—they want to force Islam down because they're scared; they know what's gonna happen."

Jawad is toying with the idea of enrolling in college, maybe majoring in political science. "You know, to help the Muslims." This is what he approaches the shaykh about after 'Isha prayer. When it is his turn to press warm lips to the shaykh's cold hand, he asks his question. When Jawad suggests political science, the shaykh says no. Politics keep you focused on this world. And then, before Jawad can thank him, the shaykh is pulled away by his other students.

Jawad shares his disappointment with one of his other teachers, who tells Jawad something much more disappointing. Jawad brings up the hadith which prophesized the generations that would follow the age of the Prophet: first, the just caliphs, and then kings, and then tyrants, and then caliphs who rule by the teachings of the prophets. Jawad was taught that we are living in the penultimate stage of tyrants, a time of oppression, and that that is why Muslims countries such as Pakistan and Jordan are so corrupt and why the West has so much power. The hadith, however, promises the return of just Muslim rulers, meaning that it is just a matter of time before the corrupt powers collapse on themselves, maybe even in Jawad's own lifetime. But his teacher disagrees: the scholars agree that the righteous caliphs were the Ottomans; their time has come and gone. Now, Muslims can only wait for the signs of the end of time.

"So it's all downhill from here on out, *baji*—until right before *yawm-al-qiyamah* [Judgment Day]," he sighs.

Those lectures and sermons back in Jersey were wrong, Jawad realizes, building a dream of a restored age of just rulers. The scholars had agreed. Now it is a waiting game, but waiting for the end of history, not for glory in history.

This is the latest in a long line of Jawad's small misunderstandings, little pinpricks of disappointment. As a teenager, someone told him that when the American astronauts first stepped on the moon, they had heard the call to prayer, that Neil Armstrong was a secret convert to Islam. "It turned out to be an urban legend." It got him praying, anyway. Maybe it was wrong to look for evidence, or maybe it was just the places Jawad looked for evidence that were wrong. Shaykh Nuh's aura ought to be enough evidence in itself.

Ambivalence in the Archive

As we saw in part 1, Muslim Americans have long been ambivalent about both the state and the American mainstream. Such ambivalence has been reflected in moral geographies that constructed the US and the umma and the Muslim world in relation to each other, articulating religious and political aspirations (and religious and political critiques) by mapping one as dystopic and the other as utopic. The transnational moral geographies produced in these networks reflect the contradictory tensions of being an American religious outsider, of being excluded from social citizenship. Outsiders stigmatize the dominant culture of the US, but simultaneously the American mainstream is also an object of desire. In these networks, the US is often constructed as a possible, thriving place for the future of American Muslims, as we see both in the ansa's suggestion of an American renewer of the faith and in Sakeena's claim that Islam's survival depends on its survival in the US. Moral geographies that map a special potential for Islam in the US, a special status for American Muslims within the global umma, also compete with a different set of moral geographies that are far more ambivalent about Islam's future in the US. However American student-travelers identify sources of traditional knowledge in the Middle East, their journeys are premised on the notion that the dynamic process by which tradition contracts and grows over time and across space pivots on their role as custodians of tradition in the present, through their engagements with other custodians, often their teachers, who reside in the Middle East. As we have seen, student-travelers encounter an earlier generation of American expats (often converts) in these pedagogical networks. These middle-aged American men and women left the US to pursue Islamic higher learning and did not intend to return to the US, such as Shaykh Nuh Keller and Ansa Tamara Gray. Even though most of their devotees plan to return to the US, such as Jawad and Fawzia, these student-travelers share a strong ambivalence about the US as a future site for their tradition to thrive. After all, their American teachers are living examples of a different way of imagining the Islamic East, not as an archive but as home, not as a detour but as a destination.

This process of debating what constitutes tradition, debates that index the social context of the present as well as particular bodies of knowledge, over time and across cultural boundaries, is what gives tradition its life from one generation to the next, from one culture to another. As we will see, the constrictive force of crisis narratives powerfully shapes and limits how American Muslims imagine the transmission process over time and space, and as a result, crisis narratives narrow the possibilities of what American student-travelers are able to do once they return to their US communities. In the crisis narratives that are reproduced in these pedagogical networks, past ruptures continue to be destabilizing forces that threaten tradition, such as colonialism, slavery, and postcolonial reforms of pedagogy in the Middle East. Other crisis narratives focus on contemporary forces that threaten tradition's transmission into the future, such as brutal Arab regimes that suppress the Islamic Revival, Western cultural dominance, the deterioration of family structures under the pressures of late capitalism, or the War on Terror. As a result of imagining a crisis, a rupture between the foundational moment of tradition and the here and now, whether that rupture is in the past or the present, those who are in the role of custodians too often seek to minimize and suppress their own role in the transmission process and to reduce tradition to a fossilized body of (Eastern) knowledge and practices.

American student-travelers construct the gap between the Middle Eastern city-as-archive (and detour) and their US mosques (as destinations) as the "natural" process of the transmission of the Islamic tradition across (cultural) space and over time. This general, default narrative about the nature of tradition's transmission—let us call it the *progressive growth narrative*—is crucial for both these processes. In this narrative, the size of the umma, in terms of numbers of adherents and in terms of cultures touched by Islam, only grows. The gaps between the umma now and the anticipated larger umma of the future are treated as "natural" features of tradition, such as the natural difference between generations of believers which grew over fourteen centuries or the naturalized (and territorialized) cultural differences that simply reflect the diversity of more than a billion Muslims around the world. In a parallel way, at the microscale of individual student-travelers, the lag time between the duration of their studies in the Middle East and their future Islamic work back in the US is constructed as a natural gap in the progressive growth of Islam in the US. In other words, the journeys and studies of American student-travelers are a means to an end as they labor toward a narrowing of the gaps: they seek both to narrow the gap of time (between the recollected past and possible futures) and also to narrow the gap of cultures (between "here" and "there").

Parallel to the default progressive growth narrative of tradition are the less optimistic crisis narratives about the possible demise of tradition. Such rupture narratives of crisis, laments about the interrupted transmission of tradition, reduce tradition to a fossilized body of (Eastern) knowledge and practices, a body forgotten or ignored or tarnished that plods forward, unchanging, through time. In some crisis narratives in these networks, the gaps between American Muslims and their tradition are constructed as unnatural, regressive, even dangerous. These narratives of crisis often pivot on a moral geography that places the relevance and applicability of American Muslims' "local" knowledge of their US communities beyond the boundaries of tradition. As we have seen, one moral geography infuses the US with the utopic possibility of tradition's growth through the efforts of the exceptional American umma, but this local iteration of the progressive growth narrative competes with another, less optimistic moral geography of the US, as a dystopia, as a place American Muslims must leave or at least temporarily escape in order to recharge spiritually. It is this latter moral geography that undermines the collective project of "establishing" Islam in the US, the collective project which drives so many American Muslim student-travelers' journeys in the first place. When tradition is reduced to a static, reified object that moves through time and space, as it is in the crisis narratives that treat the US as a spiritual dystopia, then American student-travelers can be mere carriers of tradition, maintaining tradition at best. They cannot be custodians of tradition, mediating Islamic knowledge in US mosques, engaging in debates.

As a result, the nature of the transmission of tradition, particularly the role of custodians in tradition, is sometimes suppressed and denied altogether. In other cases, American student-travelers are denied the role of mediating tradition by their peers and teachers in these networks precisely *because* they are Americans, even by individuals, such as Gray and Keller, who are American expats themselves. Such suppressions and denials of the reflexive dimension of transmission emerges out of a sense of crisis that is manifest as a lack of confidence in American student-travelers to oversee the transmission of tradition, to link the present to the past meaningfully enough such that tradition survives into the future, in a place where Muslims are not only a minority but are believed to be under siege, culturally and politically. Some of the teachers, including American teachers, in these networks do not trust American student-travelers to suture their American Muslim contexts to Islamic pasts, in part because the dominant American culture is perceived as too overwhelming. Much of the discomfort with the idea of (American) custodians who selectively expand and contract tradition is linked to fears about the idiosyncratic standards they might apply in the US, leaving off essential elements of tradition and adding ones that disfigure Islam in the name of accommodating the local needs of American Muslims, ultimately assimilating to the American mainstream. In Sakeena's case, that is precisely what she aims to do; however, Jawad and

Fawzia internalize the anxieties of their teachers and are less clear on how they might "establish" Islam in the US.

Gray explicitly offers her students the possibility of being "renewers" of the faith who could "resolve" the crisis of Islam, invoking the default narrative of transmission, the progressive growth of Islam into the future and in the US (and, importantly, led by a woman). In the same breath, she invokes the competing moral geography of the US as a spiritual dystopia; she makes it clear that her American students are carriers maintaining tradition and not mediators of tradition, and she presents the transmission process in ideological terms, as a simple preservation. As Gray imparts advice to Fawzia, she codes the maintenance of particular religious practices (such as wearing *hijab* and a modest overcoat) as a measure of one's ability to resist the pressures of the dominant American culture; she dismisses former students who fail to do so as "wimps," weak links in the chain that buckle under social and political pressure and compromise the integrity of the tradition. Rather than preparing her devotees to engage in a raging debate about modesty in US mosques, Gray draws lines in what she casts as a culture war. She dismisses changes of dress among her former devotees (what are also changes in ritual practice) as a religious failure or as a cultural concession to dominant Western norms, rather than seriously engaging the arguments that might produce such discontinuities (or, from her perspective, heterodox interpretations). In fact, she does not elaborate a legal argument to support her tradition claim for her students.

After the party, I asked Fawzia if she felt prepared to engage in the heated debates on the requirements of Islamic modesty in US mosques on her return, and she confessed with trepidation that she did not. She did note that the Qubaysi practice of concealing their hair and bodies even in the company of other women, an unusual and controversial practice in Muslim counterpublics in Syria, did confirm and authenticate what she once disparaged as her mother's "Bengali" habit of wearing a light shawl even in the privacy of her own home, a modest practice Fawzia believed to be inauthentic, merely "cultural, not Islamic." Gray taught Fawzia to see the practice of modesty even in private as a means to populate one's home with angels, as Gray teaches angels are repelled by immodest dress and drawn to Quranic recitation. While Gray is explicit that American elements must not find their way into tradition, she simultaneously prioritizes local, even idiosyncratic practices of modesty, and she encourages her students to practice and preserve them in the US. Another one of her strict interpretations of Islamic modesty, interpretations that generate heated debate in Muslim counterpublics in Damascus as well as in US mosques, is the overcoat, which she identifies as a traditional form that must be preserved, granting it the status of a universal traditional practice that transcends cultural boundaries and social contexts. In fact, the overcoat is a local, Syrian cultural form (referred to in French as *manteau*, the term itself a colonial vestige), but rather than make a case for it, Gray invokes it as a piety litmus test.

The dynamic process of evaluation, amplification, suppression, refinement, and assessment—informed by faith and energized by pragmatism—allows the custodians of tradition to unite their veneration for a sacred past with a skepticism about its relevance for the present without violating tradition.[4] However, in the context of crisis, custodians of tradition suppress skepticism and insist only on veneration, undermining the very lifeblood of tradition, its debates. Indeed, denial of custodianship, of the reflexive and dynamic qualities of tradition, is a distinctive feature of crisis. Although the American teachers that student-travelers encounter in the Middle East, such as Gray, are engaged in the work of custodianship, too often these American teachers do not transfer those custodial skills to their students and devotees. They model a particular ambivalence toward the US, a sense of outsiderhood even when they posit the US as a place for Islam's potential growth. This was an argument I had with many female scholars including Qubaysi ansas. I took issue with the inordinate amount of attention and energy spent on discussions of modesty, as though it were the singular ethical and social issue of the day, as a way to open a discussion on the reflexivity of the transmission of tradition. I challenged them to consider the responsibility of the scholars, men and especially women scholars, in skewing the religious discourse in this manner. Different amounts of gravity are assigned to some verses and not others, and so some themes in the Quran float high and others low, buoyed by the scholars' whims and inclinations, their attractions and repulsions. Again and again, they countered that it is the scholars' expertise that gives them deeper insights into which parts of the tradition are most relevant and pressing given the circumstances of the day.

While gender questions are especially likely to elicit defensive responses, as we saw in the previous chapter, debates about Islamic pedagogy and its reform are also constrained by crisis. The Qubaysi teachers are reticent to admit that their criteria for *ijaza* (licenses) in Quranic recitation reflect the needs and lifestyles of their students, such that the complete memorization of the Quran is no longer a condition for the certification of American students. Although they claim to be pure formalists, this is an example of a pragmatist, pedagogical concession. This is akin to the way the ansas "Islamicize" the lyrics of American pop songs. In both instances, Gray is engaging in the custodial work of tradition: assessing the needs of people in the present in order to amplify, suppress, modify, add, and delete various elements of tradition to ensure its survival into the future. With her invocation of crisis, her denial of the reflexivity in the transmission process actually begins to obstruct and hinder the work of tradition that American student-travelers, like Fawzia, claim they want to do when they return to the US.

Of course, there are always elements of tradition that are uncritically taken for granted, just as there are always anticritical employments of tradition that deny any human role in the transmission process. In order to be healthy, a tradition is not required to sustain an absolute transparent reflexivity. After all, in the context of a religious debate, one's claims are only enhanced by the illusion that tradition is a simple movement of a body of static beliefs and practices through time, for example, the unbroken chain of Fawzia's teachers. It is perfectly natural that over the course of debating heated religious questions, ordinary Muslims will "appeal to the notion that their way of understanding is not only 'Islamic' but 'natural' or 'God-given,' as opposed to 'artificial,' 'contrived,' 'alien,' or even 'man-made.'"[5] However, insofar as Gray hopes to produce female students who will renew Islam in the future and in the US, the consequences of her knee-jerk denial of reflexivity in the transmission process are substantial: the American student-travelers often do not accrue the religious authority they are working toward in these networks in the Middle East. This does not mean that they do not accrue any authority. After all, Fawzia is now authorized to teach Quranic recitation in the US with the sanction of a formal *ijaza* (despite the fact that she has not memorized the Quran in its entirety).

However, the ambition Fawzia articulates, her strong desire to resolve the crisis of authority in US mosques, to make religious debates more coherent, was neither nurtured nor developed over the course of her studies in Syria.

Similarly, Keller's depictions of the US as a dystopic, spiritual toxic-waste dump and his expectation for his students to relinquish their attachments to the world, and specifically *that* cultural world—in Jawad's case, politics, basketball, fast food—fails to prepare Jawad for one of his goals, returning to the US "to help the Muslims," as he puts it. Of course, relinquishment can be a useful pious practice and does not have to be punishing if an alternative, productive model is offered or developed. In other words, the teachers and peers of the student-travelers in the Middle East often offer an orientation to the US that is not conducive to the work of making American Islamic debates more coherent. Instead, debate is often suppressed, such as when Jawad's Arabic teacher convinces him that there is scholarly consensus that the Prophetic hadith promising a more just world order in the future refers to an earlier historical period. In other words, rather than trying to persuade him that one interpretation is more compelling than another (certainly the backward-looking one is a dominant interpretation, though the dignity revolutions in the Middle East might beg a different interpretation), Jawad's teacher focuses only on persuading him that there is no debate, no other possible interpretations, that scholarly consensus has made it a moot issue. Of course, the claim of scholarly consensus, whether on the interpretation of this hadith or on the relative importance and even the definition of female modesty, begs the question of how narrowly one must define *scholar* and *consensus* in order to make the claim.[6]

What is striking about the ideological claims, these abridgements of history, made about tradition in the name of crisis is not only the ways argument and critical engagement with tradition is suppressed but the ways the work of tradition itself is divorced from participation in a faith community. In other words, the options for effecting change in US mosque communities offered in many of these networks is remarkably narrow and highly individualized: teaching Quranic recitation and dressing modestly even in private for Fawzia or, in Jawad's case, designing a diet for his father based on Keller's teachings on the concentrations and absences of blessings in food. As carriers of tradition rather than custodians, as we will see in the next chapter, American student-travelers have a very limited impact in their US mosques on a communal scale, even though most of them find their journeys and studies abroad personally fulfilling. In fact, this parallels Malcolm X's experience as a student-traveler in Saudi Arabia in 1964, as discussed in chapter 3. His formal studies in the Middle East were certainly personally transformative, but they were not translated to his Muslim followers back in the US in a meaningful way. American student-travelers are too often reduced to simple carriers of sanctified, fossilized elements of the past, and in pedagogical networks in the Middle East, they are often convinced that this is all they can be.

THE UNSEEN

"The thing about having a shaykh is you have someone to take guidance from," Jawad explains. "You try to get as much of his guidance for everything: education, marriage, traveling, anything." I feel a warm, protective tug toward Jawad, but his shaykh remains an enigma to me: his quiet and stillness, the slowness of his physical movements, his reclusive habits. But Jawad hangs on every word his teacher utters. He reads a small pamphlet over and over in which Shaykh Nuh recounts his slow discovery of Islam as a young student at the University of Chicago, inspired in part by summer jobs as a deck hand and brushes with death at sea. Jawad had underlined this passage: "The great natural events of the sea surrounding us seemed to defy, with their stubborn, irreducible facticity, our uncomprehending attempts to come to terms with them. Suddenly, we were just there, shaken by the forces around us without making sense of them, wondering if we would make it through. Some, it was true, would ask God's help at such moments, but when we returned safely to shore, we behaved . . . as if those moments had been a lapse into insanity, embarrassing to think of at happier times. It was one of the lessons of the sea that . . . [man] was small and weak, the forces around him were large, and he did not control them."

The enormous importance Jawad ties to the tiny amounts of attention and direction that he gets from his sufi master troubles me. But whenever I hint at my feelings and doubts, Jawad counters that it is probably just my ego, stung by the possibility that he sees something in his teacher that I cannot see. There are few clues to Shaykh Nuh's ordinary, bookish life with his wife in their spare home. In fact, their home has very, very few personal effects at all. When one enters bathrooms in Arab homes, there are often slippers of different sizes at the doorway to be worn only there. Shaykh Nuh's bathroom has large, black rubber boots to change into instead, so as not to take even a trace of impurity from the bathroom into the rest of the house. As I stand in his tall, black boots in his bathroom, I wonder if they are like the ones he wore as a young fisherman when he saw the ocean as a sign.

Shaykh Nuh is a man who is constantly praying and constantly reading. Is that not the Prophetic way, to live as though you had seen your death, as though it had come right before your eyes? I am struck by his soft voice and his clear, hard eyes, but I am most struck that I never feel moved in his presence the way so many others do.

It is not that sufis or stillness or long silences or the idea of a sixth sense make me uncomfortable or even skeptical. My mother is a sufi, but not the kind in an order such as Shaykh Nuh's, not the kind with a formal teacher and formal assignments. My mother is her own shaykha. When good things happen to me, I wonder if they might just be divine answers to her constant prayers. For as long as I can remember, my mother has had a practice of not speaking to people between dawn and the late morning because she is in a state of silent remembrance, constantly, barely audibly breathing divine names and prayers. She still does everything: she makes breakfast, makes beds, makes lunches, makes lists on Post-it notes so that no one forgets what they have to do that day. She just does not speak to anyone but God in the morning.

Shaykh Nuh teaches and models the same kind of ethos of remembrance. I record his faint, monotone voice as it comes over the speakers: "The sign of a person whose heart is filled with the remembrance of Allah is that the person does not get bored because the *dhikr* [remembrance] has taken root. The mark of a dark soul is that you cannot talk to him for five minutes about the soul before he gets nervous and wants to change the subject to something *dunyawi* [worldly]. 'When can we talk about something that matters?'"

Shaykh Nuh reminds his students in his lectures that the obligation to remember God is not a license, a free pass, an absolving of the obligations of the world, invoking the example of his own teacher. "Shaykh AbdurRahman never had a moment's rest. He didn't have a cave in Tibet to gaze at his navel for sixty years. He was always engaged in the real world. [The eighth-century jurist] Abu Hanifa was a *tajir* [merchant]. It's not a cute anecdote. He had shops, and he provided opportunities to some to study [with his material support] anonymously. Work for a living, but don't think you are working for a living. There's only value in your work if you see Who is creating it. If you do things with the desire to see Allah, then you begin to see Allah in everything you do, phenomenally. Somebody who doesn't know how to work, who has been in a state of perpetual scholarship since kindergarten, has never gotten out of the knot of selfishness."

As Shaykh Nuh elaborates this point, I wonder how many in his audience have held odd jobs all through school the way I had, the way Jawad had. I know many of the American women I am huddled against on the floor have never worked a day in their lives. His advanced students run several successful businesses out of Amman: a magazine, a publishing house, a modest Islamic fashion line, an online fatwa site, a distance-learning course, and a newly launched Arabic program for Americans. But most of the devotees do not hold jobs in Jordan. Most of his devotees barely interact with Jordanians at all, save the few who are also Shaykh Nuh's devotees.

My mother works in a department store. She folds men's jeans into perfect flat squares and piles them into perfect, square stacks, and she joins the stacks in perfect, even rectangles lining long, white shelves. She tags and detags, prices and reprices, and she sorts and hangs and folds men's clothes five days a week. No one notices that when she is not talking to a customer or to one of her co-workers, she is remembering, praying in a voice far, far softer than a whisper, in tiny, barely perceptible movements of her lips.

Shaykh Nuh teaches his devotees about ways of seeing. A stand of trees is a forest for the poet, lumber to the capitalist, but those trees are a manifestation of the divine to the mystic. "The *dunya* [world] raises some and lowers others. 'How glorious is He who did not make anyone guided except those whom He wanted to guide.' What does [the verse] mean? There were so many contemporaries of the Prophet, *sallalahu alayhiwasalam* [peace be upon him], who got nothing out of [knowing him], and they died as *kafirs* [nonbelievers]. They didn't see him as a prophet, only as the orphan of Abu Talib." This is guidance, the blessing of being able to recognize the truth in front of your eyes.

Over the years, I have learned to see how money forms and widens an aching gap between my mother and me. Once I told her that I wished she did not work for minimum wage, folding jeans for hours and hours. She tried to show me how to see those stacks of navy-blue jeans as something else, how to see navy-blue fibers of cotton dissolve into invisible Arabic letters hanging in the air, how to see a gap between us that left me behind.

That is what came before my eyes as Shaykh Nuh closed his lesson: "Whoever is preoccupied with this world is afflicted with being humiliated in it. The sufi path does not reject working in the world, only being preoccupied with it. The *dunya* [world] is a curse, and everything in it is a curse except that in which Allah's countenance is sought."

Scripting a Resolution of the Crisis

Although very few of these American expats are as high-profile and well-regarded scholars as Shaykh Nuh Keller is, these American teachers play an important role in the debate in the Middle East about the future of Islam in the US. Keller's introductory manual outlines the rules for living in his sufi enclave in Amman; it is replete with stigmatizations of American cultural forms, simply, it seems, because they are American, such as the rule that devotees are forbidden to wear jeans even in the privacy of their own homes; they are to avoid those parts of the city that are Westernizing, restaurants, the gym, the hair dresser. Keller stigmatizes jeans as a form of aping the West and capitulating to the pressures of global capitalism, akin to the ways Elijah Muhammad forbade blacks to straighten their hair or how he forbade them from consuming traditional "soul food," what he termed "slave foods." Both religious leaders draw on the stigma of inauthenticity as a source of spiritual, psychological, and material protection for their devotees from the corrosive qualities of a (now global) dominant American culture. Although most of Keller's American devotees plan to return to the US, and they talk about their journeys and studies in the Middle East as a means and not an end, invoking the moral geography of the Islamic

East as Archive, the ubiquitous presence of American teachers and peers who have left the US permanently challenges this moral geography. After all, for Keller, the Middle East and not the US is now home; his intentional community in Amman is an escape from the spiritual dystopia of the US and the "westoxifying," "modernizing" dystopic elements of Amman. Although the Qubaysiyat, the advanced students of knowledge in Syria and Egypt, and Keller's Shadhili order in Amman are effective at teaching the knowledge and skills that satisfy individual seekers, their vocabularies are not amenable to scripting narratives that will resolve the communal crisis in US mosques. Nor do they give the student-travelers the skills and the sense of ownership of the tradition that custodianship requires.

By extracting and deterritorializing sacred knowledge, American student-travelers hope to reintroduce a common vocabulary of argumentation in their mosques, to develop a local, American expression of Islam, safeguarded from the incoherence and instability of crisis. Islamic bodies of knowledge must be made compelling and relevant to be persuasive; they cannot simply be retrieved from the insides of dusty books in dusty Middle Eastern cities. If they are to be custodians, American student-travelers must recognize the elements of tradition as well as local (in this case, American) ideas and practices that may be admitted into tradition, as they are relevant to the present and the future. This requires not only competence but also confidence in their local knowledge and their role as custodians, something that student-travelers rarely develop in the Middle East. Insofar as the Americans' project of "establishing Islam" back to the US is a communal project, it is, by their measure, a failed project; the detour simply turns into another road. American student-travelers do obtain Islamic knowledge in the Middle East, and they may develop deep relationships to teachers and peers. However, for the most part, American student-travelers fail to develop a reflexive orientation toward tradition as custodians in the pedagogical margins of Cairo, Damascus, and Amman. They fail to develop the skills and training needed to transmit that knowledge back to their US communities. They fail to engage in their mosque communities in the US in ways that facilitate a wider body of American Muslims participating in the debates that constitute tradition. Ironically, just as with the gendered debates over Islamic authority in the previous chapter, this failure to find a reflexive archive in the Middle East is directly related to the same urgent sense of crisis that drives their journeys to the Middle East in the first place.

"FIQHED UP"

Shaykh Firas recommended an introductory legal manual written in the eleventh century as a key text for me to study: the esteemed Hanafi scholar Imam Hasan Al-Shurunbulali's *The Light of Clarification*. He explained why we should read the Damascene edition of the book, which also includes Imam Al-Shurubalali's abridged commentary on his legal treatise, and he warned that the edition published in Beirut is not good, emphatically stressing how important it is to consider the publisher before choosing a text. Too often, he complained, earnest students end up studying texts littered with mistakes and, in the case of many Saudi editions, the willful distortions and omissions of ideologically driven Wahhabi editors.

The majority of our lessons were spent slowly making our way line by line through this text and excerpts from more advanced ones. Classical legal manuals all have roughly the same order of chapters. We read through an eleventh-century abridged edition of the original, even older book that summarizes its ritual law chapter: specifically, the rules of ritual purification, prayer, fasting, alms, and pilgrimage. We spent hours learning what did and did not make water ritually impure. If a bird had died in a well, it was impure, but if a lion had only submerged his paw in a lake, the water was usable. The details were often tedious and arcane, but the shaykh taught us to see the rhythms of the genre of positive law and gave us peeks into its deeper logics. Jurists often offer rulings on hypothetical "edge cases" of unlikely circumstances to make a fine legal point. Legal manuals list such hypothetical scenarios as illustrations, for example, how to determine who ought to lead the prayer as imam in a group of peers, ordering criteria according to importance. While the ones at the top of the list are reasonable, even self-evident (the prayer ought to be led by whoever had more of the Quran memorized or whoever was older or whoever lived closest nearby), the criteria become more and more arbitrary, even offensive, moving down the list. One of the last criteria I found so absurd that I wondered if it was a joke:

if all else was held equal, the man with the most beautiful wife ought to lead the prayer.

I found the human fingerprints in Islamic law fascinating but also troubling when taken for granted. Shaykh Firas always found my offhanded criticisms insufficiently deferential, but when I mentioned the example to an advanced American student of knowledge, I was surprised that he had a similar reaction. He defensively reminded me that to criticize a luminary in Islamic history such as the great jurist and author who had written the book I was reading was like criticizing a Companion of the Prophet because of the unbroken pedagogical chain. He added coolly that to criticize a Companion was to criticize the Prophet himself, and he recommended a classical text that details the proper etiquette of the student of knowledge.

When I share the anecdote with Usman, he jokes that the traditional scholars and students of knowledge in Damascus could use a public-relations campaign. "The Prophet was known for smiling, and scholars and students of knowledge are not known for smiling. I understand why, but I don't want to become like them. With the cultural warfare that's going on in the Muslim world, traditional scholars and students are on the defense, on the edge, and when you are defensive, you get negative. I've become a lot less romantic about the cultural past as I used to be. Nonetheless, a lot of religious people, and rightly so, feel that their tradition is being forced to die, that the West is stomping all over it—and also Muslims in these countries: the bourgeoisie, the elite, the secularists. Especially the moral changes, their traditional family roles, societal roles are all changing, and they are bothered. Some of it is that they don't have the intellectual tools to deal with it, or they're kind of bewildered; and for others, it is that the speed, how much things are changing and how quickly—and it's too much to handle."

Usman cannot count the number of discussions he has had over thick, fragrant Turkish coffee bemoaning those changes, too many and too fast, and mourning the losses that have slipped through the cracks. "There's been an overhaul in the way the traditional 'ulama were looked at in the past hundred years that's completely different; now, almost no respect, whatever, politically—it's completely lip service. So if they see the news or a girl dressed a certain way [or] a guy drinking, they are ready to rip [them apart]. They are justified in not liking *haram* [sinful] things, but the lashing out is not justified. In the religious circles, dogmatism turns everything into a sin, and so the students of knowledge are isolated in this bubble. All they have is their *thawbs* [robes] and their shaykhs, and their biggest problem is which [religious institute] to join. It is a very distorted, isolated experience of Damascus and elitist because everyone outside of that circle [is] these poor, poor humans infatuated with the West, and so you start feeling superior. And it's like, 'OK, this is not what I came here for. What are you doing to make it better? Walk around the city with this sour look on your face of disapproving?' So they have the crisis element, too, but less of 'How can I make an impact?'"

In the course of Usman's classical studies, he found that he had changed so much and so fast that he hardly recognized himself, a period he and his friends have nicknamed "the fiqhed-up phase." "You go through the personal crisis after a certain amount of years here; we all have. And I did start to become so harsh, like, 'Oh, that woman is wearing makeup; she's showing that body part.' And so you get into that mentality of seeing everything in terms of legal permissibility. And it can overwhelm your focus. I was to the point that I was at a *qiyam* [vigil] in Ramadan, and I'm reading *fiqh* [law]. And my friend notices, and he kicks my foot, and he's just like, '*Ya Sidi*, get up and pray.' I mean, it may be good to know *fiqh*, but if that's all you are, you're not going to change the world with that, and you're not even going to change yourself with that. So I had to get away from some of the legalism. What my teachers taught me is that it's not about who is most scrupulous to the details, who is harder on himself or others, although there are elements of that in our *din* [tradition], but that asceticism should be on the inside. It shouldn't be directed or appear outward."

Usman's frustrations with his friends grew into a personal crisis. He would sit in the circle on the floor of the mosque and watch with the feeling of sinking into the thin carpet as students competed for the shaykh's attention the way flowers compete for sunlight, silently, hungrily, movements so slight they were barely perceptible. Soon their true colors and petty jealousies were in full bloom.

"Coming out of that phase, I definitely became jaded with the students of knowledge. I would see these people doing these power politics, dirty looks, backbiting, and it's over nothing. And it's so stupid and petty 'cause nobody is getting any power or money. I'm thinking,

'You're all just a bunch of poor people in the mosque.' Or you see some-one saying one thing in a lesson and doing something totally different in his business transactions. And I came here thinking, 'These people are these pure souls.' Most of us come very romanticized: everything in the East is good, all of the *shuyukh* [teachers] are good, all the people I see at the *masjid* [mosque] are good. And if you're honest, you have a crisis because all the materialism and gossip and arrogance you were running from [in the US], you find it here. 'God, if they are petty, what chance do I have?' You get to the point where you say, 'Well, all I have is Allah,' which is the critical lesson."

Much of Usman's time in Damascus had been learning what his books did not know or could not tell him. It was more than a matter of missing pages or lack of access. In those moments, Shaykh Nuh's words rang true: "The seeker hungers for knowledge, but only as a tool of obedience."

That was all. Knowledge could be no more than a tool. And cocked the right way, it could just as easily become a weapon.

Confidence in Transmission

If tradition is conceived of as open, unfolding arguments, participation in the arguments requires a confidence in one's voice. In general, this con-fidence is not found or cultivated in the archive; the American student-travelers' inability to develop and nurture this communal confidence, as we will see, obstructs their ability to "establish Islam" back in the US. The discourse of crisis of their teachers and peers in the Middle East who sup-press and deny their own custodial work as well as the inherent reflexivity of tradition is one factor that constrains the transmission process. Ideo-logical claims in the name of crisis unnecessarily expand the domain of tradition that cannot be challenged, eliminating spaces of doubt, ambigu-ity, criticism, and reflexivity. Jaroslav Pelikan has termed this ideological suppression and abridgement of tradition "traditionalism."

Tradition is the living faith of the dead; traditionalism is the dead faith of the living. Tradition lives in conversation with the past, while remember-ing where we are and when we are and that it is we who have to decide. Traditionalism supposes that nothing should ever be done for the first time, so all that is needed to solve any problem is to arrive at the supposedly unanimous testimony of this homogenized tradition.[7]

This anti-intellectual tendency—itself a symptom of crisis—diminishes tradition even as it purports to preserve it, for it suppresses rather than nurtures engagement and argument.

Shaykh Ali Gomaa recognizes this anti-intellectual tendency to suppress debate as a particular problem for American Muslim teachers and student-travelers precisely because of their deep ambivalence about the US. He believes that in the course of living in a place such as Egypt, American student-travelers develop a sense of Islamic deficiency. As he explained this to me in his home office, he stretched his leg out from underneath his long white robe, revealing thick, black wool socks. He ran his big toe along an intricate, diamond-shaped frieze in the center of the silk rug, pointing out the perfection of its symmetry even to the tiniest details of its design.

> This, this rug, this artistry, is the mark of Islamic civilization, of Islamic genius, of thousands of years. We [in the Middle East] are surrounded by the Islamic civilization. It is in this carpet and it is in the books of law, but we may find imperfections in them. When we are steeped in our civilization, our tradition, these imperfections will not disturb us the way they will disturb someone who feels deficient. Advanced American students of knowledge often feel deficient in civilization and confuse it for deficiency in religion. Of course, American Muslims will always be deficient in Islamic civilization. They are products of American culture, which has its own system and mores. America is not empty of culture, nor is its culture the same as its products. For example, premarital sex is impermissible in Islam but an acceptable practice in the US. Even within an irreligious social order, which as Muslims we cannot accept, we should understand that Americans still have a moral system, concepts of jealousy and fidelity and manliness and skill, such that some men are "players" and others "player haters." This is the psychological complex of American Muslims who confuse culture and civilization with religion. . . . They don't know whether to be jealous of Western civilization or to be jealous of what we [Arabs] have, [immersed in] Islamic civilization.

Gomaa refers to the double consciousness and false consciousness engendered in American Muslims as religious minorities in the US, which exacerbates the sense of religious crisis. Although he concedes that American Muslims must mediate tradition, as we saw in chapter 4, Gomaa himself is suspicious of what pragmatist and reformist American students believe they are transmitting to the US, that they might be accorded an authority that they do not deserve. In other words, even among those scholars who seek to empower American Muslims, religious authority is tightly guarded and withheld from most of the American student-travelers who study abroad. It is precisely these pragmatist and reformist students who make up the bulk of the American seekers in these networks, who want to study abroad in order to impact their Muslim communities back in the US.

Although the journeys of these student-travelers are challenging and powerfully transformative at the individual level, at the communal level, it becomes quite clear that "carrying" sacred knowledge back to the US will not be enough to alleviate the American crisis of authority. Islamic bodies of knowledge must be made compelling and relevant to be authoritative, not simply retrieved. Furthermore, American student-travelers often find that the requisite local knowledge of the discursive conditions of US mosques is simply not waiting in the archives of the Middle East. The mediation of tradition, its selective preservation and modifications in the present, is not something that student-travelers are trained to do in the Middle East. Student-travelers often find that the cultural realities and discursive conditions of the religious debates in the Middle East, even if over the same religious questions, often diverge too much from their iterations in American Muslim counterpublics.

WIZARDS AND LORDS

"I'm not here for a fatwa," Asma tells Usman flatly.

Usman chuckles and reassures her that he does not make fatwas; he is only a student of the law. Immediately, Usman knows it will be a tough session by the fire in her eyes. Asma is so petite that she looks like a teenager, but she is actually twenty-six. Usman notes the absence of her wedding ring and feels weary immediately, anticipating her painful story and hot tears and not least because he had spent a good part of the day trying to remedy the damage of an electrical fire at his shaykh's house caused by the refurbished air-conditioner Usman had bought him.

The great Shaykh 'Abd Al-Rahman Al-Shaguri, the shaykh of Usman's own teacher, Shaykh Nuh, personally sent Asma to seek Usman's counsel. Usman cannot imagine how this Pakistani American woman who speaks almost no Arabic managed to get permission to visit the great "living *wali*" (saint) in the first place, but he just smiles and asks her if she likes Damascus, as his wife serves us tea and cardamom cookies. Asma made her trip to Syria in order to perfect her Quranic recitation. She wants to expand the Quran class that she teaches in her local mosque in Houston. The trip is also an excuse to get away from the highly charged and emotionally draining environment of her family and mosque community.

For the past eight months, she explains, she has been living with her parents. She left her husband of three years and has been struggling to get a divorce, which he is unwilling to grant her. She says that she wants to end "the contract [she] made before God before dealing with the lawyers." Her condition of wanting an Islamic divorce first before going through the civil courts has prolonged an already incredibly painful process.

Usman quietly asks her to explain what happened. Asma composes herself and in an exhausted voice tells the story she has told too many times. They were college sweethearts and married shortly after graduation. The first few months were fine, but then her husband got laid off. He was devastated and sank into a deep depression. He would not leave the apartment for weeks. Everyone was worried and urged her to support him and be patient. Weeks of depression turned into months, and some days he would not even change out of his pajamas or take a shower. To make matters worse, they became financially dependent on his parents, and her mother-in-law became more involved, blaming Asma for her son's depression, for being cold. Asma packed her bags and moved back home.

At first, Asma's family begged her to go back to him and even offered to support them financially. When her husband got a new job, she relented and returned, but there was so much tension between them that she came back to her parents' house after five days. He quit the new job a few weeks later. Convinced at last, her parents broached the subject of divorce, but her husband swore to them he would never grant her a divorce. They involved the local imam, who initially discouraged her from divorcing and advised her to be patient and merciful with her troubled husband. Things went back and forth for months.

Once the imam realized that reconciliation was unlikely, he advised Asma to initiate an alternative form of Islamic divorce, a *khul'* divorce, by giving up the $15,000 that had been his marriage gift to her. The problem was that since they were in the US, there was no Islamic court to officiate and enforce a *khul'* divorce initiated by a wife. Asma still had to convince her husband to let her divorce him. Her husband told her that he would decide if or when they got a divorce.

Her voice quivering with emotion, she vows, "If one more person, one more person, comes to me to tell me, 'Oh, I don't believe in divorce. People give up too easily,' or 'God, it's getting too easy to get a divorce,' I'll just, I don't know. I mean, getting this divorce has been the hardest thing I've ever done! I don't know why they think it's too easy. If anything, it should be made easier!"

We were silent for a moment. Usman's expression remained soft and thoughtful as he listened to Asma, and he had said very little. Now, in a soothing tone, he reassures her that divorce is legally permitted in Islam and that no one could argue divorce is a sin.

After weeks of trying to mediate, it was clear to the imam that Asma's husband was not going to budge. The imam brought up a new possibility. Since they were in a non-Muslim country, in lieu of a judge in an Islamic court, her imam would assemble a team of imams who collectively would wield the authority to grant her the divorce. The problem was the other imams did not think she should get the divorce. Despite her protests, they cautioned her about the high divorce rate in the US and the lack of patience among her generation. Life was full of tests, they warned, and it would never be perfect. Her husband's behavior, they conceded, was a serious problem, but nothing that could not be fixed, maybe with medication—he was, after all, a good, God-fearing man. They offered to draft a contract stipulating her return under the condition that he get a job and continue therapy and that she should meanwhile treat him nicely. Asma was shocked. After her ordeal, the imams would still not grant her the divorce she had been trying to get for almost a year.

"Why? Divorce is a halal [Islamically sanctioned] option! I'd rather be alone for the rest of my life than live with a depressed person. And they denied me this for what? A statistic? It's so unfair!" Asma's tears were flowing freely now. "What do statistics have to do with *fiqh* [law]? *Fiqh* has failed me!"

Usman pours her another glass of ice water. She drinks it in hurried gulps, but it does not calm her much. "It turns out that if I just get a normal, American civil divorce, *sharia* recognizes it anyway. That's what my imam told me right before I came to Syria. So I don't even need this *khul'* thing, really. They could have just told me that from the beginning, but instead these imams make me go through all of this just to do nothing in the end. If I had just gotten an American divorce lawyer a year ago, this whole thing would be over by now."

Asma wipes her face with a wad of tissues. "These imams don't realize what they do to people's *iman* [faith]. I was doing all of this because I thought it was the right thing to do, the Islamic thing to do. I thought I had to go through this, that God was punishing me, that Islamically I had to, but it turns out this torture of hanging in the middle is just because of nothing. Our imam told me that the purpose of *fiqh* is to make things clearer, but me insisting I wanted this whole thing handled Islamically first, *fiqh*-wise first, before the American courts, made everything a million times more painful and unclear. I mean, for months I'm going, 'OK, has my *'iddah* [postdivorce waiting] period started or not?' Even now, who knows? What you realize is that what you think of as a divine legal process is just totally haphazard and subjective and dependent on the personalities of a bunch of middle-aged men who happen to be *'ulama* [scholars]. Their reasons for denying me my divorce in the beginning was not on some religious basis. I mean their logic was 'be patient" and "there are too many divorces.' That doesn't make any sense! Does the number of divorces in your community make it *haram* [wrong]?"

Usman calmly reminds her that the pain she endured would not go unrecognized. God willing, she will be rewarded for her patience. Asma is relieved that he does not press with questions or ask her to justify her decision. She begins again, now in a quiet, tired voice. "This whole process, it just really tested my *iman*. I had so much trust in their knowledge, and then this whole thing. It was like Dorothy in *The Wizard of Oz*, you know, when she pulls back the curtain and it turns out the wizard is human just like her? That—that hurt me, that feeling of—God, I don't know. You know how in the Quran when Allah is talking about the Jews with their rabbis and Christians making their monks lords? I just—I had to separate my *iman* from *fiqh*. I told myself I am not going to make these imams my lords."

Usman tells the story of the woman who approached the Prophet in order to obtain a divorce, comparing her husband to a loose thread on the Prophet's garment to signal that she was sexually unsatisfied. The Prophet granted her the divorce, proof that her dissatisfaction was grounds enough. Asma raises her eyebrows and marvels at the frankness of this woman. Usman repeats the hadith that his shaykh always recited: "There is no shyness in matters of religion."

Asma smiles, but not with her eyes.

Resolving the Crisis of Authority

As a temporal relationship, authority binds us to something beyond ourselves, the same way that love binds us to another person. The binding of love is far from a simple choice, and yet it still feels natural, organic, and spontaneous. We do not choose to love just as we do not choose what compels us, what we consider authoritative. Asma's love for her husband dissolves, and in the course of her divorce and through the coercion of the council of imams, she comes to see the human limits of Islamic law and its material irrelevance; the authority she once granted scholars of Islamic law also dissolves. Like Dorothy in *The Wizard of Oz*, she finds she had the power all along to enact a divorce enforceable by the state and recognized by Islamic law without knowing it.

Crises of authority operate in qualitatively different ways at the different scales of the individual and the community. The fragmentation of authority, new forms of sociality, the deterritorialization of religious debates—all these pressures lead American Muslims to identify sources of incoherence in contemporary Muslim debates, sources of crisis. Insofar as a community widely recognizes its own cognitive dissonance and incoherence as a crisis, that sense of crisis remains until the community accepts a new narrative to order, and encircle, its world, a new moral geography that captures its religious imagination.[8] American

Muslims' common questions bind them to Muslim counterpublics, where through public debate they negotiate the meanings of revelation and their religious heritage, where they collectively construct narratives of crisis and resolution. The individual experience of the crisis does not require a rational argumentation the way communal debates about religious crisis do; for individual believers, their questioning is not necessarily, or even usually, confrontational questioning. For believers, the gap between what can be known and what can be proven about God can never be completely filled by reason. Asma's quest is not for rational answers but for confirmation of her faith, greater confidence in what she knows is unprovable but what she believes is not unknowable: the interior, transformative religious experience.

At the individual level, American student-travelers in the Middle East cultivate particular skills, styles, and bodies of knowledge that can allow them to inhabit their tradition in a richer way, that make the journeys very personally satisfying. But a sense of personal spiritual fulfillment does not always extend to impact the larger community. In particular, as American student-travelers return to the US, as we will see in the next chapter, it becomes quite clear that unmediated, objectified, fossilized knowledge will not be enough to alleviate the crisis of authority at the communal scale in US mosques. The fundamental tension between the individual believer and the community of believers is that the individual has access to experiential knowledge of that which cannot be proven in the public space of communal debate. American student-travelers may discover the limitlessness of their individual knowledge of the divine in the Middle East, experiences that elude practices of verification and refutation. They also learn the very real limits of what can be negotiated, acknowledged, and debated in American Muslim counterpublics, through confrontational argumentation, the rigor of logic, the force of evidence in debates over law, theology, and ethics.

Crisis forces us to rethink the future's relationship to the past and present and pushes us to create a new narrative that more adequately orders our experience. In Asma's case, in order to resolve her faith crisis, she rewrites the narrative by divorcing Islamic law (*fiqh*) from her faith in the divine, from God and the divine, ideal system of *sharia* that the human legal system of *fiqh* only approximates. Though she is disillusioned with the imams' misuse of their power and the inapplicability of Islamic law, she renews her bond to her religious tradition through the art of Quranic recitation and her individual religious reasoning. Asma believes, after all, that the Quran is the one book without a human, and thus flawed, author. Similarly, Usman experiences a sense of personal crisis by recognizing the limits of his classical education and the challenge of reinvigorating, applying, and enforcing Islamic law in the US. Asma's case teaches him that knowledge alone is not the answer to the crisis, that the mediation and application of that knowledge is the critical step in making tradition matter to American Muslims.

Usman found Asma's tragic story both frustrating and demoralizing. Despite the years he had spent mastering legal texts on marriage and divorce, much of her case did not make sense to him. How was it that an ad hoc council of imams could assume the authority of an Islamic court? There were no universally agreed-on rules of qualification of legal authority that Usman might reference from a book. What did her imam mean when he said that *sharia* recognized civil divorces? Did that make the *fiqh* of divorce obsolete for Muslims in America? What did that say about all his years of training? Usman worries that he is too out of touch with what was going on in the US. After all the years he has spent learning a legal system to raise the bar for American Muslims, American imams are brushing Islamic law to the sidelines. If Islamic law could not be applied in the case of individuals who sought it out, then what place could all Usman's classical legal training have in the everyday lives of Muslim Americans? Usman doubts Asma could discern between the scholarly credentials of a classically trained judge and her local imam, and now these titles meant even less to her. Although Usman offers her a bit of comfort by allowing her to vent her frustrations, her case deeply troubles him because he is unable to reassure her in any real way.

The crisis of authority for Muslim Americans cannot be resolved by canons and etiquette alone. Usman realizes that his classical legal training and his American upbringing, English, and cultural fluency alone will not resolve the crisis of authority for American Muslims. Like many students of knowledge in the Middle East, he is perplexed by classically trained 'ulama who have spent years studying in the Middle East and since returned to the US; some of these individuals have largely abandoned Islamic narratives of countercitizenship, of ambivalence about the US, and instead embrace their identities as Americans. These American scholars promote what Usman considers "liberal" fatwas, and they promote a vision for what he calls "American Islam or Americanizing Islam." Usman is perplexed by the changing discursive landscape in US mosques which he watches from Damascus, but he does not challenge the authority of these American 'ulama because from his point of view, these 'ulama have a "traditional pedigree" that he says he could only dream of having. He gives the example of one white Muslim scholar based in Chicago; though he disapproves of what he considers his "feminist" opinions, he admits, "Dr. Umar [Faruq Abd-Allah] is a master, not just intellectually in *aqida* [theology] and *fiqh* [law] but in *tasawwaf* [sufism]. He is a real sufi. We know how deep his knowledge goes with law and theology, and so, who are we to criticize him?"[9]

THE FACE IN THE WOOD

"You came to say good-bye?" Maryam is pleased to see me.

It is true. Back in our Giza apartment, my take-charge husband was repacking all the suitcases that I could not seem to pack. The passports and tickets were fanned out and waiting on my vanity table, along with the lipstick and gum and tissues for crying that would be tucked into my purse for the long plane ride home.

"So you're finally going home? *Akhiran* [finally]," she says, cocking her head to one side.

"Yeah. No more interviews. No more fieldwork. The end of my traveling year."

"Your gypsy year." Maryam had turned the English racial epithet for the wandering peoples of Egypt and India into an affectionate nickname for me and a way to tease her two Turkish roommates, for whom gypsy thieves were constant bogeymen.

For a year, my passport took me to Cairo and Beirut and Damascus and Amman and Dubai and Lahore and back and forth. My favorite thing about Egypt Air is that you do not need to buy the tickets in advance. You can show up at the airport the same day for the same fare. This is perfect for impulsive people like me, who travel light and make decisions on whims. Maryam always found my sudden trips and mad dashes to the airport amusing. She is better at making the road home than I am. All that homesickness, and now I feel I cannot bear to leave.

We are leaving because the bombs are beginning to drop in Iraq. Two by two, my husband's relatives in Iraq had crossed the borders to stay with us, in hopes of getting out permanently or, at the very least, of safely if anxiously waiting out the war. In Damascus, Hamada's cousin Rana and her father surprised us on our doorstep; in Amman, it was Rana's mother and her aunt. I sat through unsuccessful job interviews in office buildings and elementary schools throughout Amman with Rana, her fresh college degree in hand, and after a few weeks, we began visa applications to France and to the US. When my brother-in-law's fiancée and her brother finally arrived in Amman, we got a second apartment. We needed it. Loved ones began coming for short and tearful reunions; we even threw a simple, last-minute wedding in our living room in Amman to make a visa approval and a honeymoon come faster. Now in Cairo, we got a tearful phone call from Hamada's parents in Michigan, with FBI agents sitting in their living room asking about charities we had given money to, asking about our research overseas.

But I do not share this with Maryam for fear of worrying her. Maryam tugs lightly on my long, silk veil as I unfasten it. "You and your gypsy scarves and your gypsy eyes!" This is her way of telling me she will miss me.

"Are you calling me a thief?" And I laugh and pretend to be offended. "I have stolen some things this year. I've been stealing stories all year."

Maryam becomes serious, even stern. "Allah has blessed you, and you have learned many things this past year. Remember that learning goes all the way back. Allah taught Adam first, right, that *ittaq Allah wa 'alimukum Allah* [be God conscious and God will teach you], as if *taqwa* [God consciousness] was the condition for learning. Don't let it all fall away when you go back. Don't change back."

Maryam wants a promise, but instead I tell her a story that is not stolen.

On late nights, when I was growing up, I would often lie in bed staring at the wood grain of my closet. Sometimes a face would appear in the wood, mean and old, and even though I was afraid, I could not look away. I imagined that this face was the devil's, and I told myself that if I was good, I would roll over, turn my back to the face, and trust God to protect me. I had invented a test of my faith, and it became a nightly ritual. Sometimes it was easy, but on other nights I stayed awake, trying to stare down the face and feeling a little bit like a coward the next day.

I had nearly forgotten about this ritual test of faith I had invented, this exercise in teaching myself to better trust what I knew but could not prove. And then, one restless night, a face appears in the oak armoire in my dusty apartment one block up from the Nile. And I test myself again. Because fears and doubts still haunt me. And courage is something I could use, especially when it seems anything is possible and nothing is predictable. Mostly, though, that face is a reminder that faith rises and falls, that it comes and fades.

It can come anywhere. Any time. It can disappear and reappear.

The Aura of the Archive

One of the ways devout Muslims map Islamic authenticity onto particular landscapes is through *baraka*, or diving blessings. *Baraka* can be defined as a "beneficent force of divine origin, which causes superabundance in the physical sphere and prosperity and happiness in the psychic order."[10] It is a divine charge that permeates all of creation but is concentrated in particular temporal and spatial locations. This Islamic concept of blessings involves a transmission process whereby an individual may experience the special concentration of blessings by being in the right place at the right time, so to speak. Thus, Muslims consider the holy cities of Mecca and Medina to be imbued with more *baraka* than other geographical spaces are, as is the month of Ramadan or the last third of each night, when God is most proximate to those who are in prayer. The Islamic concept of blessings involves transmissive processes of the divine essence, which can be apprehended through Walter Benjamin's theorization of the auratic. For Benjamin, aura is a strange weave of space and time, the semblance of distance, "however close it may be," which combines the transcendence and the imminence of the divine.[11] *Baraka* is also concentrated in individuals (the prophets) and, according to the sufi tradition, in saints.

However transformative or personally meaningful such spiritual experiences might be for an individual seeker, they are not elements of tradition that can be retrieved and brought back to the US. In other words, American student-travelers may experience the aura of the Archive, but it is not something they can take back to share with their communities in the US as anything more than a personal account. If the student-travelers are going to be able to have more than just a good story to tell, if they are going to be able to shape the future of Islam in the US, then their travels abroad must be empowering in ways that translate beyond the individual religious experience.

If the mastery of "traditional" knowledge as a new, universally accepted criterion of Sunni authority is to displace the usual claims to authority in American mosques, claims based on race, class, and "professional" knowledge, that "traditional" knowledge will have to bind communities of Muslims to their tradition in an equally compelling way. The mastery of traditional knowledge must render the leaders of these communities into custodians. Only then will tradition be maintained and preserved in the US in a way that might endure. For Usman, and for many other student-travelers, the questions remain: What will bind Muslim Americans to their tradition? What are the future criteria of religious authority for Muslim Americans? Authority is not and cannot be coterminous with knowledge. To be authoritative, traditional knowledge has to touch Muslims' everyday lives. American Muslims must feel compelled to apply Islamic law because they feel its authoritative weight, because they feel bound to it even when it restricts them. And like love, that sense of being bound cannot come from persuasion, coercion, or force. It has to feel natural, organic, authentic to the self.

7

Muslim Reformers and the American Media

The Exceptional Umma and Its Emergent Moral Geography

PATHS

"Be in this world as though you were a stranger traveling a path."
 Paths wind, paths twist.
 Usman came back to the US with his wife and two sons. He got a graduate degree and a job as an imam in a leafy, suburban mosque community. But he never felt satisfied; he never felt as though he was putting what he had learned to its proper use. As an imam, he helped some troubled couples patch things up, taught a few law classes, oversaw the Islamic studies curriculum at the local Islamic K–8 school. He traveled and gave sermons at mosques and lectures at retreats and conferences to eager and attentive Muslim college students. He resolved a community conflict and prevented the mosque from getting sued by the church down the street over a parking lot they shared on Sundays and Fridays. He found coaching the mosque's youth-group basketball team most rewarding of all. Of course, he had not learned how to coach basketball in Damascus. After two years, he decided against renewing his contract with the mosque and moved back to the Middle East for a few years, to work on Islamic legal research with a consortium of other religious scholars in the Gulf. He still plans to return to the US someday, but he is gravely worried about the political climate, which is increasingly hostile to Islam and especially the misunderstood notion of *sharia*.
 If Usman has learned anything, though, it is that things can change and that all attachments are obstacles in the end, even dreams and especially ambitions. He tells me his wife has resigned herself to the fact that their family will probably never be able to make a ten-year plan, or maybe never even a five-year plan. She is a patient and resourceful woman. She holds Usman to his promises only for two years at a time.

Asma remarried; she says she "accidentally fell in love" at a cousin's wedding with a businessman based in Italy. She hopes that when the economy improves, they can move back to the United States. She tells me she no longer wears hijab and that she thinks of herself as a practicing Muslim feminist.

Sakeena confesses that the demands of married life and her three children have prevented her from keeping up with her study circles and that her Arabic has lapsed since leaving Egypt. She wishes she had more time to herself these days. Her greatest pride is the successful business she and her husband opened three years ago, a cute floral shop in a little suburban strip mall just outside Boston. She named her baby Zahra, after the Prophet's daughter, Fatima Zahra, "Rose."

Sakeena worries that African American Muslim youth in her generation are losing their faith; her own older brother frightens her with his doubts and his irreverence, his new friends and his bad habits. Their mother is shattered over the changes in him, and Sakeena wonders with trepidation what things might look like once her small children come of age as fourth-generation American Muslims. She still nurtures an ambition to be a leader in her Muslim community, but her goals are less scholarly than they were as a student in Egypt. She would rather be a shoulder to cry on than a preacher, inspiring people with love and kindness rather than speeches at conferences. Once her kids are in school, Sakeena hopes to get a degree as a chaplain, to support Muslims on college campuses and in prisons grappling with the meaning of their lives and the permanence of the afterlife.

Paths loop, crossing and recrossing.

Leila and Fawzia both teach Quranic recitation in their mosque communities and privately to female college students at local campuses. Leila remains in regular contact with Ansa Tamara, who moved to the US in 2012 with the escalation in Syria's civil war and began hosting retreats for American Muslim women in different cities. Leila continues to rise up the ranks in the order, and she also serves on the board at her mosque. She is married and has a son and a daughter. She prides herself on the fact that she has committed half the Quran to memory.

Fawzia is frustrated that she is still single and living with her parents in the suburbs of Los Angeles. A successful dentist, these days the white coat is the only coat she wears over her clothes. Her lucrative private practice allows her to support the families of Syrian friends and teachers displaced by the Assad regime's brutal suppression of his opposition; in 2012, she began regularly sending thousands of dollars to refugee camps in Lebanon and to charities in Syria.

Ahmad did not get any American acceptance letters after graduating from AlAzhar, but he did finally get a visa to come to the US and to work as an imam in a sleepy southern town. His wife likes the South better than upstate New York, where they lived for two bitterly cold months. She is pregnant. She gets nauseated, and she gets homesick; the heat and the fruit in the South comfort her, reminding her of sweet, golden afternoons in Egypt. Southerners are like Arabs, she tells me, their warmth, their hospitality. She and Ahmad are nervous as to whether they will be able to stay in the US, whether they will have to move to Canada instead or maybe back to the Middle East. Will the baby be a boy or a girl, or an American or a Canadian? Only God knows. No matter where they are, the baby will be an Egyptian. As they watch the unfinished revolution unfold in Egypt from their American laptop and television screens, they wonder if maybe it would not be such a bad idea to go home, to go back to build a better, democratic Egypt.

Paths split.

Jawad has left Shaykh Nuh's sufi order, but he assures me that he still tries to pray as regularly as he can—not as regularly as he did—but he still only eats halal meat. Jawad describes how different the old neighborhood in Amman has become. Now there is a sparkling new compound and thriving businesses run by the devotees and all kinds of people, not all religious, milling about. Now when Shaykh Nuh comes to the US to meet with his thousands of devotees, they meet in groups lumped together by what state they live in; there is little time for private guidance. Jawad cannot quite pinpoint when his heart changed, probably gradually, or maybe it was right after his father passed away. He says he lost confidence in Shaykh Nuh as his positions and rules changed over the years in ways that seemed arbitrary to Jawad. Jawad never did go to college, but he married a woman who understands his mother. They get along well, all three of them. He manages a Dunkin' Donuts in New Jersey owned by his uncle, his mother's brother.

Richard tells me he is happy, happily married, happy at his "dream job" at a growing start-up. He has kept up his Arabic over the years, and

Richard → went looking for culture, spirituality

he teaches a Quranic calligraphy class at his local mosque on the weekends. He calls his time in the Middle East his "lost" period; if he had to do it all over again, he would not have spent a year of his life there. He says he does not regret his year in the Middle East so much as he regrets spending so much of it looking for something he could not find there, a peace of mind he says he has now, a way to be himself, white and Muslim, spiritual but not that religious. *Isn't religious anymore*

There are many, many students and teachers whom I met in my time in the Middle East, men and women who inspired me with their sincerity and their curiosity about the meaning of our place in the world. Most of the students and teachers who crossed my path did not make their way into this book. Nevertheless, their prints are on these pages. Their questions and insights are here.

Good Muslim Citizens

Over the past few decades, hundreds of American student-travelers have traveled abroad to pursue religious studies in global pedagogical networks in the Middle East. Although there are no empirical studies that have produced a statistic, my estimate is conservative; one would be hard-pressed to find a mosque community in the US, which now number over two thousand, that has not produced student-travelers who have since returned to their US mosque communities. Despite the prevalence of the phenomenon, the results on the ground, in Muslim American counterpublics, have been mixed and difficult to measure. In my follow-up interviews with returning student-travelers, I found a general pattern of frustration over conflicting expectations. Although these American Muslim youth see their journeys and studies abroad as a way to resolve the crisis of authority in US mosques, on their return to the US they are often disappointed by the limited scope of their impact on their communities. In part, the student-travelers' self-assessment of limited success and even outright failure may simply be the result of having unrealistic ambitions for the potential of their studies and journeys to effect change in the first place. Conversely, American mosque congregations often make demands of returning student-travelers to act as imams or Sunday-school teachers, roles they are rarely interested in playing. The sense of "failure" is even more pronounced among advanced students of knowledge, who expect themselves (and who are expected by their US communities) to have the most powerful impact as the new generation of Muslim American religious leaders. These newly minted religious intellectuals rarely assume permanent positions as imams in mosques, despite the demand for them, and the few who do rarely report job satisfaction. They are frustrated by their limited impact on the state of discourse both in their local mosque communities and at the national level of Muslim American umma institutions. In part, their limited impact on public discourse in US mosques is a function of the discourse of crisis itself, which often leads to a suppression of debate and a denial of the reflexivity of tradition, as we have seen, reducing student-travelers to carriers rather than mediators of the tradition. However, Muslims' own discourse of crisis is not the only constraint on American student-travelers returning to the US.

Since September 11th, American student-travelers have had to reckon with the constraints of intense external scrutiny, by the US government, the mainstream media, and the lay public, on their efforts to resolve the "crisis of Islam" and to intervene in public debates about the reform of their tradition. Debates about Islamic reform are conducted both in public spaces of America's mainstream media and in the private (but never really private) spaces of US mosques. In sharp contrast to the period before September 11th, when Muslims' own religious debates were of little interest outside mosque walls, debates about reform within US mosques are now regular objects of consumption, investigation, and analysis for American audiences who have little context for them. As a result of this mediatization of Muslim debates, the discursive terrain that American student-travelers return to in the US is even more fraught and unstable than that of earlier generations of American student-travelers.

As we will see, the presence of external scrutiny, both the presumed presence of government surveillance and the mainstream media spotlight, actually transforms the ways Muslim American intellectuals and religious leaders speak to one another, profoundly shaping their debates about the crisis of authority. The perpetual threat of surveillance and punitive state policies from above and the threat of a backlash from ordinary Americans further constrict Muslim debates and produce a different kind of incoherence and sense of crisis than the one described in the previous ethnographic chapters. In this final chapter, I map the debates about Islamic reform among the generation of American student-travelers who preceded the Muslim youth we have followed in the previous chapters. I contextualize a set of media fragments about the reform of Islam that shape the way Islam is represented in the public sphere since September 11th in relation to emerging trends in Muslim American counterpublics, on the basis of my research and interviews with Muslim leaders in US mosques, trends that are rarely captured in journalistic accounts. The Muslim American leaders, most of whom studied Islam abroad in the eighties, are now established Muslim American leaders with national and international reputations among Muslim counterpublics as community activists and thought leaders; however, since September 11th, they have been thrust in the media spotlight and are grappling with the pressures of translating their reform projects and negotiating their legitimacy in the eyes of government, the general public, and Muslim counterpublics in the mainstream media, what I call the challenges of *mediatization*. By focusing on the difficulties of an earlier generation of returned student-travelers rather than those newly returned and still getting their bearings, we gain a deeper understanding of the transformations in constructions of religious authority, emergent moral geographies, and mainstreaming trends in Muslim American counterpublics that American student-travelers grapple with on their return to the US.

Despite regular media exposure since September 11th as "go-to" sources for the US government and for US journalists, these Muslim leaders-turned-spokespeople remain largely unknown to most Americans. In fact, American Muslim leaders are consistently represented in the mainstream media as skirting their responsibilities to "moderate" their communities and to condemn terror. As *New York Times* columnist Thomas Friedman noted in 2005, "When Salman Rushdie wrote a controversial novel involving the prophet Muhammad, he was sentenced to death by the leader of Iran. To this day—to this day—no major Muslim cleric or religious body has ever issued a fatwa condemning Osama bin Laden."[1] Aside from the gross misrepresentation of a fatwa as a death sentence, this is also a gross misrepresentation of Muslim American leaders, as every major Muslim organization in the US had repeatedly, publicly renounced terrorism. In a political climate often hostile to Islam, Muslim American spokespeople are in a double bind. They must demonstrate their willingness to work with the state to combat terror, flaunting their public relationships with the US government in the mainstream media as proof that they are "moderate" Muslims; but at the same time, they must downplay those relationships in their own mosque communities in order to preserve their political legitimacy and religious authority.

How Crisis Constrains Reform

After September 11th, Americans' desire to discover "real" Islam in the text of the Quran—to read the Quran for themselves, to search out the verses that had supposedly caused the attacks—paralleled the desire to learn how to "read" Muslim bodies, to learn how to recognize those who appear to be Arab, Muslim, or Middle Eastern, so that if they "see something," as the signs in American public transportation systems instruct, they could as vigilant patriots "say something." Although profiling those who look "Arab, Middle Eastern, and Muslim" is now a normalized feature of our terror culture, it is also widely understood that the racial category of "Middle Eastern-, Arab-, or Muslim-looking" people is imprecise, too fluid, too wide a net. Several of the hate crimes since September 11th, including those that ended in homicide, targeted individuals who were not Muslim but were "Muslim-looking," including Sikhs, Hindus, Native Americans, Latinos, and Arab American Christians.[2] Stories about "flying while brown" (akin to "driving while black") abound in the US. Over the years, the signs that make a person appear threatening to a crew member or that make a fellow passenger "uncomfortable" enough to get one removed from a US carrier has grown long and unpredictable: Muslim names, Sikh turbans and ceremonial knives, silk veils, a pile of Arabic three-by-five flash cards, lingering too long on one page while reading (Heidegger), a T-shirt with Arabic writing across the chest, the smell of spicy food, leather strips strapped around Jewish arms, olive-skinned bodies, "I have to go!" whispered so low and quickly into a cell phone as the flight attendant asked for electronic devices to be shut off, a phrase that, in the explanation of that flight attendant, sounded too close to "It's a go!" to be worth the risk.[3] As legal scholar Sherene Razack notes, racial profiling in the name of security becomes so routinized as to move from bigotry to a full-blown social organizing principle so that "a racial hierarchy is maintained without requiring the component of individual actors who are personally hostile towards Muslims."[4] Such security practices make Americans feel "safe enough," and the imprecisions (and injustices) associated with them are assumed to be in small enough amounts that they are tolerable. These are, as the proponents' arguments go, necessary, if not always efficacious, policies in service of national security. For example, Nixon Center policy analyst Robert Leiken argued that in order to prevent domestic sleeper-cell attacks, the government must target "the haystack [if] the needle resists discovery."[5] In fact, with the exception of the Iraq War, both President Bush's and President Obama's War on Terror policies received wide support in the public.

Even more frightening than anxieties over our ineptitude in distinguishing good and bad Muslims is the darker possibility that detecting the difference itself is impossible. With the election of Obama, amid the intertwined rumors that Obama was himself a foreigner (manifest in the demand for his birth certificate) and also that he was a Muslim, previously latent arguments in which "good Muslims" and "bad Muslims" are indistinguishable for all intents and purposes were given credence in the public sphere in a way that they never enjoyed during Bush's term. Anti-Muslim feeling and activism in the US took a dramatic upswing even though Obama was elected eight years after the September 11th attacks. This second set of American anxieties about Muslims is preoccupied not primarily with national security but with cultural domination, a "stealth jihad." Muslim Americans, writ large as a kind of sleeper cell, are slowly "Islamizing America" and the world, usurping the Constitution in small, almost imperceptible steps so that they might impose sharia across the land and, eventually, across the world. This nativist paranoia is not simply an effect of pervasive misinformation about Islam but the result of a successful industry devoted to disseminating disinformation about Islam and Muslims.

The Center for American Progress found that from 2001 to 2009 seven charitable groups provided $42.6 million to a small group of right-wing think tanks, scholars, and activists, who in turn produce books, policy reports, websites, blogs, propaganda films, lecturers, and training sessions for law enforcement (such as the NYPD), for politicians, and for the general public, materials that are xenophobic and anti-Muslim.[6] While this anti-Muslim rhetoric is not new, the organization and consolidation of resources of grassroots efforts has forged a new space and legitimacy for anti-Muslim activists, what I call *disinformation experts*, in the national debate over the place of Muslims in the US and the reform of Islam.

Drawing on old racial and xenophobic formulas, the rhetoric of the disinformation experts about Muslim inferiority and lack of loyalty to the nation requires little explanation. In fact, their anti-Muslim rhetoric is not only imprecise; it requires almost no knowledge of Islam beyond a handful of Arabic terms: *fatwa, jihad, madrasa, sharia*, which in their lay usage in the US do not correspond to their actual meaning in Arabic to Muslims in the US and around the world. The disinformation experts have been strikingly successful in manufacturing crises that quickly devolve into national media spectacles about the threat of "stealth jihad." The disinformation experts are efficacious not only in creating media controversies but in galvanizing politicians to serve their policy agendas. For example, a few anti-Muslim activists successfully disseminated "sharia creep" throughout the country as a "wedge issue" in the election cycle of 2011. Of the "sharia bans" proposed in more than thirty states that year, most were drawn from the boilerplate offered at the website of a single anti-Muslim blogger and activist.[7]

In a revealing moment, a Republican state senator named Gerald Allen, who introduced an anti-sharia measure that would bar Alabama courts from considering Islamic law in any form, was asked to define sharia by a local reporter. With some embarrassment, Senator Allen confessed he could not define the term, explaining, "I don't have my file in front of me. I wish I could answer you better." Ironically, he would have only needed an Internet browser, since the text of Allen's anti-sharia bill is lifted word for word from the first paragraph of the Wikipedia entry on sharia. The more nuanced sections of that Wikipedia entry, however, which explains that sharia is not a single set of laws like US code but a pluralistic legal system and which explains that there "is tremendous variety in the interpretation and implementation of Islamic Law in Muslim societies today," is notably absent from Allen's bill.[8] One of the alarmist "statistics" of disinformation experts that is frequently invoked—for example, by Representative Peter King in support of his 2011 counterterrorism trials of Muslim Americans—is that 80 percent of Muslim American clerics are radicals.[9] In the fraught, post–September 11th political climate, the triumphal narratives of a Muslim American Dream no longer ring out in Muslim American counterpublics as they did in the nineties. As a South African immigrant scholar and former president of ISNA noted with sadness in a speech to American Muslim youth in 2004, "American Muslims are the wealthiest umma in the world, yet we pine for dignity."[10]

Often intended as correctives to the anti-Muslim disinformation industry, there have been a slate of sympathetic representations of Muslim debates about religious reform in the mainstream media since September 11th, typically featuring the aforementioned earlier generation of student-travelers turned religious leaders. As spokespeople, these Muslim American leaders attempt to explain themselves, their religion, and the perpetual debates within their religion to government officials and to ordinary Americans. Historian Robert Orsi argues that in the dominant American culture, "true" or "good" religion is ethically singular, and, therefore, Americans feel confident that they can distinguish a "good" religion from a "bad" one (that is, a fundamentalist one), even with minimal amounts of information. Good religion, he writes, "is rational, respectful of persons, noncoercive, mature, nonanthropomorphic in its higher forms, mystical (as opposed to ritualistic), unmediated and agreeable to democracy (no hierarchy in gilded robes and fancy hats), monotheistic (no angels, saints, demons, ancestors), emotionally controlled, a reality of mind and spirit not body and matter."[11] Since September 11th, Muslim American leaders are routinely called on to publicly prove both their loyalty as patriotic citizens and to prove that they believe in a "good" Islam. Not only are Muslim Americans asked to disavow terrorism; they must disavow "fundamentalism," presumably the "cause" behind terrorist attacks. Indeed, the two isms are seen, for all intents and purposes, as inextricably linked, as opposite sides of the same coin.[12] Unfortunately, even in these sympathetic mainstream media representations, Muslims' debates, complex histories, and religious vocabularies are collapsed in on themselves so regularly that they often have no correspondence to the actual Muslim discourses and vocabularies in question.

As Muslim American religious leaders attempt to translate Islamic debates to the American public and often to US government officials, they often reproduce the logic of culture-talk themselves, with a nationalist twist, defining good Muslim citizens against bad Muslims. By accepting collective responsibility for terrorism on behalf of Muslims in general and Muslim Americans in particular, Muslim American leaders-turned-spokespeople affirm their positive identification with the US as good, flag-waving citizens, identifying Islam in terms of normative definitions of a good religion and claiming a space in the cultural mainstream through the disavowal and identification of bad Muslims and bad Islam. Muslim American spokespeople regularly highlight the "good" features of Islam (its monotheism, its rationalism, its compatibility with science, its egalitarian ethos) as well as its doctrinal and historical relationship to the other Abrahamic faiths. Over and over again, in the mainstream media and to US government officials, Muslim American spokespeople emphasize appeasing qualities of Islam: Muslims' recognition of Jesus as a prophet; the etymological relationship of the word *Islam* to *salam*, the Arabic word for "peace"; the Prophet Muhammad's elevation of the spiritual tradition of jihad (the struggle for self-improvement, the greater jihad) over the martial tradition of jihad (the lesser jihad).[13] Most of American Muslim spokespeople's discussions of Quranic verses related to martial jihad focus on contextualizing the verses in an Islamic just-war tradition that specifies rules of engagement for armies and distinguishing jihad from terrorism and vigilante justice in general. In addition to jihad, Muslim American spokespeople also defensively explain (and sometimes dismiss) those elements of normative Islamic practice that appear coercive or hierarchical to non-Muslim Americans as cultural pollutants, a kind of derivative culture-talk of their own. Sensitive points that need to be finessed for non-Muslim audiences include any elements that manifest a distinction between men and women, such as veiling or gender segregation in formal prayer, or elements that make Muslims seem irrational, such as the grainy news footage of students rocking back and forth in distant madrasas.

Consider prominent activist and reformist preacher Faisal Abdul Rauf, author of a best-selling book, *What's Right with Islam Is What's Right with America*, written as a response to Orientalist Bernard Lewis's best-seller *What Went Wrong?*[14] Abdul Rauf's efforts to demonstrate how Islamic ideals and American ideals converge and are perfectly compatible earned him a reputation as an ecumenical, patriotic, and "liberal" imam, but it did little to protect him from the intense scrutiny he received from his community's proposed real-estate development in Manhattan of a community center modeled on the YMCA and the JCC. Although, in 2009, even conservative media such as FOX News represented the proposed center as a positive step for Abdul Rauf's sufi community, which had been holding prayer services in the neighborhood for decades, within a year, the disinformation experts successfully manufactured an international crisis over what they dubbed the "Ground Zero Mosque," claiming it was really a "Trojan horse" mosque. The "Ground Zero Mosque" controversy became the most heavily covered media story about Islam in 2010. As a result, Abdul Rauf, who was himself working for the State Department in a cultural diplomacy program intended to reform Muslims abroad, fought off baseless charges in the mainstream media of building a "victory mosque" for AlQaeda and having terrorist connections. Given Abdul Rauf's direct ties to the US government and his long and close relationships to liberal Christian and Jewish leaders in New York, his fall from grace served as a reminder to all Muslim Americans, and especially Muslim American leaders-turned-spokespeople, of the fragility of the "good Muslim citizen" status.[15] The backlash against the Manhattan community center was felt acutely by lay Muslims as well; the disinformation experts launched an impressive grassroots campaign against mosques and Islamic schools across the country. While lawsuits to prevent mosques from being built in various American cities can be found as early as the 1980s, the phenomenon of a national anti-mosque coalition had no precedent until 2010, when anti-Muslim grassroots activists were being bused across state lines; their efforts pivoted on a generalized suspicion that any mosque could be a "Trojan horse" for terrorists.[16] As the disinformation experts generalize their paranoia about the specter of the Islamic threat, anti-Muslim racism narrows in order to hit the "right" targets, reshaping itself along the edges of the imprecisions and racial misrecognitions that characterize the War on Terror. The man who stabbed a Bengali cab driver in Manhattan at the height of the furor over the so-called Ground Zero Mosque took a moment before plunging the blade through his victim's brown skin to first confirm, "Are you a Muslim?"[17]

Fig. 7.1. Protesters demonstrate in opposition to the Park 51 community center. (Courtesy of Mark Peterson / Redux)

As we will see, in the process of making intra-Muslim debates digestible for imagined and real non-Muslim American audiences, the lay audiences of the mainstream media and the official audience of US government officials, Muslim American religious leaders-turned-spokespeople combine diagnoses of Islam's (fundamentalist) pathologies with admissions of their own complicity in what they describe as the crisis of Islam by not being aggressive or effective enough as religious reformers. While assimilation is so often assumed to be the decline of an ethnic and religious difference, that process of fitting in also always involves the making of difference among people who share an ethnic or religious identity, drawing a line between those who can more easily assimilate and those who are less able or unable to do so.[18] In other words, social and legal citizenship are in tension but not opposites; both conceptualizations of citizenship are discursively dependent on an avowal of (commensurable) Muslim difference and a disavowal of (incommensurable) Muslim difference. This making of difference by Muslim American leaders (primarily for non-Muslim audiences) between bad Muslims (those backward, regressive fundamentalists and potential terrorists) and good

Muslim citizens (those citizens who believe in a good, benign, and moderate Islam) is, in fact, the primary work of the sympathetic media representations of American Muslim leaders and debates about religious reform. Importantly, in these sympathetic accounts, journalists seek out sincere and well-respected American Muslim leaders rather than native informers, yet the frame of good and bad Islam remains intact. By accepting responsibility for "bad Muslims" in the public sphere, Muslim American spokespeople's defensive postures not only treat terrorism and fundamentalism as synonyms; they link the rehabilitative strategies necessary for salvaging Islam (their own reform projects) to the project of mainstreaming Muslims in the US.

What gets restaged again and again in sympathetic American media representations of Islam's crisis of authority and its reform by good Muslim citizens is a tension fundamental to American citizenship. As we have seen, citizenship as defined by US law is not coterminous with the social definition of citizenship, defined by the far more amorphous realm of cultural and racial mores.[19] Over the course of the terror decade, American journalists have offered various kinds of good Muslim citizens as solutions to Islam's crises: sufi intellectuals, feminists, blacks, and even ultraconservative (but pacifist) "fundamentalists." These diverse American Muslim spokespeople have initiated energetic programs to found Islamic pedagogical institutions in the US, promoting an emergent Muslim American moral geography with the US at its core, the American Medina as Home, eclipsing the transnational moral geography of the Islamic East as Archive as well as earlier transnational and nostalgic iterations of the American Medina moral geography in which the Muslim World figured as a Diasporic Homeland. The national moral geography of the American Medina as Home not only embraces American citizenship; it replaces outsiderhood with American exceptionalism, specifically with an emergent religious narrative that posits American Muslims as the exceptional umma, recasting American Muslims as leaders and examples to the Muslim World.

Intellectualizing Islamic Authority: Zaytuna College

Prior to September 11th, it was Hamza Yusuf's devastating political and cultural critiques of the West that had, in part, earned him his reputation and wide popularity as a public intellectual in Muslim circles around the world. Since September 11th, Yusuf has received an enormous amount of media attention in the mainstream US media, highlighting his sharp wit, his looks (he was likened to the Beatles by one journalist), his background as a well-educated white American, and his potential as a voice of reform. (As we have seen, Yusuf insists he is not a reformer but is a revivalist, reinvigorating classical pedagogical forms and bodies of knowledge for American Muslims through his lectures, writings, and his institute, Zaytuna, which embodies his formalist orientation to Islamic learning. Nevertheless, journalists consistently apply the label of "reformer" to him and other Muslim leaders.)

In the mainstream media, Yusuf has repeatedly referred to the terrorists as the "enemies of Islam" and "mass murderers," as opposed to the New York firefighters whom he described as brave "martyrs."[20] Heralded in the *Guardian* as "Islam's most able theological critic of the suicide hijacking," Yusuf was among the first to insist that Islam itself had been "hijacked" on September 11th in the mainstream media. He claimed that the religion itself was "on that plane as an innocent victim," and that Muslims had to return to "true" Islam divorced of violence and terrorism. In the wake of 9/11, Yusuf underwent what he terms a "transformation." In addition to representing "true" Islam as a victim of the crime of terrorism in the mainstream media, Yusuf also concedes that he had been complicit in the pathological "discourse of anger" that had produced September 11th.[21]

In media interviews after the attack, Yusuf readily accepted the personal responsibility of excising the "bad" elements of Islam, noting, "September 11th was a wake-up call to me. . . . I don't want to contribute to the hate in any shape or form. I now regret in the past being silent about what I have heard in the Islamic discourse and being part of that with my own anger."[22] Yusuf directed Muslims to become self-critical and introspective and to "reject the discourse of anger. Because there is a lot of anger in the Muslim world . . . about [their] oppressive [living] conditions, . . . [and] the desire to blame others leads to anger and eventually to wrath, neither of which are rungs on a spiritual ladder to God."[23] In interviews, Yusuf fused a number of defensive postures: the victimization of Islam itself; diagnoses of the collective guilt of Muslims through the redirection of his cultural criticism to Muslim communities (rather than the dominant American culture or US foreign policies); his individual acceptance of and repentance for his complicity in producing what he calls the Muslim "culture" or "discourse of anger"; and his assurances to the public and to the US government that Islam is a good religion that confirms dominant, Western, enlightened values and can, therefore, be rehabilitated. Immediately after September 11th, Yusuf met with President Bush and gifted him a Quran; he also successfully dissuaded Bush from naming his military operation in Iraq and Afghanistan "Infinite Justice," which Yusuf explained was one of the ninety-nine names of God in Islam. As a result, the military campaign was renamed "Enduring Freedom."

Yusuf's strong affirmation of his own patriotic loyalty to the US immediately after September 11th was intertwined not only with critiques of Muslim states and populations abroad but with critiques of Muslim American immigrants, critiques that had troubling, nativist valences. In one interview, Yusuf derides the totalitarian regimes and corrupt legal systems in the Muslim World through the triumphalist narrative of the American Medina; as he claims Americans are more representative of Islam than Muslims are themselves, Yusuf affirms the moral credibility of the US, the UK and Islam in the same breath. "[The] way Muslims are allowed to live in the west is closer to the Muslim way. A lot of Muslim immigrants feel the same way, which is why they are here, [but immigrants who] rant and rave about the west, they should emigrate to a Muslim country. The good will of [Western] countries to immigrants must be recognised."[24] This statement is a considerable departure from his pre-9/11 career as a Muslim preacher in US mosques, in which he characterized both the American mainstream and the postcolonial Muslim third world as dystopias. In fact, immediately after 9/11, Yusuf also came under scrutiny as a "radical imam" by reporters who dug up some of his pre-9/11 speeches and writings critical of US foreign and domestic policies. Just two days before the attacks, Yusuf addressed Muslims at a charity event and condemned the US government for its expansive military occupations and institutionalized racism, predicting that "a great tribulation" would befall the nation.[25]

Yusuf's dramatic political transformation immediately after September 11th raised questions about his religious credibility in Muslim American counterpublics, particularly his conciliatory public statements in

Fig. 7.2. After September 11th, Hamza Yusuf appeared in Western clothing in the media. (Courtesy of the *New York Times*)

the media and his role as an adviser to the Bush administration and his much commented-on abandonment of robes and turbans for two-piece suits in media appearances. In the wake of September 11th, some of his fiercest critics dismissed him as a sellout, using slurs such as President Bush's "pet Muslim" and "Hamza Useless." Even some of his Muslim American friends, colleagues, and fellow student-travelers challenged his media messaging, criticizing his representations of Islamic creeds, his softened critique of the US government, and his decision to cooperate with the government by advising President Bush.[26] These public challenges to Yusuf's authority also reflected the anger and sense of betrayal over his public criticism of Muslim immigrants, remarks made as politically vulnerable immigrants were being rounded up, detained, and deported by the government at a massive scale.

In the post–September 11th American context, the assignment of Muslims' collective guilt is not shared evenly across Muslim American populations, with brown, first-generation immigrant men suffering the brunt of racial-profiling policies, false imprisonment, and deportation. Even among brown Muslim immigrants, socioeconomic class is an important factor in determining their relationship to the state's security apparatus. The black and gray markets of working-class immigrant enclaves in major US cities are selectively profiled in ways their middle-class coreligionists in the suburbs are not. The high-profile tax evasion, smuggling, forgery, and pirated-DVD "busts" in enclaves such as Dearborn, Michigan; Devon Street in Chicago; and Astoria, Queens, in New York are not unusual for immigrants on the margins of the US economy, but, of course, bootlegging DVDs is not a crime the way terrorism is a crime; Yusuf's criticisms of immigrants in the mainstream media had a particular sting for many Muslim Americans during this time.

In addition to singling out the generalized anger and the political and economic frustrations of Muslims, Yusuf diagnosed the Muslim World with an intellectual ailment that made Muslims susceptible to fundamentalism and, therefore, terrorism. Consider this interview in which Yusuf frames Islam's crisis in pedagogical terms:

> Islam has very few scholars at very high levels. Most of the brilliant students in the Middle East now go into medicine and engineering. . . . They don't go into philosophy. . . . Almost every one of these terrorists that are identified, . . . you will not find amongst them anyone who did his degree in philosophy, in literature, in the humanities, in theology. . . . [Brilliant students are] only studying the physical sciences to the neglect of what makes us human, which is humanity, is poetry, is literature, as well as philosophy and theology. . . . I came out of the enlightenment tradition and I still believe in the best of the enlightenment tradition and I think Islam confirms and enhances that tradition.[27]

Yusuf's quote probably did not surprise many people; there have been a number of articles in US papers interrogating the ways the narrow pedagogical tracks of Muslims in the Muslim World as well as Muslim international students in the US might contribute to terrorism, including provocative headlines such as "Why Do So Many Terrorists Have Engineering Degrees?"[28]

The irony is that Yusuf's quote could be misinterpreted to mean he supports the billions of US dollars in education reform that have been spent on madrasas in South Asia since September 11th as part of the War on Terror. In fact, his invocation of the Enlightenment tradition, the humanities, and liberal arts is actually an argument and defense of "traditional" Islamic schooling—precisely the classical madrasa curriculum that arouses such misplaced fear in many Americans. Although most Americans might have missed his point, Muslim American counterpublics long familiar with his pedagogical vision and his Zaytuna Institute in Northern California did not. In the mainstream media, however, Yusuf's diagnosis of the crisis of Islamic learning is glossed as identical to US state policies' project of encouraging "liberal" Islam through educational reforms, confirming Americans' vague fears about Islamic learning in general and Muslim engineering majors in particular.

One of the most explicit examples of the ways formalist arguments about Islamic learning became wrapped in a narrow definition of social citizenship is in the writings of Abdul-Hakim Murad, a white British convert, a regular lecturer at Zaytuna Institute, and a popular sufi preacher in American mosques who is based in the UK. Murad wrote an essay about his American coreligionists living in a post–September 11th world and made a pointed religious critique directed primarily at immigrants. He chastised immigrants for immigrating to the US for economic reasons. He also rebuked them for failing to adjust to the dominant culture, arguing that a "cultural migration" was necessary and that "multiculturalism must always have some limits"; Murad argued for a social construction of citizenship rather than a strictly legal one. In his essay, Murad explained that it was probably too late "for the older generation [of immigrants] embedded either in regional folklorisms which have no clear future [in the West] or in a Movement Islam of various hues" to integrate into the American mainstream.[29] However, he urged the second generation of Muslim immigrants born in the US to review both the xenophobic history of the US and the writings of the classical Muslim philosophers, and their delineations of the proper etiquette of the guest, in order to develop the appropriate relationship to their American "hosts."

There was a backlash against the nativist valences in the rhetoric of Yusuf and other formalists associated with Zaytuna within the American mosque communities, particularly from immigrants, in the wake of September 11th. In response to this intra-Muslim backlash and the policies of the Bush administration, which Yusuf found increasingly abhorrent, Yusuf underwent a second transformation in which he softened his critique of immigrants. He also reinvigorated his public opposition to US foreign and domestic policies; a critical turning point was his damning critique of Bush and his public urging of the thirty thousand Muslims at the 2004 ISNA convention not to vote for him. Yusuf's attempts to reestablish his credibility with his mosqued Muslim base were helped by the fact that he too came under formal, if confused, investigation by the government. One journalist described an encounter a few weeks after September 11th when the FBI visited Yusuf's home in order to interrogate him, only to be informed by his wife that Yusuf was at that very moment at the White House as a guest adviser to President Bush.[30] When journalists bring up how he advised Bush to change the name of the military campaign, Yusuf quickly retorts that it was the last time Bush listened to him.[31] Such politically ironic media stories helped Yusuf reestablish his political and religious credibility and to prove that he was not "Bush's pet Muslim," as his critics had dubbed him. Yusuf began criticizing the US government and Muslim militants in the same breath: "Whether it's a president or a man in a cave, when people believe they've been sanctioned by God, they can do the most misguided things. . . . Religion is like nuclear power. It's clean, it has the power to illuminate, but it also has toxic by-products."[32] In 2010, Yusuf wrote a powerful op-ed tracing his own family's lineage to his great-great-grandfather Michael O'Hanson, who arrived in the US from Ireland in the 1840s, and arguing that "Muslims are the new Irish."[33] He encouraged Muslims to take heart and to follow the example of previous ethnic and religious minorities who successfully became a part of the American mosaic, although his pre-9/11 critiques of American racism were rarely this triumphal. Before September 11th, Yusuf was known for his stinging critiques of American racism, invoking the systematic exclusion of Native Americans, blacks, and Asians; his comparison of American Muslims to the integration of white ethnics was decidedly more optimistic. Although his political critiques of US policies after his second transformation are far less radical than those in his pre–September 11th speeches, Yusuf's authority has largely been restored in US mosques. Just as important, amid this second transformation, he has shifted to a very different moral geography, one with the US at its core.

Before September 11th, Yusuf's influential pedagogical vision embodied the antiestablishment tenor of the dominant discourse in US mosques since the eighties, which derided the creation of modern universities in the Arab world as a dilution of Islam's rich scholarly tradition.[34] After September 11th, however, Yusuf's pedagogical vision began to shift in focus, away from the Islamic East as Archive and toward the establishment of a "traditional" Islamic seminary, but one based in the US and in the form of a modern college.

In 2004, Yusuf's fledgling Zaytuna Institute expanded to a college by launching a pilot seminary program, a conscious attempt to go beyond its hodgepodge of recreational classes, which introduced American Muslims to classical pedagogical forms and texts. Yusuf's longtime intellectual partner, Imam Zaid Shakir, an African American Muslim scholar and activist, joined Yusuf in California to form the nucleus of the burgeoning Zaytuna College faculty. Shakir's reputation in American Muslim counterpublics is based not only on his scholarship but on his leadership in revitalizing poor, urban ghetto communities. Through a well-organized series of fundraisers across the country, the team successfully promoted Zaytuna as an inclusive and highly professional institution of higher learning that would be formalist in its pedagogical orientation and that would raise the bar of American Muslim discourse by offering Islamic higher education in the United States; there was little mention of the mainstreaming or "liberalizing" religious reforms American journalists presumed Zaytuna College would bring about simply because it is on American soil and run by Americans. Yusuf and Shakir's goal is to transform Zaytuna into a liberal arts college with a systematic curriculum that could be used to train the future generation of Muslim scholars in the United States. Zaytuna College's tag line is "Where Islam meets America," and the college has received sympathetic media coverage.[35] In August 2010, Zaytuna College welcomed its first freshman class. After renting facilities from the American Baptist Seminary of the West, a member of the Graduate Theological Union (GTU), one of the foremost centers for theological study in the US, Zaytuna purchased a permanent campus in Berkeley at the GTU in 2012. As the first Muslim institution of higher learning within the GTU, Zaytuna aims to grant graduate degrees in the next decade. In fact, in 2009, Yusuf began pursuing a PhD at the GTU himself, after years of discrediting the Western academic study of Islam and the "illiberal" education offered by the modern university.

Fig. 7.3. Yusuf lectures to students. Zaytuna College has received a great deal of sympathetic media coverage and attention. (Courtesy of Zaytuna College)

Yusuf's media interviews, in which his complex pedagogical philosophy and his intervention in the global debates about Islamic pedagogical forms circulate as mere affirmations of the importance of the "humanities," take on a prescient quality when we consider the dramatic transformations in his moral geography. Yusuf's mainstreaming ambitions for Zaytuna College are a sign of the shift away from the countercitizenship and the transnational moral geography of the Islamic East as Archive that he popularized. Zaytuna College's promotional literature proclaims, "Islam has never become rooted in a particular land until that land began producing its own religious scholars." Quoting an African American Zaytuna alum, one brochure reads, "The jazz composer and philosopher Sun Ra said, 'If you're not a reality, whose myth are you?' As Muslims, we need institutions that will help us define our own reality, and at Zaytuna, we have scholars trained in our tradition who can also speak to the reality here in America," invoking the national moral geography of American Medina as Home. As Yusuf pitches Zaytuna College to Muslim Americans today, he distinguishes it as a better pedagogical and cultural fit for them than the pedagogical margins of the Islamic East that he used to exalt as utopic; Zaytuna College in California, Yusuf now argues, is the best Archive of tradition for American Muslims.

Equalizing Islamic Authority: PMU and the Gender Jihad

Yusuf and formalist religious scholars like him are not the only Muslim American spokespeople to receive sympathetic mainstream media attention since 9/11 as individuals who might reform Islam and resolve the crisis of authority. In 2004, a diverse group of politically and socially liberal Muslim American activists and academics with a reformist orientation to the Islamic tradition organized themselves into the Progressive Muslim Union of North America (PMU) and quickly became a favorite source for journalists; they were celebrated for "moderating" Islam by the *New York Times*, the *Financial Times*, the *Christian Science Monitor*, *Newsday*, *Time*, and many other mainstream media. Like Yusuf, the PMU representatives took personal responsibility in the media for the reform of Islam.[36] In contrast to the angry rhetoric and crisis of Islamic learning that Yusuf isolated as the source of Islamic extremism, the PMU spokespeople located the collective guilt of the Muslim community in the social conservatism and the gender and sexual inequities of mosques and Islamic institutions and organizations in the US and the patriarchal cultures in the Muslim World. Founders, such as Sarah Eltantawi, elaborated their progressive stances against terrorism, sexism, homophobia, and religious intolerance and emphasized the group's "enlightened and positive expressions of [their] faith in the country."[37] However, it is their feminist reformist vision that garners the most media attention.

In PMU spokespeople's initial media appearances, they focused on "condemning terror" and analyzing politics in the Middle East; however, critiquing fundamentalism and what they called "conservative" and "sexist" Muslim social norms in US mosques quickly became their primary focus. PMU executive director Pamela Taylor decried American Muslim discourse as dominated by the "hyper-conservative, the very conservative, and the moderately conservative."[38] In one article, founder Ahmad Nassef claimed PMU offered an alternative discursive space for the "silent moderate majority" of "liberal" American Muslims who were ready to take on the small but powerful fundamentalist and "conservative fringe" in American mosques.[39] This invocation of a "silent, liberal" Muslim American majority drew on an inversion of the War on Terror's power of scale, what anthropologist Arjun Appadurai names "the fear of small numbers," in which a tiny minority of "conservative" Muslims wield terrible power; it also constructs the US media as aiding their cause by amplifying their voices.[40] The same anxiety characterizes nativist rhetoric of the disinformation experts about the Islamization of America and the specter of stealth jihads: Americans ought to fear the cultural domination of this potent minority of bad Muslims. In the media, the liberal spokespeople of PMU insisted that American mosques could be reformed and rehabilitated and that the liberal majority of Muslim Americans were actually already a part of the mainstream; a few even explicitly argued that bad Muslim Americans are at fault for their own social marginalization and deserve the intense political scrutiny of the Office of Homeland Security. Nassef's website, Muslim-Wakeup!, was seen as the unofficial website of the PMU and regularly featured satirical and critical essays charged against regressive immigrants "fresh off the boat" ("FOBs") and (implicitly sexist) immigrant men, emphasizing that Muslim immigrants' cultural particularities are superficial and doomed to disappear within a generation. Through these acts of disavowal, PMU distinguished its commensurable (liberal, gender-equitable) difference from the incommensurable (conservative, sexist) difference of bad Muslims for its Muslim and non-Muslim cyber audiences, promising that neither Eastern cultures in general nor Islam itself are hurdles to Muslims' entrance into the American mainstream and embrace of mainstream American gender norms.

Self-described as a collective of North American Muslims, PMU's media appearances on radio and television were invariably made by highly educated, second-generation Middle Eastern and South Asian Americans whose accentless English, trendy clothes, and up-to-the-minute hairstyles marked them as all-American. Despite their promising trappings, frequently commented on by journalists, the representatives of PMU were routinely asked to prove their loyalty in the public sphere. Bill Maher, host of *Politically Incorrect*, posed the ubiquitous question to a PMU guest on his show: "Are you Muslim first or American first?"[41] Importantly, the successful integration of minorities that the PMU spokespeople came to embody depends on the erasure and recognition of commensurable forms of difference: they cannot just be identified merely as Americans or progressives; they must continue to be marked as *Muslim* Americans and *Muslim* progressives. In other words, in the media spotlight, the transcendent power of American citizenship is displayed by first marking Muslims' racial and religious difference, their (parents') immigrant origins, in anticipation of the PMU representatives' affirmation of the success of hyphenation—that is, the transcendence of American values over the conservatism and sexism of the Muslim World and their regressive Muslim American coreligionists. The PMU narrative constructed liberal American Muslims not as religious outsiders but as the exceptional American umma, models of "liberal Islam" and citizenship for the rest of the Muslim World.

The most heavily covered and perhaps most controversial event cosponsored by PMU was the "Women-Led Prayer Initiative" on March 18, 2005, part of a larger "Gender Jihad" campaign organized primarily by Indian American journalist Asra Nomani. Although the term *Gender Jihad* had circulated in Muslim counterpublics before this, Nomani's adoption of the name for her reformist campaign to reshape American mosque communities from a feminist perspective reflected her media savvy, adopting an alliterative and provocative mantle that American journalists and publics were drawn to and found memorable.[42] Like Yusuf's promotion of the humanities as a solution to terrorism, the feminist reform project was also represented as a counterterrorism effort in the media. Nomani explicitly tied the event to September 11th in her article in the *Daily News*:

> Friday, March 18, 2005, will be remembered as the day when about 130 Muslim women and men stood shoulder-to-shoulder behind a woman on Manhattan's upper West Side and took their faith back from the extremists who had tried to define Islam on Sept. 11, 2001. I was proud to be in the front row. New York City has been a beacon to the world for its courage after 9/11. Our prayer makes New York a city of light to the Muslim world.[43]

From the perspective of the organizers, the event made American Muslim women not only leaders of mixed congregational prayers but leaders of the Muslim World, redefining Islamic authority in gender-equitable terms. As we will see, just as Yusuf's invocation of the humanities meant very different things to the American public than it did to Muslim American counterpublics, so too did the Gender Jihad campaign capitalize on the sloppy equivalences and imprecision of terms in the media to explain Islamic prayer leadership and Islamic authority.

Nomani was at the center of a similar, smaller media story when she had held a "pray-in" in 2003 for her right to pray in the men's side of her local mosque in Morgantown, Virginia, culminating in *New York Times* articles which described her as Islam's "Martin Luther" and "Rosa Parks" and characterized her conflict with the mosque's board as an "inquisition."[44] For the woman-led prayer in 2005, Nomani invited Islamic studies professor and PMU board member Amina Wadud, an African American Sunni scholar, preacher, and activist. A former student-traveler, Wadud studied Islam at AlAzhar University in Egypt in the eighties. She is the author of a popular, feminist exegesis on the Quran, published in 1999, which was widely read in mosque communities in the US and, generally, well received. Although women imams leading other women in ritual prayer is a widely accepted religious practice, a female imam leading both men and women in ritual prayer is radical. A female imam leading both men and women is so controversial that although the prayer service in 2005 was supposed to take place in a Manhattan art gallery, the outcry from lay Muslims anticipating the event created security concerns for PMU, and the location was kept secret until the morning of the event, when the location for the service was announced in a *New York Times* article and on PMU's website; those who were interested in attending were required to preregister.[45]

Anxieties over security notwithstanding, the gathering bubbled with a self-congratulatory excitement and an explicit invocation of American Muslims as the exceptional umma. Nomani excitedly told one reporter, "Today is the dawn of a new day in the history of Islam. . . . We are going to change history and the course of our Muslim World. . . . America and the West have to deal with glass ceilings; [Muslim women] have brick walls in front of us, and we are hammering them down. And it is so that we can bust open the Muslim World for a better day."[46] As imam, Wadud led Muslim men and women in a communal prayer and gave a sermon held in their alternate location, an Episcopalian church in Manhattan. Although the event, prefaced by a dramatic press conference, garnered Wadud and the participants much applause and attention in the American media as "brave pioneers," none of the journalists reported on the content of Wadud's lengthy sermon on gender equality and Islam. In fact, many reporters seemed bored, and a few used the sermon portion of the prayer as an opportunity for a cigarette break.[47] (Wadud recounts in her book *Inside the Gender Jihad* that the flashing of the journalists' cameras was so intense during the ritual prayer that she actually lost her train of thought.)[48] In the media representations of the event, Wadud was the photo op—a bold image of a (black) woman leading men and women in prayer—and Nomani and her radical feminist reform of Islam became the story. Journalists repeatedly identified Nomani as "Islam's Rosa Parks," a "Muslim Sojourner Truth," "Islam's Martin Luther," and "Islam's Martin Luther King, Jr."[49] Nomani encouraged and enacted the comparisons to Rosa Parks and Martin Luther, naming the bus for her book tour the "Muslim Women's Freedom Bus" and taping her treatise *The Muslim Women's Bill of Rights* to the door of her local mosque in West Virginia with a camera crew in tow.[50]

Like Yusuf, the media attention cost Wadud and other religious leaders associated with the PMU some religious credibility in US mosque

Fig. 7.4. Although little of Wadud's sermon was reported on in the mainstream media, the image of her leading the mixed-gender ritual prayer was widely disseminated in the media. (Courtesy of Omar Sacirbey)

communities. In American Muslim counterpublics, the event was unpopular and controversial on political and religious grounds.[51] Most Muslim American objections to the event were made in religious terms, arguing that as an unprecedented innovation in formal ritual practice, a female imam leading a gender-mixed congregation is sinful and hetero-dox. (As Wadud and other PMU leaders attempted to reestablish their religious credibility, they later emphasized to Muslim counterpublics that there was a precedent in the tradition, although the novelty had been emphasized in the press.)[52] Other Muslim American critics of the event were in fact sympathetic to PMU's feminist principles behind the Gender Jihad event, but they objected to its methods, arguing that the media circus around Wadud and Nomani's threat of involving the state by making a legal case that would go before US courts was dangerous given the anti-Muslim political climate. Robert Crane, a prominent Muslim, Native American preacher, compared the tactics of the PMU organizers to Bush's military campaign of (forced) democracy promotion in Iraq, describing the Gender Jihad as a campaign of "shock and awe."[53]

In addition to challenging PMU, many Muslim critics objected to the media's sloppy analogies, based on false equivalences between Christianity and Islam and between American racial segregation and Islamic ritual gender segregation. For example, the US press often likened the question of a female imam to the movement for female priests in Catholicism, even though it is religious scholars, not imams, who hold the highest religious ranks in Sunni Islam, and women, as Wadud's own example demonstrates, are not technically restricted from becoming religious scholars and preachers. In addition, PMU's critics argued that many non-Muslim American audiences would impose a "back-of-the-bus" reading of the segregated prayer spaces of mosques, assuming that since men pray in front of women, they are (symbolically) superior and more proximate to the divine. In contrast to Wadud and her supporters, most mosqued Muslim Americans (including many Muslim American feminists who were critical of Wadud's prayer service) attach very different meanings to gender segregation in ritual prayer, none of which were represented in the mainstream US media. In the normative, majority view, the spatiality of a mosque is not akin to a Jim Crow–era bus or a church because one's place in prayer lines does not correspond to one's intrinsic value as it would on a segregated bus and because, unlike churches, mosques do not have altars in the front. From this point of view, a Muslim's proximity to God and individual worth is increased in the spot where their foreheads meet the ground during prostration in ritual prayer, not by their proximity to the front of the congregation. Some of Wadud's Muslim critics, including other African American Muslim women, accused her of using her black skin as a sign to foreclose any other interpretations of gender segregation in prayer in the mainstream media. Wadud countered that it was Nomani who had used her as a token black while promoting herself as the "Muslim Rosa Parks" and using the event to kick off her book tour. Nomani protested that the PMU website erased her organizational efforts completely and took credit for her work. She openly accused the organization of opportunistically disassociating with her in order to establish credibility within the "conservative" majority of mosqued Muslims. As critiques mounted in US mosques on racial, political, and religious grounds, Wadud left the PMU, and the PMU distanced itself from Nomani, the first public indications of the deep fractures within this reformist organization.

Despite the unprecedented mediatization of the Gender Jihad initiative, the debate itself was not as novel as it was represented to be in the media. The vast majority of Americans mosque communities have for decades been debating and negotiating the equitable arrangement of gendered space in prayer halls, the methods of segregation, the range and quality of services offered to female worshipers, and the role of female leadership outside of ritual prayer (that is, not as imams) in the mosque. These debates took on heightened import as the Salafi movement grew in the eighties and nineties and introduced stricter gender segregation in many US mosques than had previously been the norm. Since PMU's feminist agenda targeted ritual gender segregation itself and championed the possibility of female imams in gender-mixed congregations, it did not correspond to the less radical, but more widely resonant, debates about female access to space, resources, and leadership positions in most US mosques. Since these less radical efforts were invisible in the mainstream media, the female imam issue became a kind of litmus test for non-Muslim audiences following the story. Just as the pirated DVDs bought and sold in the black markets of working-class, Muslim ethnic enclaves in Chicago and New York got caught up in the crackdown on terror, normative Muslim practices such as segregation in prayer were dubbed "conservative" or "sexist" and linked to fundamentalism in the media furor over the Gender Jihad event. When journalists reported on the death threats Wadud received from anonymous, angry Muslim critics, it only confirmed in the minds of many non-Muslim Americans that the Islam of those who opposed Wadud was the Islam of bad, violent, murderous Muslims—in other words, that gender segregation was itself a sign of fundamentalism and terrorism. Nomani makes this point explicit in a "slippery slope" argument she repeated in several newspaper articles: Muslim Americans are collectively responsible for terrorism, she argues, especially sexist, immigrant Muslim men, because their sexism creates a "slippery slope" which leads to terrorism. She claims that her feminist reform project not only makes mosques more gender equitable; it is actually an effective counterterrorism strategy. Nomani reproduces the logics of culture-talk, insisting that terrorism is best explained by the Quran, not history or politics, that Muslim men are essentially violent and misogynistic, and that conservative policies such as racial profiling are the best way for Western states such as the US to police Muslim minorities within its borders. "Profile Me!" she titled an op-ed in defense of stricter airline security measures against those who "look Muslim," at once proclaiming and disavowing her Muslim identity.[54]

As we have seen, the application of political categories such as "liberal," "progressive," and "conservative" fails to capture the varied perspectives and religious orientations of Muslim Americans. In fact, it is the imprecision in the definition of progressive or liberal politics and progressive and liberal religion that ultimately led to the demise of PMU. By the end of 2005, three founders and a large number of other scholars and activists left PMU over differences on various political issues, including some PMU members' support of the policies of President George W. Bush, specifically the Iraq War, the *hijab* ban in France, and their lack of support of the right of return for Palestinian refugees and exiles.[55] This internal split over the definition of "progressive" politics sparked the slow decline of PMU, which was essentially defunct by 2007. Although PMU and the Gender Jihad mosque campaign burned out, it would be a mistake to underestimate the impact they had on

reforming gendered arrangements in US mosques.[56] Feminist reformists like Wadud, Nomani, and other leaders associated with the PMU
never enjoyed as much authority in US mosque communities as formalists like Yusuf, and they have been far less successful than Yusuf and
Zaytuna in restoring the credibility they once had prior to the media
circus associated with the 2005 Gender Jihad prayer event. They have
also been unsuccessful in rebranding and rebuilding their organization;
however, their institutional success is not the only measure of their
marked impact on debates on gender authority in US mosques.

In the wake of the media storm, many US mosque leaders rushed
to resolve conflicts within their congregations over women's accom-
modations in the prayer hall and women's leadership in the community. The pressures and threat of external media scrutiny forced US
mosque leaders to "moderate" their congregations' policies on the questions of gender segregation and female leadership. To this end, many
national Muslim organizations released statements and pamphlets,
such as the one by ISNA's then-president Ingrid Mattson and activist
Shahina Siddiqui, titled "Women-Friendly Mosques and Community
Centers: Working Together to Reclaim Our Heritage," which addressed
the variety of more representative concerns over gender equity in US
mosque congregations.[57] Nomani extended the threat of governmental
scrutiny and punitive measures from the state in the form of her formal litigation against her local mosque's executive board and her call
for the US government to deny nonprofit, tax-exempt status to sexist
mosques, in other words, to not recognize them as places of worship.[58]
Nomani's powerfully effective strategy of policing gender segregation in
US mosques is emblematic of what anthropologist Elizabeth Bernstein
terms "carceral feminism," in which feminists and conservatives collab-
orate to promote punitive rather than redistributive solutions to contemporary social problems.[59] Nomani's call for justice through policing
embodies the rightward shift on the part of many mainstream feminists
and other secular liberals toward a politics of incarceration espoused
by their conservative collaborators. Nomani argues that the US government's punitive gestures toward those men who "look Muslim" are the
collective result of Muslim men's own sexism.

One result of this mediatization of Muslim gender debates was the
dramatic reshuffling of religious authority. Previously marginal feminist

perspectives in American mosques were empowered by the new, external measures of good Muslim citizens and bad Muslims and bad Islam through the arm of the mainstream media, such that more radical (and often carceral) Muslim feminists were apprehended as social citizens in ways that less radical Muslim feminists, whose agendas were far more representative of American mosques, were not. Furthermore, the moral geography explicated by Nomani in particular and PMU in general posits the US at its core and liberal, feminist Muslim Americans as the exceptional umma, as moral and political examples to the Muslim World and to the conservative Muslim majority in US mosques.

Like Yusuf, members of PMU have mobilized the interest in the reform project spurred by the media coverage of the Gender Jihad toward developing pedagogical networks and institutions with their feminist reformist orientation. As a reaction to the backlash against PMU over the female imam event in US mosques, one PMU member, Daisy Khan, a feminist Muslim activist and high-profile Muslim spokeswoman at the helm of the American Society for Muslim Advancement (ASMA), organized an international conference in New York City in 2006, underwritten by major grants from philanthropic agencies such as the Rockefeller and Lilly Foundations. She launched an initiative, Women's Islamic Initiative in Spirituality and Equality (WISE), which includes a muftiyya program sponsoring religious training for female and feminist student-travelers from the US with opportunities to study abroad at Islamic universities such as AlAzhar. Muftiyyas will earn both an *ijaza* and a doctorate from Union Theological Seminary. Since September 11th, many transnational and international Muslim charities had their assets frozen over charges of minor legal infractions and unsubstantiated accusations of links to terrorism groups (particularly those with international ties), with many buckling and shutting down under the pressures of policing. In contrast, Muslim organizations such as WISE, promoting a "liberal" strain of Islam and a reformist, feminist American pedagogical network, are celebrated and financially rewarded for their work, in the form of grants from philanthropic foundations and the government and by the media in the form of extensive and positive coverage. Like Nomani, Khan embraces the responsibility to reform Islam by excising the practices and norms that reflect the presumed sexism, misogyny, and inegalitarian spirit of "conservative"

Fig. 7.5. The WISE conference featured a play, "7Heavens, 7Women," that ends with a utopic monologue; a future WISE student-traveler returns to the US from Malaysia a scholar and in a triumphant speech recounts the worldwide feminist achievements of WISE's female ʿulama. (Courtesy of Jonathan Cerullo)

Muslims, especially immigrants. She also promises that her project will mainstream American Muslims; she reassured one reporter, "All religions Americanize over time."[60] She successfully mobilized a great deal of public attention and quite sizable material resources in service of her feminist reform project to train female, feminist scholars whose fatwas will "lead and reform" American Muslim communities and the Muslim World, echoing Nomani's feminist narrative and moral geography of an exceptional American umma.

Indigenizing Islamic Authority: African American Muslim Chaplains

Like American Muslims' conflicts over women's religious authority, black-immigrant divisions in US mosques have been the focus of several sympathetic mainstream US media stories since September 11th. A lengthy article in the *New York Times* described "a vast gulf" between black and South Asian and Arab Muslim immigrants, "marked by race

Fig. 7.6. A *New York Times* story about friction between African American and immigrant Muslims featured this photo of Imam Talib, pictured with a Kashmiri physician in a suburban mosque in Long Island. (Courtesy of the *New York Times*)

and class, culture, and history."[61] The article described African American Muslim communities as morally upright, focused on social justice, and based in the inner city, contrasted with suburban, wealthy Muslim communities populated by professional immigrants who fail to understand American racism and American history, typified by the strained relationship of a Pakistani immigrant doctor and an African American preacher, Imam Talib, "a thundering prison chaplain whose mosque traces its roots to Malcolm X" and whose relationship to rappers Mos Def and QTip, the journalist notes, have earned him the nickname "hip hop imam."[62] The article obscures the fact that the vast majority of Muslim immigrants in New York City live in the outer boroughs and are not upwardly mobile professional suburbanites. By equating the category *immigrant* with upwardly mobile suburbanite professionals perplexed by American culture and history, the article constructs African American Muslims as the exceptional umma, as "indigenous Muslims."

The term *indigenous Muslims* that is frequently invoked in sympathetic media coverage is part of the idiom in American Muslim counterpublics, a term popularized by Sherman Jackson, an African American Sunni scholar and university professor and a student-traveler of the same generation as Yusuf and Wadud. Jackson, arguably the most influential American Muslim public intellectual in framing the terms of debates about the conflicts and strained relations between African American Muslims and immigrants, challenges American Muslims (and blacks in particular) to develop a "literacy" of the classical Islamic disciplines that "will confer upon [American Muslims] both the right and the responsibility to develop their own body of concrete doc-trine."[63] "Literacy" here refers to a basic but conceptually rich Islamic higher education, one that will "empower" lay American Muslims to engage scripture and contemporary religious debates in US mosques. Jackson's pragmatist pedagogical vision of increasing "Islamic literacy" among American Muslims is linked to his larger vision of "indigeniz-ing" Islam in the US and his moral geography of American Medina as Home. Key to his project is the rejection of what he terms "Immigrant Islam." For Jackson, "Immigrant Islam is not synonymous with immi-grant Muslims" but rather is the uncritical embrace of Eastern sensi-bilities.[64] Jackson challenges immigrants and blacks to abandon Immi-grant Islam, which nurtures a psychological and emotional hesitance and ambivalence toward their American identities and a suspicion of American culture; he calls on them to embrace his programmatic "indi-genization" of Islam in America, which redirects Muslim Americans' ambivalence toward the Muslim World and renders suspect immi-grant Muslims' social norms that pass as universally applicable Islamic norms in US mosques. One African American Muslim complained to a journalist, "[Immigrants] say we're all brothers, but they don't always practice this in their interactions with us. . . . They always feel the need to play one-upmanship, as if they've got all the [religious] answers and we're there on the fringes in a support role."[65]

While Jackson himself defines the immigrant/indigenous binary in terms of different orientations toward Old World Sunni Islam and America, African American Muslim leaders and the journalists who quote them use the terms "immigrant" and "indigenous" as fixed, ter-ritorial, and ethnic/racial categories. In other words, Muslim American religious leaders, African American ones in particular, use the term "indigenous" as a cultural and racial or ethnic conception of American social citizenship. For some journalists who adopt this frame of indigeneity as social citizenship, blacks (and occasionally whites) have a natural and patriotic relationship to the US and practice "good" Islam, and conversely, immigrants have a presumably "natural" relationship to fundamentalism (and terrorism). Journalists teach their readers to recognize African Americans as good Muslim citizens by representing them as moral exemplars of a moderate Islam to their immigrant coreligionists. One journalist suggests that blacks' "indigenous Islam [in America] that is unique in the West" will offset the kind of political disaffection felt by Muslim immigrants in Europe by nurturing patriotic feeling in US mosques.[66] In one article, Imam Warith Deen Mohammed is the example of a patriotic Muslim. Like Yusuf, he argues that the US is more Islamic than the Muslim World is: "our form of democracy . . . may be closer to . . . Islamic justice for society than any other political ideology existing in the world today."[67] What is left out of these articles is the fact that many African American Muslims, including other black Sunnis, have a far more ambivalent relationship to the US and a far greater identification with Muslims abroad.

This language of "indigeneity" is troubling for many reasons, including the fact that it hardens the lines of social citizenship that black and white Muslims enjoy in a way that their immigrant coreligionists do not. One journalist describes a group of Muslims from the Middle East walking out of an African American mosque "because they objected to the music, claiming it was forbidden by Islam." The article goes on to describe an African American Muslim kindergarten teacher who plays music for her Muslim students; she notes that all human beings "have a natural rhythm, your heart even has a beat."[68] The article gives no context for this difference of opinion over the question of the permissibility of music in Islam except that it is a way to distinguish immigrants from African American Muslims. In other words, the article gives the false impression that African Americans are unique as Muslims who enjoy music. Such sympathetic representations of music-loving African American Muslims and their commensurable Islam are gross distortions that fail to account for the vast internal diversity among black Sunnis and render Muslim immigrants as implicit racists but also "fundamentalists" (and, therefore, potential terrorists) in contrast to good, black Muslim citizens. Importantly, African American Muslim musicians are key to the US government's cultural diplomacy with the Muslim World. Like the Cold War jazz tours, in which the US government sponsored African American musicians' concerts abroad in order to improve the image of the US, since September 11th, American Muslim rappers are part of the US government's hip hop tours in the Muslim World. Parallel to the ways American Muslim religious leaders struggle to maintain their religious authority among Muslim counterpublics alongside their awkward and close ties to the US government, American Muslim rappers-turned-cultural-diplomats struggle to maintain their street credibility and their fans despite their official ties to the government.[69]

In contrast to African American Muslims' hypervisibility in official state tours abroad, sympathetic media representations of African American Muslims in the mainstream US media are the exception. Typically African American Muslims are simply left out of mainstream media stories on American Muslims. For example, they were conspicuously absent from the media coverage of the Ground Zero mosque controversy and the related national debate over anti-Muslim racism. When they are represented, it is their blackness and Americanness, not their Islam, that is the point of interest. Even in media accounts in which it is African American Muslims who take the more strident religious posture in opposition to their immigrant coreligionists, blacks' religious motivations are always secondary. For example, journalists covered an incident in 2005, when two NOI Muslim men broke into a corner store in Oakland, California, and smashed bottles of liquor, wine, and beer with metal pipes, shattering refrigerator cases and leaving behind piles of broken glass. They stole nothing but made a statement to the store's immigrant Muslim owners: stop selling liquor in poor, black communities. In the following weeks, a number of protests by the local mosque communities ensued against Muslim-owned liquor stores across Oakland, with African American Muslims confronting Muslim store owners about Islam's prohibition of alcohol and its detrimental effect on their poor communities, while store owners, mostly Yemeni immigrants, expressed economic desperation and asserted their right to pursue a livelihood in their new country. Despite the fact that these African American Muslims clearly articulated a sense that Muslim store owners had a special, religious obligation not to sell liquor in the ghetto, journalists represented it primarily in racial terms: "In urban America, friction between poor residents and the immigrant merchants who sell cigarettes, bread, and alcoholic beverages . . . is nothing new."[70]

The efforts of African American Muslim leaders to establish their own Islamic pedagogical institutions in the US also remain largely invisible in mainstream media coverage of conflicts between blacks and immigrants in US mosques, such as Jackson's pragmatist institute, the American Learning Institute for Muslims.[71] However, other pragmatist pedagogical institutions that draw African American Muslims have received sympathetic coverage: chaplaincy programs. Chaplaincy programs offer a unique model of US-based Islamic higher education, training Muslim Americans to serve in hospitals, schools, the military, and prisons. While relatively light on classical Islamic disciplines, such as Islamic theology and law and the art of Quranic recitation, chaplaincy programs focus instead on developing applied pastoral skills such as counseling, interfaith relations, and leadership training that will be a resource not only to Muslims but to people of all faiths who seek their counsel. African American Muslim chaplains such as Imam Talib are described in the mainstream media as representing an "indigenous" and uniquely American form of Islamic authority; headlines such as "Muslim Chaplain Offers American Brand of Islam" promise that black chaplains will have an important mainstreaming potential.[72] American media representations of African American Muslim chaplains contrast them with the "typical" imam, an immigrant "*hafiz*" who was trained in the rote memorization of the Quran in an overseas madrasa and who is culturally "out of touch" and implicitly out of place in the US. Clearly, in the context of a crisis over Sunni religious authority and Islamic pedagogy, there are important implications in the standardization in training "professional" and "indigenous" Islamic authorities, but these debates over the authority of chaplains are glossed over in media accounts, such as the PBS documentary *The Calling*, which focused instead on the touching, up-from-his-bootstraps life story of an African American Muslim chaplain.[73] Interestingly, in these sympathetic representations of African American Muslim chaplains, it is the figure of the Latino Muslim that occasionally interrupts and unsettles the categories of indigenous and immigrant and challenges the racial logic of collective guilt. In one article, military chaplain Asadullah Borges advises a

Fig. 7.7. Bilal Ansari, an African American chaplain, speaks to a crowd at the ISNA convention, a moment captured in the PBS documentary film *The Calling*. (Courtesy of Kindling Group)

Pakistani-Venezuelan cadet and other Muslims not to apologize for terrorism, saying, "You can't be sorry for it because we didn't do it."[74]

(In)doctrinating Muslim Youth: AlMaghrib Institute

No Muslim debate over Islamic reform receives more media coverage than the theological and legal one over jihad, radicalization, and homegrown terrorism. The American media life of this Muslim American debate has a history much longer than September 11th; however, today American Salafis, such as Shaykh Yasir Qadhi of the AlMaghrib Institute, are offered as the solution. In the wake of 9/11, the American Salafi movement was profoundly undermined, its adherents fleeing the movement in part due to police scrutiny of their leadership, but the movement also fractured as a result of infighting over theological issues. Founded in 2002, the AlMaghrib Institute, with headquarters in Houston, has almost single-handedly revived the Salafi movement in the US among Sunni American Muslim college students, and its success is demonstrable in its high student enrollment. Most of AlMaghrib's instructors are American student-travelers who studied abroad in the nineties (the generation after the likes of Yusuf, Wadud, and Jackson), and many are graduates of the Islamic University of Madinah.

AlMaghrib has received an enormous amount of public scrutiny (it is called "Jihad U" by some conservative bloggers) primarily because Shaykh Anwar AlAwlaki, the American citizen who left the US and became the highest English-speaking cleric in AlQaeda, was a popular preacher among American Salafis. Although he was never formally associated with AlMaghrib, recordings of his religious speeches continued to be sold at AlMaghrib events, even after they were banned by AlMaghrib faculty in reaction to AlAwlaki's praise of the 2009 Fort Hood shooting. AlAwlaki was also tied indirectly to AlMaghrib because the Nigerian Umar Farouk AlMutallib, better known as the Christmas Day bomber, who had explosives sewn into his underwear that he intended to detonate on a plane headed for Detroit in 2009, claimed AlAwlaki as inspiration and was also a student at AlMaghrib. Other AlMaghrib students who have followed AlAwlaki's call-to-arms include Daniel Maldonado, a New Hampshire convert who was convicted in 2007 of training with a group linked to an AlQaeda militia in Somalia; Tarek Mehanna, a twenty-eight-year-old pharmacist arrested for conspiring to attack Americans; and two young Virginia men held in Pakistan in 2009 for seeking to train with militants.

In addition to scrutiny from counterterrorism agencies, AlMaghrib has come under attack by other American Salafi groups that were thriving in the eighties and nineties but that have since dramatically shrunk and fractured; this older generation of Salafi American preachers accuse AlMaghrib's leadership of taking "liberal" or "apolitical" positions. As a result of this external and internal scrutiny, the theologically reformist organization rebranded itself and moved away from the public use of the label "Salafi," although AlMaghrib faculty identify the organization as Salafi in ideological orientation privately. Qadhi admits that Hamza Yusuf has so effectively branded Zaytuna's pedagogical method as "traditionalist" that the AlMaghrib faculty were forced to find an alternative "brand" in order to compete. Each of the religious leaders at the helm of the emerging, US-based pedagogical projects claims to convey traditional knowledge, whether the formalist founders of Zaytuna, reformist feminists such as Wadud and Khan, or the pragmatists developing Muslim chaplaincy programs, and the reformist faculty at AlMaghrib are no exception. Forgoing "Salafi" primarily for political reasons and "traditionalist" because of Zaytuna's high profile, AlMaghrib's faculty have aggressively attempted to brand themselves alternatively as "indigenous Salafis," explicitly borrowing the mainstreaming language of Jackson, or—as explicated in a massive, eleven-page, interactive *New York Times* article about Qadhi—as representing "orthodox [Islam] with a capital O."[75] Despite the many negative connotations associated with the term *orthodox* in English (which confirm negative stereotypes about Salafi Muslims as sectarian, exclusive, and rigidly conservative), AlMaghrib's founders identify Orthodox Jews, specifically the modern Hasidic movement, as their model of commensurable American difference, and their own project of "indigenizing" Salafi Islam in the US is carefully molded after them. In other words, if Orthodox Jews are conservative and old-fashioned and exclusive (terms that Qadhi himself uses unselfconsciously to describe AlMaghrib), then equating "Orthodox Islam" to Orthodox Judaism is an effective (and conscious) branding strategy.

The AlMaghrib scholars take Orthodox Jews as a mainstreaming model in a number of ways, perhaps most visibly in their online presence. AlMaghrib's success and its slick website is comparable to the enormous success of the conservative Lubavitch Jewish community, which also represents a small strain of Judaism in the US numerically, yet its site, chabad.org, has successfully positioned itself as the gatekeeper on all things Jewish online for a global, English-reading cyber audience. AlMaghrib's user-friendly website also boasts an incredibly active forum, distance learning, and multimedia content, including cartoons starring animated versions of AlMaghrib's instructors who explain intricate details of Islamic law, much like chabad.org's "kabbalatoons."

In the company of the US government's counterterrorism officials and journalists, Qadhi positions himself and AlMaghrib as the solution to extremists such as AlAwlaki precisely because he is "Orthodox" and he accepts the collective responsibility for reforming "bad" fundamentalists. Just as critics of Nomani, Wadud, and PMU decried their invocation of the "back of the bus" as analogous to gendered space in mosques, Qadhi's critics argue that his characterization of Salafis and AlMaghrib as "Orthodox" Muslims in the media similarly exploits Americans' assumptions and misinformation about Sunni Islam. Like Nomani and Wadud, Qadhi has been accused by his Muslim critics of opportunism because

Fig. 7.8. An animated Yasir Qadhi in a grocery store promotes an AlMaghrib class on the dietary restrictions in Islamic law, which was featured in a *New York Times* spread. (Courtesy of AlMaghrib Institute)

of the way he has introduced and grossly simplified a complex debate about orthodoxy and theology in US mosques in the mainstream media, presumably using external attention as a tool in service of his own theological reform project. Naturally, Qadhi claims that he and AlMaghrib represents the "truest" or "purest" form of Islam, but his rivals and critics contest the exclusivity of his claim, particularly since the Salafi-identified mosques make up only 1 percent of US mosques as a whole, and Salafis represent a significant but small Muslim American counterpublic in general (just as Wadud and Nomani's feminist reform is far more radical and far less representative of American mosque congregations at large).[76] In reaction to the *Times* article, Qadhi's critics protested that Sunni Islam does not fit into the Reformed/Conservative/Orthodox categories of American Judaism. In fact, many Sunni Muslims (including feminist reformers) use the term *orthodox* the way Malcolm X famously did, as an inclusive, umbrella term for the Muslim mainstream, which includes both Sunnis and Shias, and not a fringe "conservative," "rigid," or "old-fashioned" sect. The inclusive, antisectarian use of *orthodox* is also significant because the reformist Salafi movement has a reputation for being divisive and eager to label other Muslims as heretics (sufis and Shias are frequent targets).[77] Furthermore, the term *orthodox* also has a particular racial valence in US mosques, because it obscures the longer legacy and history of black communities such as the Nation of Islam that laid an important foundation for contemporary American Muslims and institutions, a legacy that African American Sunni leaders such as Jackson labor to recuperate in service of the "indigenization" of American Islam.[78]

In addition to representing "Orthodox" Islam, the *Times* article also details how Qadhi represents himself as a "pacifist Salafi" to counterterrorism officials, itself a disingenuous claim in the eyes of his critics, including his former students, since he openly admits that he is not actually a pacifist and since he publicly denies being a Salafi. Just as Hamza Yusuf, who actually is a pacifist, was heralded as Islam's most able theological critic of suicide bombing, so Qadhi is held up by journalists and government officials as a particularly efficacious counterterrorism tool who can indoctrinate youth against militancy precisely because he is an "ultraconservative" and "orthodox" Muslim.[79] It is a role Qadhi embraces in the media despite its challenges.

> [In order] to offer an authoritative rebuttal of extremist ideology . . . Qadhi says he would need to address the thorny question of what kinds of militant actions *are* permitted by Islamic law. . . . If he were to acknowledge that Islamic law endorses the legitimacy of armed resistance against Western forces in Muslim territory, he could give a green light to the very students he claims he is trying to keep off the militant path. Yet by remaining silent, Qadhi says he is losing the credibility he needs to persuade them [that as] . . . American Muslims . . . [they must] abide by the laws of their country, understanding that had they been born in Palestine or Iraq, their "responsibilities would be different."[80]

Qadhi complains that he could stop extremism, "but it's not palatable for Americans," even as he insists American Muslim scholars such as himself are the global solution. "American Muslims are at the forefront in battling Islamic extremism because they have everything to lose if anything else happens," Qadhi says. "They'll lose their American identity, and they'll lose their prestige, whatever prestige remains of our religion that we would like to have in this land."[81] Qadhi posits the American umma as exceptional because they are the most invested in preventing terrorists, but they are also exceptional because they are constrained as American citizens from waging war on their "hosts." Therefore, for Qadhi, American citizenship is a productive limitation that makes American Muslims uniquely important, potentially moral examples to the Muslim World in the global religious debate about jihad and modern warfare.

The *Times* article frames this global religious debate over jihad as one over competing moral geographies, competing Muslim constructions of America:

> The central contest between Qadhi and militants like Awlaki hinges on a rather abstruse point: how to define America in Islamic terms. Qadhi likens [the US] to Abyssinia, the seventh-century African kingdom that

Fig. 7.9. Yasir Qadhi pictured before delivering an Eid sermon. (Courtesy of the *New York Times*)

gave refuge to the prophet's followers. In exchange for upholding the laws of the land, they were allowed to worship freely—a contract Qadhi equates to an American passport or visa. Breaking the contract by joining militant groups at war with America constitutes treachery, Qadhi says, which is forbidden in Islam. Awlaki, by contrast, compares America with ancient Mecca, where the prophet's followers were persecuted, forcing them to flee and later fight back. Critics take issue with the technical nature of the debate. Qadhi's students, they argue, could conclude that joining a militant group is permissible provided they renounce their citizenship. This is further complicated by his refusal to address whether the Islamist uprisings in Iraq and Afghanistan constitute legitimate jihads. Saying yes would open the door to public recriminations, denying the legitimacy of the insurgencies would fly in the face of Islamic law.[82]

In other words, Qadhi vacillates between the national moral geography of an American Medina as Home, where an indigenous (Salafi) Islam might thrive and take root in the US, and the transnational moral geography of an American Abyssinia, one that remains far more ambivalent about the US and embraces Muslims' status as religious outsiders, guests in a host country that will never be home. Both compete with AlAwlaki's moral geography of a dystopic American Mecca, where Muslims are persecuted on a domestic front in what he framed as a global war between Western governments and the Muslim World.

Despite Qadhi's lingering ambivalence toward the American mainstream, he embraces racial profiling, a far departure from the insular politics and countercitizenship narratives of an earlier generation of American Salafis. The *Times* article details the cold reception of the FBI at an AlMaghrib retreat when Qadhi surprised his students by inviting FBI officials to address them. Such dramatic and open endorsements of self-policing and racial profiling of Muslim youth not only make AlMaghrib's students vulnerable; they have diminished Qadhi's religious credibility. In reaction to the *Times* article, former AlMaghrib students expressed surprise and regret that they had taken classes in a Salafi institute without realizing it; others felt betrayed by Qadhi's cooperation with law enforcement to profile AlMaghrib students such as themselves, dubbing their former teacher "Shaykh 'Yes Sir!' Qadhi."

In the absence of being able to talk about jihad or even the slippery quality of American citizenship openly, journalists and Qadhi himself fall back on culture-talk, setting Qadhi up as a civilized, rational, good American citizen who happens to be a Salafi, in contrast to AlAwlaki, whom he represents—in troubling, racialized language—as not only militant and "crazed" but *backward*. The article portrays Qadhi as an all-American geek, a *Star Trek* fan and a graduate student at Yale University. Qadhi himself uses his status as an Ivy League student to demonstrate his embrace of his Americanness and to distinguish himself from an earlier generation of American Salafis, telling a *Washington Post* reporter, "It's unprecedented that a Salafi is doing a graduate degree at an Ivy League school. . . . Our [American Salafi] forebears would see that as anathema."[83]

Reminiscent of the coverage of the second-generation immigrants of PMU, the *Times* article lingers on how Qadhi dresses in polo shirts and drives a black Honda CR-V, vacations at Disney World with his wife and kids, and orders a coffee at Starbucks or pulls "into a Popeye's drive-through for popcorn shrimp and gravy-slathered biscuits."[84] His consumption habits render his "ultraconservative" difference commensurable. In one lecture, also featured as a link on the *Times* website, Qadhi gestures at the lush, hotel auditorium adorned with crystal chandeliers where he is speaking, and he asks his students wryly, "Should you follow a guy in a cave or a guy lecturing in a beautiful hall?"[85] In other words, in the journalist's logic of good Muslim citizens that Qadhi reproduces, it is his "mainstream" consumption habits, entrepreneurial success as a "savvy businessman," and material wealth that distinguishes him from a robed and turbaned bad, backward Salafi who lives in a cave and who fails to "indigenize."

Of course, AlAwlaki's alternative moral geography of an American Mecca is not drawing students away from Qadhi because of the appeal of his clothes or his "cave" but because of its radical politics and its promise of global social justice. While American Muslim leaders such as Qadhi and others have taken it as their personal responsibility to combat extremism, they have largely failed to address the political grievances of disaffected Muslim youth: the global Muslim suffering in which the US government is implicated that they find when they read the newspaper or watch the news or surf the Web. The silences and euphemisms and illegibilities of religious obligation that constrain Muslim American discourses on jihad are often the basis for accusations of Muslim double-talk (and, from the disinformation experts, stealth jihad). But in this article, Qadhi's evasiveness is held up as a mere hiccup in the state's counterterrorism policy. In other words, Qadhi cannot concede that if Muslim Americans were to absolve themselves of American citizenship, there would be no religious restriction (and in fact there may be a religious obligation) to join their embattled Muslim coreligionists and to fight the US military in war zones such as Afghanistan and Iraq.

Once again, the intra-Muslim debates, in this case about jihad, must be made recognizable to an imagined American audience, and so the theological and political complexity of the debate is collapsed even within AlMaghrib's private classes, even in the roster of courses the institute offers because of the government's scrutiny, whether real or imagined. As the *Times* article notes, AlMaghrib does not offer courses about jihad even though it is the most often requested class topic, yet Qadhi is held up as a solution, a tool to indoctrinate Muslim American youth against terrorism through the study of "orthodox" theology. Once AlAwlaki was assassinated by the US government, Qadhi published an op-ed in the *New York Times* criticizing the government for the targeted killing of the American citizen, arguing it was not only a betrayal of the US justice system but counterproductive in the fight against terrorism, that AlAwlaki "needed to be challenged, not assassinated," a "difficult" job that Qadhi identifies as his own. Qadhi rejects AlAwlaki's indiscriminate violence, his "message that one cannot be a good Muslim and an American at the same time," and the US government's military action while asserting his own potential to counteract terrorism as an "Orthodox" Muslim preacher.[86]

Though the mainstream media's efforts to counter the disinformation experts and to redeem American Muslims through sympathetic representations is understandable, the recurrent hope that runs through these sympathetic portrayals—that there are comprehensible Muslim social citizens in our midst who know how to stop the incomprehensible Muslims that we are scared of—can be misplaced. AlMaghrib's theological and pedagogical projects and the credibility of its faculty are alternatively enhanced for American publics and diminished in the eyes of many American Muslims by constructing jihad and terrorism primarily as a religious problem and not as a political one. Journalists construct figures such as Qadhi as solutions, as teachers who can "indoctrinate" disaffected Muslim youth to read Islamic theology and law the "right" way, the Salafi way that Qadhi describes as peaceful and "Orthodox," manifest in his national moral geography of an American Medina and even in his transnational moral geography of an American Abyssinia.

An Emergent National Moral Geography

As Muslim American religious leaders diagnose Islam's crises and promote their formalist, pragmatist, and reformist pedagogical projects in the media, their authority and legitimacy has been alternatively enhanced and diminished.[87] Muslim Americans have long drawn on transnational moral geographies in order to rethink and reimagine both the place of Islam in the US and their place as religious minorities amid the American mainstream. Since September 11th, there has been a sea change in the ways devout Muslim Americans talk about themselves in relation to the American mainstream and the global umma. An emergent narrative of Muslim American exceptionalism and a growing ambivalence toward the umma is increasingly replacing older narratives of religious outsiderhood and countercitizenship. This Muslim American exceptionalism signals both the belief that Muslim Americans are culturally distinct from (unlike, different from) the global umma as well as being morally distinct from (superior than) the global umma. It fuses a Muslim American excellence and exemplarity, and, importantly, this discourse of an exceptional American umma is profoundly depoliticized. This is a fundamental break with the countercitizenship narratives that historically characterized the transnational moral geographies of Muslim counterpublics, including the global, panethnic, and politically radical moral visions of Malcolm X, Elijah Muhammad, Muhammad Sadiq, Drew Ali, Ismail Al-Faruqi, and a young Hamza Yusuf.

The mediatization of Muslim debates reshapes Muslim Americans' moral geographies and reorients them both to the US and to their tradition, often in contradictory ways. The fear about the ways Islam might be perceived finds its way into how Muslims argue with one another even when the reporters are absent, the cameras are gone, and the mosques empty of visitors, producing a kind of double consciousness. Media representations of intra-Muslim debates become a kind of assurance that "we" (of the mainstream) are winning "the battle for [Muslim] hearts and minds"—or the "struggle for the soul of Islam," as it has been alternatively dubbed—but they also have their own pedagogical grammar, teaching Americans how to discern and distinguish and "see" what good Muslim citizens and bad Muslims look like. Issues that seem to have nothing to do with terrorism—such as whether women can be imams or whether congregations should be mixed by gender or whether immigrants were driven to emigrate by economic considerations or whether those immigrants participated in the civil rights movement— become the criteria of social citizenship. American Muslim spokespeople reframe the attention and curiosity garnered by September 11th in service of their own reform projects (Yusuf's pedagogical efforts, PMU's feminism, Jackson's indigenization of Islam, or Qadhi's "indoctrinating" of Muslims into "Orthodoxy with a capital O"). Each is calibrated as a way to make Muslim Americans recognizable as (social) citizens who could "stand for" the nation. These are not merely oversimplified media representations of intra-Muslim debates; these representations index how, in the very process of making debates about Islam digestible for American audiences, Muslim Americans spokespeople end up translating differences among Muslims using the terms of culture-talk themselves. By identifying themselves as commensurable, good Muslim citizens against an incommensurable (anti-intellectual, sexist, racist, fundamentalist, and backward) bad Muslim immigrant, they reinscribe the exclusion of (some) Muslims from American social citizenship.

Of course, questions about theology, race relations, gender equality, and the criteria by which one becomes a religious leader have driven debates in US mosques for decades. However, these intra-Muslim debates have been radically reshaped since September 11th, both through the process of becoming digestible for American publics with little context for them and through the incorporation of a narrow (and shrinking) set of binaries: liberal/conservative, hosts/guests, feminists/sexists, indigenous Americans/immigrants, pacifists/terrorists, orthodox/heterodox. These Islamic debates become interpolated into an old American debate about the universality of citizenship: the tension between the political ideal of citizenship being an inclusive legal status that transcends race and religion and the reality that social citizenship remains a privilege, a prize of social recognition granted to some people and not others depending on their race, national origin, and religion.

The figure of the good Muslim citizen defers the contradictions of American citizenship that has preoccupied Muslim Americans and all American minorities for generations, the contradiction between America's universal promise of legal citizenship and the cultural and racial bases of belonging to the nation, of social citizenship. Both the bad Muslim bogeyman and the good Muslim citizen are interlinked effects of the contradiction built into American citizenship; they together confirm the universal promise of American citizenship and displace the blame for its social and racial exclusions on the excluded populations themselves. Formalists, pragmatists, reformists, sufi intellectuals, second-generation liberals, feminist pioneers, "indigenous" African American Muslims, and "Orthodox" and "pacifist" Salafis all aggressively define themselves as American Muslim citizens and as the exceptional umma against a fundamentalist, and even pathological, immigrant Muslim Other. In the process, the most fundamental binary of all—between "us" and "them"—is hardened. As the Other that intrudes in our midst, the figure of the immigrant Muslim as a perpetual foreigner indexes and underscores the ontological distance between the US and the distant, backward, pathological Muslim World from which he came; in sympathetic media portrayals of good American Muslims, the perpetually foreign Muslim marks the ontological difference between the exceptional American umma and the umma overseas.

Obama and the Exceptional Umma

While running for president in 2008, Barack Obama promised that if elected, he would address the world's one and a half billion Muslims from a "major Islamic forum." After much media speculation around the world about where this forum would be, and the strategic implications of this or that choice, the administration chose, in President Obama's words, "the timeless city of Cairo." Obama cast the Muslim World as a place he traveled to but also an audience of over a billion people he addressed. Obama's "Cairo Address," or "Muslim World

Address" as it was dubbed in the media, was framed as a (renewed) bid for the Muslim hearts and minds that had been the "other" front in President George W. Bush's War on Terror. The speech in January 2009 was many things, but chief among them was an explicit effort to signal that Americans were not (or were no longer) "at war with Islam."[88]

Although Obama's "Muslim World" address took place at Cairo University, Obama made a point to acknowledge another cohost: "For over a thousand years, Al-Azhar has stood as a beacon of Islamic learning; and for over a century, Cairo University has been a source of Egypt's advancement. And together, you represent the harmony between tradition and progress." The symbolism of Cairo's quintessential modern, secular university and its historic, Islamic madrasa-university jointly hosting President Obama may have been lost on most Americans, but, as we now know, such a coupling would resonate with Muslim counterpublics worldwide, including with many American Muslims. American Muslims figured prominently in Obama's moral geography of the Muslim World, as the exceptional umma, as moral examples of modern, democratic, and productive citizens for Muslims in the Muslim World to emulate but also as proof to the Muslim World of the American government's exceptional benevolence and tolerance of minorities.

> Islam has always been a part of America's story. . . . And since our founding, American Muslims have enriched the United States. They have fought in our wars, they have served in our government, they have stood for civil rights, they have started businesses, they have taught at our universities, they've excelled in our sports arenas, they've won Nobel Prizes, built our tallest building, and lit the Olympic Torch. And when the first Muslim American was recently elected to Congress, he took the oath to defend our Constitution using the same Holy Koran that one of our Founding Fathers—Thomas Jefferson—kept in his personal library.[89]

Muslim Americans operated as an ideal minority throughout Obama's speech: well integrated, well tolerated, contributing members of American society. Obama highlighted the achievements of American Muslims as a parallel to the "civilizational" achievements of Muslims from a glorious, bygone age on the other side of the Atlantic.

The authors of Obama's speech included several Muslim American policy experts and advisers as well as the president himself, and every word was thoroughly scrutinized afterward in the US and abroad.[90] Was President Obama's tone too conciliatory or too critical? Was it a mark of integrity or weakness for him to admit the US's complicity in the support of oppressive regimes in the Muslim World, such as his example of the US-backed Iranian shah's brutal suppression of democratic movements in the 1950s?[91] In 2009, the US's support of Muslim dictators was rarely discussed in the mainstream US media. Just two years later, however, with the millions who poured into the streets during the Arab dignity revolutions, US complicity in the subversion of democracy in the Middle East became front-page news, with images of millions marching in opposition to the US government's "friends," including Egypt's Hosni Mubarak. The initial lukewarm reaction of the Obama administration to the Cairene protestors' appeals for freedom and democracy in 2011, including Vice President Biden's insistence that Mubarak was "not a dictator" on national television in the US, belied the conciliatory and principled message of Obama's Cairo address delivered two years earlier.[92]

Only a few miles from the Cairo University's campus is the elegant Sultan Hassan Mosque, built in the fourteenth century into the hillside overlooking the city. Just before the address, like thousands of American tourists each year, President Obama walked through the mosque's majestic arched entryway and stood alongside the stone pillars of this imposing structure, taking in the panoramic view of bustling Cairo below. The mosque's very architecture reflects the kaleidoscopic, heterogeneous, decentralized nature of religious authority in Sunni Islam and its plural legal culture: the mosque's central courtyard and domed fountain open to four large rooms with vaulted ceilings and hanging lamps suspended by long brass chains facing the central atrium; the back of each room connects to corridors leading to madrasas of each of the four Sunni schools of law.

Minutes after President Obama and Secretary of State Hillary Clinton finished their guided tour, and as the motorcade began to snake toward Cairo University, government pickup trucks swarmed the Sultan Hassan Mosque. Cairo's security had been even tighter than usual, with mass jailings and "disappearings" of devout Muslim youth in the

Fig. 7.10. President Barack Obama and Secretary of State Hillary Clinton admire the historic Sultan Hassan Mosque shortly before the president's "Muslim World Address." (Courtesy of Reuters)

weeks leading up to Obama's visit. However, the Egyptian government officers who surrounded the mosque were not on a security detail, nor did they arrest anyone. Instead, they collected the flowers and potted greens that had lined the mosque and the streets leading up to it, plants that were apparently intended only for the American visitors.[93] Onlookers watched in dismay, but without surprise, as the fragrant plants were gathered in the beds of the government pickups and driven off in a haze of exhaust fumes; some mumbled that Mubarak could have had the decency to wait at least for Obama's address to begin, while others wondered aloud if the brand new prayer rugs, padding the red, blue, and cream marble floors of the mosque, would be taken away as well, and the tattered, worn ones returned. The jokes made by devout Muslim Egyptians about those flowers disappearing before their eyes capture the banality and the emotional strain of chronic political crisis. The flowers act as an analogue for a state that rules its subjects but fails to govern, a state that can quietly disappear Muslim bodies without trace or explanation, like plants rolling down El-Qalaa Street in the back of a government pickup truck.

A Pakistani American student-traveler in Cairo relayed the story of Obama's visit, and the disappearings of both the flowers and the devout young Muslim men, to me. Only one piece of her story struck me as out of the ordinary. An American citizen studying in Cairo was jailed too, a friend of this woman's, without charges and without warning, and, like the jailed Egyptians, the American and other Western student-travelers were unceremoniously released on Obama's departure. Disappeared Muslim bodies haunt the debates and the Muslim Americans this book has followed, those that are animated by the media and the global pedagogical networks that connect the US and the Middle East. I never met the American student-traveler who was jailed for Obama's visit to Cairo in 2009 and quietly released after the fact, but I imagine, like hundreds of other American Muslim seekers studying abroad in the Middle East, he was seeking his tradition in the margins of Cairo; he was seeking a place for himself and for Islam in our world. The irony is that in seeking out the Islamic East, he came up against the proxies of the most powerful security forces of the West—his disappearance is terrifying proof of how intertwined the US and the Muslim World are.

Epilogue

American Muslims and the Place of Dissent

DIGNITY

On January 25, 2011, Egyptians from all social backgrounds—young and old, men and women, Christian and Muslim, gay and straight, middle class and working poor, Islamists and Marxists—marched in cities across Egypt and began an eighteen-day protest that captivated the world. Their calls in Cairo's Tahrir Square, and in public squares throughout Egypt, rang out around the world: "Dignity, Freedom, and Social Justice!"

I used to pray that someday my children might live to see a more just, a more stable, a more peaceful Middle East in their lifetime than the one I knew in mine. I never thought I would live to see the dignity protests and peaceful revolutions that began in Tunisia at the end of 2010. I never once dared to dream it, and I don't think I even ever prayed for it.

I thought I had finished this book in the last few cold weeks of 2010, before the footage on CNN and Aljazeera of Tunisia and then Egypt made me rethink and rewrite so much of it. It was beautiful and frightening and heartbreaking and inspiring to watch from so far away. Um Ali and Maryam and I have lost touch over the years, as phone numbers and emails have changed and disconnected. I wondered if my two strong-willed friends were in Tahrir Square during Egypt's revolution. Maryam, if she still lives in Cairo, probably was not, but Um Ali, if she still lives in Cairo, probably was, chanting and praying, defiantly. Once the protests that had been beyond the limits of my imagination began, I was sure that change was on the horizon, but worries about what might happen next, about whether it was all fleeting, hung over each small victory.

On February 2, at 4:36 in the afternoon, a fatwa crawled across my screen on the Aljazeera ticker. I had been waiting for the Azhari scholars to finally break their silence. "Ali Jomaa, the Grand Mufti of Egypt, tells all Egyptians to go home: 'I greet President Mubarak who offered dialogue and responded to the demands of the people. Going against legitimacy is forbidden (*haram*) [sinful]. This is an invitation for chaos. We support stability. What we have now is a blind chaos leading to a civil war. I call on all parents to ask their children to stay home.'"

Muslim hearts and minds. I know many, many Muslims in the US and in Egypt who once took Shaykh Ali Gomaa as the ideal Sunni scholar: brilliant, articulate, pious, courageous, a man with an impeccable intellectual pedigree and political integrity. Minds can change in an instant, in the speed of a few television frames. Hearts can change in an instant, in the duration of a turning page. Disenchantment sets in before you get to the remote, to the power button, before the very last spot of white in the center of the screen goes black.

It is true that more diplomatic, conciliatory gestures were made by Shaykh Ali Gomaa later; he offered open office hours to the protesting youth, and he dug up an old fatwa of his, sanctioning peaceful protests. But in the most critical hours and days, in his public statements, he never called on the state to restrain itself. Stronger, more hard-line positions were taken by the Obama administration against Mubarak as the days wore on, also belated and unsatisfactory, not enough to erase the administration's open ambivalence over democracy in the region.

As I watched and waited, I grappled with a quiet anger at myself for being so politically naïve. President Obama had actually disappointed me; Shaykh Ali Gomaa had actually disappointed me. I should have known better than to expect anything besides what looked so predictable in hindsight. I imagined what their moral and political calculus was at the time, its logics, its constraints. Their awesome responsibility meant they could not risk the possibility that Mubarak would not fall, or they could not risk what it might take to make him fall, or they could not risk not knowing the political landscape that might emerge if he fell.

Hope, too, forms itself in an instant, in the time it takes high heels to click off a television sound stage. When an Egyptian state television news anchor, Shahira Amin, quit in disgust on live television and joined the protestors, I thought of all those Azhari shaykhs in Cairo who had complained to me so many times about how unvalued they were by ordinary people, especially by the youth. I had spent so many hours recording and writing about how their expertise went unappreciated, how badly they wanted to be relevant. Here was their opportunity; they just had to follow her lead. A few prominent scholars did. Many famous ones outside Egypt did. Most of the popular Sunni scholars in the US came forward publicly to support the protesters in writings and sermons, detailing the long tradition of Sunni dissent, the long lists of scholars who were tortured and killed for speaking truth to power. But in Egypt, too many learned men remained silent.

Some American Muslim leaders, such as Imam Suhaib Webb, expressed open disappointment with those 'ulama in the Middle East. Webb, a young, white preacher with a popular following, was a former gang member turned student-traveler. He had graduated from AlAzhar University, and six months earlier, Shaykh Ali Gomaa had praised him for his intellectual achievement on the stage at the annual ISNA conference. Shaykh Hamza Yusuf shared the stage with them too that night and on his blog, and I was surprised that he was only mildly critical of Shaykh Ali. Shaykh Hamza reminded American Muslims that even if they disagreed with the 'ulama, they ought to "maintain a good opinion of the scholars." They were scholars, after all.

I am not considered a scholar in that world of intellectuals. But I have casually flipped through enough Islamic law manuals to know that the chapters on political rebellion do not apply so clearly to the dignity revolutions. I have read enough to understand that the quietism of some Sunni scholars is built on an interpretive jump that equates the premodern caliphate and a modern police state. In those next eighteen days, as we wondered whether Mubarak would actually fall, I waited for those scholars too. I could not help thinking, "If their trained minds are so nimble, if the tradition is so dynamic and alive, then why are these scholars so slow?" Was the tradition so heavy on their backs that the revolution in Egypt was over before they decreed it was permissible?

It did not look to me like the kids in Tahrir needed anyone to teach them about courage and justice and faith, anyway. They certainly were not waiting for a fatwa from AlAzhar, the way so many American Muslim youth were, glued to their computer and television screens.

We all make miscalculations. We all have moments of cowardice and weakness, we all follow the wrong instincts, sometimes. And if those moments remain concealed, it is a mercy from outside of us. Sometimes they do not, and only our intentions or confusions or regrets are in the shadows. Credibility is vulnerable. Legitimacy is fragile. Authority is slippery. Leadership is a performance. Achievements, charisma, expertise—these things cannot hold trust together if the sands shift, if dignity cracks.

I had earned my disillusionment. That is what I was thinking one afternoon, drained from waiting and waiting for a dictator to fall. And I was trying to soften myself with the thought that no one is perfect, that nothing is ever perfect—except this one book, this one verse that I found, that spoke to me: "Oh God! Possessor of the dominion, You give reign to whom You will, and You take reign from whom You will, and You endue dignity in whom You will, and You humiliate whom You will. In Your hand is the good. Truly, You are able to do all things."

The next day, Mubarak lost his power. Millions and millions, in Egypt and around the world, felt that their prayers had been answered, that their dignity was restored. I could not help but think of Shaykh Ali Gomaa in that celebratory moment, wondering if his relief was tinged with anxiety about the way responsibility and blame might be assigned once the happy tears were dried, once the next chapter in Egypt's long history began.

Dissent

This book maps a series of overlapping, global debates among American Muslims about the criteria of Islamic authority, debates shaped by the profoundly geographic religious imagination of American Muslims. As we have seen, for American Muslims, the question of who defines Islam today is intertwined with questions about their identities as a national religious minority and as part of the umma, a global majority. American Muslims' religious debates over defining Islamic authority and their obligations to the umma are also ethical interrogations of American citizenship. Their transnational countercitizenship reflects their ambivalence as a national minority, fusing their critiques of the state with their desire for a place within the American mainstream. Despite Muslim Americans' longstanding ambivalence toward the US, and the diverse and complex ways in which they have embraced religious outsiderhood, today we see Muslim American leaders mainstreaming their communities at an unprecedented scale. As a result, the very flavor of debates about religious authority within American mosques and the dominant moral geographies promoted by a diverse set of American Muslim leaders are increasingly reflective of the proclivities of the dominant culture and the US government. Since September 11th, Muslim Americans' debates over the crisis of Islamic authority are constrained by external pressures, by scrutiny (even when sympathetic) from the mainstream US media, by the need to explain themselves to the American public, by surveillance from the US government. As the War on Terror systematically undermines transnational charitable, intellectual, and migrational networks that connect American Muslims to their coreligionists abroad, many American Muslim leaders are increasingly calling for the muting, or even the breaking, of those same ties to the global umma.

This mainstreaming trend is evident if we look at the emerging landscape of Islamic pedagogy within the US. On the one hand, given the growing number and range of pedagogical institutions developed by Muslim American leaders on US soil, it is likely that in the future far fewer Muslim American youth will feel compelled to travel abroad in order to access traditional knowledge than the hundreds, perhaps even thousands, who did so in the last few decades of the twentieth century and the first decade of the twenty-first. Furthermore, with the political instability brought on by the dignity revolutions, the Middle East will likely be less attractive to American Muslims as a pedagogical destination in the near future. On the other hand, if American Muslim pedagogical institutions, including Zaytuna College, AlMaghrib Institute, the WISE muftiyya program, and chaplaincy programs, are too closely aligned to state projects, if their pedagogical programs are perceived by devout Muslims as compromised and constrained by the US government, then they will likely lose their religious legitimacy in the eyes of Muslim counterpublics in the US and abroad. The same fate that met Islamic pedagogical institutions in the postcolonial Middle East in the twentieth century could replicate itself in the US in the twenty-first century. Conversely, as Islamists assume greater political control in the wake of the dignity revolutions, Islamic pedagogical institutions in the Middle East may reinvent themselves as politically autonomous, and they may be able to reestablish the religious credibility they lost operating under state control and by suppressing political dissent.

The debates about the crisis of authority that this book maps are haunted by the figure of the dissenting Islamic scholar. A global Sunni debate over the proper role of dissent has been reenergized in the wake of the dignity revolutions. This debate pivots on a seemingly simple question: does oppression make political revolt an Islamic imperative? Some Muslim scholars see the fight for social justice as paramount, no less than a religious obligation; they are in solidarity with the protests and activists engaged in the unfinished dignity revolutions in Egypt, the Middle East, and beyond. Other Muslim scholars argue that preserving social and political stability is the religious virtue that has primacy, even when the political leadership is suboptimal, and they offer the bloodshed in Syria as a counterexample to the (partial) successes of the peaceful dignity revolutions in Egypt and Tunisia. Although the Syrian protesters demanding dignity and political change were also peaceful, Assad's violent and murderous crushing of dissent led to the organization of a countermilitary opposition to his regime and, ultimately, a full-blown war, proof, these Muslim scholars argue, that stability under a dictator is a better public good than the anarchy of civil war.

The dignity revolutions revealed that many of the 'ulama were not as "peripheral" to the state as Muslim counterpublics in the Middle East and the US believed them to be. Although many of the intellectuals and teachers in these pedagogical networks publicly have supported the peaceful protestors, many others are studiously silent. Two of the most revered and well-respected public intellectuals that I met in Egypt and Syria, Ali Gomaa and Said Ramadan al-Buti, respectively, both sided with and defended their autocratic regimes in the name of political stability during the respective revolutions. Even once Mubarak stepped down and many revivalists and 'ulama returned to Tahrir to peacefully demand that AlAzhar regain its political and institutional autonomy from the state, Gomaa, as the official Shaykh AlAzhar and the Grand Mufti, took the unpopular position that the institution should be kept under governmental control.[1]

Since figures such as Gomaa and al-Buti loom large in American Muslim counterpublics, many American Sunni leaders felt compelled to respond to their public statements and fatwas, which delegitimized the protests as sinful and outside the pale of orthodoxy, another attack on

Fig. E.1. This widely circulated photo of the Qubaysiyat leadership meeting with Bashar Al-Assad was tweeted on December 11, 2012, and provoked a strong condemnation of the apolitical movement in the diaspora.

the tradition of dissent within Sunni Islam. While a few Muslim public intellectuals in North America and Europe took strong, critical positions against the statist ʿulama such as Gomaa and al-Buti in the Middle East, others defended them, noting that the debate over political dissent was among the oldest and most divisive questions in the tradition. One of the most extraordinary forms of the apologetic defenses offered by American Muslim intellectuals for the quietism of ʿulama in the Middle East reproduced the logic of American exceptionalism: since ʿulama in the Middle East are not familiar with cultures of dissent, it is only in the West, and the US specifically, that the Sunni scholar is "free" to speak his or her mind, to speak truth to power. What is extraordinary about this particular narrative of the exceptional American umma is that it erases the long lists of historical Sunni heroes and heroines who were tortured at the hands of the state, who died for their acts of dissent, who lived long before 1776.

Ironically, in a moment when the possibilities of dissent and social change are opening across the Middle East at a massive scale for the first time in decades, the possibilities and spaces for dissent are shrinking in

Fig. E.2. After Mubarak's fall, Grand Mufti Ali Gomaa, pictured here giving a sermon in Sultan Hassan Mosque, struggled in the Egyptian press to defend his initial lack of support for the peaceful protesters. (Courtesy of Shams Friedlander)

the US, for Americans in general and Muslim Americans in particular. After all, today the term *radical* is a slur in US mosques, and the narrowly defined *moderate* is held up as the only kind of Muslim eligible for social citizenship. Nearly all Muslim efforts at "reform" in the US today are either an implicit or explicit effort to create "moderate" Muslims, good Muslim citizens. Like the dignity revolutions in the Middle East, which are national movements animated by a transnational vision, the mainstreaming reform projects in US mosques require scholars to account for the ways the nation continues to shape the collective memory, political aspirations, and religious identifications of devout Muslims in an increasingly global age. These reform projects all reflect a narrowing of possibilities for dissent. This shrinking place of dissent in US mosques brings together many of the threads of this book: the competing constructions of Sunni religious authority, the significance of religious knowledge, the relationship of devout Muslims to the state, the diversity of the umma, and the place of Islam in the US and in the world.

These debates between and about Muslims are happening as the US government draws on the figure of the Muslim terrorist to mobilize a wide range of constituencies domestically and abroad in service of a new age of American empire, whether sanctioning perpetual war and the establishment of the US as a global security state, legalizing torture, or suspending due process. Throughout, the suppression of dissent is essential. "People of interest" in the War on Terror find themselves not only in Arab prisons that are theaters of rendition or in detention centers under America's jurisdiction even if outside its borders but on American soil too: in American mosques, American prisons, and American ghettos.

Luqman Abdullah, an African American imam of a small mosque community in one of the poorest neighborhoods in Detroit, Michigan, was such a "person of interest." On October 28, 2009, he was shot twenty-one times in an FBI raid after he allegedly refused to get down as ordered and because he shot and killed an FBI dog, Freddy, that had mauled his face and hands. The surveillance video shows how Freddy was carried to safety as Abdullah, handcuffed, was left to die on the floor of the warehouse. Though a fierce critic of the US government, Abdullah was not a terrorist. An FBI informant who infiltrated Abdullah's community in 2005 and tried to persuade him to bomb the Super Bowl in Detroit for five thousand dollars reported that Abdullah rejected the suggestion outright, angrily denouncing such a plot as against the spirit and laws of Islam. Abdullah was certainly a radical, committed to self-policing the few blocks of Detroit that he and his followers lived in, to keep local drug dealers and prostitutes out. He was deeply attached to a transnational vision of social justice, sending whatever financial support he could to Muslim charities serving Palestinians in Gaza, charities he knew many Muslim Americans no longer felt comfortable donating to after September 11th, not for lack of support of the Palestinian cause but due to their fear of the scrutiny such charitable giving might draw from the US government. The FBI was suspicious of his affiliation with an umbrella organization of inner-city mosques called UMMA, led by Jamil al-Amin, a prominent African American Sunni preacher who was known in the sixties as H. Rap Brown, a civil rights leader, chairman of the Student Nonviolent Coordinating Committee, and Justice Minister of the Black Panthers. For the FBI, these ties to radical antiracist politics and to racial and religious communities that transcend the nation are the kinds of things that made Luqman Abdullah a person of interest.

Fig. E.3. Media coverage of Luqman Abdullah's death focused on his "radical" politics. (Still from *Death of an Iman,* courtesy of Geri Zeldes, Brian Bowe, and Salah Hassan)

I always thought he was an interesting person. Imam Luqman was my Sunday-school teacher as a kid. I remember him as soft-spoken and smart. I remember how he read verses of the Quran in a melodic voice; I remember how he criticized the American government with quiet anger. He was a radical, but he was not a terrorist.

This book has been written as a kind of a fragmentary map, a mediation and meditation that crosses scales, hemispheres, realms. This book links accounts of institutions and individuals, social structures and subjects, histories and biographies, pasts and futures, in order to interrupt the sharp division between the social and the individual, the abstract and the real, the analytical and the imaginary, our here and their there. The point of this critical, fragmentary map is not to reach a finite destination, a conclusion in the perpetual argument about how Islam might be reformed, but rather to guide us toward alternative intellectual and political futures, to remind us of other possibilities. The point of a map defines its points; the point of this map is to imagine a better destination, a better destiny. This map is an invitation to a journey.

NOTES

Notes to the Introduction

1. Pew Research Center, *Muslim Americans: Middle Class and Mostly Mainstream* (Washington, DC: Pew Research Center, 2007); "Poll: 1 in 4 U.S. Young Muslims OK with Homicide Bombings against Civilians," FoxNews.com, May 23, 2007, http://www.foxnews.com/story/0,2933,274934,00.html; Michelle Boorstein, "From Muslim Youths, a Push for Change: Participants at Unprecedented Summit with US Officials Confront Extremist Images," *Washington Post*, July 15, 2007, A15.

2. Debbie Schlussel, "Meet Your 'Moderate,' 'American' Muslim Neighbors: New Study Shows US Muslims Are Extremists," Debbie Schlussel's blog, May 23, 2007, http://www.debbieschlussel.com/1323/meet-your-moderate-american-muslim-neighbors-new-study-shows-u-s-muslims-are-extremists/. Her blog post was read aloud on conservative talk-show host Rush Limbaugh's nationally broadcast radio show also on May 23.

3. See Pew's follow-up study and a similar study by Gallup: Pew Research Center, *Muslim Americans: No Signs of Growth in Alienation or Support for Extremism* (Washington, DC: Pew Research Center, 2011); Muslim West Facts Project, *Muslim Americans: A National Portrait* (Washington, DC: Gallup, 2009).

4. Benedict Anderson, *Imagined Communities: Reflections on the Origins and Spread of Nationalism* (New York: Verso, 1991), 7.

5. Michael Shapiro, "Moral Geographies and the Ethics of Post-Sovereignty," *Public Culture* 6, no. 3 (1994): 482.

6. Donald E. Pease, *The New American Exceptionalism* (Minneapolis: University of Minnesota Press, 2009), 166.

7. Edward Said, *Orientalism* (New York: Vintage, 1979). Said argues that although Orientalism is attached to Western imperial projects, it cannot be reduced to an expression of raw political power or a nefarious imperialist plot; rather, Orientalism is itself "a certain *will* or *intention* to understand, in some cases to control, manipulate, even to incorporate, what is a manifestly different . . . world" (12).

8. For rich accounts of the multiple ways the region has been made a political and cultural interest to American publics in different periods of US history,

including as an analogue for domestic debates about gender and race, see Melani McAlister, *Epic Encounters: Culture, Media, and US Interests in the Middle East since 1945* (Berkeley: University of California Press, 2001); Brian Edwards, *Morocco Bound: Disorienting America's Maghreb, from Casablanca to the Marrakech Express* (Durham: Duke University Press, 2005); Timothy Marr, *The Cultural Roots of American Islamicism* (New York: Cambridge University Press, 2006).

9. McAlister, *Epic Encounters*; Sohail Daulatzai, *Black Star, Crescent Moon: The Muslim International and Black Freedom beyond America* (Minneapolis: University of Minnesota Press, 2012).

10. Edward Said, *Culture and Imperialism* (New York: Knopf, 1993), 289.

11. Pew Research Center, *The Future of the Global Muslim Population: Projections for 2010–2030* (Washington, DC: Pew Research Center, 2011).

12. W. E. B. Du Bois, *The Souls of Black Folk* (New York: Dover, 1994), 202.

13. Mahmood Mamdani, "Good Muslim, Bad Muslim: A Political Perspective on Culture and Terrorism," *American Anthropologist* 104, no. 3 (2002): 766–75.

14. I am not using the term "Muslim-looking" as a catch-all, umbrella term but to capture what legal scholar Leti Volpp points out is a "consolidation of a new racial identity that groups together persons who appear 'Middle Eastern, Arab, or Muslim,'" an identity that is formulated through the alignment of Orientalist tropes, the exclusion of Asians from social citizenship, and government practices such as racial profiling and immigrant dragnets. Leti Volpp, "The Citizen and the Terrorist," *UCLA Law Review* 49 (2002): 1575. Muneer Ahmad extends Volpp's argument by documenting a "logic of fungibility" in which the equation of "Muslim" and "terrorist" captures "not only Arab Muslims but Arab Christians, non-Arab Muslims (such as Pakistanis and Indonesians), non-Muslim South Asians (Sikhs, Hindus), and even Latinos and African Americans depending on how closely they approach the phenotype stereotype of the terrorist. 'Looking,' not 'Muslim,' is the operative word in 'Muslim-looking.'" Muneer I. Ahmad, "A Rage Shared by Law: Post–September 11 Racial Violence as Crimes of Passion," *California Law Review* 97 (2004): 1278–79. See also Inderpal Grewal, "Transnational America: Race, Gender, and Citizenship after 9/11," *Social Identities* 9, no. 4 (2003): 535–61.

15. Andrew Shryock, Nabeel Abraham, and Sally Howell, "The New Order and Its Forgotten Histories," in *Arab Detroit 9/11: Life in the Terror Decade*, ed. Andrew Shryock, Nabeel Abraham, and Sally Howell (Detroit: Wayne State University Press, 2011), 382.

16. Richard Sobel, "Anti-Terror Campaign Has Wide Support, Even at the Expense of Cherished Rights," *Chicago Tribune*, November 4, 2001; "Anti-Muslim Sentiments Fairly Commonplace: Four in Ten Americans Admit Feeling Prejudice against Muslims," Gallup News Service, August 10, 2006.

17. Muneer I. Ahmad, "Homeland Insecurities: Racial Profiling the Day after 9/11," *Social Text* 20, no. 3, 72 (2002): 101–15.

18. Andrew Shryock, "New Images of Arab Detroit: Seeing Otherness and Identity through the Lens of September 11," *American Anthropologist* 104 (2002): 917–22.

19. Andrew Shryock, Nabeel Abraham, and Sally Howell, "The Terror Decade in Arab Detroit," in *Arab Detroit 9/11: Life in the Terror Decade*, ed. Andrew Shryock, Nabeel Abraham, and Sally Howell (Detroit: Wayne State University Press, 2011), 4–10.

20. The Asian Exclusion Act was passed by the US Congress in 1924 as part of the Immigration Act of 1924 and has its roots in the 1882 Chinese Exclusion Act (renewed in 1892 and 1902), preventing immigration from China and then Asia, respectively. The Immigration Act was also designed to restrict the freedom of movement of immigrants within the US based on their race and national origin. The Asian Exclusion Act was repealed in 1943 with the passing of the Magnuson Act, which instituted quotas for immigrants from around the world, institutionalizing a preference for white immigrants. In 1965, the Immigration Act passed the House and the Senate by a large margin, and it abolished quotas for immigrants based on national origin.

21. Moustafa Bayoumi notes the ironies in contemporary representations of race, arguing "that while Arabs and Muslims are increasingly racialized as black (in ways that approximate Cold War images of African-Americans), African-Americans are emerging in popular culture as leaders of the American nation and empire. Moreover, this depiction revolves fundamentally around the idea of black friendship with Muslims and Arabs, a friendship not among equals but one reflecting a modified projection of American power." Moustafa Bayoumi, "The Race Is On: Muslims and Arabs in the American Imagination," *Middle East Research and Information Project*, March 2010.

22. Moustafa Bayoumi, *How Does It Feel to Be a Problem? Being Young and Arab in America* (New York: Penguin, 2008), 5.

23. For a rich historical account of the impact of "white flight" on Detroit, which of course, included many immigrants who were not quite white, see Thomas Sugrue's *The Origins of the Urban Crisis: Race and Inequality in Post-war Detroit* (Princeton: Princeton University Press, 1996).

24. Raphael Patai, *The Arab Mind* (1973; repr., Long Island City, NY: Hatherleigh, 2002).

25. Jose Limon, "Representation, Ethnicity, and the Precursory Ethnography: Notes of a Native Anthropologist," in *Recapturing Anthropology*, ed. Richard Fox (Santa Fe, NM: School of American Research Press, 1991).

26. A number of Said's critics have pointed out that he was not the first to make this critique but was only its popularizer. Postcolonial scholars, including Said himself, expose some of the limitations of Orientalism and pursue a number of intellectually productive (and unresolved) lines of questioning. Examples include the nature and persistence of discourses about cultural Others, whether postcolonial theorists could themselves exist outside of such discourses, and how disciplines devoted to cultural analysis might reinvent themselves.

27. Edward Said, "Representing the Colonized: Anthropology's Interlocutors," *Critical Inquiry* 15 (1989): 225.

28. James Clifford, "On Ethnographic Allegory," in *Writing Culture*, ed. James Clifford and George Marcus (Berkeley: University of California Press, 1986). Clifford's essay is a thoughtful exploration of anthropologists' fieldwork fantasies about rescue missions and disappearing objects.

29. For a response to Said's specific critiques of anthropology, see Nicholas Thomas, "Anthropology and *Orientalism*," *Anthropology Today* 7, no. 2 (1991): 4–7.

30. Increasingly, anthropologists find themselves sharing distant, exotic field sites with area studies specialists, political scientists, and others. Similarly, ethnography, the compression of talking and listening onto pages, has become the genre of choice for scholars from sociology to religious studies armed with audio recorders.

31. Arjun Appadurai, "Global Ethnoscapes: Notes and Queries for a Transnational Anthropology," in *Recapturing Anthropology: Working in the Present*, ed. Richard Fox (Santa Fe, NM: School of American Research Press, 1991).

32. Ruth Behar, *The Vulnerable Observer: Anthropology That Breaks Your Heart* (Boston: Beacon, 1996), 5; Ruth Behar, "Ethnography and the Book That Was Lost," *Ethnography* 4, no. 15 (2003): 15–39.

33. "Native" anthropologists were among the first to point to the ways Western academic training often transforms students with diverse cultural perspectives into practitioners of a standardized anthropology based on Western theoretical assumptions that reproduce the colonizing gaze. They argue anthropology's method itself creates an instability in the anthropologist's relationship with the subjects since the object of research is what subjects consider taken-for-granted aspects of life. Kirin Narayarin, "How Native Is a 'Native' Anthropologist?," *American Anthropologist* 95, no. 3 (1993): 671–86; Hussein Fahim, *Indigenous Anthropology in Non-Western Countries* (Durham, NC: Carolina Academic Press, 1982).

34. Hamid Dabashi, *Brown Skin, White Masks* (London: Pluto, 2011), 12. Dabashi's term is a forceful reminder of the ways the informer's betrayal and the (native) informant's insider authority operate as parallel imperial tools. There is a large body of postcolonial criticism on the figure of anthropology's native informant. See Gayatri Spivak, *A Critique of Postcolonial Reason: Toward a History of the Vanishing Present* (Cambridge: Harvard University Press, 1999), ix; Mahmut Mutman, "Writing Culture: Postmodernism and Ethnography," *Anthropological Theory* 6, no. 2 (2006): 153–78; George Marcus, "How Anthropological Curiosity Consumes Its Own Places of Origin," *Cultural Anthropology* 14, no. 3 (1999): 416–22.

35. Irshad Manji, *The Trouble with Islam: A Muslim's Call for Reform in Her Faith* (New York: St. Martin's, 2003), 3.

36. Mamdani, "Good Muslim," 767.

37. Manji, *Trouble with Islam*, 31, 136, 137.

38. For critical scholarship on Manji's book and others in the same genre in addition to Dabashi, see Tarek ElAriss, "The Making of an Expert," *Muslim World* 97 (January 2007): 93–110; Moustafa Bayoumi, "The God That Failed," in *Islamophobia/Islamophilia*, ed. Andrew Shryock (Bloomington: University of Indiana Press, 2010), 79–93; Sherene Razack, *Casting Out: The Eviction of Muslims from Western Law and Politics* (Toronto: University of Toronto Press, 2008), 98–103.
39. Manji, *Trouble with Islam*, 185.
40. Saba Mahmood, "Secularism, Hermeneutics, Empire: The Politics of Islamic Reformation," *Public Culture* 18, no. 2 (2006): 323–47; Mayssoun Sukarieh, "The Hope Crusades: Culturalism and Reform in the Arab World," *Political and Legal Anthropology Review* 35, no. 1 (2012): 115–34. The US government's shift in focus from religious reform in the Middle East toward cultural reforms such as the "Hope Crusades" under the Obama administration is an important one; however, the notion that the reform of Islam is a national interest remains intact.
41. Bernard Lewis, *The Crisis of Islam: Holy War and Unholy Terror* (New York: Random House, 2004).
42. Manji, *Trouble with Islam*, 2.
43. Wael Hallaq, "Was the Gate to Ijtihad Closed?," *International Journal of Middle East Studies* 16, no. 1 (1984): 3–41; J. A. C. Brown, *Hadith: Muhammad's Legacy in the Medieval and Modern World* (Oxford, UK: Oneworld, 2009). In Manji's more recent book, she responds to the common criticism that her dismissal of the Islamic sources of revelation leads Muslims to dismiss her by including long passages of Muslim fan mail, references to widely recognized Islamic authorities, and, most importantly, a passionate reverence toward the Quran and the Prophet Muhammad. She maintains her claims about *ijtihad* and her singular moral courage as well as her financial ties to Nina Rosenwald, who is widely known as an anti-Muslim bigot. Irshad Manji, *Allah, Liberty, and Love: The Courage to Reconcile Faith and Freedom* (New York: Free Press, 2011); Max Blumenthal, "The Sugar Mama of Anti-Muslim Hate," *Nation*, July 2–9, 2012.
44. Manji, *Trouble with Islam*, 149.
45. Ibid., 11.
46. Jaspir Puar, *Terrorist Assemblages: Homonationalism in Queer Times* (Durham: Duke University Press, 2007), 92. Puar argues that Manji's queer identity does complex cultural work as she offers herself as a tool in the global reform of Islam, situating her in a larger set of queer Muslim public figures and organizations complicit in authenticating Orientalist narratives of Muslim sexuality in the service of US imperial projects and narratives of American (sexual) exceptionalism.
47. Manji, *Trouble with Islam*, 199. She also insists that America is a benevolent superpower, and she even characterizes the Israeli government as "compassionate" toward its Palestinian welfare cheats, plagued with the delusion that they are refugees. In *Brown Skin*, Dabashi writes,

> [Native informers] feign authority while telling their conquerors not what they need to know but what they want to hear. (In return, American and

European liberals call them "voices of dissent.") [They] have learned the art of simultaneously acknowledging and denying their Muslim origins. . . . [Populations] targeted for liberation (Afghans, Iraqis, Somalis, Palestinians, Iranians) [are told] that [the US intends] to invade, bomb, and occupy their homelands for those populations' own good. But the primary target of this propaganda is first and foremost the Americans themselves, who need to be assured that they are a good, noble, and superior people adorned by their creator to rescue the world from its evils. (16–18)

48. "She's Got Chutzpah," *O*, May 2004, 234, 240.

49. Robert W. Hefner, "Introduction: The Culture, Politics, and Future of Muslim Education," in *Schooling Islam: The Culture and Politics of Modern Muslim Education*, ed. Robert W. Hefner and Muhammad Qasim (Princeton: Princeton University Press, 2007), 2.

50. The anthropological canon is filled with classic ethnographies and autoethnographies that attest to the instructive qualities of emotions, making them the point of analytical departure: Malinowski's hatred and lust, Abu-Lughod's shame, McCarthy-Brown's inadequacy, Rosaldo's grief, Behar's anger, and Mahmood's repulsion are a few prominent examples. Bronislaw Malinowski, *A Diary in the Strict Sense of the Term* (1967; repr., Stanford: Stanford University Press, 1989); Lila Abu-Lughod, *Veiled Sentiments: Honor and Poetry in a Bedouin Society* (Berkeley: University of California Press, 1986); Karen McCarthy-Brown, *Mama Lola: A Vodou Priestess in Brooklyn* (Berkeley: University of California Press, 1987); Renato Rosaldo, *Culture and Truth: The Remaking of Social Analysis* (Boston: Beacon, 1989); Ruth Behar, *Translated Woman: Crossing the Border with Esperanza's Story* (Boston: Beacon, 1993); Saba Mahmood, *The Politics of Piety: The Islamic Revival and the Feminist Subject* (Princeton: Princeton University Press, 2005).

51. Fernando Coronil, "Pieces for Anthrohistory: A Puzzle to Be Assembled Together," in *Anthrohistory: Unsettling Knowledge, Questioning Discipline*, ed. Edward Murphy, David William Cohen, Chandra D. Bhimull, Fernando Coronil, Monica Eileen Patterson, and Julie Skurski (Ann Arbor: University of Michigan Press, 2010), 303.

52. Ibid., 310.

53. In writing in this public way, I have brought my readers into a space that anthropologist Andrew Shryock characterizes as beyond insider and outsider, a space where the interpretive and intimate trespassing of ethnographic moments is projected. It is these awkward postures and the risks they entail that emerge when intimate social worlds are held up to public scrutiny, he argues, and they are at the heart of ethnographic knowledge, "rooted in the contradictory demands of intimacy and mass mediation that define ethnography as a genre." Andrew Shryock, "Other Conscious / Self Aware: First Thoughts on Cultural Intimacy and Mass Mediation," in *Off Stage / On Display: Intimacy and Ethnography in the Age of Public Culture* (Stanford: Stanford University Press, 2004): 13.

54. Said, "Representing the Colonized," 213.

Notes to Chapter 1

1. This ethnography is based on fieldwork in Amman, Jordan; Damascus, Syria; and Cairo, Egypt, before September 11th in 2001 and afterward in 2002–3, over the course of which I interviewed more than one hundred student-travelers. Most subjects were American Muslims studying abroad, but I also interviewed their teachers and peers. The ethnographic fragments are primarily based on interviews, letters, and subjects' diaries and even poems that were generously shared with me; all of the quoted material is directly from these sources. I have edited conversations and subjects' writings, and I have condensed quotes recorded by tape or by hand without always marking them with ellipses. Due to the sensitive nature of the material, pseudonyms are used throughout with the exception of internationally recognized scholars who are also teachers in these networks. In addition to pseudonyms, I lightly fictionalized inessential details in these accounts. Since the number of student-travelers I interviewed in the field was ten times more than the pool of student-travelers featured in this book, I drew from the accounts of similar subjects when taking liberties with specific details. I did not invent dialogue or plots or the thoughts and emotions attributed to the subjects. In 2001, 2010, and 2012, supplemental and follow-up interviews were conducted in the US with American Muslim public intellectuals and over one hundred students associated with US-based institutes such as Zaytuna, AlMaghrib, and the American Learning Institute for Muslims.

2. Salman Rushdie, "Imaginary Homelands," in *Imaginary Homelands: Essays and Criticism, 1981–91* (London: Granta, 1991), 9.

3. Estimates vary, but according to Ihsan Bagby et al., over half the American Muslim population is "mosqued." Ihsan Bagby, *The American Mosque 2011* (Washington, DC: Council on American-Islamic Relations, 2012). Not all "mosqued" Muslims are engaged in this set of global debates. Sunnis in Deobandi communities in the US are deeply engaged in a different (but related) set of global debates about Islamic authority and knowledge, but their primary interlocutors are Deobandis around the world, not their American coreligionists. Dietrich Reetz, "The Deoband Universe: What Makes a Transcultural and Transnational Educational Movement of Islam?," *Comparative Studies of South Asia, Africa and the Middle East* 27, no. 1 (2007): 259–81; Barbara Metcalf, *"Traditionalist" Islamic Activism: Deoband, Tablighis, and Talibs* (Leiden: ISIM, 2002).

4. A. L. Kroeber, *Anthropology* (New York: Harcourt, Brace, 1948), 11.

5. Zareena Grewal, "Reclaiming Tradition," in *Anthrohistory: Unsettling Knowledge, Questioning Discipline*, ed. Edward Murphy, David William Cohen, Chandra D. Bhimull, Fernando Coronil, Monica Eileen Patterson, and Julie Skurski (Ann Arbor: University of Michigan Press, 2010).

6. Talal Asad, "The Idea of an Anthropology of Islam," Occasional Papers Series (Washington, DC: Georgetown University Center for Contemporary Arab Studies, 1986), 14; Alasdair Macintyre, *After Virtue: A Study in Moral Theory* (Notre Dame: University of Notre Dame Press, 1981).

7. Asad, "Idea of an Anthropology of Islam," 14. In the forties, scholars first introduced the schema of dividing Islam into "Great" and "Little" traditions to differentiate between the textual canon of religious elites in Islamic urban centers and the "popular" practices of the urban and rural masses, but this framework ultimately reproduces the unhelpful binary oppositions of oral/ literate, rural/urban, local/universal, and syncretic/authentic. As a corrective to the division in scales of analysis, "middle-ground" ethnographic works that sit between particularistic "tribal" Islam and universal Islam or between doctrine and practice (i.e., those who replace orthodoxy with orthopraxy) treat Islam as a distinctive historical totality or system, a determining force that dictates various aspects of social life. Scholars who work in this mode treat Islam as a body of rules and restraints enduring through time, contrasting tradition against the agency of their Muslim subjects. Asad shifts the focus of the field away from finding the right scale of analysis of Muslim societies toward finding the right theoretical tools for cultural analysis.

8. Ibid., 8–9; on Geertz's need for his Moroccans to "behave correctly," see Edwards's *Morocco Bound*, 295.

9. Asad, "Idea of an Anthropology of Islam," 16.

10. Bagby, *American Mosque 2011*, 13–14.

11. Although the focus of this study is on Sunni networks, in the initial phase of research, I participated in comparable Shia pedagogical networks that attract American Muslims in Beirut, Lebanon. India and Iran also offer a wide range of pedagogical networks for Shia American student-travelers, from beginners to the most advanced students, which share many features with the Sunni networks documented here.

12. Thomas Kuhn, *The Structure of Scientific Revolutions* (Chicago: University of Chicago Press, 1962).

13. Nuh Ha Mim Keller, *As a Rule: Kharabsheh August 2001* (Amman, Jordan: Wakeel Books, 2001), 2.

14. Mahmood, *Politics of Piety*, 3n. 5; Carrie Wickham, *Mobilizing Islam: Religion, Activism, and Political Change in Egypt* (New York: Columbia University Press, 2002).

15. The Islamist militant networks do not overlap with the pedagogical networks under study here, as they work primarily toward military training in remote areas, not language, scriptural, legal, and theological training in cities. Metcalf, *"Traditionalist" Islamic Activism*.

16. Shabana Mir, *Muslim American Women on Campus: Undergraduate Social Life and Identity* (Chapel Hill: University of North Carolina Press, 2014).

17. One important exception is the Islamic University of Madinah, which maintains relative credibility in the eyes of the students it attracts. Even in this case, Muslim American student-travelers who are alumni glorify an earlier era, the university's "golden age" of intellectual autonomy in the eighties and nineties,

a period when the Saudi government was far less involved in setting the curriculum.

18. Another manifestation of the village effect is an artificial isolation from other Americans and larger trends in US history. For a relational history that attempts to correct this, see Kambiz GhaneaBassiri, *A History of Islam in America* (New York: Cambridge University Press, 2010). Scholars undermine the village effect by focusing on how ethnic and racial boundaries are both maintained and transgressed by different, proximate Muslim communities. See Zain Abdullah, *Black Mecca: The African Muslims of Harlem* (New York: Oxford University Press, 2010); Louise Cainkar, *Homeland Insecurity: The Arab American and Muslim American Experience after 9/11* (New York: Russell Sage Foundation, 2009). Multisite ethnographies destabilize the scholarly tendency that persists even in works centrally focused on transnationalism to isolate Muslim Americans from the Muslim World. Michael Fischer and Mehdi Abedi, *Debating Muslims: Cultural Dialogues in Postmodernity and Tradition* (Madison: University of Wisconsin Press, 1990); Karen Leonard, *Locating Home: India's Hyderabadis Abroad* (Stanford: Stanford University Press, 2007); Junaid Rana, *Terrifying Muslims: Race and Labor in the South Asian Diaspora* (Durham: Duke University Press, 2011).

19. Furthermore, scholars often exaggerate the regional differences of different Muslim communities in the US, another element of the village effect, so that "their" subjects are uniquely important and interesting and different from Muslim Americans as a whole. Such overemphasis on social distinctions between Muslim American communities might be characterized as a kind of scholarly "narcissism of petty differences," to borrow Sigmund Freud's term, in which scholars fetishize minor cultural variants as the basis of their subjects' identities while ignoring the underlying similarities and often unexpected relationships.

20. Michael Warner, "Publics and Counterpublics," *Public Culture* 14, no. 1 (2002): 49–90; Charles Hirschkind, *The Ethical Soundscape: Cassette Sermons and Islamic Counterpublics* (New York: Columbia University Press, 2006), 106–7. Hirschkind expands Warner's conceptions of counterpublics in his definition of an ethical, Islamic counterpublic, but his definition diverges from other "subaltern counterpublics" which emphasize an oppositional, rather than ethical, quality.

21. Hirschkind notes how the common practice of playing Quran tapes and sermon tapes in taxis, shops, cafes, and even crowded buses in Cairo reshapes the moral architecture of these spaces because they require a deferential comportment which, if violated, draws public censure. He argues that this is more than just an index of a religious-minded Egyptian public but that these aural texts "contribute to the creation of a sensory environment that nourishes and intensifies the substrate of affective orientations." Hirschkind, *Ethical Soundscape*, 125.

22. Keith Basso, *Wisdom Sits in Places: Landscape and Language among the Western Apache* (Albuquerque: University of New Mexico Press, 1996), 109.

23. Hirschkind, *Ethical Soundscape*, 124.

24. Kevin Dwyer, *Arab Voices: The Human Rights Debate in the Middle East* (Berkeley: University of California Press, 1991), 27–28.

25. For a prominent example, see Janet Abu-Lughod's *Before European Hegemony: The World System AD 1250–1350* (New York: Oxford University Press, 1991).

26. See Aziz AlAzmeh, *Islams and Modernities* (New York: Verso, 1996).

27. Lara Deeb, *An Enchanted Modern: Gender and Public Piety in Shi'i Lebanon* (Princeton: Princeton University Press, 2006), 15.

28. Caren Kaplan, *Questions of Travel: Postmodern Discourses of Displacement* (Durham: Duke University Press, 1996).

29. The differences between travelers and tourists contained important forms of English class and gender divisions that separated working- and middle-class "day trippers" from the upper-class traveling explorer. Such social distinctions continue to be manifest in the contemporary constructions of cosmopolitan travelers as qualitatively different from tourists.

30. John Urrey, *The Tourist's Gaze: Leisure and Travel in Contemporary Societies* (London: Sage, 1990).

31. Michel de Certeau, *The Writing of History*, trans. Tom Conley (New York: Columbia University Press, 1988), 232.

32. Mary Louise Pratt, *Imperial Eyes* (New York: Routledge, 1992), 4.

33. Inderpal Grewal, *Home and Harem: Nation, Gender, Empire and the Cultures of Travel* (Durham: Duke University Press, 1996), 4.

34. Such a simple embrace of the romance of travel not only reproduces the Eurocentric discourses of objective science and anthropological self and other; it also erases the darker histories of travel: the legacies of forced migration, political and economic immigration, deportation, indenture, and slavery. Ibid.

35. Dale F. Eickelman and James Piscatori, preface to *Muslim Travellers: Pilgrimage, Migration, and the Religious Imagination*, ed. Dale F. Eickelman and James Piscatori (Berkeley: University of California Press, 1990), xv.

36. Veena Das, "If This Be Magic," in *Religion: Beyond a Concept*, ed. Hent de Vries (New York: Fordham University Press, 2008), 259–82. Das reflects on this scholarly bias, arguing that her previous research on religious violence depleted her ability to analyze issues relating to the religious aesthetic of life because she could only see religion flatly, as a flight from the ugly realities of political projects animated by religious ideologies.

37. Eric Hobsbawm, "Inventing Traditions," in *The Invention of Tradition*, ed. Eric Hobsbawm and Terence Ranger (Cambridge: Cambridge University Press, 1983), 1.

38. Michael Oakeshott, *Rationalism in Politics and Other Essays* (London: Methuen, 1991).

39. Marshall Hodgson, *Venture of Islam: Conscience and History in a World Civilization* (Chicago: University of Chicago Press, 1974).

40. Richard Handler and Joyce Linnekin, "Tradition, Genuine or Spurious," *Journal of American Folklore* 97, no. 385 (1984): 273–90.

41. Asad, "Idea of an Anthropology of Islam."

42. Roxanne Euben, *Journeys to the Other Shore: Muslim and Western Travelers in Search of Knowledge* (Princeton: Princeton University Press, 2008), 9–19.

43. Barbara Tedlock, "From Participant Observation to the Observation of Participation: The Emergence of Narrative Ethnography," *Journal for Anthropological Research* 41 (1990): 69.

44. Mahmood, *Politics of Piety*, 36–37.

45. Asad, "Idea of an Anthropology of Islam," 15. Some scholars have mistakenly read Asad's ethnographic prescription for documenting the constitution and reconstitution of orthodoxy by Muslims as his employment of a "native" category of orthodoxy that references a singular, text-based, transhistorical body of beliefs and practices.

46. Courtney Bender, *The New Metaphysicals: Spirituality and the American Religious Imagination* (Chicago: University of Chicago Press, 2010). Bender offers a fascinating account of the ways the "Ivy League Professor" is "caught" in the cultural "entanglements" of a community of mystics in Cambridge, Massachusetts. Bender is assigned roles, responsibilities, privileges, collaborations in the community's own (imagined and real) debates about the nature of spiritual experience, which she initially fails to recognize. "Understanding the role of scholarly activity in the genealogies of religious experience in fact leads us to see that scholars . . . have been far more than spectators on the sidelines" of their subjects' religious debates and that what academics presume are neutral ethnographic practices such as listening, documenting, and observing, and the act of research itself, are assimilated and apprehended by the subjects into their worlds of spiritual and religious experience (12).

Notes to Chapter 2

1. Malcolm X, *Malcolm X Speaks*, ed. George Breitman (New York: Pathfinder, 1965), 27.

2. Nikhil Pal Singh, *Black Is a Country: Race and the Unfinished Struggle for Democracy* (Cambridge: Harvard University Press, 2005).

3. Paul Gilroy, *Black Atlantic: Modernity and Double Consciousness* (Cambridge: Harvard University Press, 1993). Gilroy presents the watery border space of the Atlantic as a model for subverting disciplinary assumptions about the nation as a unit of analysis and for modeling the study of transnational phenomena. A number of his critics have pointed out that Gilroy ultimately replaces one geographic element (the bordered land of the nation-state) with another (the Atlantic ocean), and thus his project complicates but does not actually subvert the scholarly habit of linking the construction of identity to geographic terrains. In a religious context, however, references to "imaginary homelands" are not necessarily literal or worldly.

4. Alex Lubin, "Locating Palestine in Pre-1948 Black Internationalism," in *Black Routes to Islam*, ed. Manning Marable and Hishaam D. Aidi (New York: Palgrave, 2009), 19. Lubin tracks the different cultural meanings of Palestine prior

to the creation of Israel for pan-Africanists, black civil rights activists, and black Christian Zionists, alternatively imagined as a place in need of colonial intervention and a geography of liberation.

5. R. Laurence Moore, *Religious Outsiders and the Making of Americans* (New York: Oxford University Press, 1986). On the one hand, Moore challenges us to read past the consensus history of American religion that posits that religious difference bubbled away in the melting pot leaving only a bland and common civil religion that merged with an uncritical nationalism. On the other hand, he also questions histories that represent religious conflict and diversity as bordering on anarchy by showing us that outsider status has itself been a kind of unifying thread for religious communities in the process of becoming Americans. Moore reminds us that Will Herberg's canonical consensus history *Protestant, Catholic, Jew* was not a celebration of cultural assimilation but rather a celebration of dissent as quintessentially American, demonstrating "that American society was most dynamic when it encouraged people to preserve, not their ethnic identities, but their genuine religious peculiarities" (19).

6. Rather than taking theological doctrine or (black) nationalism as the analytical point of departure, the category of tradition allows us to think about subjects inhabiting multiple religious traditions simultaneously, and the overlapping of discursive traditions and modalities of authority. This is especially helpful in examining the Moorish Science Temple of America (MSTA) and the Nation of Islam (NOI) of this period, communities that identified with, rather than against, the Islamic East and the global tradition of Islam, in contrast to contemporary Black Religion Muslim communities such as the Nation of Gods and Earths (also known as the Five Percenters) that often have an oppositional relationship to the global tradition of Islam.

7. Gayraud Wilmore, *Black Religion and Black Radicalism: An Interpretation of the Religious History of Afro-American People* (Maryknoll, NY: Orbis, 1983), ix.

8. Sherman Jackson, *Islam and the Blackamerican: Looking toward the Third Resurrection* (New York: Oxford University Press, 2005), 31–32.

9. Susan Nance, "Mystery of the Moorish Science Temple: Southern Black and American Alternative Spirituality in 1920s Chicago," *Religion and American Culture* 12, no. 2 (2002): 123–66.

10. Ernest Allen Jr., "Identity and Destiny: The Formative Views of the Moorish Science Temple and the Nation of Islam," in *Islam on the Americanization Path?*, ed. John L. Esposito and Yvonne Haddad (Atlanta: Scholars, 1988).

11. Herbert Berg, "Mythmaking in the African-American Muslim Context: The Moorish Science Temple, the Nation of Islam, and the American Society of Muslims," *Journal of the American Academy of Religion* 73 (2005): 705–30.

12. Moore, *Religious Outsiders*, xi.

13. Richard Brent Turner, *Islam in the African-American Experience* (Bloomington: Indiana University Press, 1997), 92.

14. Nance, "Mystery of the Moorish Science Temple," 126–27.

15. Turner, *Islam in the African-American Experience*; Judith Weisenfeld, "Spiritual Complexions: On Race and the Body in the Moorish Science Temple of America," in *Sensational Religion: Sense and Contention in Material Practice*, ed. Sally Promey, Richard Meyers, and Mia Mochizuki (New Haven: Yale University Press, 2013).

16. "Moorish Science Temple of America Membership Card," Moorish Science Temple of America Collection, Schomburg Center for Research in Black Culture, New York Public Library.

17. Charles Taylor, "The Politics of Recognition," in *Multiculturalism: Examining the Politics of Recognition,* ed. Amy Gutmann (Princeton: Princeton University Press, 1994).

18. Peter Lamborn Wilson, *Sacred Drift: Essays on the Margins of Islam* (San Francisco: City Lights Books, 1993), 16–19.

19. Weisenfeld, "Spiritual Complexions."

20. During this period, Irish, Polish, and Italian immigrants and others were fighting to be recognized as whites, and urban legends of nonwhite immigrants from India, the Middle East, and Africa being granted a temporary racial immunity and allowed to trespass into segregated, white-only social spaces circulated in MSTA communities. Nance, "Mystery of the Moorish Science Temple," 136–37.

21. Turner, *Islam in the African-American Experience*, 101–6.

22. Aminah Beverly McCloud, *African American Islam* (New York: Routledge, 1995), 11.

23. Martin Marty, *Modern American Religion: The Noise of Conflict, 1919–1941* (Chicago: University of Chicago Press, 1989), 1–14. Turner rightly notes that Marty underestimates the impact of the MSTA on the public debates about American religion. Turner, *Islam in the African-American Experience*, 73.

24. Nance, "Mystery of the Moorish Science Temple," 136.

25. Turner, *Islam in the African-American Experience*, 112.

26. Moustafa Bayoumi, "East of the Sun (West of the Moon): Islam, the Ahmadis, and African America," in *Black Routes to Islam*, ed. Manning Marable and Hishaam Aidi (New York: Palgrave, 2007), 71.

27. Turner, *Islam in the African-American Experience*, 115.

28. Nance, "Mystery of the Moorish Science Temple," 152.

29. Muhammad Sadiq, "If Jesus Comes to America," *Moslem Sunrise*, April 1922, 55–56.

30. McCloud, *African American Islam*, 21.

31. Z. I. Ansari, "Aspects of Black Muslim Theology," *Studia Islamica* 83 (1981): 137–76; Jackson, *Islam and the Blackamerican,* 6; Susan Nance, *How the Arabian Nights Inspired the American Dream, 1790–1935* (Chapel Hill: University of North Carolina Press, 2009).

32. Despite thin evidence, several historical accounts overstate how exceptional the Ahmadis were relative to the "assimilationist" Muslim immigrants in the US in this period who abandoned Eastern dress, Anglicized their names, and

remained insular, rarely taking an interest in community outreach. Yvonne Haddad, ed., *The Muslims of America* (New York: Oxford University Press, 1991). Recent historical scholarship counters the narrative that before 1965, Muslim American immigrant communities were apolitical, isolated, or religiously lax. These panethnic, diverse communities were often deeply invested in domestic and foreign (particularly anticolonial) politics and were also passionately invested in religious practice and education. GhaneaBassiri, *History of Islam*. For example, early Arab and Indian immigrants' battles for citizenship included Muslim immigrants and entailed a complex negotiation of radical transnational politics, domestic racial alliances, and postcolonial campaigns in their countries of origin. Gary R. Hess, "The Forgotten Asian Americans: The East Indian Community in the United States," in *The Asian American*, ed. Norris Hudley Jr. (Santa Barbara, CA: Clio Books, 1976), 169–71; Sarah Gualtieri, *Between Arab and White: Race and Ethnicity in the Early Syrian American Diaspora* (Berkeley: University of California Press, 2009); Vivek Bald, *Bengali Harlem* (Cambridge: Harvard University Press, 2013); Edward Curtis, "Islamism and Its African American Muslim Critics: Black Muslims in the Era of the Arab Cold War," in *Black Routes to Islam*, ed. Manning Marable and Hishaam Aidi (New York: Palgrave), 53–55.

33. Patrick Bowen, "Satti Majid: A Sudanese Founder of American Islam," *Journal of Africana Religions* 1, no. 2 (2013): 194–209.

34. Du Bois, *Souls of Black Folk*, 3.

35. Roel Meijer, introduction to *Global Salafism: Islam's New Religious Movement*, ed. Roel Meijer (New York: Columbia University Press, 2009), 3–13.

36. Bernard Haykel, "On the Nature of Salafi Thought and Action," in *Global Salafism: Islam's New Religious Movement*, ed. Roel Meijer (New York: Columbia University Press, 2009), 34–37.

37. Abdin Chande, "Islam in the African American Community: Negotiating between Black Nationalism and Historical Islam," *Islamic Studies* 47, no. 2 (2008): 221–41.

38. Elijah Muhammad, *Message to the Blackman in America* (Chicago: Muhammad's Mosque No. 2, 1963).

39. Edward Curtis, *Islam in Black America: Identity, Liberation, and Difference in African-American Islamic Thought* (Albany: SUNY Press, 2002), 72–73.

40. Elijah Muhammad, *The Supreme Wisdom: Solution to the So-Called Negroes' Problem* (Newport, VA: National Newport News and Commentator, 1957), 29–30, 31, 33, 35.

41. Malcolm X, "Arabs Send Warm Greetings, to 'Our Brothers' of Color in the U.S.A.," *Pittsburgh Courier*, August 15, 1959, 1.

42. Muhammad, *Message to the Blackman*, 31.

43. Ibid., 88.

44. Edward Curtis, *Black Muslim Religion in the Nation of Islam, 1960–1975* (Chapel Hill: University of North Carolina Press, 2006), 69.

45. As Melani McAlister argues, this scriptural interpretation did complex cultural work for the NOI: by removing Jews from the stories of the Old Testament, they reflected the racial hostilities between Jews and blacks and authenticated the NOI's selective use of the Bible (*Epic Encounters*, 98). She argues that Gilroy's emphasis on the significance of the common experience of slavery/diaspora between Jews and blacks and his corresponding omission of Islam glosses over the different meanings Jews have had for blacks over time since—in different moments of African American life, Jews were identified not by their suffering but by their power, both in Israel and the United States—and that the Arab and Islamic Middle East competed alongside the Jewish exodus model in the black religious imagination (ibid., 123). Edward Curtis, "Islamizing the Black Body: Ritual and Power in Elijah Muhammad's Nation of Islam," *Religion and American Culture* 12, no. 2 (2006): 167–96

46. Jackson, *Islam and the Blackamerican*, 46–47.

47. Curtis, *Islam in Black America*, 73.

48. GhaneaBassiri, *History of Islam*, 261–62.

49. Curtis, "Islamism and Its African American Critics."

50. James Tyner, "Nightmarish Landscapes: Geography and the Dystopian Writings of Malcolm X," in *The Cambridge Companion to Malcolm X*, ed. Robert E. Terrill (New York: Cambridge University Press, 2011), 140.

51. Malcolm X, *By Any Means Necessary: Speeches, Interviews, and a Letter by Malcolm X*, ed. George Breitman (New York: Pathfinder, 1970), 57, 46.

52. Malcolm X, *Malcolm X on Afro-American History*, ed. Stere Clark (New York: Pathfinder, 1967), 24–25.

53. Quoted in Louis A. DeCaro Jr., *On the Side of My People: A Religious Life of Malcolm X* (New York: NYU Press, 1996), 97.

54. Muhammad's political vision was a much more radical critique of domestic and foreign US policies, particularly in the Middle East, where Israeli Jews were increasingly viewed as imperialists rather than victims of history by American blacks, despite the persistence of black Christian leaders' identifications with them. The NOI used Israel as an example of diasporic return less and less frequently, and after Malcolm X's little-known trip to Gaza in 1964, he never referenced Israel as a model again. DeCaro, *On the Side of My People*, 225.

55. Curtis, *Islam in Black America*, 81.

56. Herbert Berg, *Elijah Muhammad and Islam* (New York: NYU Press, 2009).

57. Elijah Muhammad, "This I'll Never Forget," Salaam Magazine, July 1960; Curtis, "Islamism and Its African American Muslim Critics."

58. DeCaro, *On the Side of My People*, 201.

59. Curtis, *Black Muslim Religion*.

60. Curtis, *Islam in Black America*, 84.

61. Malcolm X and Alex Haley, *The Autobiography of Malcolm X* (New York: Penguin, 1965), 307–15.

62. Quoted in DeCaro, *On the Side of My People*, 213.

63. Ibid. Later in the interview, Malcolm did discuss elements of NOI theology, although with a new reservation and hesitancy. Immediately after taping, Arab international students from the UCLA Muslim Students Association confronted Malcolm over points of NOI theology that he had discussed on the show.

64. "2,000 at Moslem Feast in Harlem," *New York Amsterdam News*, July 20, 1957, 26.

65. Haley and Malcolm X, *Autobiography*, 330.

66. Malcolm X, "Travel Diary," 1964, Malcolm X Collection, Schomburg Center for Research in Black Culture, New York Public Library.

67. Haley and Malcolm X, *Autobiography*, 343.

68. Ibid., 354.

69. Malcolm X to Alex Haley, April 25, 1964, Grove Press Collection, Syracuse University, 3–5.

70. Haley and Malcolm X, *Autobiography*, 341–42.

71. Azzam's son was Malcolm X's host in Saudi Arabia. Malcolm X studied with Shawarbi over several weeks and wept in Shawarbi's presence when the Quran was recited. DeCaro, *On the Side of My People*, 203.

72. Cheryl Clarke, *"After Mecca": Women Poets and the Black Arts Movement* (New Brunswick: Rutgers University Press, 2005), 2–3.

73. In Lebanon, he was scandalized by the immodest dress of Lebanese women; like antiblack racism, he explains it in terms of French colonial and neocolonial influence. Haley and Malcolm X, *Autobiography*, 355.

74. Curtis, "Islamism and Its African American Muslim Critics," 104.

75. DeCaro notes: "To Malcolm X, Islam was the solution, but not as a rational formula or an idealistic answer. Quite the contrary, Islam became a question, a challenge, a test that required the Muslim to work out brotherhood by the practice of faith, which undoubtedly included the struggle against injustice. Malcolm X had begun to develop his own way of being Muslim—a way that distinguished the practicing Muslim from those who reduced Islam to a religion of ritual and tradition." DeCaro, *On the Side of My People*, 237.

76. Kevin Gaines, *American Africans in Ghana: Black Expatriates and the Civil Rights Era* (Chapel Hill: University of North Carolina Press, 2010), 170.

77. Malcolm X, *Malcolm X Speaks*, 62–63.

78. Manning Marable *Malcolm X: A Life of Reinvention* (New York: Penguin, 2011).

79. Quoted in DeCaro, *On the Side of My People*, 255.

80. Ibid., 239.

81. Marable's *Malcolm X* and DeCaro's *On the Side of My People* provide detailed historical accounts of this time abroad. In those eighteen weeks that Malcolm X was working to learn Arabic, what he called "the spiritual language of the future," he also dreamed of learning Chinese, what he predicted would be "the most powerful political language of the future." Interestingly, in the contemporary period, popular Muslim American memory conflates both of

Malcolm's trips to Mecca, and Malcolm X's religious tutelage is emphasized and exaggerated.

82. DeCaro, *On the Side of My People*, 239–41. Malcolm X's Saudi teacher was Shaykh Muhammad Sarur Al-Sabban, a man whom Malcolm X described as a black man and an ex-slave who rose to power as minister of finance and secretary general of the Muslim World League. This is yet another indication that Malcolm X was familiar with the hierarchies, social inequities, systems of slavery, and constructions of difference in the Muslim Middle East and Africa, but he recognized that these social inequities did not map onto skin color in simple or straightforward ways, evinced by Al-Sabban's rise and prominence as an internationally recognized Sunni authority.

83. Malcolm X, *February 1965: The Final Speeches*, ed. Steve Clark (New York: Pathfinder, 1992), 22.

84. Malcolm X, *Malcolm X Speaks*, 61.

85. Quoted in DeCaro, *On the Side of My People*, 236.

86. Daulatzai, *Black Star*, 47. One notable exception is Malcolm X's influence on John Walker Lindh, who was convicted of treason for taking up arms against US forces in Afghanistan in 2001. Osama bin Laden invoked his own radical Malcolmology upon the election of Obama, whom he dubbed a "house negro."

87. Bayoumi, "East of the Sun," 73.

Notes to Chapter 3

1. Amaney Jamal and Nadine Naber, "Introduction: Arab Americans and US Racial Formations," in *Race and Arab Americans before and after 9/11*, ed. Amaney Jamal and Nadine Naber (Syracuse: Syracuse University Press, 2008), 1–45.

2. Richard Bulliet, *The Case for Islamo-Christian Civilization* (New York: Columbia University Press, 2004); Dale Eickelman and Jon Anderson, "Redefining Muslim Publics," in *New Media in the Muslim World: The Emerging Public Sphere*, ed. Dale Eickelman and Jon Anderson (Bloomington: Indiana University Press, 1999), 1–18.

3. Garbi Schmidt, *Islam in Urban America: Sunni Muslims in Chicago* (Philadelphia: Temple University Press, 2004); Omid Safi, introduction to *Progressive Muslims: On Justice, Gender, and Pluralism*, ed. Omid Safi (Oxford, UK: Oneworld, 2003), 1–31.

4. Similarly, at the turn of the century, Irish Catholics railed against Catholic Germans, Poles, Slovaks, and Italians who developed national parishes in order to preserve their languages and cultures from the cultural dominance of Protestants and Irish Catholics. Moore, *Religious Outsiders*, 64; Although Bagby defines *mosque* far more narrowly than I do, his 2000 and 2011 findings confirm that less than half of US mosques have imams with formal religious degrees; the vast majority who do have a bachelor's or more in Islamic studies were trained overseas. Bagby, *American Mosque 2011*.

5. Sally Howell, "Inventing the American Mosque: Early Muslims and Their Institutions in Detroit, 1910–1980" (PhD diss., Rackham Graduate School, University of Michigan, 2009).

6. Gulzar Haider, "Muslim Space and the Practice of Architecture," in *Making Muslim Space in North America and Europe*, ed. Barbara Daly Metcalf (Berkeley: University of California Press, 1996).

7. Many Muslim immigrants repeated the patterns of nineteenth-century Catholics who, indignant about the ways Protestants and assimilationists from their own ranks cast particular features of the church as foreign and backward, "insisted on treating 'foreign' elements in the church as integral parts of the universal faith rather than as anachronistic survivals from the past" (Moore, *Religious Outsiders*, 49).

8. McAlister, *Epic Encounters*.

9. Three founders of the MSA were Muslim Brothers, but the MSA was never an outreach of any foreign institution; it took inspiration from overseas movements, such as the utopian Muslim Brotherhood motto "Islam Is the Solution," but developed its own, American revivalist rhetoric. GhaneaBassiri, *History of Islam*, 263–70.

10. "We do subscribe to [the revivalists'] view that present day ideologies are outmoded, that the crisis in human spirit is deepening and any solution short of a total Islam will only accelerate the fall of humanity down a precipice. That's why we consider the leaders of Ikhwan and Jamaat as benefactors of our ummah, and we don't feel shy to quote them." Tariq Quraishi, "Vision of the MSA," *Islamic Horizons*, April 1978.

11. Larry Poston, "Da'wa in the West," in *The Muslims of America*, ed. Yvonne Yazbeck Haddad (New York: Oxford University Press, 1991), 131. Umma institutions are separate and distinct from the existing ethnic, diasporic, or political campus organizations that also draw Muslim international students.

12. Roger Waldinger and David Fitzgerald, "Transnationalism in Question," *American Journal of Sociology* 109 (2004): 1177–95. As Waldinger and Fitzgerald point out, connections between source and destination points are inherent to migration. In this sense, then, immigrants' lingering attachments to their original nation and sustained social networks are not a new or necessarily transnational phenomenon.

13. John Esposito, "Ismail R. Al-Faruqi: Muslim Scholar-Activist," in *The Muslims of America*, ed. Yvonne Yazbeck Haddad (New York: Oxford University Press, 1991).

14. Tariq Quraishi, *Isma'il al-Faruqi: An Enduring Legacy* (Plainfield, IN: Muslim Students Association, 1993), 25.

15. Ilyas Ba-Yunus, "Al-Faruqi and Beyond: Future Directions in the Islamization of Knowledge Project in Its Second Decade," *American Journal of Islamic Social Sciences* 5, no. 1 (1991): 14.

16. Behrooz Ghamari-Tabrizi, "Loving America and Longing for Home: Isma'il al-Faruqi and the Emergence of the Muslim Diaspora in North America," *International Migration* 42, no. 2 (2004): 61–84.

17. Ismail Al-Faruqi, "Islamic Ideals in North America," in *The Muslim Community in North America*, ed. Earle H. Waugh, Baha Abu-Laban, and Regula B. Qureshi (Edmonton: University of Alberta Press, 1983), 270.

18. Gutbi Mahdi Ahmad, "Muslim Organizations in the United States," in *The Muslims of America*, ed. Yvonne Yazbeck Haddad (New York: Oxford University Press, 1991), 17–18.

19. "A Session with Yusuf AlQardawi," *Islamic Horizons*, June 1979.

20. Al-Faruqi and AbuSulayman's ideas have had more traction overseas. Mona Abaza, *Debates on Islam and Knowledge in Malaysia and Egypt: Shifting Worlds* (New York: Routledge, 2002).

21. AbdulHamid AbuSulayman, *Crisis in the Muslim Mind* (Herndon, VA: International Institute of Islamic Thought, 1993).

22. Zareena Grewal and R. David Coolidge, "Islamic Education in the United States: Debates, Practices, and Institutions," in *The Cambridge Companion to American Islam*, ed. Omid Safi and Juliane Hammer (New York: Cambridge University Press, 2013).

23. Ghamari-Tabrizi, "Loving America," 72.

24. Ismail Al-Faruqi, "The Path of Da'wah in the West," *Muslim World League Journal* 14, nos. 7–8 (1987): 54–62.

25. From a normative perspective, there is an important distinction between *sharia*, which is understood as God's law, the ideal way for Muslims to live, and *fiqh*, the pluralistic, fallible human efforts (educated guesses) to understand and articulate God's law (especially those areas not directly answered by the plain text of the Quran and the Prophetic hadith. Thus, when Muslim Americans talk about "sharia law," they usually mean *fiqh*.

26. Yusuf Talal DeLorenzo, "The Fiqh Council of North America," in *Muslims on the Americanization Path?*, ed. Yvonne Yazbeck Haddad and John L. Esposito (Atlanta: Scholars, 1998), 85.

27. Curtis, *Islam in Black America*, 116.

28. Ibid., 122.

29. Carolyn Rouse, *Engaged Surrender: African American Women and Islam* (Berkeley: University of California Press, 2004).

30. Herbert Berg, "Mythmaking in the African-American Muslim Context: The Moorish Science Temple, the Nation of Islam, and the American Society of Muslims," *Journal of the American Academy of Religion* 73 (2005): 698.

31. Curtis, *Islam in Black America*, 121; Howell, "Inventing the American Mosque," 272.

32. W. Deen Mohammed, *Challenges That Face the Man Today*, vol. 2 (Chicago: W. D. Muhammad Productions, 1985), 86–87.

33. Ibid., 29–36.

34. W. Deen Mohammed, "National Imam's Meeting: Yusuf Analogy" (Calumet City, IL: WDM Publications, 2000).

35. Ibid.

36. Curtis, *Islam in Black America*, 126.

37. Maher Hathout, "Islam, Pluralism, and Social Harmony" (lecture delivered at Islamic Society of North America, July 1, 2011).

38. The Abduh quote is sometimes attributed to another revivalist, Rifa'a Al-Tahtawi. Regardless of the source, the sentiment is pervasive. Consider cultural critic Amitava Kumar's description of a conversation he had with his driver in Pakistan shortly after September 11th, once the driver learned that Kumar lives in the US:

   > [Qasim] turned his face to me and said in Urdu, "The Americans are the true Muslims. . . . The Americans have read and really understood the message of the Qur'an." I was baffled. But Qasim explained his point to me. . . . "The Americans treat their workers the right way. They pay them overtime." Ah, overtime! Fair wages, just working conditions, true democracy. There was little place on American television in all that talk of terrorism for this plain man's sublime understanding of his religion. . . . As far as Qasim was concerned, it was others in his own country, his fellow Muslims, who were oppressors. On the other hand, the fair-minded employers of the poor in America, such as they were, when they died, were going to be gathered in the arms of the angels and wafted to heaven.

   Amitava Kumar, *Husband of a Fanatic: A Personal Journey through India, Pakistan, Love, Hate* (New York: New Press, 2005), 230.

39. Stacy Mattingly, "Special Report: Muslims Attempt to Forge Uniquely American Identity," *Newsroom* (DePaul University), July 2001.

40. Matthew Frye Jacobson, *Roots Too: White Ethnic Revival in Post–Civil Rights America* (Cambridge: Harvard University Press, 2006), 11–71.

41. Jackson, *Islam and the Blackamerican*, 72.

42. Ihsan Bagby, "American Muslim Identity: The Challenges to Harmony" (lecture delivered at Islamic Society of North America, July 3, 2011); Ihsan Bagby, Paul M. Pearl, and Bryan T. Froehle, *The Mosque in America: A National Portrait* (Washington, DC: Council on American Islamic Relations, 1999).

43. GhaneaBassiri, *History of Islam*, 350–52. This trend to focus on domestic social justice issues in ISNA's *Horizons* was already happening at umma institutions' periodicals at the local level. Juan Eduardo Campo, "Islam in California: Views from The Minaret," *Muslim World* 86, nos. 3–4 (July–October 1996): 311.

44. Bagby, Perl, and Froehle, *Mosque in America*.

45. Jackson, *Islam and the Blackamerican*, 80–81. Jackson ascribes to post-'65 immigrants arriving in the US the status of legal whiteness and the motive of adopting the whiteness of their colonial masters, obscuring the far more complicated legal and racial status of Middle Eastern and South Asian immigrants. While the 1965 Hart-Cellar law abolished national-origins quotas, nothing in

its statutes rendered these newcomers "white" in any legal sense as he claims. Jackson ignores the reconfigured terrains of the post-civil-rights era, on which white privilege operates not as the object of desire but as a mediating force that encourages ethnic particularism, particularly for immigrants in Muslim counterpublics, who are more ambivalent about the American mainstream.

46. Sunaina Maira, *Missing: Youth, Citizenship, and Empire after 9/11* (Durham: Duke University Press, 2009), 15–17.

47. Consider the large cohort of Bengali pharmacists who immigrated in the late seventies but were forced into service-sector jobs instead. Nilufer Ahmed, Gladis Kaufman, and Shamim Naim, "South Asian Families in the United States," in *Family and Gender among American Muslims*, ed. Barbara Bilge and Barbara Aswad (Philadelphia: Temple University Press, 1996), 155–72.

48. Jacobson, *Roots Too*, 26. In the eighties and early nineties, Salafi, Wahhabi and Taliban Muslim "fundamentalists" were known in the US as the *mujahidin*, heralded by mainstream American media as noble "freedom fighters" in the battle against Soviet invasion of Afghanistan. Mamdani notes that throughout the Cold War, Islam-based opposition to the atheism of the communist enemy was never depicted as fundamentalist or regressive; it only came to be represented unequivocally as bad (dangerous, violent, and fundamentalist/puritanical) by the American media and the US government when it was no longer in the service of US interests. Mamdani, "Good Muslim," 768–72.

49. As-Sufi was formerly Ian Dallas, a Scottish playwright, actor, and producer for the BBC who converted to Islam in the late sixties and became the head of the global Murabitun sufi order.

50. Hamza Yusuf, *Classical vs. Modern Education* (Hayward, CA: Alhambra Productions, 2003).

51. Ultimately, Hanson's Islamic education spanned over ten years, and he studied with prominent Islamic scholars in several countries outside the Emirates, including in Saudi Arabia, Egypt, Algeria, Morocco, and Mauritania. His private tutors included esteemed teachers such as Shaykh Abdullah Ould Siddiq, then the mufti of the Emirate Abu Dhabi, and Shaykh Ahmad Badawi, the famed Sudanese hadith scholar.

52. Hamza Yusuf, "Another Mother of the Believers" (Hayward, CA: Zaytuna Institute, 2009).

53. Hamza Yusuf, "Quranic Sciences" (Albuquerque, NM, June 27, 1995).

54. Hamza Yusuf, *Agenda to Change Our Condition* (Hayward, CA: Zaytuna Institute, 2001). This pamphlet, published before September 11th, fuses theology, pious practices, and a critique of modernity with only general references to sufism in a style typical of Yusuf. In 1996, in New Mexico, Yusuf spearheaded a "nonaggression pact" among American sufi shaykhs who taught at the Deen Intensives, asking them to agree not to take (and compete) for formal devotees or to promote their orders. A few prominent American sufis refused and as a result no longer participate in the Zaytuna and Deen Intensive programming.

55. Hamza Yusuf Hanson, "Lambs to the Slaughter," in *Beyond Schooling: Building Communities Where Learning Really Matters* (Toronto: Ihya Productions, 2001), 18–19. Scott Kugle demonstrates that Yusuf's philosophy and politics is a recuperation of the thought of Ahmad Zarruq. Scott Kugle, *Rebel between Spirit and Law: Ahmad Zarruq, Sainthood, and Authority in Islam* (Bloomington: Indiana University Press, 2006).

56. Hamza Hanson, "Nomad," in Steven Barboza, *American Jihad: Islam after Malcolm X* (New York: Image, 1994), 352.

57. *Faces of Islam: Hamza Yusuf*, BBC, 1999.

58. Hannah Cross, *Migrants, Borders, and Global Capitalism: West African Labour Mobility and EU Borders* (New York: Routledge, 2013); Noel Foster, *Mauritania: The Struggle for Democracy* (Boulder, CO: First Forum, 2011).

59. *Faces of Islam.*

60. Gilroy, *Black Atlantic*, 3.

Notes to Chapter 4

1. Michel de Certeau, *The Practice of Everyday Life* (Berkeley: University of California Press, 1984), 87.

2. Dale Eickelman, *Knowledge and Power in Morocco: The Education of a Twentieth-Century Notable* (Princeton: Princeton University Press, 1985), 163; Thomas Pierret, *Religion and State in Syria: The Sunni Ulama from Coup to Revolution* (New York: Cambridge University Press, 2013).

3. For an overview of how Islamic education has been standardized and put in the service of state policies throughout the modern Middle East, see Eleanor Doumato and Gregory Starrett, eds., *Teaching Islam: Textbooks and Religion in the Middle East* (Boulder, CO: Lynne Rienner, 2007).

4. Samantha Shapiro, "The Telegenic Face of Conservative Islam," *New York Times*, April 28, 2006.

5. Hefner, "Introduction," 35.

6. Bulliet, *Case for Islamo-Christian Civilization*, 92.

7. Daniel Crecelius, "Al-Azhar in the Revolution," *Middle East Journal* 20, no. 1 (1966): 31–49.

8. Gregory Starrett, *Putting Islam to Work: Education, Politics, and Religious Transformation in Egypt* (Berkeley: University of California Press, 1998), 31, 47.

9. Heather Sharkey, *Living with Colonialism: Nationalism and Culture in the Anglo-Egyptian Sudan* (Berkeley: University of California Press, 2006), 53.

10. Gilles Kepel, *Jihad: The Trial of Political Islam* (Cambridge: Harvard University Press, 2003), 53.

11. Bulliet, *Case for Islamo-Christian Civilization*, 65.

12. The raw numbers of madrasas in countries such as Pakistan have grown, not receded, in the modern period, and AlAzhar still serves a massive population of students in Egypt. Morocco is one case in which historic pedagogical systems are essentially diminished. Carter Vaughn Findley, "Knowledge and Education

in the Modern Middle East: A Comparative View," in *The Modern Economic and Social History in Its World Context*, ed. Georges Sabagh (Cambridge: Cambridge University Press, 1989), 130–54.

13. Brinkley Messick, "Media Muftis: Radio Fatwas in Yemen," in *Islamic Legal Interpretation: Muftis and Their Fatwas* (Cambridge: Harvard University Press, 1996), 310–20.

14. Muhammad Qasim Zaman, *The 'Ulama in Contemporary Islam: Custodians of Change* (Princeton: Princeton University Press, 2002). Historian Zaman argues that the 'ulama's ambivalence toward the state has come to serve them well in aiding their maintenance and restoration of religious and political credibility. They have been able "to pursue, with considerable flexibility, several options simultaneously: they have continued to press the state on its Islamic promises, but at the same time, they have gradually expanded the scope of their own activities at the grassroots level of society" (108). Ironically, Zaman argues, this renewed credibility is a result of Nasser's reforms. "The Azhar's structural reform in 1961 and the consequent incorporation of the modern secular sciences into its educational concerns meant that it was not long before its graduates began speaking in new ways not just to the conservative segments of society but also to the modern-educated ones. . . . With exposure to new forms of education, the 'ulama and the [secular] university-educated Islamists were able to comprehend and interact with each other much more effectively than they had ever done before" (145).

15. Malika Zeghal, "The 'Recentering' of Religious Knowledge and Discourse: The Case of AlAzhar in Twentieth-Century Egypt," in *Schooling Islam: The Culture and Politics of Modern Muslim Education*, ed. Robert W. Hefner and Muhammad Qasim Zaman (Princeton: Princeton University Press, 2007), 109.

16. Hirschkind details how under Mubarak's rule Egyptian revivalist preachers' steady stream of their mass-produced cassette-tape or YouTube sermons were "frequently interrupted by periods of incarceration, house arrest, and the suspension of [the imam's] right to preach, [which] places serious limitations on the marketability of their tapes" but also served to further cement their authority as religious figures (*Ethical Soundscape*, 60). This process of state censorship redefined the uses and significance of mosques "in panoptic terms, as structures for the localization, control, and supervision of bodies. In a dramatic shift, mosques [became] sites where the state [could listen] to the audience for the incipient rumblings of contestation and militancy" (50).

17. The op-eds are translated by Gomaa's students, as he does not write in English.

18. Asad notes that the formation of the social was key to the secular conception of religion as discrete and divisible from other parts of the totality of society: "What we now retrospectively call *the social*, that all-inclusive secular space that we distinguish conceptually from variables like 'religion,' 'state,' 'national economy,' and so forth, *and on which the latter can be constructed, reformed, and plotted*, didn't exist prior to the nineteenth century. Yet is was precisely the

emergence of *society* as an organizable secular space that made it possible for the [modern liberal] state to oversee and facilitate an original task by redefining religion's competence." Talal Asad, *Formations of the Secular* (Stanford: Stanford University Press, 2003), 190–91 (emphasis original).

19. Andrew Abbott, *The System of Professions: An Essay on the Division of Expert Labor* (Chicago: University of Chicago, 1988), 3.

20. Dale F. Eickelman and James Piscatori, *Muslim Politics* (Princeton: Princeton University Press, 1996).

21. Dale F. Eickelman, "Mass Higher Education and the Religious Imagination in Contemporary Arab Societies," *American Ethnologist* 19, no. 4 (November 1992): 650.

22. Hefner, "Introduction," 33.

23. Zaman, *'Ulama*, 99.

24. Nuri Friedlander, "Interview: Sheikh 'Ali Jumu'a," *Islamica* 12 (2005): 43–44.

25. The analogy between the danger of failing to recognize the religious expertise of the 'ulama and the danger of failing to recognize a medical doctor's is pervasive. In one of Shaykh Muhammad Sa'id Ramadan al-Buti's polemical essays against Salafi revivalists, he compares his Salafi interlocutor's direct reading of revelation to the perilous consultation of a dictionary by the father of a sick child. "If physicians tell a father, whose child has got a serious infection, not to give him penicillin, otherwise he will die, and he finds in dictionaries that penicillin is a medicine against infection, then gives him the medicine, but the child dies, . . . he caused the death of his child. . . . [By denying that the father should be tried in court as a criminal] you have left the consensus of the whole Islamic community!" Andreas Christmann, "Islamic Scholar and Religious Leader: A Portrait of Shaykh Muhammad Sa'id Ramadan al-Buti," *Islam and Christian-Muslim Relations* 9, no. 2 (2007): 169.

26. Partha Chatterjee, *Nationalist Thought and the Colonial World: A Derivative Discourse?* (London: Zed Books, 1986).

27. Muhammad Qasim Zaman, "Bridging Traditions: Madrasas and Their Internal Critics," in *Islamophobia/Islamophilia*, ed. Andrew Shryock (Bloomington: Indiana University Press, 2010), 120.

28. Hussein Ali Agrama, "Ethics, Tradition, Authority: Toward an Anthropology of the Fatwa," *American Ethnologist* 37, no. 1 (2010): 2–18; Sherine Hamdy, *Our Bodies Belong to God: Organ Transplants, Islam, and the Struggle for Human Dignity in Egypt* (Berkeley: University of California Press, 2012), 115–38.

29. Frederick Schauer, "Precedent," *Stanford Law Review* 39 (1987): 594.

30. John Pocock, *Politics, Language, and Time: Essays on Political Thought and History* (Chicago: University of Chicago Press, 1989), 247–49.

31. Ibid., 270–71.

32. Sayyid Qutb, *Milestones* (CreateSpace, 2005). "The fountain from which later generations imbibed was mingled with Greek philosophy and logic, ancient Persian legends, Jewish scriptures, and traditions, Christian theology and remnant of other

religions and cultures. . . . All the subsequent generations which arose after this first one were saturated from this mixed source, hence the perfect and pure generation like the one of the companions of the Holy Prophet (s.a.w.) never arose again" (56).

33. Pocock, *Politics*, 236.

34. Khaled Abou El-Fadl, *Speaking in God's Name: Islamic Law, Authority and Women* (Oxford, UK: Oneworld, 2001).

Notes to Chapter 5

1. Yvonne Yazbeck Haddad, Jane I. Smith, and Kathleen M. Moore, *Muslim Women in America: The Challenge of Islamic Identity Today* (New York: Oxford University Press, 2006), 41.

2. For examples of scholarship on African American Muslims that is gender specific, see McCloud, *African American Islam*; and Rouse, *Engaged Surrender*.

3. Haddad, Smith, and Moore, *Muslim Women in America*, 44.

4. Ibid., 45–46.

5. Bagby, Perl, and Froehle, *Mosque in America*. For anxieties around white female converts, see Annelies Moors, "The Dutch and the Face-Veil: Politics of Discomfort," *Social Anthropology* 17, no. 4 (2009): 393–408.

6. I draw on Talal Asad's discussion of the inherent directionality and relations of power in cultural translations such that ethnographers translate "weak languages" into "strong languages." Talal Asad, "The Concept of Cultural Translation in British Social Anthropology," in *Writing Culture: The Poetics and Politics of Ethnography*, ed. James Clifford and George Marcus (Berkeley: University of California Press, 1986), 158.

7. My discussion of legibility draws heavily on Judith Butler's discussion of gendered norms of intelligibility. Judith Butler, *Gender Trouble: Feminism and the Subversion of Identity* (New York: Routledge, 2006); and Butler, *Giving an Account of Oneself* (New York: Fordham University Press, 2005). Butler draws on Foucault's "grid of intelligibility" (*dispositif*) but revises his paradigm through attention to the "social dimensions of normativity that govern the scene of recognition" (*Giving an Account*, 22).

8. Hannah Arendt, "What Is Authority?," in *Between Past and Future* (New York: Viking, 1961). The essay was originally in the past tense: "What Was Authority?," which is more fitting for her argument about the seismic shift from the classical period to our contemporary, modern one. In the contemporary world, Arendt argues the loss of such "authentic and indisputable experiences common to us all" has resulted in a hollowing of once stable and robust notions such as obligation, duty, and legitimacy (91).

9. Ibid., 93. Arendt details how Plato discounted persuasion as insufficient for the guidance of the body politic to truth. Instead, Plato explored relationships in which expert knowledge could compel obedience. "What [Plato] was looking for was a relationship in which the compelling element lies in the relationship itself and is prior to the actual issuance of commands; the patient became

subject to the physician's authority when he fell ill, and the slave came under the command of his master when he became a slave" (ibid., 109).

10. I draw this analogy not to suggest that love and intimacy are singular, universal, or "simple" social forms. Elizabeth Povinelli demonstrates that intimacy is a key site by which we can critically explore how the liberal, binary concepts of individual freedom and social constraint fail to apprehend marginalized, alternative practices of intimacy. Her ethnography of aboriginal kin networks in Australia and radical queer faerie networks in the US traces "which forms of intimate dependency count as freedom and which count as undue social constraint; which forms of intimacy involve moral judgment rather than mere choice; and which forms of intimate sociality distribute life and material goods and evoke moral certainty, if not moral sanctimoniousness. This approach to intimacy and governance does not collapse these two worlds; it does not make them two versions of the same thing. Instead it allows us to see how their differences emerge diagonally to the deafening drum of liberal figurations of freedom and its others and their racial and civilizational inflections." Elizabeth Povinelli, *Empire of Love: Toward a Theory of Intimacy, Genealogy, and Carnality* (Durham: Duke University Press, 2008), 3.

11. Ludwig Wittgenstein, *On Certainty*, trans. Denis Paul and G. E. M. Anscombe (New York: J&J Harper, 1969), 144.

12. Talal Asad, *Genealogies of Religion: Discipline and Reasons of Power in Christianity and Islam* (Baltimore: Johns Hopkins University Press, 1993), 57–58.

13. Colin Campbell, "Detraditionalization, Character and the Limits to Agency," in *Detraditionalization*, ed. Paul Heelas, Scott Lash, and Paul Morris (Malden, MA: Blackwell, 1999), 162.

14. Mahmood, *Politics of Piety*, 11–12.

15. Ibid., 15.

16. Lila Abu-Lughod, "The Romance of Resistance: Tracing Transformations of Power through Bedouin Women," *American Ethnologist* 17, no. 1 (February 1990): 43.

17. I thank Barbara Von Schlegell for directing me to the series *Man Malakat Aymanukum (Concubines)*.

18. Despite the many strands and differences within feminism (radical, socialist, liberal, third world), the feminist tradition's analytical and political coherence derives from the premise that insofar as patriarchal structures serve male interests, the result will be either neglect, or direct suppression, of women's interests.

19. Abu-Lughod, "Romance of Resistance," 52.

20. Mahmood, *Politics of Piety*, 9.

21. Sherine Hafez, *An Islam of Her Own: Reconsidering Religion and Secularism in Women's Islamic Movements* (New York: NYU Press, 2011).

22. Mona Hassan, "Women Preaching for the Secular State: Official Female Preachers (Bayan Vaizler) in Contemporary Turkey," *International Journal of Middle East Studies* 43, no. 3 (August 2011): 451–73.

23. The Moroccan government launched a similar, highly publicized program in 2004. The PBS documentary *Class of 2006* follows the Moroccan government's first cohort of female muftis, and the narrative arc of the film is decidedly triumphant, despite the fact that in scene after scene we witness how the women scholars' close affiliation with the state actually undermines their religious legitimacy in the eyes of the publics they serve.

Notes to Chapter 6

1. Walter Benjamin, "Theses on the Philosophy of History," in *Illuminations* (New York: Schocken Books, 1969), 255.
2. Pocock, *Politics*, 264.
3. Sherman Jackson, *On the Boundaries of Theological Tolerance in Islam* (New York: Oxford University Press, 2002), 20.
4. Ibid.
5. Ibid.
6. Ebrahim Moosa, "The Unbearable Intimacy of Language and Thought: Aporetic Discourses in Imagining Religion in Islam," in *How Should We Talk about Religion?*, ed. James Boyd White (Notre Dame: University of Notre Dame Press, 2005), 300–326.
7. Jaroslav Pelikan, *The Vindication of Tradition* (New Haven: Yale University Press, 1984). Quote from interview in *US News and World Report*, July 26, 1989.
8. Alasdair MacIntyre, "Epistemological Crisis, Dramatic Narrative and the Philosophy of Science," in *Paradigms and Revolutions: Applications and Appraisals of Thomas Kuhn's Philosophy of Science*, ed. Gary Gutting (Notre Dame: University of Notre Dame Press, 1980).
9. Umar Faruq Abd-Allah, *Islam and the Cultural Imperative* (Chicago: Nawawi Foundation, 2004).
10. *Encyclopedia of Islam*, 2nd ed., ed. H. A. R. Gibb (Leiden: Brill, 2001).
11. Walter Benjamin, "The Work of Art in the Age of Mechanical Reproduction," in *Illuminations*, 243n. 5.

Notes to Chapter 7

1. Thomas Friedman, "If It's a Muslim Problem, It Needs a Muslim Solution," *New York Times*, July 8, 2005.
2. Stephen Lee, "A Chronology of the 'War on Terror' and Domestic Hate Crimes," *Asian Americans on War and Peace*, ed. Russell C. Leong and Don T. Nakanishi (Los Angeles: UCLA Asian American Studies Center Press, 2002), 205.
3. Ibid.; Jeanne Meserve and Mike Ahlers, "Passenger Who Had Arabic Flash Cards Sues over His Detainment," CNN.com, February 10, 2010, http://www.cnn.com/2010/CRIME/02/10/arabic.flash.card.suit/index.html; Volpp, "Citizen and the Terrorist," 1586; "Iraqi Peace Activist Forced to Change T-Shirt Bearing Arabic Script before Boarding Plane at JFK," *Democracy Now*, August 21, 2006, http://www.democracynow.org/2006/8/21/

iraqi_peace_activist_forced_to_change; Kathy Matheson, "Flight Diverted after Confusion over Prayer," *Standard Examiner*, January 21, 2010; Tony Perry, "Muslim Woman Sues Southwest Airlines after Being Taken Off a Flight," *Los Angeles Times*, October 5, 2011.

4. Razack, *Casting Out*, 9.

5. Robert Leiken, *Bearers of Global Jihad? Immigration and National Security after 9/11* (Washington, DC: Nixon Center, 2004).

6. Wajahat Ali, Eli Clifton, Matthew Duss, Lee Fang, Scott Keyes, and Faiz Shakir, *Fear Inc.: The Roots of the Islamophobia Network in America* (Washington, DC: Center for American Progress, August 2011).

7. Ibid.

8. Justin Elliot, "GOPer Wants to Ban but Can't Define Sharia Law," *Salon*, March 7, 2011.

9. In a 1999 talk at the US State Department, a sufi shaykh, Muhammad Hisham Kabbani, offered this unscientific and self-serving statistic, which is based only on his personal impressions of antisufi bias in US mosques. King and other disinformation experts regularly cite it. GhaneaBassiri, *History of Islam*, 355.

10. Muneer Fareed, "Applications of Islamic Law in America" (lecture at American Learning Institute for Muslims, December 27, 2003).

11. Robert Orsi, *Between Heaven and Earth: The Religious Worlds People Make and the Scholars Who Study Them* (Princeton: Princeton University Press, 2006), 188.

12. Mahmood Mamdani challenges this logic that frames the Quran as the "cause" of September 11th. "Could it be that a person who takes his or her religion literally is a potential terrorist? That only someone who thinks of a religious text not as literal, but as metaphorical or figurative, is better suited to civic life and the tolerance it calls for? How, one may ask, does the literal reading of sacred texts translate into hijacking, murder, and terrorism?" (*Good Muslim*, 767).

13. The distinction between the martial tradition and one's inward spiritual struggle are derived from the hadith that recounts how Muhammad, after a battle, said, "We have returned from the lesser struggle [*al-jihad al-asghar*] to the greater struggle [*al-jihad al-akbar*], the struggle against oneself."

14. Feisal Abdul Rauf, *What's Right with Islam Is What's Right with America* (San Francisco: Harper, 2005); Bernard Lewis, *What Went Wrong? The Clash between Islam and Modernity in the Middle East* (Oxford: Oxford University Press, 2002).

15. Rosemary R. Hicks, "Religious Pluralism, Secularism, and Interfaith," in *Cambridge Companion to American Islam*, ed. Juliane Hammer and Omid Safi (New York: Cambridge University Press, 2013).

16. Kathleen M. Moore, *Al-Mughtaribun: American Law and the Transformation of Muslim Life in the United States* (Albany: SUNY Press, 1995); Kathleen Foley, *"Not in Our Neighborhood": Managing Opposition to Mosque Construction* (Washington, DC: Institute for Social Policy and Understanding, 2010).

17. "NY Official: Stabbing Suspect Had War Journals," *NBC News*, August 26, 2010.

18. Waldinger and Fitzgerald, "Transnationalism in Question," 1179.

19. Mayanthi Fernando, "Exceptional Citizens: Secular Muslim Women and the Politics of Difference in France," *Social Anthropology* 17 (2009): 379–92.

20. Richard Scheinin, "American Muslim Scholar Declares: Terrorists Are Mass Murderers, Not Martyrs," *San Jose Mercury News*, September 16, 2001.

21. Jack O'Sullivan, "If You Hate the West, Emigrate to a Muslim Country," *Guardian*, October 8, 2001.

22. Ibid.

23. Scheinin, "American Muslim Scholar."

24. O'Sullivan, "If You Hate the West."

25. Hanna Rosin and John Mintz, "Muslim Leaders Struggle with Mixed Messages," *Washington Post*, October 2, 2001.

26. Muhammad Al-Shareef, "Open Letter to Hamza Yusuf: Answering Controversies," *Islamic Awakening* forum, August 21, 2007.

27. Yusuf interviewed by Michael Enright on *The Sunday Edition*, CBC, September 23, 2001.

28. Benjamin Popper, "Build-a-Bomber: Why Do So Many Terrorists Have Engineering Degrees?," *Slate*, December 29, 2009.

29. AbdalHakim Murad, "Tradition or Extradition? The Threat to Muslim Americans," *Contentions* 8 (2003).

30. Rosin and Mintz, "Muslim Leaders Struggle."

31. Laurie Goodstein, "American Muslim Clerics Seek a Middle Ground," *New York Times*, July 18, 2006.

32. Andrew Santella, "Modern Lessons from an Ancient Faith," *Elmhurst College News*, February 22, 2010.

33. Hamza Yusuf, "Amid Mosque Dispute Muslims Can Look to Irish Catholics for Hope," *Christian Science Monitor*, September 16, 2010.

34. Yusuf Hanson, "Lambs to the Slaughter," 18.

35. Scott Korb, "American Islam," *Chronicle of Higher Education*, March 18, 2012.

36. Bill Powell, "Struggle for the Soul of Islam," *Time*, September 13, 2004.

37. Clyde Haberman, "A Little Late, but a Stand against Hate," *New York Times*, November 16, 2004.

38. Ibid.; Nabiha Syed, "Exclusivity and Its Politics," *Critical Islamic Reflections*, April 15, 2006.

39. Ahmad Nassef, "Listen to Muslim Silent Majority in the US," *Christian Science Monitor*, April 21, 2004.

40. Arjun Appadurai, *The Fear of Small Numbers: An Essay on the Geography of Anger* (Durham: Duke University Press, 2006).

41. *Politically Incorrect*, season 9, episode 39.

42. Amina Wadud, *Inside the Gender Jihad: Women's Reform of Islam* (Oxford, UK: Oneworld, 2006), 264.

43. Asra Nomani, "My Answered Prayer," *Daily News*, March 20, 2005.

44. Laurie Goodstein, "Muslim Women Seeking a Place in the Mosque" and "Woman's Mosque Protest Brings Furor in the U.S.," *New York Times*, July 22, 2004.

45. Juliane Hammer, *American Muslim Women, Religious Authority, and Activism: More than a Prayer* (Austin: University of Texas Press, 2012), 13–55.

46. "Woman Leads Controversial US Prayer," *AlJazeera*, March 19, 2005. The event was widely covered in international press with hundreds of articles from newspapers and online news sites around the globe, particularly in Muslim societies in South Asia and the Middle East.

47. Juliane Hammer, "Performing Gender Justice: The 2005 Woman-Led Prayer in New York," *Contemporary Islam* 4, no. 1 (2010): 91–116.

48. Amina Wadud, *Inside the Gender Jihad*, 252.

49. Jordan Lite, "Loosening Their Religion: Sick of Silence Muslim Women Are Shaking Up the Boy's Club," *New York Daily News*, March 3, 2005; Rose Marie Berger, "Men Only?," *Sojourners*, June 2005.

50. Although Wadud participated in the press conference on March 18, she avoided most media invitations after the event. Hammer, *American Muslim Women*, 34.

51. Ibid.; according to a survey conducted by *Azizah* magazine, widely read by mosqued American women, 82 percent of its readers reported that women should not lead mixed-gender congregation prayers; 85 percent felt that the woman-led prayer in March did not advance the cause of Muslim women; and 71 percent felt that there were more important issues facing Muslim women.

52. This was not the first woman-led mixed prayer, Wadud's first woman-led mixed prayer, or even the first woman-led mixed Friday prayer in North America. When Wadud decided to stand in front of a mixed-gender congregation, she, according to Nassef and Eltantawi, was repeating history, not changing it. Their insistence on the grounding of the prayer event in early Muslim history and Prophetic practice was intended to legitimize the event and provide traditional support for their position. Even Nomani began to argue for precedent, telling journalists that "Muhammad was the world's first feminist." Hammer, *American Muslim Women*, 13–55.

53. Ibid., 52. Crane's militaristic metaphor decried the divisive effects of the PMU's initiative, challenging Wadud's religious authority and the PMU's political authority, as some PMU members supported President Bush.

54. Asra Nomani, "Profile Me, Please! Peter King's Hearings on American Muslims Are No Witchhunt," *Daily Beast*, March 7, 2011.

55. "A Comment on the PMUNA," *CommentPMUNA* (blog), November 12, 2004

56. Hammer, *American Muslim Women*.

57. Shahina Siddiqui and Ingrid Mattson, *Women Friendly Mosques and Community Centers: Working Together to Reclaim Our Heritage* (Tempe, AZ: Islamic Social Services Association, 2005).

58. Asra Nomani, "End Gender Apartheid in US Mosques," *USA Today*, July 10, 2011.

59. Elizabeth Bernstein, "Militarized Humanitarianism Meets Carceral Feminism: The Politics of Sex, Rights, and Freedom in Contemporary Antitrafficking Campaigns," *Signs: Journal of Women in Culture and Society* 36, no. 1 (2010): 45–71.

60. Hicks, "Religious Pluralism, Secularism, and Interfaith."

61. Andrea Elliot, "Between Black and Immigrant Muslims an Uneasy Alliance," *New York Times,* March 11, 2007.

62. Ibid.

63. Jackson, *Islam and the Blackamerican,* 8.

64. Ibid., 42.

65. Caryle Murphy, "Bountiful, Blessed Month: Ramadan Offers Black Muslims a Chance to Strengthen Ties," *Washington Post,* November 16, 2001.

66. Katrin Bennhold, "For U.S. Muslims, It's the American Way," *International Herald Tribune,* November 8, 2006.

67. Murphy, "Bountiful, Blessed Month."

68. Ibid.

69. Hishaam Aidi, "The Grand (Hip Hop) Chessboard: Race, Rap, and Raison d'Etat," *Middle East Report* 260 (Fall 2011): 25–39.

70. "Vandalism Underscores Differences among American Muslims," Associated Press, December 15, 2005.

71. Grewal and Coolidge, "Islamic Education."

72. Jamie Tarabay, "Muslim Chaplain Offers American Brand of Islam," *Morning Edition,* National Public Radio, May 20, 2008.

73. *The Calling,* dir. Daniel Alpert and Musa Sayeed (PBS Independent Lens, 2010).

74. Corey Kilgannon, "Muslims in Gray," *New York Times,* November 25, 2001, 1.

75. Andrea Elliot, "Why Yasir Qadhi Wants to Talk about Jihad," *New York Times,* March 17, 2011.

76. Bagby, Perl, and Froehle, *Mosque in America.*

77. Conflicts between Zaytuna Institute students and AlMaghrib Institute students on college campuses led to a kind of nonaggression pact, with many American Sunni preachers as signatories. Despite officially friendly relations with Zaytuna faculty, Qadhi considers the sufi scholars associated with Zaytuna beyond the pale of orthodoxy (although not apostates) because he claims they subscribe to the Ashari school of Sunni theology. Yusuf, in fact, does not identify as an Ashari Sunni but has an eclectic approach to Sunni theology. In my interview with Qadhi, he claimed that Yusuf and Shakir viewed his theology as incorrect and that he was no more and no less tolerant than they were by labeling them heterodox; however, when I posed the same questions to the three core Zaytuna faculty, they all confirmed that despite their theological disagreements with Qadhi, they considered him and others associated with AlMaghrib Institute well within the fold of Islamic orthodoxy.

78. Sunni black intellectuals such as Sherman Jackson are revising lay Muslim American histories that erased the NOI from the story of Islam in the United States, albeit in terms of a religious evolution that culminates in the majority of African American Muslims being Sunni by the eighties. Jackson reminds American Muslims that despite the disavowal of Sunnis and Shias, "proto-Muslims" such as the NOI are responsible for establishing Islam's legitimacy among

black Americans, which is why, in contrast to Europe, Canada, and Australia, the US saw "the phenomenon of *communal conversion*" (Jackson, *Islam and the Blackamerican*, 6).

79. Although it is overstated in Elliot's *Times* article, there was a fierce rivalry between AlAwlaki and Qadhi. Ironically, the *New York Times* had previously held up AlAwlaki as an example in the same way as Qadhi, noting that AlAwlaki represented "a new generation of Muslim leader capable of merging East and West." Laurie Goodstein, "The American Muslims: Influential American Muslims Temper Their Tone," *New York Times*, October 19, 2001.

80. Elliot, "Why Yasir Qadhi."

81. Ibid.

82. Ibid.

83. Caryle Murphy, "For Conservative Muslims, Goal of Isolation a Challenge," *Washington Post*, September 5, 2006.

84. Elliot, "Why Yasir Qadhi."

85. Ibid.

86. Yasir Qadhi, "An Illegal and Counterproductive Assassination," *New York Times*, October 1, 2011.

87. Brigitte L. Nacos and Oscar Torres-Reyna, "Muslim Americans in the News before and after 9-11" (paper prepared for "Restless Searchlight: Terrorism, the Media & Public Life," Harvard University, August 28, 2002).

88. Barack Obama, "Remarks by the President on a New Beginning," White House Office of the Press Secretary, June 4, 2009.

89. Ibid.

90. Christi Parsons, "The Crafting of Obama's Cairo Speech to World Muslims," *Los Angeles Times*, August 2, 2009.

91. For an analysis of Obama's speech addressed to the Iranian people in which Obama's ecumenical tone recasts culture difference as commensurable by framing it in terms of American exceptionalism, see Brian T. Edwards and Dilip Parameshwar Gaonkar, introduction to *Globalizing American Studies*, ed. Brian T. Edwards and Dilip Parameshwar Gaonkar (Chicago: University of Chicago Press, 2010), 22.

92. Dan Murphy, "Joe Biden Says Egypt's Mubarak No Dictator, He Shouldn't Step Down," *Christian Science Monitor*, January 27, 2011.

93. Shima Aadil, "The Government Removes Flowers and Decorations Thirty Minutes after Obama's Departure from Sultan Hassan," *AlMasry AlYoum*, June 9, 2009.

Notes to the Epilogue

1. Noha Elhannawy, "Al-Azhar Clerics Hope for Their Own Revolution," *Egypt Independent*, July 21, 2011.

Zareena Grewal is Assistant Professor of American Studies, Religious Studies, Middle East Studies, and the Program in Ethnicity, Race, and Migration at Yale University. She is a historical anthropologist and documentary filmmaker and has directed and produced two films for television, *By the Dawn's Early Light: Chris Jackson's Journey to Islam* (2004) and *Swahili Fighting Words* (with Mohamed Yunus Rafiq, 2009). She is also Director for the Center for the Study of American Muslims at the Institute for Social Policy and Understanding.

Made in the USA
San Bernardino, CA
20 February 2017